W9-CRX-167

Year	Area	Mountain Climbed/Route	Leader/Companions
1964	European Alps	Co-Leader with Dale Johnson on first Colorado Mtn. Club European Outing to Alps	
	Dolomites	Marmolada (10,968') North Face, Normal Route	Howard Snyder, Dale & Brad Johnson, Ardis Rohwer, Karen Cole, Janet Johnson, Julia Kassanchuk, Phil Eggleston
		Civetta East Face	Dale & Brad Johnson, Edith Eilender, Johanna Guard
	S.W. Suisse	Matterhorn, Swiss Ridge (unsuccessful) To cables. Ice all the way.	Leader: John Filsinger. Others: Ardis Rohwer, Samuel Alfend
	Colo. Rockies	Apache	John Whitbeck

1965-1966 Nat'l Ski Patrol Rocky Mtn. Div., Arapahoe Basin Ski Area

1965-1967 Graduate School kept me very busy.

Year	Area	Mountain Climbed/Route	Leader/Companions
1968	New Zealand	Co-Leader with Dale Johnson on Colo. Mtn. Club New Zealand Outing Ruapehu, Normal Route Mt. Cook, (unsuccessful), avalanche conditions	
	Wyoming, Big Horn Mtns.	Cloud Peak, N.E. Couloir Ice & Snow Route	Dale Johnson, Brad Johnson Jerry Stowall
	Colorado, Gore Range	Peak C Snow Couloir	Mike & Sue O'Brien, Midge & Bob Working, Dale Johnson
1969	East Africa	Co-Leader with Dale Johnson on Colo. Mtn. Club African Safari Mt. Kilimanjaro (19,340') South side to saddle, then west to summit.	Dale and Brad Johnson, Joanna Ganong. Rest of party made it as far as Gilman's Pt., 18,300'.
	Wyoming, Snowy Range	Medicine Bow Peak	Dale & Brad Johnson

Member of the CMC since 1962. Secretary for Boulder Group in 1962.
Coordinator of Peruvian Issue of *Trail and Timberline*, CMC monthly Dec. 1963

Year	Area	Mountain Climbed/Route	Leader/Companions
1977	Japan	Mt. Fuji (12,388')	Dale Johnson
2008	Colorado At age 80	Courthouse Mountain (12,152')	Dave & Elaine Hill

The Jungfrau, Switzerland.

Whatever You Do, Don't Fall In!

VOLUME 2: 1990-2017

BY JULIA M. JOHNSON

Peaks & Places Publishing
Ridgway, CO

My beloved 1930 Model A Ford with Fred Quist in the rumble seat.

I would not have been able to complete this project without the help of
Laurie Casselberry, art director, designer, and project coordinator;
Bonnie Beach, compiler and wordsmith extraordinaire;
and Fred Quist, computer wizard.

© 2017 Julia M. Johnson
All rights reserved in whole or in part.

ISBN: 978-0-9758606-3-2

Library of Congress Control Number: 2017955525

First edition
Printed in Canada

Cover and book design by Laurie Goralka Design
Cover photo by Sue O'Brien

For more information:
Julia M. Johnson
juliamj28@gmail.com
970-626-4317

Brad Johnson
bradjohnson@peaksandplaces.com
970-626-5251

WELCOME BACK!

I am so happy I still have your attention. We are continuing on with my autobiography in the year 1990.

As a reminder, or if you are just joining us (and if you are, please go back and read Volume 1 first), here's a word on how these books were put together: There are two volumes divided into sections by decade, except for the very first section that covers my formative years, 1928 to 1949. At the bottom of each page is a series of years, and the corresponding year in which the story takes place is highlighted. The first volume ends in the year 1989, and this volume starts with 1990.

It's been fun reliving so many adventures experienced over my lifetime, and I hope you will enjoy them. In 2018, I will celebrate the completion of my autobiography *and* my 90th birthday!

—*Julia*

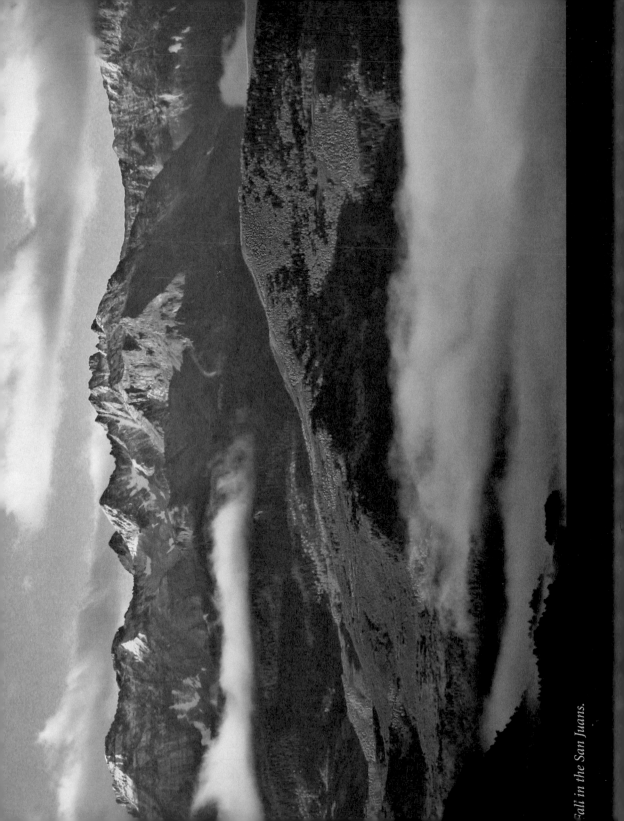

Fall in the San Juans.

TABLE OF CONTENTS

Playful grizzlies, Alaska, 1988.

Gorilla, Rwanda, 1990.

Nepal, 1997.

1990-1999

AFRICA WITH BRAD,
RAFTING THE ZAMBEZI

Wednesday, June 6

After the Anasazi Basketmaker Symposium, Brad and I were winging our way via business class to Zimbabwe, Zambia, and Rwanda.

Our tickets indicated the plane left at 12:50 p.m. but, in fact, it left at noon. Sitting in the lounge at 11:40, we were called for boarding. Brad had disappeared to mail a postcard, and I could imagine myself alone on the plane with Brad having wandered outside, since we thought there was still an hour before departure. I asked them to page him quickly, but it was five-or-more minutes before they did. Fortunately, he was just around the corner in the bookstore and he heard the page. But it was a close call: He was the last to board.

Service was excellent en route, with the food plentiful and good and lots of liquids. The seats were spacious, and I was really grateful to have a lot of space in business-class seats. However, we couldn't remove the middle armrest, so we couldn't lie down.

Between New York and Bangui, I asked if I could go up into the cockpit. Believe it or not, they let me do just that after dinner. The view was enormous! The first officer (the captain) was a Brit, the copilot and navigator were Zimbabwean and young, and the pilot was near retirement age. The amount of instruments was mind-boggling. Half of the ceiling between the seats was fuses; the right-hand wall was covered with dials. There were so many different dials in the front that it took me a while to find the airspeed, altimeter, and compass. We were flying 120° at 350 mph at 28,500 feet! And that's about all I could figure out. While I was there, the captain called in our position. On a chart, he showed me our route north of Bermuda and south of the Azores.

Back in my seat, I slept fitfully for a little over seven hours (a small child cried most of the time). In the middle of the night, we stopped at Bangui, north of Monrovia, but because there was a civil war going on, we had to go elsewhere. So we sat on the plane and waited an hour for refueling.

The second leg was another seven-plus hours. A little after 8:00 a.m., they woke us up to have breakfast. I got out my little alarm and discovered it was 2:50 a.m. in Boulder.

Brad struck up a conversation with a rabbi in our cabin. While we were eating our breakfast which—by the way—was high protein (eggs, sausage, ham, and beans), he put together what Brad called the rabbi's "owned synagogue." The rabbi wrapped a long tape, plastic looking and a half-inch wide, around his arm starting above the bicep where there was a square box-like thing attached. He had taken one sleeve of his suit jacket off in order to do this. He put another same box-like thing on his forehead and wrapped the tape around his head. He had a lovely white shawl with black stripes that he placed over his head, Arab style. Before doing all this preparation, he had gotten dressed with his hat and jacket as if on the way from home to the synagogue. Then, for 45 minutes, he performed a ceremony and, at one point, stood in the corner. When he was finished, which was about the time we finished our breakfast, he put everything carefully away and put his jacket back on. All this time, he had to readjust his "beanie."

One gal in our section was on her way to Zambia to do a trip for a trekking outfit. She'd been running trips for six years in Africa and liked Zambia the best. One of the reasons was that there was more freedom in the game parks. There were also two young guys in first class who, like us, were on their way to do a safari in Zimbabwe. They'd be going to Harare to start.

We landed around 10 a.m. The airport was being enlarged, so there was all kinds of construction and no order. Jackhammering was going on, and it was so loud that you couldn't hear. Fortunately, the plane was not full, which would have been worse.

A young lady, Catherine, ran into Brad—literally—and made him step into a pothole of water. He was quick enough to recover so his foot didn't get wet. She said she was looking for Brad Johnson. What a coincidence! She helped us through customs, which took about an hour to get our luggage and do paperwork.

A van with a driver waited for us, and we drove to Pamodzi (which means "togetherness") Hotel, where we'd stay on our return. We reconfirmed our reservations there, picked up a lunch for the road, and drove into town to the office of the travel agent. We got $5 worth of kwacha at the airport but never needed it. After paying in advance ($211) for the three-hour drive from Lusaka to Kariba, we rode in the van with the manager, Evelyn. The country we drove through was very hilly and covered with small trees. The border crossing was at the dam at Lake Kariba, an immense body of water. We were not allowed to stop, so no photos. At the Zimbabwe side, there were monkeys, and Brad said he saw elephant dung along the road at the turn into the Cutty Sark Hotel.

Evelyn discovered, and so did we, that we could have done a tour in Zambia instead of spending three days in Kariba. She claimed there was a denser population of animals in Zambia than Zimbabwe. Oh well, this was a "fam" trip, so we'd discover what we should have done differently.

Abercrombie and Kent have private offices in the hotel, parts of which were quite old. Our room, #63, smelled like mildew because it was so humid. There was a balcony overlooking the lake, and schools of fishing boats dotted different areas. There was a swimming pool with no ladder and lined with something like flagstones. Our air-conditioning didn't work, so a repairman came to fix it. Brad collapsed on a bed, one of two twins.

1990 1991 1992 1993 1994 1995 1996 1997 1998 1999

The sun was setting and, across the lake, the evening mists revealed a series of hills, one behind the other in hues of evening gray. A flat houseboat skimmed along in front of our room with crowds of tourists perhaps returning home from a tour and picnic, which was available. A long trail of minute ants zigzagged across the top of our stuccoed wall and window, down one side of the door, under the doorstep, up the other side, and even across the top of the top. Their destination was unknown to me. The grounds had various flowers in bloom, which seemed strange for "winter" time. Birds sang and crickets creaked. The full moon, high in the sky, was partially covered by sparse clouds.

I wondered how the water (lake) had changed the climate here. The Kariba dam was completed in 1967, having taken three years to build. Below our room and to one side was a tennis court. Three small thatched roofs on a central pole were on one side of the court, possibly for shade.

After dinner, with music in the background, we headed for bed and I died immediately.

Thursday, June 7

We were awakened by a knock on the door and tea. The sun was up and the lake was a bit windy. Last night, we talked briefly with a pilot who told us to fly out to Bumi Hills on the other side of the lake. After breakfast we looked into it and discovered a cancellation at the lodge, which meant we could leave momentarily. Rushing to pack, cancel our room at Cutty Sark, check our bags, and leave the laundry, we got a ride with the lady in charge of the office for the airlines. She and her husband had come here for five years and stayed 34. He was retired and had just completed building (himself) their home on the lake on one acre they bought for $10,000.

We saw our pilot friend but another flew us out to Bumi. Along the way, we saw several large herds of elephants as well as some buffalo and antelope. Approaching Bumi, we flew level with the cottages on the hillside and were very low, swooping left to land on the dirt strip behind the main hill.

Bumi Hills Lodge sat on a hill nestled among the trees where it overlooked the lake by several hundred feet. On the flats below the terrace dining room, we watched two lone elephants bathe and a small herd taking a bath.

Peter, the manager of wildlife trips, allowed that we could join the crew going out to the houseboats to ready them for evening guests. It was about a 20- to 30-minute trip by canoe. Among some deadwood near the shore were six to eight houseboats, each arranged for two people with twin beds and a basic bath and shower. The water was heated solarly, but I couldn't understand the toilet situation. One houseboat served as a dining room.

From three to sunset, we went on a cruise to see game. We saw a lot of birds, some bushbuck and waterbuck, kudu, buffalo, and crowned crane. We tied up to a snag to watch the sunset. After dinner, around nine, we went on a game drive. We didn't see any cats, but we did see a lot of elephants, bushbuck, and small deer-like animals. We got back by eleven and were tired, so we were off to bed.

1990   1991   1992   1993   1994   1995   1996   1997   1998   1999

Friday, June 8

Brad got up at 6:00 a.m. to photograph the sunrise. I stayed in bed until 7:20, and at 7:30, we went on a morning game drive. We saw zebra, bushbuck, elephants, birds, antelope, and crocodile. After returning at eleven, we packed up and looked at one of the lower cottages that overlooked the waterhole. It could open into an adjoining room, had a shower and tub, two bunk beds, two twins, and was carpeted. Very nice for $83 US for each bed and breakfast.

I visited a craft shop and sunned for awhile, then read and had lunch.

August, September, and October were good game-time months. The leaves fall off the trees, allowing you to see into the brush more easily. Starting in October and going into November and December, it was hot, hot, hot! 120°! It was so hot that the roads steamed after a rain.

At three, we flew back out in the Beech Baron with another chap. We passed the "Islander" on the way, even though we took off 10 minutes late.

Neither of us wanted dinner. I had a bacon-and-tomato toasted sandwich and went to bed by 9-9:30. Brad decided to see what the computer conference crowd was doing while I read, and I soon was fast asleep. At midnight, or really 12:30 a.m., I woke up and found no Brad. I decided to look for him, as he had no money. The entire compound had gone to bed. A guard was posted in the parking lot, so I explained why I was up at such an ungodly hour. No one had seen Brad, although the office clerk was just doing up a dinner charge, so at least he had eaten. They thought he might have met someone who was going to the casino, and I hoped that was the case. The office clerk actually called there and had him paged. I could imagine that someone had hit him over the head or a hippo had run him down out in front of the rooms. He could have gone down to the water's edge in hopes of finding one. After 15 to 20 minutes, I decided there was nothing else to do. They wanted to know if he was used to getting drunk! I no sooner was back in the room when there came a knock. It was Brad, who had come back while I was gone and was unable to rouse me (or so he thought). I was looking for him and he was looking for me. By the time we were back together and trying to sleep, it was 1:30 a.m.

Saturday, June 9

We were supposed to be picked up the next morning by Charles and Teddy, our Wilderness Safari leaders. The alarm had gone off but I didn't even hear it. At 7:30, our breakfast arrived, although we hadn't ordered it. It was a good thing, for we were just ready when the guides showed up.

We waited a bit for Brad to write a letter, then we were off to pick up two Dutch chaps at 9:40. It turned out that the plane was very late, arriving after eleven. So I went back to the hotel and sent a telex to Evelyn at Lusaka Travel, asking her to change our flight out of Vic Falls and book us into Luangwa National Park in Zambia between the end of our safari and going to Rwanda. Charles and Teddy said this was a bad time to raft the Zambezi and that there was nothing to do in Vic Falls once you see the falls. We'll see.

Once the plane arrived, we boarded and had a short flight that landed near Mana Pools National Park at about 11:30, picking up our ride into the interior from there. When we reached park headquarters and had signed in, it was well past noon and we were delighted to finally stop on the escarpment for lunch at a pull-out. They told us the Zambezi Valley stretching far below us in both directions might soon be flooded like the Kariba Lake area—such a pity.

We finally turned off on a dirt road, fairly straight, and drove a long way. Several herds of elephants crossed our path, and we saw lots of impala and bushbuck, kudu, baboons, and monkeys. Finally, Brad spotted a lioness next to the road. All the rest of us had missed her. Charles found a place to turn around and we slowly pulled up in front of her. She looked like she would charge, tale twitching, but she never did. At last, we left her and went on to camp.

It was almost dark by the time we hit camp and set up tents under a large natal mahogany tree. The hippos were yawning and making their funny noises, and the elephants were crossing the Zambezi River. While dinner was being made, we could take a hot shower behind a green three-sided tent. The pail of water was heated, raised by a rope above one's head, and you could adjust the spray with a regular outdoor water handle like we use on the hose. The moon was full and it was so bright outside you didn't need a light. Lion, hippo, and hyena called in the distance. They said we should expect something to be in camp during the night, whether lion, hippo, or elephant.

Dinner was a one-dish meal the cook called "lasagna with broccoli." We also had strawberries and coffee.

1990 1991 1992 1993 1994 1995 1996 1997 1998 1999

Thirsty lioness.

We sat around the fire for a while to discuss our morning plans of rising very early, having tea, biscuits, and perhaps a banana before leaving to pick up a guide for a morning walk.

Sunday, June 10

We heard Cleaver, our camp helper, call "wakie wakie" at 5:30 a.m. The Dutch "boys" were hard-pressed to get up and ready, and Charles had to call them a second time. We had a banana, a couple of "biscuits" (cookies to us), a cup of Milo (chocolate-like drink), and were off by six.

You could hardly begin to see things. At 6:15, we were at headquarters trying to find a guide. Michael, who has been with the park for three years, showed up in a minute, and by 6:30, we were on our way again. We didn't go far before we parked. Following closely behind Michael, we trudged across the dry countryside in search of black rhino spoor. At a long pool, glistening in the early morning sun with bulging eyes and twitching ears, were a large group of hippos.

The birdlife was abundant, and we even saw a pair of owls in broad daylight. There was a large herd of hippos with a couple males fighting for supremacy. Whoever won bred all of them as long as he was king. Stray males tried to come into the herd, and some succeeded. Before returning to camp, we left the Land Rover a second time to view the remains of a buffalo that had been killed the day before. We discovered six lions feeding on it. By 10:30, we were back at camp eating a hearty breakfast of scrambled eggs, tomatoes, toast, jam, greasy fat bacon, and coffee. Then it was nap time or sunning time, or whatever. Three large elephants crossed the Zambezi while we were eating. A croc came up on the opposite bank to sun himself, and a hippo was half out of the water near the shower tent. What a great camping place!

1990   1991   1992   1993   1994   1995   1996   1997   1998   1999

Herd of impala.

From three to dusk, we drove again to see what we could see. At one point, we walked to some ponds where a large croc lay in the sun on the opposite bank. Otherwise, we didn't see much.

Our dinner was stir-fried chicken and potatoes, which was really good. Cleaver didn't feel well today and could be sick with malaria. He doesn't take the pills. Again, the moon was very bright, and by its light we could see a parade of elephants crossing the river. We counted eight. We went to bed about nine after we had all taken a shower. Pretty incredible to be standing near the edge of the Zambezi River, the pink sky reflecting in the water where hippo eyes and bulging backs glisten in the moonlight. Our shower tent had this view. The night noises were just beginning, with the lions in the far distance mingling with the cry of the hyena. No sooner were we headed to sleep than the bugle of an elephant along with much thrashing of the underbrush could be heard 150 yards away. Something was frightening the elephant, perhaps a cow with a baby. Brad was fast asleep when the band of eight who earlier had crossed the river could be heard again splashing back across. The splashing lasted a long time, and although I couldn't actually see them, I could in my mind's eye.

Monday, June 11
Before I knew it, I heard Teddy call "wakie wakie." We were up again as quickly as possible.

It was colder today. Breakfast was as usual—a banana, biscuits, a hot drink—but no park guide.

Plan B: drive around to find him. While we waited for Charles, we heard a lion. Charles had a new guide, Nicholas, who we'd pick up in an hour. We decided to follow the noise of the lion and—lo and behold—spotted two. After pictures and when they were too far away, we returned to park headquarters to pick up Nicholas. We tried to track down the lion, walking several hours, but had no luck.

After some lunch, all of us walked to several pans (pools to us) where we hid in the brush, observing the birds. A lone impala came to the edge of the "gest" (brush), looked around carefully, then left. Soon, some baboons also came to the edge of the gest. Carefully looking all around the water's edge, a lone kudu came in to drink. I moved to a better spot for pictures. A sudden baboon ruckus came from the gest not too far distant. The kudu became very alert, even ran a few steps in the direction of the noise. At last, it decided to leave in a hurry. Charles thought there might have been a lion or leopard in the area, which would make the baboons get excited.

Teddy and Charles Brightman had both worked as guides for some time and for different companies. Teddy once had her own Land Rover when she was a guide for another outfit. They have only been married three months and feel they will continue as guides as long as they can. They're both from Harare. They had a small wedding (60) somewhere in a national park signifying their love for what they're doing. Her father used to be a farmer but gave it up for sale not too long ago and was now recycling mine dumps. She said that to be a very lucrative business, they should bring in anywhere from Z$25,000 to Z$40,000 every two weeks. She's in charge of the food and Charles seems to be the guide. He knows an incredible number of birds and seems like a better guide than the park guides we had to take with us on our walks.

This will be our last day in Mana Pools. We will be up and on our way to go across Lake Kariba on Tuesday by 7:00 a.m.

Tuesday, June 12

Somehow, we left by nine minutes to seven. We stopped at Cutty Sark, where Brad and I were sure we'd have a reply to the telex we sent three days ago to Africa Bound in Lusaka. However, there was no reply. We couldn't believe it! Noticed the telex said Zambia Airways and discovered most companies use someone else's telex because they don't have their own. We sent another but still had no reply.

We also found out how incredibly poor or even nonexistent their communication system was. It was said that Zimbabwe was a very poor country because all the money was used by the heads of government. Anyone who rebuffed or complained was shot. Even with that, the people still wouldn't leave and move somewhere else. There was no place like home, and here they could have servants. It was a pretty good life, regardless of all the inconveniences and high cost of certain items. For example, we wondered why they used wood to cook over rather than bottled gas. I guess it was even difficult to find a bottle, and then the gas was way too costly.

We were to be at the dock by one and were a little early, but the ferry didn't arrive until 2:15 p.m. Typical. Teddy was very upset, because now we would be camping in the dark. The trip across took four hours and cost Z$600 one-way. Even though they booked it three days in advance and called to say we'd be waiting at the dock, it wasn't there. Then, after it arrived and Charles managed to back the trailer onto it, the ferry sprang an oil leak. No telling when we'd go then. We had our lunch while we waited.

Here are some things Charles told us: the male Egyptian goose quacks and the female hisses; impala and wildebeest can both suppress delivery of their young as

1990   1991   1992   1993   1994   1995   1996   1997   1998   1999

long as two to three months if the rains don't come; an elephant trunk holds two-plus gallons of water.

The village of Kariba was crawling with elephants. In fact today, the lady at the airline office told me about a friend of hers who was building a house, and there was a lot of noise where the cement mixer was running. It turns out that two elephants were munching in her garden just below the house.

No one swam in Lake Kariba unless they were out in the middle where it was cold and deep. There was a microscopic bug called "bilharzia" which got into your intestines and, over the years, destroyed the walls. It was always fatal. Halfway across, the Dutch boys wanted to swim, so the ferry stopped and they dove in and very quickly swam, and we were on our way again. This bug wasn't in water that was constantly moving or cold, so it's not found in the Zambezi except in eddies. Water was supposed to be potable in all of Zimbabwe.

One evening—the last, I guess—I spotted a giant eagle owl, the largest owl on the continent. It was very late and the light was poor, but I tried a silhouette shot.

By 9:15 p.m., after a big dinner of pork chops, broccoli, and potatoes, I was beat and went to bed.

Wednesday, June 13

We camped on a peninsula of Lake Kariba where there were many dead trees sticking up in the shallows. Across the bay to the west was Bumi Hills. Last night, as we sat by the campfire, we could see so many lights that you would've thought there was a village across the way. But the lights were from a string of fishing boats.

Our morning call came from Teddy about 10 minutes of six. By 6:20, we were driving to the park headquarters to pick up our guide, Maxin. By 6:30, we were stomping through the underbrush, which was very noisy because of the dried leaves having fallen (like our fall hunting season). It was impossible to be quiet. We kept looking for spoors of the churo elephant, the largest in all of Zimbabwe. His footprint was identified by three distinctive creases which, in the sand or soft dirt, were raised areas. He also left dishpan-sized droppings. For 2½ hours, we tromped here and there following footprints and sometimes droppings, sometimes broken branches. We got close to two other elephants, and I was about ready to give up when the big fellow was spotted. We watched for a while and, finally, he took off with us running behind, the vines catching our feet and branches snapping us in the face. It was amazing how fast he could move. We followed him across the airstrip, where I took two close shots with Charles in the foreground. We continued for a while and got very close when suddenly he charged, ears held wide to appear larger than his already immense presence. He made no noise but crashed through underbrush that we thought was enough to stop or at least deter him. The trees were big—six to eight inches across—and they just gave way to his massive shoulders. It really seemed that he would be upon us in a moment. Some of us bolted (I did) while others stood their ground. Apparently, there's usually a couple of bluff charges and then—watch out! We didn't stay around to see what would happen next. In 30 minutes, we were back at camp having breakfast at 10:30 a.m.

1990   1991   1992   1993   1994   1995   1996   1997   1998   1999

Left: Tracking elephants with our guide. Right: Found one!

Photos by Brad Johnson.

Woodland Kingfisher.

About 2:15 p.m., we left with Maxin our park guide. Within an hour and a half, he had spotted the elephant near a road on his way to water. We all sat down in the road to wait for him to appear. It was about 10 minutes later when he emerged from the *jesse* (plant thicket) on the left. He stopped, looked at us, and took his time crossing before finally disappearing into the cover of the *jesse* on the right. We headed back to the truck.

From there, our destination was a watering hole, only we never got there. We stopped and let Maxin out to scout while we sat visiting and having a drink, either beer or pop. It was 4:00 p.m. Soon, Maxin came back and said he'd spotted black rhino spoor and would stalk a bit longer. After a very long time he reappeared ahead of the car, all wide-eyed and excited. He had surprised the rhino just 50 meters or less ahead of us, asleep, under a tree within sight of the road. If only we had stopped a bit further along to wait for Maxin! Such was luck.

Tashinga Camp on the Zimbabwe side of Lake Kariba was very large with fireplaces, water spigots, and an ablution building (showers with hot water and toilets).

1990 1991 1992 1993 1994 1995 1996 1997 1998 1999

It was kept clean. The water was filtered but not advisable to drink without boiling or treating it. The toilets flushed, but the handle attachment was broken so a wire ran down to the bulb, and a stick was attached to the end so you could pull up on it to flush it. The shower floors were cement with the walls white-tiled. The hot water was on the right instead of the left.

There were no lion noises here in the night. You might hear a hyena far in the distance, and waterbuck, buffalo, and impala came in camp during the night. There were a lot of birds.

Brad and I were very concerned with the lack of proper hygiene in the kitchen. Dishes weren't washed in hot soapy water, no Clorox was used, and Teddy's hands were anything but clean. No telling about Cleaver's, as he was already black.

Thursday, June 14

Again, our wake-up call was at 5:45 a.m. Brad and I planned for a 7:30 departure but, before we knew it, we were on our way at 7:09. After arriving in camp yesterday, Charles decided to check the oil and other things on the truck. By nightfall, it was in worse condition than when we arrived. Today was to be a full, long day. In one hour 45 minutes, we'd only gone 25 miles. It took 3½ hours to go 81 kilometers. The country was covered with *jesse* down all the gullies and the truck crawled along. About noon, we came to a long bridge over a lovely gorge. The South Africans (Joburg) we passed earlier were right in the middle of finishing lunch. We, of course, stopped, and Brad and I both took pictures. I heard a bird and asked Charles to identify it. Without thinking, he tried to start the engine—no luck. He and Cleaver got out the tools while Teddy got lunch ready. We were already an hour behind schedule. Soon, we decided to try pushing the truck to start it, as the battery was now dead from so many attempts to start it up. Last night, they glued the distributor head together with a local weed silicone and then wired it on. We had no luck pushing it forward so we tried backwards, and there was a terrible transmission gearbox noise. Teddy said she had a four-wheel-drive Nissan, and one time when she had tried to start it going backwards, she had broken the gearbox. At any rate, now it was really out of commission. Cleaver and Charles took water, hats, and money before starting out on the 42-kilometer walk for help, which was in the form of a police radio. Obviously, we would be camped here at the Sengwa River at least tonight.

Near the bridge was a platform on stilts with a ladder. Perhaps it's a bus stop-shaded place? Under the bridge was a small stream, parts of which were moving. There was a well-beaten path down the middle, right through the water, where we saw several groups of native Tongans coming and going. Women were carrying baskets on their heads, men were carrying reeds that they used for making baskets. One woman was carrying a small black pot with a handle on her head and a baby on her back. Her two front teeth were knocked out, a tradition in the tribe done by the husband so his wife wouldn't be attractive to another man. The lady with her had a strange-looking pipe.

Well, the trailer was in the very middle of the bridge now, blocking all traffic. We all got behind the truck and managed to push it to the end of the bridge and almost off to one side so a car could pass. With a little more pushing, we made enough room

One of the many safari vehicles used on this trip.

for us to even push the trailer through. With Clemens lifting the front and the four of us pushing, we got the trailer halfway up the hill into some shade. The two Dutch guys went off down the river. Brad and I decided to go in the opposite direction where several said there was a village. Some said 10 minutes away, some said 30 minutes. We had to go through the water, and I was reluctant to do that because of the tiny microscopic bug that goes through your skin and causes bilharzia. Brad went on alone and I returned to the truck. Soon, a flatbed truck arrived, and they said they'd pull the truck up the hill. They managed to pull it well past the platform. Unfortunately it wasn't level, which made the freezer crooked and not work as well. No matter, they couldn't do better. Around five, I decided to set up a tent, struggling to get the mattresses and tarps out of the trailer without having the roof up. Just as it was almost dark, the fellows returned. We all decided to move the trailer up to the campsite (which was the major tribal highway). With Clemens lifting the front and the four of us pushing, we managed to get the trailer all the way up the hill and into the old roadway, where it was level and we could make a fire. It didn't matter that all this was in the middle of the main route to the village.

Then Clemens got the bright idea to put the truck in neutral and let it roll back to the campsite, thereby dispelling our fears of thievery during the night. It worked beautifully! About dark, a couple trucks and the bus zoomed past. One of the trucks stopped momentarily, then continued on. Earlier, when the truck moved our truck, a police car had come by and stopped. He wasn't much help.

Some dinner was cooking—potatoes, canned peas, and beef filet with garlic cloves. We had just finished eating when a truck arrived with its turn signal on for turning in. The truck which had stopped earlier and then gone on had come across Charles and Cleaver and gone to a lot of trouble to drive them back the 20 miles they had walked. Both were in bad shape, limping, footsore, and bone tired. Charles had a tooth that really hurt, and with no food or drink, he had vomited quite a bit along the way. For the rest of us, we soon were all in our tents and asleep.

Friday, June 15

This was the first day we didn't have to get up early. No place to go! People began to travel on the highway. One fellow had a rugged cargo bike. We asked if he would take a message to the police. He said "no" very quickly because he had many things to do and would be too busy. So Charles and Clemens are going to walk again to where there was a radio. Charles refused to wear socks—said he never wore socks—so he got blisters and sores. The rest of us will wait or, perhaps, go to the village.

Brad and I went down the river to the village. Cleaver was taking the dishes down there to wash them. The first bit of stream was a challenge for me to jump over, so Cleaver carried me. Brad just stood there, grinning and watching. I said, "Where's your camera?" So Cleaver carried me back and started over so Brad could take a picture, and all the while Cleaver and I were laughing.

At the village of a few thatch-covered structures, we found a young girl with a small child on her back. She was singing as she picked cotton, stashing it in a large-sized bale under one shoulder. There was a modern spray can nearby, probably used for bugs that kill their crops. Walking on over the hill, we discovered a 25 year old working in his garden. His wife was washing clothes in a very small irrigation ditch; a younger girl was his sister. His wife was sick with fever and aches—maybe malaria. We wondered if she'd survive without attention.

We went further to a larger grouping of thatch-covered structures. There were goats, lots of newly born chickens, two cats—one black, one white—two dogs, and six children, all very shy and reluctant to talk or smile. All the coaxing we did kept them all the more sober until I imitated the rooster crowing, which sent them into peals of laughter. There were three very large and extremely heavy mortars and long pestles for grinding corn, along with a bundle of twigs tied together for a whisk broom. The latch on one door was reminiscent of the type of latch our Pueblo Indians used on their doors: a loop with a rod through it.

Cotton: 100 kilos = 220 lbs. = $140/bale. In one year, they might get five to six bales. This year was a drought, which meant they'd only get 1½ to two bales.

Through a hole next to a door, we could see in the dark mess a sewing machine, corn hanging from the rafters, and a place to sleep. Very basic. One of the little girls was trying to knit with two straws and a few short pieces of yarn she had found. There were no adults around.

There were voices coming from the river so we headed that way, past the young farmer who, by this time, had completed his 5X10 plot in which to plant some more cabbage. His father had seven wives and we could see them all hoeing. When we got there, we saw they were removing a very high bank because the soil at the base was fine and loamy. They all had large short-handled hoes and would flail them into the dirt, then throw it out behind them. Brad introduced me to the man, and all the wives came over to shake my hand, saying, "*Ta pauah mapanah hune.*" That's their greeting to say hello, how

1990   1991   1992   1993   1994   1995   1996   1997   1998   1999

are you, I'm fine. Now I must be careful what I do with my right hand until I wash it. The father picked up one of the children who had on a yellow sweater and a tie around its wrist with a large white button on it. The child's navel was badly ruptured, an inch and a half around and two inches long. Brad and I wondered if it would be repaired.

We went on further to watch a couple more people cutting reeds and stripping them of their leaves. We had seen men carrying them on their heads yesterday.

I decided it was too hot and time to go back to camp. Brad stayed on.

When I got there, all was quiet. I read, wrote in my diary, and slept. Then I heard a car. It was the same police who had stopped yesterday when the flatbed was about to pull the truck up the hill. The policeman told Teddy he would radio or phone for help and bring Charles and Clemens back.

Brad returned just as we were eating lunch. We had onions, tomatoes, cheese, crackers, pineapple, beef filet leftovers, cucumbers, and pickles. He had stayed with the family while they made and ate lunch. Sometime during the lunch, the old man offered one of his daughters to Brad for Z$6,000. The 25-year-old son of the old man said he paid Z$600 for his wife, which was the standard price.

Around three, people began to come out of the woods. There was a lady carrying her child on her back and several men, one of them the young man we had visited with whose wife was sick. He was coming to say good-bye to a friend. Then there was a man carrying some reed mats. He insisted on unrolling them and showing us the patterns created with the natural colors of the reeds. Teddy purchased a small one for Z$12. Then about five to six men appeared carrying bundles of split reeds. They all seemed to be waiting for the bus. We thought we heard it coming, and when it turned out to be a truck, we all groaned. The men with the reed bundles took off.

When we were setting up camp that night, we needed a spanning wrench. Teddy called it a "hobby john spanner." We asked if the threads went the same way as ours. She said, "Lefty-loosey—righty-tighty."

Now the people waiting for the bus have been there an hour and a half, from three to 4:30. The night bus comes just at dusk, about six or 6:30.

Some facts about the animals in East Africa: In Kenya, the last five white rhinos in the national parks were shot in the last two years. Rhinos had become used to the pump that supplied water to the watering holes, so when they heard it running, they went toward it to drink. The last white rhino in Zambia had recently been shot. The differences between the black and white: The black were very aggressive, the jaws were different, and the diet was different. Poachers got $27,000 US for a rhino horn. It was used in the Far East as an aphrodisiac and, in Saudi Arabia, a young male didn't become a man without a knife of rhino horn.

In bygone days, big elephant tusks were shot off or the elephants were killed, destroying the gene pool, so today's large elephants had short tusks. Elephants had six sets of molars at three to four years old, so they could tell their age that way.

A banana-beaked bird was a yellow-billed hornbill.

Hippos spent most of the day in water because of sunburn; they came out at night to browse.

1990 1991 1992 1993 1994 1995 1996 1997 1998 1999

The giraffe never slept very long because of vulnerability to predators. They slept soundly for only four minutes. When they lay down, the valves in their neck closed to prevent too much blood from being sent to their brain. They had the same number of vertebrae in their necks as other mammals—seven. They sometimes folded up their legs and found a crotch in a tree to rest their neck in for a while. They're the only mammal born with horns—two over their eyes, one on their forehead, and two behind.

The white on the back of a whitetail's ears was theorized to help them follow each other when they're in danger.

Crocodiles can slow their metabolism down to one heartbeat per minute, allowing them to go a year without eating.

Just after darkness fell, Michael and Shawn came from Vic Falls with a brand-new truck, which wasn't as nice as the one we started in. There were three rows of three seats, and the ones in back were higher so all those in the front could see was the back wall of the cab or the sides. There wasn't any floor space because the seats were mounted on boxes and were hinged forward. They had mounted the hinges wrong so when the seat was tilted forward, its full weight was on the strap, not the hinge. Consequently, they were already coming apart.

We had to spend one more night camped along the road near the Sengwa River. As soon as we got everything transferred to the new vehicle, we were on our way again. We now would have to bypass Chizarira National Park and go directly to Hwange, which they said would be cold. The drive was most of the day, but we arrived before it got dark.

The buildings there were either black-tiled roofs or thatched. Of course, the main ones were thatched and very inviting. The buildings were painted light green or tan to blend in with the scrubby growth and trees. Our camp spot was at the end of the area (a dead end), so no one was constantly driving by. Each spot had a stone and masonry fireplace and a water faucet. This was the first place where we could brush our teeth with the water. They said it came from boreholes, which I guess was the same as wells. Our spot under a large shade tree was far enough away from the kitchen and the bathhouse so we wouldn't be kept awake or woke up early. This place and Tashinga Camp both had hot water and showers but this place, unlike Tashinga, was spotlessly clean and waxed. You could actually take a bath in the tub and stand on the floor barefooted and not worry. The water was boiling hot.

As we pitched our tent, three warthogs strolled through without taking notice of us at all.

The first night, Charles' parents joined us for dinner. They were both guides for an outfit called "Touch the Wild." There was a large estate adjoining the park where they worked, and they took on clients who stayed in the lodge there.

It was too late that first night to go out, so we looked around the shop, restaurant, lounge, and grounds, then had dinner and were soon ready for bed.

By six the next morning, we were getting ready for our first game drive. We didn't get started until 6:35 but we found elephants, rhinos, giraffe, sable, kudu—quite a lot of animals. I took an entire roll of film of the rhinos only to discover that it never wound and went through. By the time I discovered it, they had moved on.

1990 1991 1992 1993 1994 1995 1996 1997 1998 1999

We went for an afternoon drive and seemed to go a long way without seeing much. The bushes were so thick that you couldn't see into them. There were only a few savannah-like places. This time of year was fall, the leaves were turning, and we were supposed to be able to see better than when the rains came and everything greened up. This was also their dry season, besides having had a recent drought.

In 1928, India gave the national park system water pumps to pump water into the drying-up waterholes, but the park had a difficult time getting enough money to pay for the diesel fuel it took to run them. Some were not running now and wouldn't begin until the next month. They did this to keep the animals from migrating into neighboring countries, mainly Botswana, where they would only be killed. It didn't take the animals long to learn that the noise of the pump meant water.

Another night, which lived up to the expectation of being cold, we had another game drive that was less fruitful. We saw hardly any game at all. I said it was too cold.

I forgot to comment on an afternoon drive yesterday. After two hours, we arrived at a "pan" at the end of the road where a ranger, his wife, and two small children lived. We picnicked there after spending some time watching a large herd of "el" in the waterhole. They splashed, drank, and two rolled in the muddy water. Fun.

Back in camp for breakfast, I decided to call Don. I got through OK but—after spending Z$4.50 to get him, quickly give him the numbers to call me back, and waiting 20 minutes—Brad told me it was 4:00 a.m. there. Oh, dear! Poor Don! I thought it was 8:00 a.m.

At 3:30 p.m., we went for our last game drive. I spotted the notorious rhino on the left in some bushes, and when we backed up to see if he'd come out in the open, we spotted the female and baby. We watched a long time but never got a good look at them or the big one, so went to the viewing platform which was crawling with people and cars. We stopped short to keep out of the noise. There was a large herd of buffalo

Photographing the notorious black rhino.

1990   1991   1992   1993   1994   1995   1996   1997   1998   1999

at the pond and some giraffe that seemed to desperately need a drink. However, they were very cautious because of the vulnerable position they have to get into to drink. At last, one of them drank, front legs splayed to the sides. To get up, they throw their long neck up and kind of hop their front legs back together. We left to go back to where we saw the rhino and watched a while longer before going back.

Charles' parents came again for dinner. There was lots of talk about poaching and no money to do a good job. Charles also told a story about a friend of his who was dragged by his feet by a hyena from his open tent in Mana Pools Park. He was asleep with his hands behind his head on his back when this happened. He remembered his 18-inch flashlight near his head, grabbed it, and hit the hyena over the head, saving his life.

We played thought games around the fire: A man was found in a room in the middle of the desert hanging by his neck, and there was no furniture in the room. How did he hang himself? Also there was the one about Romeo and Juliet who were found dead on the bed in a room locked from the outside. The window was open and there was no sign of violence except broken glass on the floor.

The headline in Zimbabwe papers was "Poaching Under Control," which the Zimbabweans said was propaganda. When we got to Hwange, Teddy said their friend—who we stopped to talk with at the intersection where we would have to turn to go to Chizarira—told them there had been a war going on in the park the two days we would have been there if we hadn't broken down. Poachers had killed four rhinos, and anti-poaching troops were out looking for and tracking them—all activities which would have stopped us.

The visit we had to the village along the Sengwa was probably better than staying in the park.

Some Thoughts about East Africa

My very first trip to East Africa was to Uganda in the late sixties. While there, we fell in love with the people, the land, and the multitude of animals. Brad and Dale stalked some large birds in a swamp near where we stayed one night and, shortly thereafter, Dale came down with malaria. We had an adventure in itself in going to the Kampala hospital to get him taken care of.

Our visit was long before Idi Amin, at a time when Uganda was the breadbasket of East Africa. All the vegetables they needed were grown there. The lodges for animal viewing were the most beautiful we had seen. We understand that Amin's soldiers destroyed them, along with hundreds of animals—elephants, hippos, etc. What a crime.

Any contact with Ugandan women was very fascinating. The last time I visited Kenya, I met a gal who worked with them. She said they had no rights and that money funneled into the country to help with problems was given only to the men. Her findings also indicated that the women were the wood gatherers and users who needed more wood and different kinds of wood than the men. The women used it for cooking, the men needed it for fence material. It was interesting to listen to her stories.

A friend of ours, who has since died (earlier than his time), worked for the Ford Foundation. He was trying to convince the people of Kenya that they needed to domesticate one of their wild animals (I can't remember its name). It was very large, grey, and had a hump on its neck. Because it could survive better than their cows and did less damage to the ground, it was important to help them survive. That idea didn't go very far.

I wasn't at all surprised when someone commented about the security problems there. I remember when we stayed with our Ford Foundation friends in their house in Nairobi. It was a daily occurrence to have a murder or two in their neighborhood. They didn't have their sleeping quarters locked off from the rest of the house, so they had a 24-hour guard, and it was hoped that he wouldn't fall asleep.

1990   1991   1992   1993   1994   1995   1996   1997   1998   1999

Rafting the Zambezi

The following story about the Zambezi River was one of the biggest adventures we took part in on this trip, along with several walking/camping safaris.

Up early again, we had a very small, quick breakfast and were on our way to Victoria Falls. It was a long, dull ride. Some roads were boringly straight with only heavy woods on either side. Occasionally, a sign would warn drivers of elephant or impala crossings. Along one stretch were curio stands. Zimbabweans were trying to sell wood carvings of rhino, hippo, giraffe, drums, salad forks, etc. Brad bought a rhino for $10!

At noon we arrived at the Rainbow Hotel, a couple of long blocks from the main street and perhaps six long blocks to the Victoria Falls Hotel. Things looked very different from my memory of 16 years before; I think it was even longer ago than that. It seemed that the railroad track was not so near the hotel as it now was, just in front on the other side of the drive and some grass. The hotel no longer resembled what I remembered it to be. Only the main lounge and patio were the same.

We ate lunch at poolside. Charles picked us up to go to the falls. I remembered walking down a wooded path from the hotel to the falls before, but now a road led to a large entrance of three thatched-roof structures. You parked in a large lot across the street, bought a ticket for a dollar, then looked through the museum. You then could go either left to a statue of Livingstone or right to a trail running along the falls. When emerging from the wooded path at the statue with the thundering of the river and falls becoming louder, suddenly the trees opened and you could see the falls, the spray, and a gorgeous rainbow. What a thrill! How impressive and spectacular. Cameras were soon clicking, as the amount of spray and sunshine changed to create either a dim or bright rainbow or, sometimes, even a double rainbow.

We took pictures of the statue and the two plaques then progressed along the trail, stopping at each viewpoint to take more pictures until the spray became so intense we had to put the cameras away. I put on my rain jacket, but soon my shorts began to get

Victoria Falls.

Photo by Brad Johnson.

wet because the rain—or the spray—was running off the bottom of the jacket onto them. It must have been about two hours before we got back to the gate where Charles met us and returned us to our hotel.

We showered, changed, and were ready when Charles picked us up for dinner. Compared to our camping clothes, we were dressed up. Dinner was on the immense patio where colored lights were strung all around, making it very colorful. There was a long buffet where there were all kinds of salads, vegetables, and many choices of meat cooked over coals. It was out in the open and I was a little cold. If I had worn pants instead of a skirt and my wool sweater, I would have been fine.

It was now too late before we got back to the hotel to prepare for tomorrow's adventure. We had tried in vain to reach Mr. Mamba of Africa Bound in Lusaka to change our plans to go earlier to Zambia rather than spend time here or go to Botswana. The Wilderness Safari organization runs trips into Botswana, and Brad felt they were a good outfit and wanted to use their Botswana itinerary.

Wednesday, June 20

We got up early and got a ride with Charles to get rafting reservations for the Zambezi today. I stayed behind to try again to reach Mamba in Lusaka. The phone system was impossible, if not nonexistent; it was best to have confirmed reservations before coming over. I had no luck and, before I knew it, Brad was back, saying we had reservations and had to go pay and be at Victoria Falls almost immediately. No reply from Lusaka.

After paying and rushing to the Vic Falls Hotel, we waited for at least an hour before loading into Land Rovers and taking off. We had to sign our lives away because of the dangers of the river, crocodiles, etc. They said we'd walk down a very steep trail—that it was the "steepest trail of your life"—and the young guide also explained how dangerous the river was. He told us it was 2,700 kilometers long, emptying into the Indian Ocean after going through Mozambique, and at this time of year, it ran at about 400,000 to 500,000 cfs. Where we would raft from rapids numbered 11 through 19, the water was about 200 feet deep, which this year was low compared to other years. We would see the high waterline later.

1990 1991 1992 1993 1994 1995 1996 1997 1998 1999

The fellow read the liability form, which theoretically said if you were hurt or killed either by drowning or crocodile, they were not responsible, and we knew what we were getting ourselves into. Then they passed a form around for each of us to sign.

Finally, we loaded into vans—12 people per van—and drove 30 minutes out of town through some low forest country and to the steep trail that would lead us to the river some 400 feet below. First, we packed up our life vests, which came in S, M, and L. We were told to get a good tight fit and have someone else tighten it up. If you could lift it by the shoulders and it came up around your ears, it wasn't tight enough. We left our tee-shirts and rain pants behind and the employees would meet us at the getting-out place.

The trail was steep. They had tried to make it into stair steps using three- to four-foot logs, but some places were too steep. Now and then there would be a snag to hold onto, and the steeper it got the more difficult it was for the soles of worn-out sneakers to hold. Some people, not knowing the conditions, wore sandals and had even a worse time than I. I was the oldest person among the 30 who had signed up. Later, all of the Dutch boys told us they overheard that sometimes, they have had people who were 45 years old go on the trip. We all got a good laugh out of that.

I reached the bottom first and was told to sit on some rocks that were in the shade. There were four Zodiac-type rubber rafts tied in a small inlet. Above us was what must be a lovely waterfall during the rainy season. At the bottom was a large, clear pool where the water would land before traveling out into the Zambezi. The area had ferns and vines that grew around and clung to large, sharp-edged rocks. If one had to climb out from here—400 feet to the rim without a trail—I doubt they would be able to make it.

Eight Zimbabweans, skin as black as their hair, sat above and to the left of the trails. Nearby, a fire was smoking under a large black teakettle; the campfire pot spouted steam. Thirty orange plastic cups were placed on a triangular bamboo tabletop they had laid across some rocks. A few spoons out of a jar of sugar and powdered creamer completed what was necessary to serve tea, which almost everyone drank.

We were told not to sit on our life jacket. Another guide stood up, got the attention of everyone, and began telling us the rules. There were three things to remember: One was to hang on at all times; two was to always face the front of the boat, which was the direction in which it was going—if it was going backwards in the current, then that became the front; third, if you were dumped and not hanging onto the boat, try to keep your knees and your feet downstream to help in fending off anything below or from hitting a rock or a wall.

There were seven in a boat—three in back and four in front. Brad, the two Dutch fellows, and I went up front. Heath was our oarsman, and we had a trainee in back named Andy plus two others on the tour, so we really had eight passengers in our boat.

Heath rowed us out into the river. There was a large eddy at the mouth of the inlet, so we didn't go far. He explained boat language to us: "High side" meant the front of the boat, "low side" meant the bottom rear, then there was left or right.

He showed us how to hang on to the braided rope that went all the way around the raft. We could also hold on to the 2½-inch aluminum frame on which the oars were attached and the oarsman sat. We had to line up four abreast, crossing an arm behind the person next to us and grabbing hold of either the shoulder of his jacket or a strap on the back. The purpose was to be always holding onto the boat and a person when in rapids.

Then he gave us commands: "high side now" or "left now" or "right now." Our response was to fling our entire body in that direction, which meant someone would be in the bottom. I tried not to be on the bottom.

Finally, we were all instructed, and the boats took turns going into each rapid. We started off with Heath at the oars. He commanded us really well, and I came out at the end of the first rapid without even getting my hair wet.

I can't remember which rapid was worse, but when Andy took the helm a couple times, we didn't feel nearly as secure. He lacked aggressiveness and didn't tell the passengers what was expected. Sometimes we had to guess what we should do. As a trainee, we allowed that he'd learn and get better in time. One time when he was rowing, he missed getting into the mainstream, and our boat was sucked left around a large island rock.

Heath and he debated who should do the really big rapid, and Heath, fortunately, won out. He gave us fantastic directions, and we got soaked but made it through better than he had ever done it before, congratulating us on our good work in following his directions.

Finally, we pulled ashore where the men who served us tea at the beginning now had prepared lunch. The 2½ hours had gone way too quickly. A couple of us helped butter bread, and we made our own sandwiches of chicken, onion, tomato, and cheese, and had some hard candy for dessert, and tea.

When everyone was reasonably dried out, I decided to start up the trail, which was similar to those in Nepal: very steep with fewer trees acting as stair steps. It was very warm out and only took us about 20 minutes. I let some younger, faster ones pass me but, surprisingly enough, the other two American gals who were in the Peace Corps and from Boston said I had set a good pace; they'd stayed behind. At the top, there were cold drinks and a ride back to town.

This would be our last night in Victoria Falls, as we would be in Lusaka tomorrow night. Renne, Clements, Brad, and I decided to see the traditional dance program from seven to eight, then have dinner. The program was at the edge of an area where they re-created several types of Zimbabwean villages. They had a small seating area and spotlights to light up the stage area. A large group of men came out in warrior garb and put on the dance that was usually done before they went into battle. They wore white, something to look like straps crisscrossing their chests and shirt-length miniskirts. They had a white stripe down the shin area and some kind of large seed pods grouped together at the ankle so when they danced, they rattled. The dance was accompanied by drummers with stick drums and wooden block cymbals that a large group of women banged together.

They had several other dances which included very large heads made of a papier-mache type of material with weird faces painted on them and some with grey rag-type hair, some looking like a rag mop. One head was a plump elephant's, others were a hyena and a sheep. Some headdresses were so large they had to turn sideways to get through the door. It would have been great on a video. There were lots of strange music and movement. At the end, a man and a boy came out to lift two iron bars (railroad track sections): The large one weighed 77 pounds and the small one weighed 25 pounds. They lifted them with their teeth by placing a cloth around a narrow section and biting on it. After they demonstrated this two times, a woman from the audience came down and tried to lift the bars, just to prove how heavy they were. With both hands, she could barely do it.

Thursday, June 21

Brad and I had reservations for a flight of the Angels at 10:30; we had to be out of our rooms by ten. An air taxi picked us up for a 15-minute ride that cost about $43.70 each. Brad sat up front to take pictures but was disappointed because the engine or wings were usually in the way.

I decided to rent the entire plane so we could spend the whole time at the falls if we wanted. The flight went much quicker than we thought and ended with a very low pass—about 50 feet—above the river, where we spotted hippo and elephants in the water. We told the pilot where we wanted to be, and although we didn't always have a rainbow, it was pretty spectacular. The best time of day for rainbow photos was early

Victoria Falls from the plane.

Here I am holding a baby crocodile at Spencer's Creek Crocodile Farm.
Photo by Brad Johnson.

morning; we were out there at high noon.

When we got back to the hotel, it was late. We had a quick lunch, paid the bill, and got a taxi out to Spencer's Creek Crocodile Farm. This was a huge park where they raised crocs of all ages and sizes in a large pool, and there was a shop where they sold crocodile purses, belts, etc., which were made right there in a small building.

The taxi came back for us and took us to the border crossing between Zimbabwe and Zambia. We knew we had to pay at least $50 US each for reentry visas, so we consciously saved six $20 bills to get through the border. We filled out the usual forms and then presented our $100. The central officer then explained the rules: You can only take $50 each across or out of the country. We weren't about to give him our extra $20; it wasn't all that much to us, but it was a lot to them. Brad had been chatting with a lovely lady from Zambia. She had been shopping in Zimbabwe (Vic Falls) for food, which was so scarce in Zambia that many people crossed the border for supplies. Brad and the officer were in a heated conversation about the money when the officer turned away, saying that it was the law. So while his back was turned, Brad pressed the extra $20 bill into the lady's hand. She saw what was happening and said softly that she would meet us on the other side and give it back to us. When the officer returned, we showed him that we had only $50 US each. "What did you do with the other $20?" he growled. "I gave it to someone who needs it more than you or I," snapped Brad. He suspected we'd given it to this lady, because he had seen Brad talking to her, but he couldn't prove anything now. He let us pass.

1990 1991 1992 1993 1994 1995 1996 1997 1998 1999

The guard at the gate, who had been tipped off by the central officer that we had more than the $50 each we had showed him, stopped us to check for the money. But the people from Africa Bound had a van and were waiting for us, so the guard finally had to let us go. The young woman, close behind us, was also detained. We were concerned that she could get into trouble, but now there was nothing we could do. The people from Africa Bound didn't think this would be a problem, as she was allowed to have the money on her.

As we approached the bridge, Brad asked if we could stop for a photo. "No, it's against the law," was the response. "We can drive slowly and you can take a photo out the window, but don't photograph soldiers."

On the Zambia side, there were papers and reentry fees to pay, and now we were short $20. They had a sheet of costs for visas and wanted us to pay for entirely new ones, which was four times the cost of the reentry visa. Ours were good for six months, but the official was concerned about the words "within six months," which meant that if we went out within six months, we'd need new ones. During all the arguments, the young woman showed up, having walked across the bridge—a long way. She gave us the $20 and we paid the officer.

Mr. Mumba and a lady met us and took us to the Livingstone airport, where we had about an hour's wait before we flew to Lusaka. The airport terminal was dark and drab, so typical of Third World countries. Livingstone, not a clean city, was about the size of Denver. The contrast between Zimbabwe and Zambia economically was evident. The tour people told us that they lived in Zambian Airways housing and had a percentage taken out of their pay as rent. The woman lived in a flat—one bedroom, living room, dining room, kitchen, and bath. They took 20% of her pay, which she said was about 200 kwacha. So we figured she made about 4,000 kwacha a year, a little bit more than $1,000 US. Mr. Mumba lived in a house which cost 40,000 kwacha, or a little more than $10,000 US, and no one could afford to own a house.

Kathy, the guide with Africa Bound, met us in Lusaka along with Alek, the driver. We got through customs fairly easily and were surprised at how nice the domestic area of the airport was compared to where we arrived when we came from New York in the international section.

We stayed overnight at the Pamodzi Hotel and went to the Africa Bound office the next day. We paid a little over 900 kwacha to go for two days to Chibembe Lodge. We had to fly to Kafue, where we were met and taken on a three-hour drive in an open Toyota—and I mean OPEN. They had deliberately removed the windshield and the side window glass in the doors, and built two raised three-person seats in what was the back of a pickup. At first I figured it would be OK, but when we started up and were going 30 mph, the wind was so bad that I could barely keep my eyes open. My hat would have been long gone had I not tied it down under my chin securely. *Three hours* after a 20-minute stretch of pavement, miles of incredibly rough dirt roads, three miles of burning or burned grassland in the Luangwa National Park, and passing many thatched-roof villages, we arrived at Chibembe Lodge, a lovely spot on a river under large trees. There were only two other people with us. The camp was nice enough with individual two-bedded cottages, but the people who ran the camp were most unfriendly. We were joined by Geoffrey Saunders and his daughter, Jennifer, from London for a 4:00-8:00 p.m. game drive. He was Irish but she had been born in Lusaka, had just graduated from "farm A," and he was showing her where her life had begun. We had only about 30 minutes to get ready to leave, and none of us had had any lunch. Breakfast had been sparse at seven, so we were famished. They set out some cold pizza and tea for us, which quickly disappeared. We ate as we watched some local hippos appear and disappear in the river before us.

Zambian guides drove in at breakneck speed along the heavily brush-covered country dirt road. Brad commented that we were on a "high-speed" game drive. Going through the villages, the children waved and some called out "ha-low," running along in our dust. Women carried five-gallon pails of water on their heads; a homemade chair appeared occasionally made of large bamboo, a very clever design. Their homes were usually round, some made of bamboo sticks set and tied vertically. Some were plastered like daub and wattle. There were some we saw with painted designs similar to our Indians, such as the Greca House Ruin, for instance. Others were basic zigzag designs in black or brown.

Although we didn't notice much for 30-or-more minutes after we entered the park and went off the main road, we soon began to see things. Brad spotted a leopard on an ant mound at the same moment that we saw a bushy-tailed mongoose. The mongoose was headed toward the leopard, who was very alert, and we thought he would attack the mongoose, but perhaps our presence held him back, for he stayed put.

We stopped by the river just as the sun was beginning to set. There were many hippos right in front of us, some giving great yawns. The view and the sounds were quite impressive. We waited until it was too dark for photos. Now it was time to turn the spotlight on. The spotter did a good job of finding the eyes in the night. There were civet cats and genet cats, mongoose, and owls, and we heard a large group of baboons chattering in distress. Following their noises, we discovered another leopard that had just made a kill. The driver left the road, going over deep ditches; we were concerned about getting stuck. Suddenly, a ditch with water prevented us from getting close. All of us looked for a place to cross, gave the driver directions, and told him to cross at an angle. At last he took the plunge and did it, spinning only a little. As we approached, the leopard quickly left his kill, a young puku (a type of antelope). We had seen all the eyes together, so we felt it was strangling the animal just when the baboons were screaming loudest. After pictures were taken with a flash, we left to discover a lion on its casual way in the direction of the kill. He paid no attention to us or the kill and was so nonchalant that we couldn't believe it. He didn't even change his pace or pause even momentarily. He went beyond the kill, possibly to make sure the leopard was not near. Another vehicle came onto the scene just as we decided to leave.

We had a hair-raising drive back to the camp. We were supposed to be there at eight, but it was more like 8:45. We were exhausted from the dust, bugs, tsetse flies, and the bumpy road. There was no hot water, and we had wanted to bathe before dinner. A knock on the door meant it was time for dinner, which we were told would end at nine, and it was already 9:30. So we went to eat. With lights out at 10:30, there wasn't much to do but go to bed. We'd be up at six to go on a walk from seven to ten.

Saturday June 23

We left camp around seven, a half hour after daylight. Our gun bearer led the way past the area where the help lived. Suddenly, we were in the bush in single file, and a hush descended upon us as we realized we were no longer in civilization but out in and part

of the wild. Before long we emerged at the edge of the river, where we dropped down a steep dirt embankment to where a dugout type of boat awaited. We were told to step in the middle. One of the men paddled us across very near a sizeable group of hippos.

Soon we arrived on the opposite bank, which was the Luangwa Park. Again, there was a hush that was obvious as we obediently followed the leader and tried to be quiet, despite the dry leaves that were covering the ground at this time of the year—their fall.

The leader pointed out birds to us and otherwise stopped us when there was something to see. A lily pond we arrived at was also a hippo pond and bird-feeding place. After pictures there, we continued on around the end and into an open area. The most we saw was a heard of antelope and a large group of baboons. At ten, we began to get thirsty. The messenger—John—who didn't say much and was not nearly as informative as Charles, finally said we'd stop for tea. The tea bearer, who had carried water, tea, sugar, cream, cups, saucers, a tablecloth, and a teakettle, built a small fire, heated the water, and served tea and biscuits.

On the way back to camp, our rifle bearer came upon a lion in the grass only 10 feet ahead of him. We all were taken by surprise, and before we could get our cameras up, she was on her feet and quickly moved through the grass in a small ditch where she had been lying.

We were able to relax around camp a few hours before starting on another drive mid-afternoon. This time, the driver was the manager of the game drives, so we thought we'd really see a lot. Quite the contrary, he went into the interior of the park away from the water, so there was even less game. We arrived at a natural hot springs out in the open, just at sunset. There, we all had a beer as we listened for sounds of lion in hopes of locating one. When we started up again, it was time for the spotlight. The driver thought he had heard one not too far away. There seemed to be nothing then, suddenly, on the road directly in front of us, was a large male walking toward us, very unconcerned about our light or our vehicle. He passed on our right 25 feet from the car, never changing his gait or looking our way.

Again, we were late returning to camp and dinner, and the lights went out at 10:30. I had left a candle burning for Brad, and he came in long after the lights went out. He had told me that a bat had been flying around in the room our first night there. He went into the bathroom with his flashlight and discovered the bat hiding in the lampshade that dangled from the ceiling. It came out and began to fly around the small room. Brad quickly opened the door, trying to get it to fly out. At one point he closed it back in the john, then saw it was trying to come through a crack in the door so he let it out. I covered my head with the sheet each time it swooped my way. Finally, it flew out. Brad went back out, sat by the fire, and listened to the night noises. On his way back, around 1:30, a hippo browsing between two cottages scared him half to death.

Sunday, June 24

The next morning, I slept in while Brad went on another game walk; I took pictures of hippo and birds that were right in front of the dining room. By 9:30 we were on our bumpy, teeth-rattling way back to the Kafue airport, arriving two hours later. Just before boarding, I bought a large basket for $3.

We stayed at the Pamodzi Hotel where Brad quickly made friends with Gertrude, the dining room hostess. After a light meal of soup we got a taxi to the market, where we hoped to buy baskets. The market covered an entire city block. The filth was incredible and, with it being at the end of the day, there were a few young boys trying to sweep up some of the dirt. Consequently, the air was filled with a fine dust. There were chickens in cages, vegetables, fruit, and fish, all mixed together. The fish market seemed to be run entirely by women, who were standing on 18-inch-high boxes behind counters that were built on an angle to display the fish better. There were some fish, like bluegills and bullheads, which were on the floor under the other fish. They smelled dreadfully fishy and were covered with flies. One area made things out of tin— chicken feeders and coal burners. Everyone cooked with wood, and there were signs encouraging people to buy a type of burner that conserved energy. As we left there, we spotted a woman selling chickens. One breast bulged out of her blouse where a small child was sucking on it. All of this was matter-of-fact. Such was life in Africa.

There were wooden items, spoons, clothes of all kinds. We couldn't find the baskets so we asked and were directed to the "other" entrance. We found our way through very narrow aisles with people bumping into us, giving us surprised looks. Brad thought we may have been the first white people in the market. On the other side, in the street, we found baskets but not like we wanted. The various odors were more than I could take and were making me feel very ill. We decided to get a taxi and go back to the hotel. We had heard at the Pamodzi from some other Americans that the Ridgeway Hotel had a gift shop but was closed. It turned out that the Ridgeway was only across the corner from the Pamodzi, and we could walk there. Paying off

1990 1991 1992 1993 1994 1995 1996 1997 1998 1999

the driver, we told him we'd walk home. This way we could walk by the shop, which wouldn't open until eight in the morning.

I didn't want a big dinner, as we'd had a hamburger around four. I went back to my room, watched TV, read, and wrote in my diary. At about midnight, the phone rang. It was Gertrude wanting Brad to meet her at the staff gate. I was awake now, not knowing where Brad was. Thinking we were above the entrance and thinking she had said "stop gate," I thought she or he might be out there. Instead, we were over the swimming pool, and there Brad was, in the light. I called down to him about Gertrude. No sooner was I in bed and dozing when the phone rang again, asking for Brad. It sounded like the same lady. I asked if it was Gertrude, and she said no. Who was it? How many ladies had he made a date with? A third time, the phone rang; not long after, Brad came back. We had to be ready to go to the airport at 8:30 the next morning.

Monday, June 25

We hurried over to the shop at the Ridgeway, but it wasn't open. About 8:15, a lady came to open up. We saw many beautiful baskets we'd like, but they were too large to take home. Brad chose two lovely smaller ones and we bought five trays. All this was $49. They had nothing to wrap them in, and we thought it would be difficult to carry them unwrapped. They did have some thin but strong string. Brad asked if they had a needle so they could weave the string through the two baskets to at least hold them together, and they managed that. By 8:30, I had paid and waited for Brad to return with the driver and our luggage. Now we had the problems of the airport tax and crush of people at the airport. The flight to Nairobi was about two hours.

On the way to Nairobi, we stopped in Dar es Salaam. The plane was almost an hour late because of the lack of a system and manpower at the Kenya Airways ticket counter and baggage check. The pilot, however, apologized and said the delay was beyond their control. Hogwash!

At Nairobi, we hired a Kenatco van (a man next to me from the UK said they were good) to drive us through the Nairobi National Park on the way to our hotel. For this, we'd pay per kilometer, which turned out to be way less than the 270 shillings they wanted us to pay to get to the hotel straight.

We were in culture shock with all the cars, people, pollution, and noise. The Ambassadeur Hotel had hammock beds, cockroaches, no hot water, and was too noisy. The price was about $45. That night, we ate at an Indian restaurant just around the corner where I remembered having eaten when I was here with the photo group. Afterwards, we walked to the New Stanley, which many still called the "Thorne Tree." We saw many people bundling up in doorways to sleep for the night. Later on, the streets were deserted and we were eager to get inside. We stopped at the Hilton and looked at a room, booked one, and decided to leave some of our baggage there while in Rwanda.

We watched the World Cup soccer games in the TV room for a while, then went on to bed.

Tuesday June 26

Our same driver picked us up at 8:30 a.m., stopped at the Hilton long enough to leave some baggage, then headed to the airport. We were there about an hour ahead of our

1990 1991 1992 1993 1994 1995 1996 1997 1998 1999

10:30 a.m. departure, which was not enough time to get good seats. I almost left my small bag at the x-ray control and had to dash back after it.

The Rwanda airport was a pleasure, for a change, plus we would meet up with some old friends who lived here, Tom and Ruth. We were met by Charlotte, who was Tom's best friend here. She and the driver took us into town to a very nice hotel where we had lunch.

At 2:00 p.m., the office opened, we signed for the car (Suzuki), got our itinerary, and were led to our hotel at a breakneck pace for a three-hour drive, climbing up, up into the hills and going along the ridgetops. We saw groves of bamboo, tall stands of eucalyptus trees, and people carrying wood, water, potatoes, cabbage, hoes, everything on their heads. There were hillsides of tea in neat rounded beds surrounded with deep, chest-high gullies where the water would go during the rainy season to keep the plants from drowning. There seemed to be potatoes, cabbage, and some other root plants—maybe carrots, sweet potatoes. There was a lot of grass, maybe the stuff they made baskets out of, and acres of bamboo and sugar cane, some pineapple, loads of bananas. Large five-gallon-size, yellow plastic water bottles or jugs were everywhere. Almost everyone was carrying one, and there was a smaller gallon size that kids carried. Today, we saw a kid with a homemade conveyance to carry two-, three-, and five-gallon jugs. The wheel wasn't really a wheel, but an oblong cylinder with a hole through it. As crude as it was, it worked.

The stands of eucalyptus on the mountain had obviously been cut many times. They were fast growing and would start new growth once cut. Some areas had piles of wood stocked alongside the road, probably for sale. Occasionally you'd see a lady carrying just a hoe or just one piece of cane, six to eight inches long, with a six-foot-long log on her head. Most of the men seemed to sit around.

At 7:00 p.m., after driving on a paved road, but with many human obstacles, we arrived at an unbelievable hotel called "Meridian." Had I known it would be on a lake (you could swim in) and had a pool, I wouldn't have left my bathing suit behind in Nairobi. The place was large, clean, and quiet, and overlooked the lake. We had hot water and TV so were quite content to stay put for a day.

Wednesday, June 27

Our free day we slept late, ate late. I discovered a boutique across the street where there were some lovely baskets and a long stick with a sharp knife inside. I was sure Brad would want it, as he had always searched these out in other countries. When he arrived and tried to pull it apart, it wouldn't give. The store was crowded, and it happened that the manageress of the hotel was there. I told Brad to pull hard, and the next thing I knew, he had dropped both pieces and was bent over in agony, or so it seemed. He said he had cut his little finger bad and would need stitches. The manageress heard us, knew we were staying at the hotel, and immediately became almost hysterical. She insisted we follow her to the hotel, where she discovered the hotel van was gone. We told her we had our own transportation, so she rushed us to the car and directed us to the hospital. Brad had just come from the beach, where he had met the local surgeon's daughter, a Belgian. The manageress knew both doctors, but the Belgian doctor, René Wolf, had the day off. As time ticked away with our frantic French hotel manager trying to get us help, we were ushered into a most filthy room where they wanted to at least disinfect it, but Brad wasn't about to let them even look at it. He said he thought it was cleaner as it was than it would be if they did something to it.

Now our manager said let's go to the beach, find the daughter, and see if she knew where her father might be. She came, got in our tiny car with the manager, and directed us only a few blocks to their lovely home with a German police guard dog and a dachshund. The front door was locked and the daughter had to knock.

Soon Mrs. Wolf came, let the daughter and manager in, listened to our tale, and phoned somewhere two times. She found her husband at an auto repair place, and when she got the location, we left the daughter, who had been sunbathing and we had disrupted. We drove to town, where we found the doctor. He was a short, bespectacled man, partially bald with a rather large nose, but most pleasant. The two women said they'd walk home, so we drove ourselves and the doctor to the hospital. This time we went into a surgical building where things were more reasonably clean.

We were both concerned about AIDS and hepatitis, but Dr. Wolf assured us it was alright. I went back to the hotel to get Brad's health certificate to see how old his tetanus shot was, which was 1982. When I returned, they had Brad sitting on an operating table with sterile green cloths draped around his hand and Dr. Wolf had on rubber gloves; we had seen him scrub first. Brad was a bit faint from the Novocain, and he hates needles so much that the doctor smiled—Brad called himself a "wimp," which was a new word to the doctor. Since the tetanus shot was so old, the doctor recommended a booster shot. Finally, he began to stitch the cut closed using a large curved needle with black thread. He had a difficult time getting through the skin and commented that Brad had tough skin. As Brad was still feeling faint, I told him to put his head between his legs and breathe deeply. I blew on the back of his neck, and he managed to hang on until there were three stitches and a large bandage on his left pinky. The doctor refused any payment, said he'd been glad to help and would come by the hotel at five with the tetanus shot.

On the way back to the hotel, we had a flat but were able to make it into the hotel parking lot. Immediately, there were four or five black Rwandans on the scene to change it…so we let them. Then another Rwandan in a Suzuki drove up and took the wheel off to be repaired. He said he'd return in half an hour but, after an hour and a half, I decided to walk over to the town center. I couldn't find him, but I did find the marketplace and took some pictures, then headed back. There, the Rwanda Travel guide spotted me, jumped into his car, and came after me. He said they were just now finishing the tire, that it had three holes in it! I couldn't believe how they were attempting to repair it. They had taken the valve stem out and shoved a rubber hose over the valve, then held onto it tight by hand while another fellow started the compressor. Once, it blew out of his hand because he couldn't hold it tight enough. Finally, he thought there was enough air in it, clamped a finger over the opening, and quickly inserted and screwed up the valve stem. Now it needed more air, so he got a gauge with a clamp on the end and hooked the rubber hose to it, clamped the other

1990   1991   1992   1993   1994   1995   1996   1997   1998   1999

end to the valve, and again held the connection tightly while the compressor was started up. Slowly, ever so slowly, the gauge moved upward. The Rwanda Travel man didn't feel they had enough air in it, so we started the process over. At last, the gauge satisfied everyone and we paid 600 francs for their efforts, which was $8.33.

I was pretty upset when this flat occurred. I was angry at myself for not checking the tires before we left and angry at the Rwanda Travel people for giving us a car with poor tires. And now the entire day was gone with no sightseeing—no buying of souvenirs and no surfing or swimming for Brad. Too bad. We hung around the hotel until 6:00 p.m.—not 5:00 as he had said—when Dr. Wolf came with the shot. We went to our room to do it. Brad actually found it not too bad. And again—no charge. So we got his name and address to send him something or perhaps send a small item through Tom or Ruth.

I asked Dr. Wolf what had brought him here 23 years ago, and he replied that he wanted to do all kinds of medicine, not just OB/GYN or surgery, but everything. And like it was in the U.S., you had to specialize. So when he came here, he was the only doctor for 300,000 people, and now there were about 14 doctors.

Then I asked if he had ever been in the U.S. One time, for only a short time, not even a day, he said. There had been a priest here who had been severely injured by an electric saw blade that came apart and went right across his sinuses and skull. He was rushed to Dr. Wolf, who did what he could, removing some splinters. The man recovered to some degree but never was really right, so he flew with the priest to Canada to his home church, which was half in Canada half in the U.S. Dr. Wolf put one foot into the U.S. before returning to Rwanda.

We said goodbye again, but he and his wife stayed in the hotel to have drinks with the management. Brad joined them, talked with them about coming to the hotel with his groups, how to get a permit, and when the weather was best.

We had to get up at five and eat at 5:30 to leave at six for our day with the gorillas. Therefore, I tried to get to bed early, but it was 11:00 p.m. by the time I had paid the bill and discovered that the daytime desk clerk had not ordered either our wake-up calls or our picnics.

Thursday, June 28

We were up at five and ate a very skimpy breakfast at 5:30 to be off by six, again at breakneck speed, even after we left the pavement. The road coursed through gardens and long narrow paths, then finally to a diversion in the road where we waited a while for a guide. When he didn't come, the main van drove off to find him and soon returned. Now we followed in their dust up the side of the volcano until the road seemed to end. All of us got out, were given a porter, and started up the steep trail through people's gardens and very near their homes. All eyes were on us, as we were a curiosity. The children were shy, although when we waved or said "bonjour," they smiled and responded.

1990 1991 1992 1993 1994 1995 1996 1997 1998 1999

After walking 30 minutes, we rested; after the second rest, I said I'd much rather walk slowly and not stop. They let me set the pace but still stopped. The going suddenly became more difficult as we left the gardens and entered the jungle. So dense was the growth that there was no penetrating it off the trail without a machete. The undergrowth was beat downhill and, being green, was slippery. Tall or short growth was everywhere, occasionally going through my long-sleeved tee-shirt and my khaki pants. Occasionally, my porter would take my hand, now in a leather glove as advised, and pull me up. I was beginning to get a feel for what Dian Fossey had gone through on her introduction to gorilla land. Vines crept across everything, so your feet would suddenly stop forward movement and you'd try to catch yourself before falling. Now and then my leg would disappear into a hole. My porter would hold tight to my hand and pull until I recovered. The sweat ran down my temples and my shirt and pants stuck to my

body. My kerchief tied around my forehead kept the sweat from running into my eyes. An hour and a half later, we came to the spot where the Susa group had been the day before. We continued on for another 30 minutes. Finally we could hear them, and a moment later

we saw a dark form among the brush ahead of the guide. Some people who were right behind the guide got a better look than I. Continuing on and dropping into a dry riverbed with enormous moss-covered boulders, we came onto the black-backed gorilla. Again, I was not in a good position for pictures.

The guide let us stay there about 10 minutes then suggested we go back to find the others, as there were only five or six in this group. The guide knew how to make gorilla sounds and kept getting answers. Finally he came to the silverback, but he kept moving, circling around us, and went in the direction of the first group we'd seen. We seemed to be in hot pursuit, thrashing our way through the jungle. I was being pulled by my porter and felt like a gorilla being towed. At last we were back where we had started in the riverbed, and they continued to move on up a sheer cliff with all of us trying to follow. Our guides finally said it was too steep and dangerous and we had to retreat.

Going down was easy. We had our lunch, shared with the porter, once we were out at the top of the agricultural area in sight of the cars. The guide said it was a good day

1990 1991 1992 1993 1994 1995 1996 1997 1998 1999

and a bad day, because we saw the gorillas but they left. We tipped the guides 200 F each and the porters 300 F each.

We took our time now, with a porter in the back who would show us where the Kinizi Guesthouse was. Late afternoon, we arrived there, having stopped along the way for various pictures. One was of a lady with a huge bundle of something on her head, so much you could scarcely see her face. She was very angry with me for taking a picture. We also stopped for pictures of honeycombs like the Nepal hives, made from a hollowed-out log.

The guesthouse was on the flanks of one of the volcanoes. The road leading to it was bone jarringly rough for 30 minutes, and the dust was unbelievable. We felt sorry for those on foot, who we could just begin to see in the late-afternoon light. All the valleys were filled with smoke, especially early morning and late evening when everyone was cooking. All the houses looked like they were on fire, as smoke poured up through the thatch or out the ends of roofs.

The guesthouse itself was made up of two square brick buildings, each side having five bunks, two showers, and two toilets. We were both so tired that we couldn't face the situation. Besides, we had consolidated our luggage into one bag, so we needed a room together, and they could only give us separate rooms. After a brochette that was so tough I couldn't chew it and some beer, we felt better and decided to check in at park headquarters, then go to Ruhengeri to see if there were better accommodations.

We also needed gas. At the filling station, we saw a white lady getting gas. She was in an imported-looking truck. It turned out that she was part of the research center, knew Tom and Ruth, and told us of a good hotel to try. She said there would be a lot of people from the center's board there for a meeting starting next week, so the research center would not be, and usually was not, open to tourists.

We got gas and found the hotel, which was OK. At least it was clean and had lots of hot water. The jolting 30-minute drive down seemed worse than on the way up.

After a shower and clean clothes, Brad and I happened to see Bernard, the Belgian who had been with the girl from Mali we met at the Meridian pool. Brad and Bernard drove over to the home of the Mali girl; later, Brad came back and said he'd had dinner with them. I went to bed early after talking with some naturalized Americans, Presbyterian missionaries from Cameroon.

Friday, June 29

After a late breakfast, we took a look at the grass strip airport just behind the hotel and our room #6 at Hotel Muhabura. Then we went to the post office, where Brad wanted to buy stamps for his postmaster. There, an old toothless, grey-haired man with a small cap came up to Brad and began speaking fairly good English. Brad finally went into the post office and, while he was in there, the man attacked me (verbally) with his sad tale of wishing for a handout, which some tourist must have given him a previous time.

I took telephoto shots of people going by, some who saw me and didn't like it.

When Brad was finished, we drove to the hospital where he was to find a Dr. Tassi, who was recommended to change the bandage on his finger. I waited, mostly because

1990 1991 1992 1993 1994 1995 1996 1997 1998 1999

I was too obviously taking pictures and people really got angry. While in front of the hospital, three ladies spotted me, and one came over very angrily demanding payment. I professed to not understand her, which I didn't, but I knew very well what she was talking about.

We then went up to the park headquarters to see about paying for tomorrow's trip. The road wasn't any better, and clouds of our dust caused the women to turn their backs to the road and cover their faces. There was no other way to do it.

The Peace Corps guy and his group were at the guesthouse when we arrived there from park headquarters. They were closed until 2:00 p.m. and it was now 1:30. After a short time, a couple of the Americans (the mother) returned, and I decided to go see if the guide was still at headquarters. He was and said I should pay today to be sure to get on tomorrow, but the girl refused to take our money. A Swedish lady said if we didn't pay today, we'd probably lose our space. So I tried again, this time talking with a man. I asked him if he knew Tom K. He did and referred to him as "boss." After showing him the letter with Tom's name, they said we'd for sure get on group nine tomorrow.

Brad had gone up to a house across the road and talked with a lady (young) whose husband worked for the research center. They lived in a tiny four-room place—we noticed she had a servant. She didn't have much to do, which she admitted.

On the way back to town, we picked up hitchhikers, Anastasia from Michigan and a fellow named Tom from Australia.

Back at the hotel, I wrote in my diary to finally get caught up.

Saturday, June 30

This was to be the day—or not at all—that we could get some time and pictures with the gorillas. We left Hotel Muhabura at 7:00 a.m. Some students who stayed at the hotel last night were kind enough to charge one of our large batteries for the video.

By 7:30, we were again at park headquarters. The road was still as bad as ever, although not as dusty, for it appeared to have rained in the night. The people were out again everywhere we looked, going about their daily chores of hoeing the fields and carrying water; women were in colorful clothes with baskets of potatoes on their heads, some carried wood or sugarcane. They all had the most beautiful smiles I've ever seen…so white.

There were a dozen or more tourist parties waiting outside the office, hoping to get on a trip through a cancellation. The lady in charge of the tickets recognized me but still refused to take my money until 8:00 a.m., so we waited. Finally, a van from Rwanda Travel arrived. I immediately approached him and gave him my 1,900 francs (22:1), and we continued to wait. It was 9:15 before we started out by car, retracing our bumpy path through the small village where only men seemed to congregate (we found out later that it was to drink beer all day), then instead of turning toward Ruhengeri, we turned up the road toward the mountains. It's hard to believe that the road could be any worse than the one leading to park headquarters, but it was. At first it went straight as a die through potato fields, fields of peas and beans loaded with bright-red blossoms, and endless acres of daisy-like plants called "pyrethrum" that were used to make an

1990   1991   1992   1993   1994   1995   1996   1997   1998   1999

organic pesticide, one of Rwanda's major exports. The road most surely was disguised as a test for truck tires. There were several roads we could take, and I commented that we could never find the trailhead on our own. Probably 30 to 40 minutes later, we arrived at several mud-and-stick buildings where, again, there was a large congregation of men. (Obviously, beer was for sale in one of the buildings.) Here, we chose a porter who would accompany us until the group of gorillas was located. His job was to carry my camera gear and help me through the jungle underbrush when necessary.

The trail was out across a large field, beyond which was uncleared land. When we reached the edge of the field, the guide told us we were now entering wild country. There would be wild buffalo and possibly some smaller animals, and from here on we should be quiet so as not to frighten or alarm the gorillas.

It was a relief to find the terrain very gentle, the complete opposite of where we tried to locate the Susa group. The trail was even less jungle-like at first. Leslie, who had been with us on the Susa trek, also said what a welcome relief it was. Gradually, the trail rose over a small pass then down the other side into more dense jungle.

Cobwebs occasionally would grab a foot or cross my face, and the going became more difficult, so at times we had to bend over to go through what at first appeared to be impenetrable underbrush. One whack with a machete and the guide would open a path for us. On and on like this we went in single file, now and then even going on hands and knees and sometimes dodging gorilla or buffalo dung. After an hour and a half, it was beginning to look like the gorillas had disappeared and we would turn back disappointed.

When there was an over-thick growth of vines

Making our way through the dense growth in search of the gorillas.

and brush, the porter would lend me a hand. It was mid-morning and beginning to get hot, but I didn't dare push up my sleeves for fear of being brushed by the sharp barbs of something like a wild rose thorn. Unlike our Susa guide, the group nine guide made no gorilla sounds; rather, he would stand and wait while the other guides scouted out the area. We had not passed as much dung as with the Susa group, but there were only seven to nine in this group compared to 32 to 39 in the Susa group. Just how often does a gorilla relieve itself?

The guides continued to confer with one another and shake their heads. We crawled, sometimes on our bellies. The sky had cleared and the temperature had gone up. I had worn long pants, wool socks, climbing boots with lug soles, long sleeves for protection from the prickly nettle, and gloves for the same reason. I was soaking in my own perspiration and everything was sticking to me. At one point, my guide was dragging me through a difficult spot and he suddenly let out a small cry of shock, let go of my hand, and began to swat and brush himself off. Suddenly I knew why, because I was doing the same thing. Fire ants had come out of nowhere and dropped on my neck, shoulders, and in my hair, and I was being bitten time and time again. We began to swat and brush each other as we moved along so as not to be left behind. Several in my hair continued to bite, so I finally stopped and motioned for him to search like a monkey or baboon through my hair. He found one and we ran on to catch up with the others. One of the children was throwing up—just what the guides were trying to avoid, because they had lost so many gorillas to human diseases and illnesses. We stumbled up at one point above the undergrowth then went back down on our bellies, going under it.

At last, the guides stopped and gave us our packs, indicating that the gorillas had been found. Quickly, we followed the guide and found him only a few feet from the silverback, but he disappeared under some brush before I could get a picture of anything but his butt. Circling around almost to cut him off, we followed the guide again. This time, he carefully pulled some weeds away to expose about five of them. The large one in front was on his back, arms and legs spread-eagled to cool off, and the giant silverback was back in the dark recesses of some bushes. Several young ones were sprawled around in various positions. We noticed some part of them touched another. It was difficult to take pictures, because there were eight of us all trying at once. They didn't seem to mind our presence at all. There wasn't much movement and only an occasional low rumble of noise. Earlier, when the guide spotted them, we heard a huge gorilla "fart," and all of us smiled. After a long period of picture taking, the large female in the front got up and moved across in front of us toward where I had left my pack. I never realized one of them might make off with it. Quickly, the guide snatched it up, and not a moment too soon. As this fiery lady moved noiselessly across the underbrush, the sun glistened on her nose and forehead. What a surprise to see them perspire, too! They were so close, I could have reached out and touched the hand of one, but I knew I shouldn't.

An hour with them flew by, then suddenly we had to leave. Now for the long walk back. Brad kept saying we were headed in the wrong direction, because the sun was

Silverback gorilla.

directly ahead of us. He was sure we were lost. Now the going got worse again, with more hands-and-knees crawling. Thank goodness the terrain was level and not at all like the area where we were in when looking for the Susa group!

It was 1:00 p.m. when we finally located group nine, and we had started walking at 9:45 a.m. At two, we had to start back. Now and again the guide hacked out a new trail, all the time Brad saying we had to go left. Finally, we took an abrupt left, crawling under some bushes, while Brad and his guide went another way. Soon the guides were calling to one another, Brad's guide looking for directions. All of a sudden our tracks joined, and we were all back together. Brad apparently had spent most of the time literally crawling on his belly. Earlier, before we found the gorillas, Brad had lost the eyepiece to the video—the thick brush had knocked it off—so now it would be difficult to take pictures. It was loose to start with so we should have taped it on.

On we trudged. Now and then there would be a bridge—a great relief from the heat. Soon, there was a good, well-used trail going in the direction Brad had thought we should go. I had hoped we weren't far from the vehicles. My hope didn't prove to be right, but the terrain opened some and there were a variety of flowers along the way. At one point, we heard a rumble of the earth and brush being trampled. The porters appeared frightened and almost ran toward the gun bearer. Buffalo! Buffalo!

On and on, one foot ahead of the other. In the distance, I heard a mooing cow, so we were getting close but not close enough, for now two hours had elapsed since we began our retreat. The trail came out onto a road, the same cinder-strewn type as all the roads. Now we began to see people, the children running out from the thatched-roof homes to call "bonjour" and wave their hands. The minute I held up my camera as if to take a picture, they'd scream, cover their faces, and scurry off.

Finally, about a quarter mile more, I saw part of the van protruding from behind a building.

Everyone paid off their porter with 400 francs and guides at 250. We bought a beer for 100 F and shared it. Our guide wanted a ride and rearranged our baggage so he could fit in the back. Now, for the 30-minute, bone-rattling trip down the highway. How good it would be to be done with these rough roads!

Because it was so late—five—we would not reach Kigali until after dark—7:30. What a relief to find the Hôtel des Mille Collines without too much trouble and have a long, hot shower. Even the sagging bed felt good!

We actually slept in for a while in the morning. Unfortunately, it was Sunday, so we couldn't buy anything—the stores were closed. We got ourselves over to Rwanda Travel to return the car and Brad wanted to talk to the manager, who just happened to be there. He let us forego filling the car with gas because they owed us 600 francs for the tire repair. One of their drivers took us to the airport, where Charlotte met us with our tickets.

In Nairobi, we got a Mercedes Kenatco taxi to town and got our luggage out of storage. I repacked, we ordered dinner in our room, and we watched soccer and died.

Back at the airport in the morning, we had the usual hassle. When we got out to the gates, no one was there. After inquiries, we discovered the flight would be 2½ hours late. After figuring out the time change, we figured we'd have plenty of time to make our connection—at least we were on the plane, just very late. The pilot indicated that the problem was beyond his control. Stupid Third World countries and their lack of systems.

The flight was about two hours long. Because we were late leaving Nairobi, at least we wouldn't have a long wait in Lusaka.

When we got there, we were herded into an overcrowded, smoky, noisy waiting room. At 10:30, we wondered why they didn't let us board. When at last we were in the business-class section and ready to go, it was still delayed because of food service. Seems the chef had already gone home and they needed more food.

At last—we taxied out, got into position, and the engines roared down the runway. It was as bumpy as the road we had left behind in Rwanda! Things didn't sound exactly right, and suddenly there was a dreadful sound—things came crashing down and forward as the reverse thrusters were spoiled, engines cut, and the brakes were slammed on. I was in back of the bulkhead between business class and first class, alone in the middle seat of the middle section. I quickly put my feet on the wall in front of me, expecting a crash as we careened off the end of the runway, but it never came and, finally, things were quiet. Obviously, everyone was scared spitless and wanted to know what happened. For the first time in all my flying experience, I had a panic feeling of wanting to get off and go on some other flight, or even some other airline. It seemed an eternity, after two airline men ran forward down the aisle shortly after the incident, before the captain calmly came on the speakers and said they'd figure out the problem.

Everyone just sat with their own thoughts and fears; all was quiet. At last, it was announced that a "panel" had not been seated properly, and that the plane was perfectly airworthy and safe, so we would taxi and start again. The whole incident was a bit unnerving, to say the least.

I immediately tried to settle in, using blindfolds and taking only a drink of fruit juice. I gathered a couple blankets and pillows, spread one blanket on the floor, and actually slept almost the entire seven hours of the flight. On the ground, we refueled for 20 minutes then were off again to New York. I forced myself to sleep but finally awakened 6:30 New York time, just in time for breakfast. I felt pretty good and read until breakfast.

The customs in New York was a breeze, and we caught a shuttle bus right away and were at La Guardia in 20 minutes for $8.50 each. We checked in and had a 2¾-hour wait, during which we had lunch.

On boarding, they were overbooked, so Brad decided to stay until the 5:30 flight to get a free RT flight anywhere in the U.S. There was a last-minute crush to get his hand luggage back to him and his ticket. Finally the loaded plane departed, and we were in the air, winging our way to Denver—a flurry of an ending to a month-long odyssey.

1990   1991   1992   1993   1994   1995   1996   1997   1998   1999

The Trip to Pakistan

In late August, I joined a good friend and neighbor, Don Eicher, and spent a month in England. Our base of operation was in a 14th-century hunting lodge which looked more like a giant castle. We did some walking in the Cotswolds, in the Lake District, and in Scotland, then we flew off to Pakistan, which was the highlight for me. My Canadian friends from four or five years ago when Brad and I were in Peru—Nicole and Phillip Tresch—were living in Islamabad, the capital of Pakistan. We were not sure this was a good time to visit that part of the world, but the Tresches were in a position to know on a daily basis what was happening in the country. So we chanced a trip there and had a fabulous time.

My companion, Don, and I arrived at Heathrow a little before 6:00 p.m. There was no line for checking in, and a blonde British lady and a Pakistani checked us in. She argued with him as to where we should sit, and I agreed with her that directly behind first-class next to the bulkhead and toilets would be best, even with smokers. She also allowed us to use the first-class lounge, which made it really nice not to deal with the noise and crowds. They called for us to board at the last minute, so there was no pushing and shoving. Although we did leave a little late, the British lady was in charge and saw to it that everything moved along.

The plane wasn't full because we stopped in Manchester to take on gas, and the majority of the passengers got off there. The flight to Manchester was 45 minutes, then all hell broke loose with Pakistanis hugging and kissing and in the wrong seats. We sat on the ground up until 1:00 a.m., which would really make us late arriving in Islamabad. They kept apologizing for the delay; I decided to go to sleep and only woke when, at 5:00 Islamabad time, we took off from Manchester. I refused dinner and slept until ten, when they began to serve breakfast. So I had a total of about seven hours of sleep, which was a surprise. We flew over a vast expanse of desert—many sand dunes and no vegetation, no sign of life for an hour or more. Finally, we saw some small enclaves of either mud huts or tents and a few watering holes.

At last, we were coming to Islamabad. We flew over a long range of mountains, some with snow on them. I forgot to have my camera out, so perhaps we flew over some Himalayan mountains.

The PIA pilot made a very smooth landing and we were soon out in the open air and on a bus. Nicole met us and we waited a good 45 minutes or more for our bags. They were on the bottom of the last wagonload of a 747...*groan*.

I cashed $200 at the airport. Shortly after, we were through customs without a glance and met Phillip. It was so great to see him! They rushed us to a Friday-only market on the street after we unloaded at their lovely home and had some tea and lunch. James, the cook, was a smiling, mustached man with a funny bowlegged walk. Great cook, very efficient.

At the market, there were endless rows of rugs (carpets) and another of jewelry. I bought an old lock for Phillip, who collected old locks, and it cost 80 rupees. A hundred rupees was $5. We went on a quick tour of the city and then got back to their home where we saw their daughters, Sarah and Marian. James served a great dinner—lots of veggies.

On Saturday, we had a brunch around ten with Wendy Miller, a friend of the Tresches. She and Nicole worked with an aid organization, and they were going out on a mission Monday in Gilgit, which we hoped to be able to go on. Wendy was a newly married lady, very much in love, with a very good sense of humor. Her hair was cut very short. She was staying at the Holiday Inn.

Once she joined us, we all went to the copper man's house in Rawalpindi to buy copper. The "shop" was in various rooms of his home. The grandmother was lying on her bed, watching people come and go. We got there around mealtime and soon there were so many Canadians, Brits, and Americans elbowing through the rooms that it was difficult to see what was there. I bought a large brass tray which needed a 36-inch folding leg set. I also bought a large vase the size of a wastebasket, a toy, two boxes, and some bells. I would pick them up later. We took Phillip and Nicole to dinner after we toured the lake and returned Wendy to her hotel.

Pakistan was an exciting place to shop. They had marvelous rosewood furniture and there were gorgeous kilims (brightly colored woven Iranian and Afghanistani rugs), Persian rugs, and brass items. Sunday, Nicole took us to the bank and the "wood" furniture shop. Good night! What gorgeous things, but how to get them home? We both bought far more than we thought we could bring home without paying over-baggage. As we were on our own in the afternoon, James' son got us a taxi. I bought two rugs—one runner and one 4X6. We drove to a place called "Threadlines" but didn't see anything worth buying. I walked to pick up the rugs then took a taxi home. We ate early and went to a party given by Fred and Dimetria, who was a fantastically funny lady. Everything she said made you laugh. As Nicole described her, she was a Bette Midler, only not as caustic, more refined. Their backyard was surrounded with the Pakistani "tent" material—very colorful with lots of Christmas lights. There were tables and chairs all around and lots of people. Their speakers were blaring music through a window. The minute you arrived, someone came to give you a drink and tray after tray of food. We had said we'd stay only until nine, so just as we were leaving, they brought out a tray of éclairs, tea, and coffee. We left without having any.

There were fascinating people there. There was a man named Mo who will be on our Khunjerab trip if the plane got in. Some of Phillip's colleagues were there, as well as another man who politely asked about my Anasazi project.

Back at the house, I saw a jackal at the driveway before going to bed.

1990   1991   1992   1993   1994   1995   1996   1997   1998   1999

Monday, October 1

We were up at 5:30 and eating breakfast at 6:15. At seven, a van came to pick us up. We would be able to go with Nicole, Louise, and Wendy by helicopter to Gilgit, which was a 15-hour drive by car and a two-hour flight by chopper. The weather looked absolutely perfect and we all were feeling great about the flight. At the airport, we all were searched, as was our luggage. Then we entered and had a short drive to the helipad, where two Bell 10-passenger, two-pilot helicopters were parked. We all met the pilots and then were told it was raining in Gilgit. We had to wait perhaps until nine when hopefully the storm would lift, and if we had a mile of visibility, we could go. They served us tea then we had to go to the john, which was just behind the trailers in the weeds.

At last, we boarded the helicopter. Fortunately, I got a window seat on the right-hand side of the craft—the best seat in the house because all the high peaks were on my side of the flight. At first we flew over the city of Rawalpindi, then Islamabad, and I spotted the mosque, the foothills, and the valleys behind them. A large lake appeared on the left. Soon, a large river that emptied into the lake was crossed, and we followed it the entire way to Gilgit. Along the way, the terrain was exceedingly steep. Many small villages were perched in places you would think an animal couldn't even stand. There were many long and wide alluvial fans. As we got deeper into the mountains, at 8,500 feet, we began to see snow-covered peaks in the direction of Nanga Parbat.

The Gilgit Valley runs east and west and was, to some degree, the trade route between China and Pakistan. Like in all Third World countries, Gilgit was a bustling town with dirty streets and gutters, sometimes running with water and everything else. "The Bazaar" was really all the streets in the center of town. At the opposite end of town from the Hunza Tourist Hotel was the polo field and the china shop, where there really was some china.

A view from the helicopter.

Local breadmaker.

We had lunch at the Hunza Tourist Hotel then watched a documentary about the mission project. It was very well done. Then the education and training consultant, Dr. Shahida Jaffrey, invited us to tea. We could see they were busy, so we left as soon as we had finished. We did some walking around through fields, took pictures, etc., then went back into the bazaar and hotel, sat in the sun, and talked with a girl journalist traveling alone and some others.

Soon, they dug a hole in the middle of the yard, built a fire and, with chairs all around, started a chicken barbecue. We weren't sure we were to have any but asked for our chicken to be cooked without any oil. I was hoping for veggies to go with it, but they had the same dahl made from lentils, onions, and spices, along with chapatis. They fed us early, presumably to get rid of us before the mission's people gathered. Drummers and a flutist arrived about 7:30 and played raucous music until 10:30. I finally fell asleep before then and, unbelievably, slept very well all night.

October 2

We were up at 6:30 in order to be at the airport by 7:50. The day dawned almost clear, so we felt certain the PIA flight would come. I had heard a plane—an earlier one—and was ready in plenty of time to get to the airport. Don lagged behind but was ready by the time a second flight arrived. A Waljis Travel man met us and took our bags to the van. I suggested we choose seats then or we'd be in the middle with 11 people coming.

It was a great group and most were our age: Zane and Mo were from Canada; Paul and Mary Lou were first-timers to a Third World country. Mary Lou and food were not getting along very well. Marni was the one who complained about everything; she had emphysema and smoked (always one in the crowd). Jean had a Brit accent, and Jeff was a nice guy—a camera buff. Christine, from Norway, was very young and blonde. There was one black lady named Marian who was a very nice addition—jolly, etc.

1990   1991   1992   1993   1994   1995   1996   1997   1998   1999

But we ended up driving right back to the Hunza Tourist Hotel for a cup of tea and the use of the john! We could have stayed there in the first place and enjoyed the sunshine and wrote letters! Apparently there was a problem with the plane, so we would be doing the trip by van.

Later, they drove us to the Memorial Shrine for the Scouts, who helped defend Gilgit in 1947. Next was the suspension bridge, the longest in Asia at 600-plus feet. I barely took a photo of it, instead placing my dark glasses on a little boy and on a lady who came along a trail to one side. Sorry I didn't get a picture of me.

The china market was next, where the prices had not been set so no one could buy anything. Then, for over an hour and a half, we wandered through the marketplace taking pictures. Some folks bought tablecloths which were very large, with six napkins hand-embroidered, for $15.50. I found an old man in the block behind the main street with some garnets. Soon, we went back to the hotel for a 30-minute rest, then had lunch.

After lunch, we climbed into our van and headed north to Gulmit, our first stop overnight at the Marco Polo Inn. It sounded great. The drive was to be five hours, so we would arrive about 5:30, depending on the number of pictures we stopped for. About a half hour out, our first flat suddenly occurred. All of us piled out, thinking we'd be 20 minutes, but in about five we were on our way again. Within 30 minutes more, the same tire started going flat and the driver began to speed up. We all hung on for dear life, realizing the consequences of the flat at high speed. Soon we came to a police outpost, where we slowed down. We all expressed our thoughts that they'd have a way to fix a flat, but the van only slowed and passed on. Then a village of sorts came into view. I kept poking my head out the window to see how the flat was coming when, all of a sudden, it went completely flat out on the outskirts of the village. The driver hopped out and ran toward the village while the rest of us climbed out for a stretch. Just then, there was another van that came barreling up the road and stopped to help. Amazingly, he gave us a tire. So, again, we were quickly back on the road. Before long, though, we stopped again to fix the tires. We weren't making much headway.

At last, we continued on our way—Chalat and Karimabad, then finally Gulmit. We all were in hopes of a great hotel—after all, it *was* called "Marco Polo." Our bath had a one-holer with two footplaces, like in France. There was no hot water till later and the bed had wooden slats with a two-inch foam mattress over it. It wasn't all that uncomfortable, and the heavy, colorful quilts were really warm. The shower got the entire bathroom wet. Our dinner was not all that great, but it was edible. The moon was full and the night was very bright with snow glistening in the sky. We took a walk up through town.

October 3

Breakfast was very basic—cornflakes, hot milk, green or black tea, coffee, and some kind of fried bread. Then we were off to the China border, a five-hour drive. The peaks, covered with snow that we'd been able to see up the side valleys the day before, now were lost behind the narrowing valley walls. On both sides of the valley were remnants of the original Silk Road (Marco Polo). The cliffsides it clung to were so steep you couldn't imagine how it stayed there, and the amount of rock wall holding the road up was incredible. We wondered how long it took to build the road. We were watching on either side of the road, knowing that the KKH (Karakoram Highway) took 20 years to build.

We had to stop at a police checkpoint where our passports were taken until we returned from Khunjerab Pass. None of us liked that. There were barriers everywhere and just men—some in beards, more young than old. There were rows of wooden stalls on one side of the road and a restaurant and a couple more stalls on the other. Everything was grey and nothing was growing.

As we continued on, the weather worsened. We passed a tractor and wagon tipped over because it lost the front wheel. A dozen men were attempting to right it. The wagon was very near the edge, and there was also a landslide near the same area. Every once in a while, there was a group of men and tents who were police road maintenance. The valley became ever so narrow at several points where, between the two walls, were the road on one side and the river on the other. There were more and more switchbacks and, finally, we were very near the top when it began to snow.

When we reached the top, there was only one other vehicle and a couple signs indicating that we were at the China border, as well as a soldier who was no doubt frozen to death. A fellow in our group spoke to him and he said, yes, it's very cold. They were on that kind of duty for one month. How god-awful it must be! A short way down the Pakistan side was one tent where he and his buddies lived.

We all took pictures and, in 15 minutes, were winding down to warmer weather and some kind of shelter where we could have lunch. We stopped at a deserted stone building. The sun was now out and we sat against the building on a tiny foundation ledge. Lunch was an egg, a large chunk of beef, some of their flat bread, four biscuits, and a box of juice.

Back down the road, retracing our path, we arrived five hours later in Karimabad where, at a turn in the road, we loaded into Jeeps and drove up an incredibly steep narrow path (not a road) to the Mountain View Hotel. We could see why they wanted to get there before dark, because the road was so narrow and steep that it was difficult to navigate in the daylight, let alone at night.

Just before dark, we were able to see all the peaks. The valley ran east and west, so it was behind the hotel where two 6,000-meter peaks (Ultar Peak 1 and 2) rose, shrouded in snow with a jutting finger called "Ladyfinger" but referred to by locals as "Tower of the Queen." In front of the hotel, high on a steep slope overlooking the valley, we could see the Golden Peak far in the distance to the southeast. In front of us was Diran and to the southwest was Rakaposhi (locally called "Dumani").

We soon learned that they didn't have any water piped in for showers. I spotted two young men stoking a large black boiler and jokingly said they were probably going to carry it up the long set of stairs in buckets. Just then, one fellow carried one up and, surprisingly, took it to our rooms. I had told Don all this was going to happen, and then it did! He was the only one to get any. So after dinner, I took our bucket down with Paul following and filled it myself. No one saw us, or so we thought, but the next morning a two-tiered layer of blocks was in front of it. At least four of us got baths by hauling our own water.

The moon was almost full. We went walking up the road, reading all the signs along the way. We found a store open and browsed around. We went into the Mir's Castle grounds where three men were coming out. I asked whether we could see it and, basically, the answer was that special VIPs could stay in a portion of it for 800 rupees ($40), with breakfast being 50 Rs, lunch 70 Rs, and dinner 90 Rs. That would be the place to stay.

October 4

We were up early and out for pictures of the peaks and Mir's Castle. I was glad, because they didn't take us there later on the tour. The peaks were bathed in the early morning light, and the valley was coming alive with women herding their goats out to pasture and some men with sheep. The shadows formed in the lower-angle light gave the countryside and mountains deep shadows and relief.

Hunza River Valley.

After an eight o'clock breakfast, they took us to the Altit Fort by Jeep—around the mountain and down into the valley, then back up to the fort. We tried getting pictures of women there, but they didn't want their pictures taken. The orchard entrance to the fort was lovely and green with many apples. A family was the caretaker and lived at the entrance stairs at the upper end of the orchard. Altit Fort was 500 years old, perched as it was on a thousand-foot rocky cliff at the edge of the Hunza River. A bumpy mile Jeep ride from Mountain View got you there. The road took you through a large archway in the aqueduct feeding Karimabad. This was only a short distance above the present Mir's Castle. From the arch, the road wound down into a deep gorge where there was a hanging bridge. After several hairpin curves, you finally arrived in the polo grounds of Altit Village. This, like most other off-surface roads, was not for the fainthearted, for it was rough and steep.

There was a commanding view from the fort of the entire Hunza River Valley with a backdrop of snow-covered peaks: Golden Peak to the left or southeast and then Diran

1990 1991 1992 1993 1994 1995 1996 1997 1998 1999

with Rakaposhi on the right. The fort was built during feudal times when the Mir ruled. In times of enemy attacks or in times of need, the Mir provided for the people, giving grain from his stores and allowing them to run to the fort for protection.

Mir royalty had the luxury of a toilet, which cantilevered out over the wall of the castle with a considerable drop to the ravine below. This, of course, was only a square hole in the floor over which one would squat and aim. A long carved veranda or balcony overlooked the life at Altit Village where apricots, corn, and tomatoes were laid on the roofs to dry for winter use.

Another fort we visited was higher still on the mountain and perched on a singular hill with a commanding view of the valley below the Ultar glacier. It had 53 rooms in all.

We were back at the Mountain View Hotel for lunch then off to Gilgit, where we'd spend our last night before the Jeep trip. We stopped along the way to search the rocks for garnets. They were everywhere! On the way into Gilgit, we stopped at Serena Lodge Hotel where a double was $40. The Hunza Tourist Hotel in Gilgit was $16 plus meals for $4.50.

We had a fairly good meal with our new friends; I really liked Mary Lou and Paul Brandt from Pennsylvania. Their son went to school in Peshawar as a geophysicist.

Another view of the Hunza River Valley, with Altit Fort in the center of the picture.

Apricots, corn, and tomatoes are laid on the roofs to dry for winter use.

October 5

At seven, the guide came to pick up the group. We said our good-byes and waited for him to return with our Jeep, cook, and driver.

Once in town at the tour agency, we could see they had not loaded the Jeep, so I went with our 20-year-old guide, Amin, to find scarves. The hotel man gave me a clue that it was really dusty and we'd want to be covered up. I also bought 12 bottles of mineral water. By 8:45 we were squeezed into the backseat of this long-bed Jeep, along with the food and camping equipment stacked high behind us, our duffels and packs on either side of us, and sitting or leaning on our sleeping foam pads. We were off! We stopped to pick up the water and had to stuff it into corners and under the seat to get it in. The thin guide Amin, the fat cook Da du, and driver Azijon—who was so tall he had to duck his head to see out—were crowded into the front.

Indeed, the road was rough, like a typical bad Jeep road in Colorado, and parts of it hung precariously on the sides of cliffs along the Gilgit River. The amount of rock work that had been done on the roadbeds was unbelievable. On the opposite side of the river and canyon was another, older road with more curves and more hanging cliffs than ours. We made several stops for lunch and tea and, of course, lots of pictures. There were many burros carrying loads of corn stalks so large that the burro was not even seen under it. One of the couples on the Silk Road trip told of their experience in asking a farmer to stop the burros for a picture. He kept saying no, but they persisted, and when the burro stopped, he collapsed!

Our drive to Gupis was seven hours (67 miles), so it was obvious we made only 10 miles an hour. There were many suspension bridges that made you wonder how they were made. Amin said either a man swam across with a rope tied to him or they went in a boat to get the cable across.

1990   1991   1992   1993   1994   1995   1996   1997   1998   1999

We arrived at Gupis National Guest House where they pitched our tent in the "garden." It wasn't half bad! We were able to use the bathroom, where there was running water and a water heater, but it never heated up. There also was a foot toilet.

Dinner was at seven and consisted of soup (chicken broth) that was made from the smallest chicken I've ever seen that Amin found in town for $6. It was so tough we couldn't eat it. We had mixed veggies on rice and awful boiled potatoes. After dinner, we walked down to the suspension bridge in the full moonlight, then went to bed about 9:30.

Saturday, October 6

Got up at 5:20 then had breakfast at six—porridge, thank goodness, along with coffee and freshly made chapati bread. I walked over to the village while the breaking of camp and packing took place. I took pictures of a colorfully decorated house and stopped in a shop to get shots of an old man, but he said no. I talked to schoolboys who wanted their pictures taken and exchanged addresses with them. I watched men winnowing dahl and took photos, especially of the lovely pitchfork.

The road from Gupis to Shandur Pass was indescribable. Most of it had been blasted out of sheer cliff walls above the Gilgit River bed; it was at all levels with sharp, blind curves. Don was frightened and worried. We stopped a few times to take pictures of a large lake (man-made). We had to walk across a suspension bridge that wasn't all that good. Soon afterward, we came to the building of a suspension bridge and three men called out and honked the horn. The men were friends from Hunza.

Going up higher and speeding around a corner, we were suddenly stopped by a stalled tractor and trailer. About 10 men were trying to get it going. An hour and a half

An example of a typical road cut into the mountainside, and a bridge that we went across on our journey.

later, we were able to finally get by all of the tractors. Being late, our driver drove like crazy to make up time. The trouble was the road was hung on a cliffside and was very narrow, so narrow at times that we thought we'd slide over the edge because the gravel was loose and the Jeep would skid on the sharp curves.

When we finally reached Shandur Pass, we saw the polo field and small cottages where every July they hold a big polo match between Gilgit and Mastuj. The wind was blowing a gale, the clouds were boiling up a storm, and we were freezing. It was so bad that we didn't stop for pictures but just wanted to get the day over with. The road going down was as bad if not worse than the road going up to the pass. Finally, we crossed a bridge at 5:15 and were told we were almost to camp. When we suddenly made a right turn, it appeared like we were going to drive right over the cliff, but instead drove down an incredibly steep narrow road to the river bed, then drove a mile or two before turning into the tourist cottage gate leading to a Garden of Eden with fruit trees, closely clipped green grass, and a couple of wide streams meandering through. There was no place for a bath, but it was a pleasant place. Little kids appeared immediately but were told to keep their distance. Once unloaded, Amin discovered his bag and all of the important travel documents plus his clothes were missing. He and Azijon

Captivating local children.

Another example of the type of road we traveled on.

decided to drive back up to Shandur Pass and look for it, because at the checkpoint there, Amin had seen it. So the locals and I helped the cook put up the cook tent. Then I put up their sleeping tent, only getting help from one of the local boys. By 7:30 we were eating soup with rice, dahl, and chapatis with tea or coffee.

As I said, we didn't have a place to bathe, but Don had found a path down to the river before dark. After dark, he led me down there but couldn't find the way, leading me across tilting river-washed boulders and swampy areas, then through some brambles, but never finding the way. I decided to go back before one of us sprained an ankle. There was water closer to camp, and Azijon had a pan of hot water for me in the end.

I got to bed by 8:30, just when Amin and Azijon returned. They were jubilant because a Jeep coming in our direction had found the bag, and 10 kilometers this side of the pass had met up with them. Amin could now have a good night's rest.

Sunday, October 7

I didn't get up as early today because we only had six hours to go to Chitral. After the usual breakfast, Don and I started walking in the direction we were going so they'd pick us up. They were supposed to be along in 30 minutes, but it was 1½ hours before they started from camp, by which time we'd walked our way back to see what the problem was. On the way, we stopped at a mill where Don saw for the first time the way they ground the flour, just like in Nepal. Water ran under a house where it turned a horizontal wheel. On the axle of the wheel, they placed a large grinding stone with a hole in the middle. Over the stone was a large funnel-like thing into which the wheat went and dropped down into the hole. Somehow it got thrown out under the circular stone between it and the base grinding stone. It came out as flour that they swept up into bags.

Don and I, wrapped in scarves to protect ourselves from the dust while traveling.

At noon, we stopped for lunch and again were the object of puzzlement. This day we actually sat on the ground and had a picnic. Yesterday, we stopped at a government house overlooking Phander Lake. The caretaker opened up the place so we could eat inside the living room. We had tuna fish with tomato sauce and canned cheddar cheese on crackers with tea, peaches, and cookies. Pretty tasty. Today we had tuna with curry and cheese, the same stuff. Fresh chapatis were brought from the restaurant, along with black tea. Again everyone, including a cocker spaniel and a goat, watched us. I took pictures of a bearded man then two chaps with white hats. Then a man with a bow (*jgame*) sat to watch us as I used the small Urdu section of the Pakistan handbook to talk to them and make them laugh. Finally I took a picture of the man with the bow, then asked if I could try it. When I missed and put a ding in it, he wanted it back. I felt badly, so I bought it for 50 Rs ($2.50).

On we went, and it wasn't far before we came to our first landslide and a full, long stop. Dust, dust, and more dust. It was about 2½ hours before they got it cleared, everyone directing traffic and watching. When the dust settled, the lorries coming in the opposite direction had lined up two abreast, so the entire road was blocked. There was no order, no one directing traffic, and horns began to honk. Our driver had made his way to the front of our line, probably so we wouldn't have to eat anyone's dust. We managed to get through the rockslide but the two lanes of oncoming cars halted us, and we had to be satisfied to sit until a lane was cleared. Finally, we were through, with one Suzuki behind us honking, and when our driver veered to one side it sped by, leaving us

1990   1991   1992   1993   1994   1995   1996   1997   1998   1999

in its dust. My nose and throat were feeling the effect of breathing so much dust, and I was beginning to cough.

At last we were in Chitral and at the PTDC (Pakistan Tourism Development Corporation), a government tourist hotel. Our room was large, clean, and had a sit-down toilet. There seemed to be hot water, as our room was on the back of the hotel near the water boiler. The only bad thing about it was that it kept filling with smoke from the stoking of the boiler. Dinner was reasonably good—tomato and radish salad, soup, chicken and rice, and some veggie dish, apples, and black tea. I also had sprile for the first time.

A journalist fellow was eating dinner alone, so he struck up a conversation. He was freelancing in Peshawar and had been here four years, with a six-month forced vacation due to malaria that his Tucson doctors could not diagnose.

I forgot to mention about meeting the campaign truck just west of Shandur Pass, which was broadcasting for the National People's Party, or National People's Democratic Alliance. There was no one in sight to hear their broadcast, but they were doing it loud and clear anyway.

My bath was a luxury and just the right temperature. I also did a small washing, then got to bed early.

October 8 to Kalash Valley

After a short walk to the police station, we waited 30 minutes to get registered. Then we walked through the upper market for a while until, suddenly, Da du and Azijon appeared. Time to get on the road, which was surfaced. I fell asleep for some reason and had done the same thing yesterday. Hope I don't have some illness. Partway up the canyon, off of the Bamboret River, there was a small landslide, which must have held us up for three hours—at least it was 1:00 p.m. before the men who were hand-shoveling it were finished and we could get through.

We then made another short stop for a permit to go into Kalash Valley, and then we started up the very narrow, dusty road. If we had thought some of the road from Gilgit over to Chitral was narrow, this was even more narrow and precipitous. There were many curves where the sides of the Jeep almost touched the wall on the inside.

Kalash locals.

Our "garden hotel" was about the worst we'd had so far. It was small with a lot of white iron chairs and tables in a garden with fruit trees and roses. There was also a green-and-white umbrella over a concrete table surrounded by eight chairs. At the back was a row of rundown, stand-up-in tents that they rented out and a green wooden building with a squat toilet but no way to flush it other than pour water in. The garden had three terraces, maybe four. We chose to put the tent right in the middle of the lawn chair section. The cook tent was nearest to the Jeep.

The town of Kalash was very small, with just a main dusty road, an occasional shop and flour mill, and homes that were larger than those in the Gilgit Valley, which were made with smaller stones and wood.

Since it was very late, we ate our usual cheese, tuna, crackers, and fruit lunch with green tea, then Amin took us on a tour of what was there. We stopped at the tourist hotel and picked up a guide who had organized a dance of the women later in the day, which we would pay 400 Rs for. We also paid 10 to 15 Rs every time we took a picture. I stole some with my telephoto lens.

The women there wore gloriously colored necklaces and headdresses, even in the fields. They were very shy and didn't like their pictures to be taken. But at the dance—which consisted of women in black dresses with red beads, standing side by side and arm in arm— pictures were allowed. The women danced

Kalash woman with elaborate necklaces and headdress.

1990   1991   1992   1993   1994   1995   1996   1997   1998   1999

Close-up of headdress beadwork.

one way first and then the other to the beat of a couple of drums. There wasn't much to it, but it gave me a chance to get some pictures.

There were three valleys where about 3,000 of these Kalash have made their home. As a vanishing culture, it was special to see them.

Back at camp, I washed up and we had dinner.

October 9

Amin said the road would be worked on early in the morning, so we'd better get an early start. At first they said to wake the cook, Da du, at 4:30, then changed that to five because Da du said it would be dark at 4:30. Well, it would still be dark at five, but we agreed.

It was a long night, going to bed at 8:30 because of the cold, the coldest it had been. Just before five, Don awakened Da du, and after I was packed, we took down the tents to help hurry things along. We didn't want to sit two to 13 hours while they repaired the road. I kept after them to hurry, and we really drove away about seven minutes early. It only took us 30 minutes to get past the landslide area, so it paid off to hurry everyone.

The train, fields, houses, rocks, everything was such a contrast to the KKH side that I found it dull. The road itself continued to be hair-raising. Periodically, I slept. The houses were built on the sides of cliffs, just like those of the poor people in Mexico. Everything was grey, the color of the rocks. The roads clung to the hillsides, some under rock overhangs that had been blasted out for the roadway. There continued to be a lot of corn stalks stacked high on rooftops in preparation for winter. A short distance down from the pass, a cluster of buildings had more than we could count, plus stacks and stacks of wood. God, the winters must be dreadful.

Once off the pass and into the valley, things greened up. There were cornfields and rice paddies and tree-lined roads, along which were many kinds of orchards. Some looked like oranges. The day was very hot and, when we had lunch, we were able to shed some clothes from the morning drive in the shade. At that point, we saw some other tourists going the other way to Chitral. One lady was all in white, and I wondered if she knew what lay ahead—dirt and cold.

Finally, we reached the Pameer Hotel where we could have a hot shower, relax, and put on clean clothes. We went out and I bought a local outfit for 430 Rs. When I tried to put it on, I couldn't get it over my head. So I went back into the store and found a young man sitting on the floor surrounded by sewing machines, some Singers. I demonstrated that the hole was too small, and he immediately went to work to enlarge it. Using a long 12- to 18-inch scissors, he cut the threads, showed me how long he'd cut it, and that he only had white backing. In 10 minutes he had it fixed, perfectly topstitched and all. He didn't want any rupees, but Don insisted and gave him 10 Rs.

We took a short walk through the streets then had dinner at the

Don outside one of our accommodations.

Pameer, which was really bad—we couldn't even eat the rice! We finally hit the sack.

October 10

Breakfast was better than dinner, and Amin came to take us around the bazaar (streets). By nine, we had taken a group photo and were headed for Islamabad. We had one stop for lunch where we decided to eat bananas and granola bars and have soda pop, since we were still well. The traffic had increased and the roads were paved. There were donkey carts, horse-drawn wagons, camels, lorries, buses, cars, and wheelchairs, all on the same highway, dodging one another. This went on for six hours until we were back in Islamabad. We stopped to see if Don's boots were there, then went on to Nicole and Phillip's to take a shower and have a dinner that James had made. Right after my shower, Amin returned with Don's boots in a taxi. We gave him 50 Rs for the taxi and 50 Rs for his trouble.

I packed and did laundry, etc., that evening to get ready to go to Quetta the next day.

1990   1991   1992   1993   1994   1995   1996   1997   1998   1999

October 11

We went to the bank to cash $400 = 8,000 Rs and toured the city some, then had lunch. We were picked up at noon and driven to the airport. There were 30 hashers gathered there with luggage, including several large boxes of beer. It was a waiting scene, and we could finally check in and get onto the plane. I got a window seat.

The desert community of Quetta was surrounded by rolling, sandy hills, mile after mile of cliffs and terrain—similar to that of Comb Ridge in our Southwest—that turned into higher mountains. Made up of the Salt Range, the terrain had large anticlines and synclines—such beautiful flowing lines. A large river, the Indus, flowed through here. The wind blew and it wasn't uncommon to find yourself in a dust storm or see dust devils rising on the horizon. Being very close to the Afghanistan border, there were numerous refugee villages on the outskirts of town. Canvas flapped in the wind and make-shift structures of cardboard, tin, plywood, and canvas formed the only shelters these homeless people had. With no sanitation facilities, disease was rampant.

A Serena van met us and drove us to the gorgeous Serena Lodge Hotel of Quetta, a look-alike of the Santa Fe adobe hotels, even down to the mountain backdrop. The hotel won an international architectural award and took seven years to design, research, and produce what it was today. A Canadian woman was the architect and interior designer. With the fabrics,

Woman carrying a kid.

1990   1991   1992   1993   1994   1995   1996   1997   1998   1999

rugs, pull-string drapes, bedspreads, headboard circular designs, inlaid wooden furniture, and lamps, it took 1½ years to complete. The walls were done by locals by hand. The local people didn't like the hotel because it was nothing new.

We met the executive assistant manager, Qasi M. Mohsin. He was the one who did three years of research and had 3,000 pieces of paperwork on designs for fabric and lamps. The lamp pattern was taken from the window latticework of the Balochistan adobe homes. The carpets were woven in two parts, the center and the border, so they could be laid in uneven halls, etc. The circular embroidered pieces on the heads of the beds in different colorful patterns were made in Sibi. The people were given a sort of plastic to do them on. They didn't tell them what colors to use so they'd be original. The heads of the beds had 13 circles and the dresser had seven on the lower section, set in squares. The carpets had similar patterns. The five hanging lamps in the dining room were taken from the latticework of the homes. They were brass and hung at different heights. Some ceramic ones were bedside lamps. The drapes were extremely heavy and lined. Next to the window was a lace curtain; a large valance with a pattern similar to some of the rugs and throws were over each window. The floors were marble and heavily waxed, so in sneakers, every step was a loud squeak. You couldn't sneak up on anyone! The colors were green, red, yellow, burgundy, lime green, orange, purple, light blue, white, brown, and rust. Some patterns were zigzag and arrow, similar to Navajo rug patterns. The doors were heavy and wood-paneled. Hall lighting was recessed with a square piece of marble over the bulb which, when on, was translucent. All corners

Serena bazaar.

Bazaar vendor.

were curved. Each room had a tiny alcove that was surrounded with colorful beads and had a graceful branch with leaves, presumably indicating east for prayers.

Amazingly, in this desolate land, this modern hotel was an oasis with a fire alarm in the ceiling and modern window hardware. A lot of ceramic pottery tilted on its side in various places, and air conditioning was present in each room. There was even water that they said you could drink! TV, too, with two stations.

The first evening we hurried to the bazaar, a crazy place with everything mixed together. There was the fruit market with its red-and-green apples piled neatly and high, some covered with a canvas shade; the shoe market; the butcher market with carcasses hanging and covered with flies and dust; and the nut area with almonds, walnuts, peanuts, pistachios, etc.—mounds and mounds of them. Red boxes for 75 Rs. Dust was everywhere mixed with diesel fumes, gas fumes, urine odor, putrid meat, body odor, horns honking, people shouting, hawkers of their wares, hardware, stationery, snow cones, kebabs, and smoke from large pans (three feet across) where they fried bread.

Later that night, we were driven to a private home where the Hachers were having their reunion. There were lots of people in a yard surrounded by multicolored patchwork tents (walls and covers) and a large buffet, any kind of drink, and there was loud music. It was very cold and I stood by the barbecue fire to keep warm.

October 12

We were up in time to have James' sweet rolls and juice and coffee with Nicole and Phillip, then we met the group at eight, waiting 30 to 40 minutes for one person. Then

Nomad camel caravans making their way south.

three carloads headed for Bolan Pass and Sibi, where the nomads were migrating to the south. Now we saw the landscape up close—it was so like New Mexico and Arizona with desert for miles, dust devils, and periodic tunnels for the train that went up the canyon and over the pass.

Once a year, nomad camel caravans come through the edge of Quetta on their way south. They leave the high country, where it will soon be cold, to make their home on the other side of the mountains where the weather is milder during the winter months. The scene here was straight out of a movie set, with sand in every direction back-dropped with distant mountains. Long lines of camels—some carrying people, some carrying chickens tethered with one leg—ambled through the heat-wave mirages with dust devils rising behind. Their robes flapped in the wind, their dogs barked and nipped at the ankles of the camels. Pans clanged, blankets flapped over carpets—all their worldly possessions were tied to a wooden framework on each camel. The women covered their faces, as was the custom. We saw some women with babies, but there were mostly men who wore turbans fashioned from yards of cloth wound around their heads. When the wind and sand became too severe, the tail end of the turban would be used to protect their face and eyes. What a scene! What an experience! We stopped for photos several times and turned around at Sibi.

We got back to the hotel for lunch and, therefore, missed the Jumma Market, which closed for prayers by three. Don lost his camera, so we took a taxi to the site

1990 1991 1992 1993 1994 1995 1996 1997 1998 1999

Here I am with a caravan guide.

but it wasn't there. We hoped to find it in the car tomorrow. The hotel had a pool, two squash courts, and two clay tennis courts, many conference rooms, two restaurants, and some shops with carpets and jewelry.

We had dinner in and talked with the manager of the boutique, which was very interesting. Got to bed at midnight.

October 13

I was unable to see anything on the flight to Karachi. We were 20 minutes late due to the stretcher case they brought on board. Stewardesses asked a nine-year-old girl to give an elderly man her seat as he wanted a window. That upset me. The girl was Danish, and I spoke to her to see if she was OK. Then the old man asked my seat partner to move in her place. Soon after she got settled, some idiot came over and tried to get a bag into the overhead. It wouldn't fit and fell out, landing on the girl's head. Her parents lived in Denmark—the father was Pakistani and the mother was Danish. They boarded her in a school in Quetta, of all places, to learn English. Poor thing! She was on her way to live with her aunt and go to school in Karachi now.

We were met by a van from the Avari, a five-star hotel—quite nice but not as posh as the Serena. We bought eight lamps, five for me and three for Nicole. Phillip took them back to Islamabad with him on an earlier flight. Five cost $162.

Nicole called her friend, Marilyn, a nurse. She and her roommate, Nancy, a Peace Corps person, came in Marilyn's car and took us to an American club for dinner. It was a plain place but had excellent food. She wouldn't let us pay.

After dinner, we got in a cab and drove to Hawkes Bay Beach to see the giant turtles. It was about 10:00 p.m. when we found a little shack with a light and a Turtle Foundation guide to take us out on the beach where, between July and November, turtles come in to lay their eggs. There were only two or three other places in the world where they continue to do this, and thank goodness the Pakistanis know enough to protect these age-old creatures. Soon, we were seeing the three-foot-wide "tractor" tracks they leave in the sand. The guide pointed out one of them, digging her hole. Sand spewed up 10 to 12 feet into the air as she flicked her flippers to dig a large five-foot-diameter hole. Once dug, which usually took 30 minutes to an hour and a half, she would finally begin to lay her eggs. If disturbed before that episode began, she would return to the sea without laying the eggs and try a different section of the beach. So it was important to be quiet and not shine the lights on her.

We stood lower on the beach than the cottages, which were on a small rise, and because the city lights were in that direction, we could see the outlines of several turtles as they flicked the sand to make a nest. Many "tractor tracks" came out of the Arabian Sea and made a beeline for the hilltop, which was about 150 feet. The tide was coming in, and there was enough light on the wet beach for us to make out the shadow of a turtle as it came up to the beach.

Finally, the guide motioned to us to come, as he thought one was about to lay her eggs. Sure enough, she was! And once she started, you could flash the light, talk, take pictures, etc. She had a really deep hole dug right under her tail. It seemed to be about a foot or 18 inches deep and a foot across. Already there were a pile of eggs—there must have been hundreds—a little larger than a ping-pong ball, and there was saliva-

A group picture with our guides on the trip.

like stuff on them. Sometimes two to three came in rapid succession. The guide told us she'd lay 200 to 250 eggs then cover them and herself up. She'd rest for an hour or so and then return to the sea. He would gather the eggs and keep them in an incubator so they'd hatch in 45 days, then they were let go to go back into the sea. He pulled a couple handsful out of his pockets. They were the size of a silver dollar and their little flippers were flailing in the air. When they were put onto the sandy beach, they sort of headed out toward the sea with all four legs frantically paddling. The entire experience was like nothing I'd ever seen before.

By midnight, we were back at the hotel.

October 14

We met Nicole at ten and started walking to the markets. We ended up with a horse and buggy, trotting our way to a rosewood factory. There was child labor everywhere there, but the wood products were incredibly beautiful. Then we went on to a carpet shop, ending up there for a couple hours. We each bought a carpet, not Persian but Afghani—such bright colors. By then, we were all melting in the heat and needed lunch.

Elaborately decorated trucks were a common sight on this trip.

Carpet vendors.

We returned to the hotel, lunched, changed into jeans, and then off in the hotel van we went to the harbor to catch crabs. Nicole had made the arrangements with the son of Mr. Avari, the owner of the hotel. At the harbor, it turned out the bell steward would go with us, so the four of us followed the boat owner, Captain Mack, through throngs of filthy people to an area where there were some old sailboats. Ours had colorful cushions in the back and red Persian carpets. We could kick our shoes off and lay back in laziness.

Soon the sail was raised, and one man used an oar to move us along faster. The oar was a round disk on the end of a long pole. He didn't have an oar lock but just put it against a section where the mast was tied down, sat on the deck, braced his feet against the plank, and rowed. The other mate climbed either the mast or a rope with his toes to help navigate and to unfurl the sail. Out past the Pakistan Navy boats we went, not very far to an area off a small village where there were many fishing boats and a small local ferry dock. It was not an area where we would have thought we'd catch crabs, but we dropped anchor, and that was it. Because of the Navy ships, I couldn't take pictures. Bummer.

We each were given a piece of wood, sort of an oblong block with line wound around it, on the end of which was a heavy weight and two hooks baited with pieces of fish. After flinging them over the side, we were to feel a crab on the end and slowly pull it in. Nicole caught more than anyone. Don caught one, and finally I got one large blue

1990 1991 1992 1993 1994 1995 1996 1997 1998 1999

one, but the captain let it get away! I can't believe it! That was after they had built the fire (Primus stove) in the center of the boat and cooked a dinner of onions, potatoes, tomatoes, cabbage and—of course—crab! Anyway, it all was a neat, relaxing experience, and at six we started back to the dock, a huge orange sunset over the village and another sailboat moving along the shore.

We went to the market to get elephant pillows just in the nick of time, as they were closing. Then we went on to a leather place, but we were so hot, sticky, and dirty that we ended up back at the hotel at eight to go to bed. On the boat, Don's passport fell out of his hip pocket. Nicole happened to see it, or who knows what would've happened next.

Now it was time for Don and me to prepare to return home via England.

We happened upon some snake charmers at one of the bazaars.

Flying from Islamabad to London via Dubai

We were soon flying on a TWA 747. It was one of those planes with an upstairs to the cockpit and a few first-class seats. Arriving at the airport, two baggage carts in tow, we approached the check-in counter holding our breath. Acting as though it was normal to have two giant boxes (two oversized-cubic-feet each) and two oversized leaden suitcases to check in, I handed the female agent our tickets and waited. Finally, she said we were 58 kilos overweight. Nothing was said about how many rupees that cost (we only had 200). I said I had phoned the cargo department and was informed that, flying internationally, we could have two bags any size and weight. The agent called her supervisor.

The waiting seemed to take forever. The airport tax was only 200 Rs each rather than 300, so all we really had was the 200 left from the 600 we'd kept out. Finally, a stern-looking man appeared, mumbled that since we were stopping in London the rule stated that we'd have to pay over-baggage…however, this time he'd overlook the WHOLE SITUATION! The four pieces were checked through!! To London!! We were halfway home-free!!!

As we were boarding, a man who looked like a pilot came up with his bags. I asked if he was the pilot. He said no, he was the purser. He wondered if I needed some assistance. I said no, but we had wanted bulkhead seats. I gave him my boarding pass and asked if the seats that we were given were those. He confirmed my suspicion—they weren't. "We'll see if we can make some kind of an adjustment," said he as he hopped on the shuttle ahead of us. Neither of us were looking forward to the long flight. Our seats turned out to be a few rows back from the bulkhead with a group of people who appeared to be quiet, so we made no fuss, even though the purser offered to move us before taking off.

Because of the poor quality of food in Islamabad, the route we took included a stopover in Dubai to pick up food there. The scenery south and west of that city captivated both of us. We were glued to the window the entire way, oooohing and aaaahing at various geologic formations. Everyone around us kept looking out to see what we saw that was so impressive. I'm sure all they saw were the desolate sand and mountains.

The stop in Dubai was such a contrast to Islamabad! After landing, they allowed everyone to exit the plane and visit the duty-free shops of the airport while food was loaded onto our flight. Only 20 minutes was allowed, just enough time to whet one's appetite and make you want to return. We didn't want to visit the duty-free shops and so stayed aboard, periodically playing Scrabble.

While we were waiting, I asked the stewardess if I could go upstairs to have a look around. I was surprised to find quite a few people there and asked how they got seated up there. It turned out to be business class. As long as I was there, I poked my head into the cockpit ("flight deck" is the better term) and asked what the chances were of coming up during the flight, that we were both pilots. Well…he—I think it was the navigator—who was the only one there, just asked what seats we were in, and he would see!

We actually took off on time (as we did from Islamabad) and, again, we both glued our heads to the window, trying to figure out where we were, and saying wouldn't it be great to fly in a small plane over some of the terrain like we do in our Southwest?

We were supposed to stay awake to avoid jet lag, so several Scrabble games and lunch later—and much to our surprise—a stewardess came to get us! She asked if we were pilots, and when we said "yes," she said the captain wanted to see us, then she led us to the flight deck. Wow! We couldn't believe they actually let us in there—especially Don…he would've wished to do it but would never have asked. So there we were on the flight deck, sitting right behind the captain and co-pilot at 35,000 feet, flying 560 mph somewhere over Austria by then, headed for Frankfurt and 1½ hours before touchdown in London. We had a magnificent view of the setting sun, causing the clouds to be shades of pink and orange, with an occasional snow-covered peak poking its head above everything far, far in the distance.

So there we were on the flight deck, sitting right behind the captain and co-pilot at 35,000 feet, flying 560 mph somewhere over Austria by then, headed for Frankfurt and 1½ hours before touchdown in London. We had a magnificent view of the setting sun, causing the clouds to be shades of pink and orange, with an occasional snow-covered peak poking its head above everything far, far in the distance.

The number of controls and dials was mind-boggling, and the conversation was great! What did we fly? When and where did we learn to fly? Then we asked them questions, and it turned out that they had learned to fly in west Texas. The pilot had trained for his "heavy" rating in Denver 11 years ago with United Airlines; the copilot had been in Denver once, and his favorite small plane was a Cessna 210. We told them we'd give them a flight over the Rockies if they were ever in Denver again. They said we should come back to Pakistan and they would give us a ride that we wouldn't soon forget up to Skardu, similar to where you fly from Kathmandu to start hiking to climb Everest. The talk was about mountains, comparing theirs with ours, and flying

1990   1991   1992   1993   1994   1995   1996   1997   1998   1999

to Lukla, where the copilot got his training for flying Fokkers into Skardu. A great experience.

So I made a couple new acquaintances which may turn into something down the years. Who knows? Don still wasn't over the fact that we got into the flight deck of the 747 IN FLIGHT!

Touchdown at Heathrow was on time at 6:15, and we both had stayed awake and felt good. We got a porter who helped us get our bags and boxes with a large four-wheel cart. He was a jolly Irishman who knew the ropes and whisked us through the customs area, where no one even made a suggestion of looking at or into our luggage. We left most of it at "Left Luggage" for 1.70 pounds per piece, then took a shuttle to our hotel for a late dinner and early bed.

I couldn't let our experience with the Irishman pass without saying to Don that he had worked at Heathrow, helping people through customs and getting transportation for 20 years. When Don began to doubt that a free shuttle would come to pick us up and wanted to get a cab rather than wait for 10 minutes, our jolly Irishman said, "Give me 10 women any day against one man, and I'll take the women. They don't worry, fret, and stew if things don't happen right NOW, but the one man? He's always in a hurry and doubts my word every time." Even when he told Don a taxi to the hotel, which was less than two miles away, would cost $40, Don was so impatient he almost hailed a cab. About that time, the shuttle arrived and the Irishman said, "Ya see?"

The Ibis Hotel was, indeed, a stone's throw from the airport. It had a lovely restaurant and a great show. After a late dinner, we slumbered away for 11 hours! Opening the double-soundproof windows in the morning, we saw that we were right across the road from the end of runway 27 right. We watched several "biggies" take off, one for Singapore, and later I heard an incredible noise that made me say, "Boy, that's a big one." It turned out to be one of the Concordes which reminded me of my one flight in one from Paris to Kennedy, where we left at 10:30 a.m. and got to New York before we took off the same day, at 9:30 in the morning.

After a late breakfast, we were back at terminal three, Heathrow. This would be the acid test. We got the loot out of Left Luggage, again with a porter who knew the ropes (they were worth their weight in gold). We seemed to sail through several checkpoints, our man pushing the cart along with us. A lady asked us who packed the boxes and where they were packed. She wanted to know if we were carrying any gifts or packages that weren't ours but were for someone else. We were holding our breath. Next came security checks, then the check-in counter. There, we couldn't believe that they took our two suitcases and told the porter to just put the boxes on the trolley without even weighing them! We probably could have brought the entire lot back with no trouble. Oh, well—we couldn't handle any more. We had done it all the way to New York!

All's well that ends well, but an unexpected turn of events just about ruined the entire two-month trip when we checked into our Kennedy-to-Denver flight. As I reached into my carry-on bag for my stuff sack filled with exposed film to have it hand-checked, it was GONE!!! I had left it at the last security check before going into the duty-free shop and lounge in terminal three. How dumb!

1990　1991　1992　1993　1994　1995　1996　1997　1998　1999

There was just 30 minutes before the flight left. I grabbed my boarding pass and dashed off to TWA bagging services. After an interminable wait for my turn, I explained what happened and they sent off over their computer tracer to Heathrow. Needless to say, I was SICK! In Denver, I again went to baggage services and they did the same thing—sent a message over the wires. I happened to wake up at 3:00 a.m. the next morning so I called Heathrow inquiries, which directed me to security. They had a record of it having been left, and they would check with TWA right away. There was no ID on the stuff sack other than a North Face label, but the film was mostly out of its can and numbered with a magic marker, so it was easily identifiable.

From Saturday morning through Tuesday night, there were three more calls to London, two to New York—one in which the lady hung up on me—and several calls to Denver. Finally, at nine Tuesday night, Denver TWA called to say they had it!! Don and I drove in to pick it up, not taking any more chances that if they gave it to a delivery service the next day, something might happen to it. It's now being developed and I hope it didn't go through every x-ray machine between Heathrow and Denver! We'll see.

So, again, all's well that finally did end well! We can't say enough good things about our three weeks in Pakistan. We heard this morning that Bhutto lost the election and that there was a 6.6-point earthquake near Kabul which affected Peshawar and the Hindu Kush.

Back from Pakistan, A New House

So I came home from Pakistan to find Peaks and Places set up for business in the basement of 1965 Dartmouth Avenue, my home. Brad had moved in, and Peaks and Places was an adventure travel business he and his partner, Jose Guzman, had set up. They thought I'd be moving out by Christmas and were surprised to find that it would be February before that happened. Closing had not happened yet on a house I was purchasing on Vassar Circle, which would be in December.

I wasn't even looking for a house when my friends from Pakistan had visited Boulder last summer. They wanted to look at real estate, and as we were driving around to show them Boulder, we came onto this house on Vassar which I had admired for 20 years. I had always said that if it ever came on the market, I would buy it. Well, lo and behold, there was a sign on it which had just gone up! I was the first person to see the house and make a bid, which they accepted. I didn't want to have an empty house while I was in England and Pakistan but, as it turned out, the owners didn't want to move until my return. It worked out well for both parties. Had my Pakistan friends not visited when they did, and had they not wanted to look at real estate, I would never have known the house was on the market. I guess it was meant to be.

Brad had secured a loan to keep Peaks and Places going for another year in hopes they would be able to make a go of it. Jose was in the house every day by eight and sometimes didn't leave until six. Things were a beehive of activity, as they were trying to put together a new catalog.

Carl Darnell, Brad's partner in another of his businesses—the Gamow Bag—was in another office on the west end of Boulder's downtown area near the mouth of Boulder Canyon. The Gamow Bag was a portable chamber, something like a sleeping bag, to treat someone who had high-altitude sickness. The business had suffered and so had Brad's well-being, so he had decided to give up teaching skiing in Sun Valley. I know that was really hard for him, although he said not. He was looking forward to having some free time, mainly weekends, when he could play and unwind, hopefully. He spent some time at the business downtown and some time at my house.

I had begun to pack, trying to make room for some of Brad's things. I felt sorry for him that he couldn't just move in and get settled. But that would come.

The Holiday Season

Brad was on the Colorado River with his father before Thanksgiving and about froze to death. He said he would never do that again at that time of year. No sunshine down in there, not even enough for lunchtime. He wore a dry suit the entire time. Not only that, but the water was so low that all the boats ended up being damaged, and one gal broke her back going through a rapid. I guess Dale had a radio and could call to a passing airplane, who called for an emergency helicopter evacuation for the next morning to take her out.

I had about 11 people for Thanksgiving dinner. I did the bird and everyone else brought a dish of something. I did the same thing for Christmas Eve dinner and managed to get through the holiday season pretty well. Christmas day was bad because I was alone, but the weather was so beautiful that I went for two hikes.

By December, we were in the midst of an Arctic low, with the wind chill plunging us down to -50 degrees. I can't remember when it had ever been that cold. The streets were glassy and people lost it on the corners. It had been snowing for a couple days, so I had almost 12 inches on the deck. Finally, December 17 came and I signed the papers to the Vassar Circle house. Remodeling would start after the first of the year, since everyone was busy with the holidays.

Brad bought himself a fantastic book on the mountains of Pakistan for Christmas. What a beautiful book! It made me want to go again. I wanted to see Peshawar and Lahore and do some more shopping!!

MY NEW HOME

Waiting on the remodel before occupying my new house, I gave an "empty open house" at the Vassar home on New Year's Eve day from three to seven. I hoped most people would come while it was still daylight so they could experience the fabulous view.

The next few months were taken up with the remodel, which at that point looked like it would be very expensive, but I had to continue to tell myself that it was a great investment. I would eventually be able to recover my investment by selling if I decided not to live out the rest of my life there.

I took this picture of a Rocky Mountain goat on one of my many hikes.

GAMBLING IN NEVADA

I sprained my ankle just before I took off for San Francisco to pick up a new car. It hurt like heck when I did it, but it didn't swell up and didn't hurt to walk on. The x-rays showed that it wasn't broken, thank goodness. Ski boot pressure made it uncomfortable, but after Christmas I was able to grin and bear it.

So a gal friend, Mary Reich, and I flew out to California to pick up the car. On our way back, we gambled our way across Nevada and spent the last night on the border two hours west of Salt Lake. After signing in and getting a cheap overnight room, we had dinner then I decided to play the dollar slots.

I walked into a small room where there was just one person—a woman—playing four machines at one time. All four buckets below each machine were filled with metal dollar pieces. I was so amazed and asked how much one of them held. She said that it was only about $500, and if I thought that was something, her husband had just taken a couple out to the front desk to exchange for the real thing. I told her we had just come from a place west of there and didn't know they were going out of business, and had lost all the gambling money we had. After further conversation, she said they lived nearby and came often. She apparently won most of the time. I asked if she thought I could play and win, and after thinking over my question, she pointed to a slot near hers. She said to be sure to play three coins, not just one. After about $9, the bells went off! People gathered around me and I said, "What happened?" They all said, "You won!" I said, "What did I win?" They said, "A thousand dollars!" I couldn't believe it!! So we didn't go home penniless.

BACK IN BOULDER: WAITING ON THE REMODEL, WE LOSE JESSIE

It had been very hard to make any decisions about the new house, which had been slowly remodeled but still wouldn't be ready for occupancy until at least May. On top of all that our dog, Jessie, became ill, rapidly went downhill, and died. Oh, how sad that was for everyone—the friends who walked her, neighbors who cared for her, and we who saw her born and raised over the last 11 years.

Brad, too, had been very depressed about his life in general. Sharing what I was going through over the remodel was bad enough, but when Jessie died, it was almost more than we were able to handle.

I tried to keep busy and be away from Dartmouth Avenue as much as possible. I went to Santa Fe with a friend, spent oodles of money on the sofa and chaise covered with an indigo and a dhurrie, respectively. I went skiing for five days and hit the jackpot with a foot of new powder, which hadn't occurred all winter. What fun!

SPRINGTIME

It was March, and Brad would leave in two weeks for Nepal. He was taking his father and new wife to Island Peak on a trek (three weeks total). He wasn't looking forward to that. Just a month ago, he went to Chile to raft the Bio Bio River. Great adventure!

The end of April and the first part of May, I went back to Grand Gulch for a brainstorming session regarding the exhibit that the Utah Museum of Natural History would have in 1995 on the Anasazi Basketmaker project. Then I celebrated my 63rd birthday by jumping rope with some Indian children! Two other gals and I did a five-day Indian trading post tour, during which much jewelry and many Indian rugs were purchased. I also went on a canyon trip, part of an all-woman writing workshop, into Canyon de Chelly, an area where no white man had been until the mid-1800s. I took another trip over Memorial Day Weekend near Mesa Verde and up a canyon the Wetherills explored in the late 1800s.

Since starting the remodel, my life has been one ordeal after another. I guess things might have gone better if I had been able to keep my sense of humor about everything that was happening. Even the contractor said, "In my 20 years of doing remodels, there have been only five jobs I never should have taken, and this is one of them." That *really* made me feel good. It seemed like everything that could conceivably go wrong did.

On the Thursday before Memorial Day, I moved over 50 boxes in my station wagon. I had planned to have a pizza-and-beer box-moving party, but there were still so many workers coming and going that day that I couldn't face the idea of a party. So I did it alone. Then Friday, I rented and drove a U-Haul truck, hired two workers to help, and we moved the furniture.

SUMMERTIME AND THE NEW HOUSE

I had been in the Vassar house for three weeks. The remodel was basically done but not everything was finished. Most of my time had been spent packing, moving, unpacking, organizing, and rounding up subcontractors to come back and redo things they didn't do right in the first place. But that was slowing down, and the place was beginning to look like and feel like "home." It was lovely, and I was pleased with the way everything turned out. Its completion had occupied all my time and kept my mind off other things. It had been good to get away from Dartmouth Avenue, too.

I heard through the grapevine that while traveling in Nepal, some friends ran into Brad right before he had to leave for the airport. They, too, were all sick, just as Brad's group was. This trip was the worst he'd had, with everyone sick from both ends. Perhaps the illness was from the water in Kathmandu, as the doctor they saw said that usually he had five to six people get sick, but he'd had more than 30, and they had traced it back to Kathmandu's water. One man got sick twice and came home before they ever did the climb. That left Brad, his dad, and the new wife all very weak but determined to climb Island Peak. In doing so, Brad's dad had to use the Gamow Bag to acclimatize to the altitude. After another week, they all summited Island Peak.

Recouping from the Remodel,
More Trips

Compared to the lives my friends led, I'd become very lazy and had procrastinated about doing many things that needed doing. I guess just finishing the house and finally getting moved in at the end of May depleted any energy I might have had to do anything more than keeping in shape, both body and mind. I'd done a lot of bike riding, usually between six and seven in the morning, on a 10-mile circuit I discovered. It was a good workout in just under an hour.

So I began to slow down and take it easy, even do some fun things. My friend, Lorraine (also my decorator), and I went to Glenwood Springs for the July 4 weekend. Another friend owned a darling Victorian house there and rented it out to us cheap, so we stayed there.

In July, I took part in an annual ladies camping trip for a week down in the San Juans, where we were above timberline almost the entire time. I supplemented the meals situation there by fishing in the lakes.

I took several trips. As usual, the Wisconsin EAA trip was a waste of time. The only good thing that came out of that was that I played golf with my niece and several nephews. I hadn't played in 40 years but did as well as one of the nephews who played all the time. Consequently, I decided to take up the game. Upon getting back to Boulder, I bought a half set of clubs and had fun getting back into it again. I even took one lesson, which put my score on nine holes in the high fifties. One added bonus in playing was that when some friends visited me for five days and I wondered what we would do, I learned that they were already golfers and interested in playing while they were here. That took up the better part of two days.

In early August, right after the Wisconsin trip, I was in Idaho where Brad and I attended a fabulously fun wedding for Ben Chidlaw, Jr. Brad took his parasail along and did some flying. The weather cooperated and it was a great three-day weekend.

The Bolshoi Ballet troupe was in Vail again this year, and in the middle of August, I attended a beautiful performance with a friend. She and I had been going out for dinner every Friday evening followed by a movie, and we'd seen most of the latest films by doing this. Now that fall was here, we'd signed up for a concert series given at the university in Macky Auditorium. There was usually one concert per month, and last month's was Sarah Chang, a 10 year old from Thailand. She played here two years ago, at which time Don and I saw her practice as well as perform. She was cute as a bug and incredible on the violin. This year, she'd grown almost a full head and was more mature in her face. Her performance was spectacular and flawless. The concert for this Friday was a young pianist.

Thus far this year, I'd been to a Michael Crawford concert and planned to see *The Phantom of the Opera* in December. I did a little flying, but not as much as I would like. Lots of early morning 10-to-20-mile bike rides.

The wildflowers above timberline are spectacular in July.

Trekking in Switzerland
with Kate Prager

The end of August I flew to Switzerland with another friend, Kate Prager, who lived in Washington, D.C. She and I met years ago on a long-distance bike trip. She wanted company on a hut-to-hut, two-week hiking trip. We started in Lauterbrunnen outside of Interlaken and went northeast. The trip consisted of walking with our 35-pound packs as well as taking buses, trains, taxis, and—in one instance—hitchhiking. It was a great trip with cloudless skies.

We arrived at the Zurich airport and were met by Brad's friend, Franca. She was smiling as usual but—oh—was very thin. She had gotten very sick from bad water in Pakistan and had had to come home. Apparently she became very dehydrated and was hospitalized there. Finally she sent an SOS home, was brought back, and had lost a lot of weight. She had just heard that three of her friends, one a woman, had reached the summit of their peak. What a disappointment for her not to have been with them.

Franca Caiocca and her friend, Franco Demarchi.

Franca playing with a local cow.

Franca's school started and she was supposed to be in a meeting, but told her boss she would not be there. To meet me, she had to get up at 5:30 and drive 2½ hours to Zurich. What a gem! Then she said it would be best for her if we saved our visit to Bern till the end, when she'd be able to be with us over our last weekend. Therefore, she drove back to Bern and we left on the train for Zurich, where we found maps to guide us on our way.

Kate had had a seatmate named Katie (a coincidence), who arrived about 15 minutes after we did. Katie helped us find lockers and be on our way.

We made the decision to skip Appenzell and go to Lauterbrunnen because our tickets would take us there, and it cost less using them instead of going to Appenzell. So we were on our way to Lauterbrunnen, changing trains in Bern and Interlaken.

At Lauterbrunnen by mid-afternoon, we decided to stay and recover from jet lag. Kate found a great room with a balcony overlooking the valley. After unpacking and reorganizing, we took a swim in their pool—we were glad we took our suits—then rode up to Wengen for a dinner of spaghetti, our last part of the beat-the-jet-lag requirement. The late 9:30 train got us back to our hotel and in bed by five to ten, and we died!

August 28

I couldn't believe we slept until after eight! During the night, someone's car alarm went off three or four times right outside our window. We had thought we'd go to Kleine Scheidegg today so we ordered our breakfast in a bag. Then we realized we'd be exhausted, so we had our lunch for today and would buy breakfast.

So we got a very late start and decided to go to Schilthorn, but we instead wandered around Mürren—where I bought a belt—and we didn't go to Schilthorn. By noon, it was too cloudy. We stopped and checked prices at a mountain hostel: 6.50 SFr per night plus 1 SFr for a hot shower outside. It had bunk beds for 40 people, two large rooms, a kitchen, water closet, and hand-wash troughs, plus some private rooms. We looked in the windows of a newly constructed house listed at $180,000 (250,000 SFr).

We walked down to Gimmelwald, where I had skied with the Madison Ski Club. Then we walked on to Stechelberg and Trümmelbach. It was 7 SFr to see the 10 falls—

1990   **1991**   1992   1993   1994   1995   1996   1997   1998   1999

pretty impressive! The water was from the Eiger, Mönch, and Jungfrau mountains; 20,000 tons of rock a year came down from them.

We walked back to Lauterbrunnen by seven, just as a bell was tolling. Along the way, we enjoyed waterfalls and green fields, which looked manicured. We swam and had dinner at the Schützen Hotel; there was no music tonight, only on Tuesdays. Dinner was 21 SFr and consisted of soup and a veggie plate that was excellent, then 5 SFr for dessert and coffee at 2.50 SFr. Got to bed by eleven—a long day.

August 29

We got up early. It was difficult, but we actually caught the 7:05 bus (3.60 SFr) to Stechelberg. There, we had an expensive breakfast in the hotel (25 SFr for two), then we were off up the trail to Oberhornsee, supposedly a 4½-hour hike. We started at 8:30, made only a few stops for pictures, and arrived at the lake at 12:30. We lunched at the edge of this very clear, cold lake, then were off to Schmadri Hutte, which turned out to be only a shelter. By 1:30 we started down to catch the 5:35 bus back to Lauterbrunnen.

The mountains surrounding us were the Eiger, Mönch, and Jungfrau to the north and Breithorn, Tschingelhorn, Wetterhorn, and Gspaltenhorn to the east and west. Waterfalls were everywhere; glaciers were tumbling down and there were occasional rumblings from avalanches. Kate saw one, her first.

We had been in Lauterbrunnen two full days and nights and had become spoiled by a swim every night after returning from our daily hike. The Hotel Jungfrau had a spectacular view from the front balcony of our room. As we ate dinner, the alpenglow of sunset set the snow on fire. The clouds seemed to spill in and around the peaks every

Franca and me.

1990 **1991** 1992 1993 1994 1995 1996 1997 1998 1999

Franca, me, and Kate posing on a bridge on one of our hikes.

evening; the mornings were clear. There wasn't a central parking *platz* (place) because there was no place to park. Further up the valley was a large camping *platz*. There were huge buses there, and one with a patio on the roof had everything, including the kitchen sink and the children's playground. Everyone was two to three feet from his neighbor. What a vacation.

There was basically one street in Lauterbrunnen, and the railroad came from Interlaken to Kleine Scheidegg and Grindelwald. There were several cable cars out of town to Schilthorn via Mürren and Grindelwald. We were again disappointed that we didn't get up to Schilthorn, as it was still cloudy.

Our hotel room had a balcony, sink, and closet. We went out to the water closet and down one flight to swim and take a shower. While there, they'd fixed the pool shower so it got only cold water!

August 30, Friday

It was difficult to get up at 6 a.m. We were up until midnight, packing and unpacking, wondering what to leave behind and send on to Altdorf. Once up and moving, we knew we had done a long walk the previous day. We hurried to the train station, checked our bags to Altdorf, and bought two one-way tickets to Kleine Scheidegg (KS). Our Swiss pass ($79) had more than paid for itself, as all our tickets had been half price. The normal ticket back to Lauterbrunnen (LB) from KS was 20.80; we paid 10.40.

The day was cloudless. We couldn't believe it: It was a perfect day to go to Jungfraujoch. But there were many Japanese tourists, and the poor conductors couldn't communicate with them. They just stood still as if to say, "When in doubt, don't move."

1990   **1991**   1992   1993   1994   1995   1996   1997   1998   1999

We found an elevator to the Sphinx before going out on the glacier to the Mönch Hutte. The walk over was 45 minutes, so we decided to do that instead of taking the elevator. We got there before it did! I couldn't believe how it had changed from 25+ years ago. The cost to get up there from either LB or Grindelwald was $80. They had trains going every half hour and they were always full.

The three hours from nine to noon evaporated quickly. Soon we were back at KS, sitting on a grassy hillside eating some lunch. About 1:30, we started down out of the crowd of tourists to Alpiglen. Uncertain what we'd find, it was a delight to discover a flower-festooned restaurant surrounded by colorful umbrellas. Our guidebook indicated they had *matratzenlager* (mattresses, aka sleeping spaces for rent), and sure enough, they did! Kate was eager to try it, so we had our pick of 30 mattresses on the floor. We chose two under the windows. The place was relatively new, wooden, with lacy curtains, clean, no water, no bathroom, but we could use the one at the restaurant. The price was right—25 SFr with breakfast. If we had wanted a room inside the restaurant, it was up two flights with big down comforters for 37 SFr, including breakfast.

Everywhere we'd been, the flowers were magnificent—red geraniums, petunias, orange marigolds, lobelia without the white center, Elaine's daisies, the geraniums like Lorrance's. The prettiest combination was the purple lobelia and red geraniums. The daisies with lobelia without white centers were also nice.

Someone came to the Pension des Alpes (now a hotel) with a huge bouquet of blue mountain gentian that they called "enzian" and which could be made into

schnapps. We had them on our table for dinner and breakfast. Since we arrived mid-afternoon, we sat in the garden amid the flowers and in the sun for several hours—our first real leisure afternoon.

We turned the lights out around ten, the earliest we'd gone to bed. I vaguely heard the Frenchman come in and cough one time during the night. Great night's sleep.

August 31, Saturday

Woke at 6:45; had a great breakfast of cheese, coffee, milk, hot chocolate, jam, and butter. Got on our way to Grindelwald at 8:30. Manicured fields, flower-decorated chalets, green fields, rushing streams, electric train to KS, watering troughs, well-marked trails, some asphalt, some gravel, a piece of paradise. A better place to be I do not know.

In the village, we got money, postcards, and stamps ($1.54 to send a postcard and stamp to U.S.). Fruit, cheese, bread, and sausage was 9 SFr each for two days; candy for 2 SFr. We hiked to Milchbach below the glacier coming off Wetterhorn, bought two iced teas each (5.60 SFr per), ate our lunch, hiked down to the Wetterhorn Hotel and Restaurant, and paid 4.60 SFr (half price) for the bus.

Being a Saturday, there were no rooms left, so we rode the bus to Schwartzwaldalp where a lady with a very bad attitude and a broken arm met us. We had to sign without seeing the *matratzenlager* in no uncertain terms. That was not necessary at all, but we did it. Then one of the cooks showed us the place in an outbuilding. We were squeezed into a corner next to some climbers, even though there were a couple empty beds out in the open near the window. I knew it would be a bad night, so I suggested we walk up the road to a farmhouse and ask if they had a *zimmer frei* (available room). It turned out they sold cheese that we had seen a couple signs for. They told us to go to the inn. We said we had gone there and were thinking of going to Rosenlaui. They offered to call. Their daughter was using the phone, so she got off, we called, and they had a room—*matratzenlager*. The Swartzenlager was 20 SFr, cold water, and no shower. Rosenlaui was 30 with a hot shower and more atmosphere, art, antiques, and friendly people. We told them we'd be there on foot in 30 minutes or so. It was an easy, pleasant walk, and we were delighted at our decision to leave the other place. *Gulasch suppe* and salad for dinner, hot shower, lots of water, and a third-floor back room that was quiet.

September 1, Sunday

The next day, we left at 9:40 to climb to Dossin Hutte, 1,300 feet above Rosenlaui. Everyone warned us it was a long way and steep with cables and ladders. We would go as far as we could. It was, indeed, as described. Kate did really well, although she was anxious about the ladders and cables. But we kept going. Once in sight of the hut, I wanted to keep going. We were on a very steep ridge and Kate was beginning to weaken, so she stayed behind while I continued 30 minutes to the hut. I took a wrong turn up a scree slope and under the outhouse, ending a hundred feet or more above the hut. I was grateful for a trail down to it! I stopped only long enough for a couple photos and didn't even look inside the hut. Clouds were moving in rapidly and I was fearful of losing trail markers as the day darkened. Up in 5¼ hours and started down at 2:55. I found a note left by Kate, who was inching her way down, clutching every object on the way. I had to keep her moving or it would be dark by the time we got back to the hotel. Finally got there at six to find they closed the dining room on Sundays at 7:00 p.m. We had *Gulasch suppe* again with salad and beer and got to bed by eight, exhausted. (Lunch was 12.50 each for a salad plate, ice tea, ham on lite.)

September 2, Monday

We got up too late to get the mid-morning bus to Meiringen, so unless we hitched a ride, we'd have to wait two hours. A busload of children came up and one car with all the food, so we asked if we could get a ride with the man who was driving. He was nice enough to take us in to town where the stores had just closed. We window-shopped, bought some lunch stuff, visited the church and cemetery, and ate a great lunch—an omelet and salad. Then we took the bus to Engstlensee where we stayed in a *matratzenlager* for 22 SFr, with breakfast.

There was a cluster of houses and a kiosk as far as the bus went. Our quarters were separate from the hotel and other buildings with it, again, being over the barn.

The lake was the best fishing in Switzerland with pictures in the hotel showing trout two feet long. The water was the clearest I'd ever seen. I picked enough blueberries for putting on ice cream and sauce with hot milk in the morning. We ordered trout and potatoes, which really was a great meal with a salad. We were in bed early again.

September 3, Tuesday

It takes Kate about an hour more—or longer—to get ready than it does me. We were late starting up the side of the lake where, on the pass, we could see the lifts described in the guidebook. The trail was gradual and, once on top above the Trübsee at Jochpass, there were at least five or six lifts going in all directions. The flowers (purple) were covering the hillside down the Trübsee side. There, we were amazed by a concrete road between two lift houses. There were many people coming and going—grand central station. The Titlis Glacier towered over us and I told Kate we'd come this far, so we should go to the top. There were four sections of two six-passenger cabins from the valley floor to Engelberg and two large trams holding 80 each from there on. A sign in one building indicated they were building

Kate, me, and Franca.

the world's only revolving tram, probably like the smaller cabin type but with an 80-passenger capacity. By the time we reached the top at 1:30, the clouds were rolling in and we couldn't see very far.

They had an underground exhibit about how glaciers are formed, grow, and move. One tunnel was almost 400 feet long. We could look out the south side of Titlis, having come up the north side. The cost was $21, which we thought was well worth it.

We didn't get to Engelberg until 4:30, when we made one phone call to Stäpeli and another for a taxi. The taxi was 11 SFr to the end of the road, then we hiked 55 minutes to Stäpeli. Their *matratzenlager* had separate rooms over an old barn, a common washing room—his and hers—with cold water. It was very nice ($35 each).

At first, there were only two other women in the dorm, but two young men—one from southern France and the other Yugoslavian—arrived and were using the same guidebook. The Yugoslavian was a guide in the Sierra Club.

We went inside the restaurant after dark. It was cold! I read in the lamplight, got to bed at 9:30, but couldn't sleep. At 11:15 a couple arrived, laughing and talking and clomping in the hall. I thought snoring was bad—this was worse!

September 4, Wednesday

We had small pieces of cheese and jam for breakfast then were off up to Surenen Pass. The way was steep but the views great. Near the halfway point was a huge cirque with a church and small farm with fresh milk—1 SFr—and one *matratzenlager* for 12 SFr above a new (10 year old) barn. There was a young mother with her child of six months and a grampa. Some ladies from Stäpeli were just leaving. We went on to the pass for lunch, where there was a crowd of geology students. We had *schweineschnitzel, rösti,* salad, coffee, rhubarb cake, rum, and tea. The view was all the way to Altdorf, which was a lovely place nestled in a valley surrounded by mountains. It was two hours and 45 minutes and a long, steep way to the top of the lift. On the way a man, three young ladies, and two children we had passed farther up the trail were sitting on a patio having lunch. They recognized us and asked us to join them. They gave us a bowl of soup and a cup of coffee. It turned out that they were from East Berlin, and it was the first time they had been out of their country on a vacation. Also, another coincidence, the three women were all seamstresses in a one-year-old business making sleeping bags, parkas, and backpacks. The name of the company was Yeti. We did the best we could translating, learning that many people were out of work and that there were many problems in communist businesses—they failed, making way for independent businesses to start up. Finally, as we left, we took their picture and they waved until we were out of sight. The lift was self-serve—every 30 minutes, get in and it goes.

At Altdorf, we took a bus to the train where we picked up our bags and went right next door to the Bahnhof Hotel, recently redone and OK. We had good hot showers, washed our clothes, and walked to the restaurant for dinner. By the time we had dinner it was dark, and we had a hard time finding our way back to the hotel.

September 5, Thursday

We spent the morning looking around the city, taking pictures, looking in the cemetery, and buying groceries at the last minute (the *migros* closed at noon). Altdorf is a nice city with clean streets and shopping areas that are clustered in one spot. There were some lovely old churches, and everything was easily reached on foot.

We caught the train at 2:30 to Bellinzona. Franca was a little late, but she arrived shortly in a large white Nissan van with two bikes in the back. Oh, how thin she is from being ill in Pakistan and China! She's lost perhaps 30 pounds but has gained back nine or 10.

We drove to her flat in the lower level of a friend's parents' home. The house was very near the river on a corner. While there, Franca set up a ride for me to do piggy-back parasailing. However, the day we were to do it, the wind picked up and the clouds rolled in—the first bad weather we'd had in two weeks—so it was canceled. I was really disappointed.

After a short visit with Franca and her brother, they helped us get our flight back to the U.S. It was a great trip!

Chaco Canyon, Indian Country, the Florida Panhandle

The end of September I was back in the desert visiting Chaco Canyon, a large Indian ruin south of Durango, Colorado. At one time, it was thought that 5,000 Indians lived there in what appeared to have been a central trading center. From the air, old roads are discernible going in every direction. Trade beads from Mexico, California, and elsewhere had been found there. Our guide, whose name was Florence Lister, did a great job. Her husband, Robert, had recently passed away, but they had written several books about the canyon, and she was a storehouse of information. It was also she and her husband whom I had bought my new house from.

Six of us left there and went further west to Navajo country, where an Indian took us into a canyon off-limits to whites. There, we spent an hour or so photographing and poking around a room called "Poncho House" because, years ago, they found a poncho there. That was exciting, because it was obvious not many people had been there before.

I no sooner got back home from that trip when I flew to the Florida Panhandle, where I helped some friends work on their rental house. I had a working vacation, more or less. I like to work though, so it was fun. They had friends who played golf, so I played one day.

Chaco Canyon ruin.

THE AMERICAN ALPINE CLUB

The first weekend in December, Brad and I went to the American Alpine Club annual meeting in Seattle. They had a gathering of 10th Mountain Division men there showing old pictures and telling stories of their experiences during the war. The 10th Mountain originated in Colorado near Vail, where they taught the men mountain survival with what we now call "very antiquated equipment." As a matter of fact, one of the men in that division, Gerry Cunningham, came out of the service and started what we knew then as the Gerry line of outdoor equipment. Back before Frostline, Dale and I were in business with Gerry Cunningham in Gerry Mountain Sports.

A couple of pages from a Gerry catalog.

TRIP TO ST. THOMAS, LOST LUGGAGE

January 11 I flew to Dulles in Washington, D.C., where I stayed overnight with the lady I hiked with in Switzerland last fall. The next day I flew out to St. Thomas in the Virgin Islands and went on a long Windjammer cruise. The thing that made that trip different was that I did it sans luggage. I had picked up the wrong bag at Dulles but didn't realize until four hours later that it wasn't mine. I had put all my slides from the Switzerland trip in the suitcase, for lack of space in my carry-on with camera and film, intending to share them with Kate in Washington because she had never seen them.

When I was ready to leave Dulles for St. Thomas and still didn't have a bag, I called Brad at 5:30 a.m. and asked him to go over to my house and get a bathing suit and shorts and call Lorraine (the gal I was going with) because she was leaving that day for St. Thomas. So at least I would have that much for the cruise. Well, bless his heart! He also sent along two bras and panties! Even though they were my ratty camping undies, I was impressed that he would think to do that so early in the morning.

The day we were to get on board when the bag still hadn't turned up, I went shopping (United said they'd pay for half of whatever I bought). I bought a pair of cheap flip-flops, a sweatshirt top and bottom, a pair of dressy-type shorts to wear at the captain's dinner, a shirt to match, and a tee-shirt that ended up matching the shorts Brad sent down.

Once on board, another lady passenger had three bags, so she loaned me another baggy lightweight shirt to pull over my bathing suit and get out of the sun in, as well as a looooong eight-inch-wide black cloth belt I wore as a bra. I twisted it in the back and tied it in front with a long piece of yardage I fashioned into a sarong skirt for costume night, making it into a short skirt; I just added beads for the captain's dinner party. Everyone commented that for someone who didn't have their luggage, I was doing pretty well!

The only other thing that I really needed was my snorkeling stuff. I had even taken my refresher course in school before I left and bought a new pair of prescription goggles which were in the luggage. Fortunately, the ship had goggles, fins, and snorkels. I got to them first and found the only pair of goggles that were not meant for a giant. There was one place, St. John, where three of us went to a dive shop and had an entire morning of diving. The dive master I had with me was really great. He took my word that I was certified, didn't make me fill my mask with water (I didn't want to lose my contacts), and I was such a low breather that he and I stayed down 15 minutes longer than everyone else because we had more air. That was the highlight of the trip for me.

1990   1991   **1992**   1993   1994   1995   1996   1997   1998   1999

BACK IN COLORADO

Boulder experienced the driest winter I have memories of, and summer started a month early. It had been very strange weather, but it was great for getting outdoors a lot. Skiing, biking, and getting ready for two trips had kept me busy.

I also got involved in two local organizations, volunteering. I joined the Colorado Music Festival group of "Friends." They do various things during the year to make money for the festival. It was a summer version of the Boulder Philharmonic Orchestra which operated only in the winter. The festival took place at Chautauqua Park. That had taken up a lot of my time.

I also joined an organization called "Women of the West." We were trying to raise enough money to build a museum in the Boulder area that would be devoted just to women who have been instrumental in some way (arts, culture, music, etc.) in the development of the West. It never had been done before and it was a great idea. That, too, had been time consuming.

Brad Starts his Makalu Trip

Friday, I took Brad to the airport. He flew up to Canada to do his annual helicopter ski week with his wealthy ski client from Paris. He would leave March 12 for Nepal and wouldn't be back until June 20. I asked him how I would be able to stand not talking with him all the time. His reply was that I should fly over and go to the base camp. I just didn't want to do that and would be happy with a couple of desert trips instead.

He was going to attempt to climb Makalu for the second time. Two years ago, he made it to within 1,200 feet of the summit solo, turning back because of dangerous avalanche conditions. When he finishes with Nepal this time, he'll go to the Philippines for two weeks to visit another ski client living there. Later, perhaps mid-summer, he'll go to Paris to visit Claude, who he was with this week in Canada. I had the idea that perhaps I could fly to England and visit a friend at that time, then go on to Paris to meet Brad. From there, we could go to Nairobi for a short time and then on to Botswana, where we wanted to go the time we went to Zimbabwe, Zambia, and Rwanda.

Brad had sold his share of the hyperbaric bag business back to his partner. He still had an investment in it, but he finally decided that he was miserable doing what he was doing and was going to get out. Now he wanted to try to make a living with his photography. Funny, I told him to do that years ago because he had a real talent there. He had about five friends who were doing that and were willing to help him get started. I hoped it would work. The African trip would be a "working" photographic trip. We'd want to sit around a lot and wait for things to happen.

After I took a flight in a private plane to Pueblo for lunch and got back to Boulder, I stopped by Brad's house to check on the damages that a small fire had made, and I found him there! I couldn't believe my eyes! United had canceled his flight, so there was no use in going on the next or earliest next flight, because he would have already missed his connecting flight out of Seattle to Bangkok. So he opted to come home for the weekend and start over Monday. The flight out of Bangkok to Kathmandu leaves only on Tuesdays, Thursdays, and Saturdays. The second attempt got him there.

By that time, he was four days behind his expedition of eight fellows. He arrived in Kathmandu the day before they were to leave, and he had four days of business to attend to before getting on his way. He did his business, flew to Tumlingtar, and arrived two days after they had passed through there. With his long legs, he caught up with them in a day and a half!

The climb over the two passes was far more difficult than he had remembered. Until they had snow, he was extremely hot, and I'm sure—like the last time—he lost a few pounds. At the last village before the two passes, the 77 porters went on strike for more money. A British team funded by a British TV (possibly the BBC) had gone in before them and overpaid the Sherpas. Consequently, that put Brad's team in a bind, because they were paid only twice the going rate. After a half-day of negotiating, they came to some agreement. Pushing on over the passes, they were then faced with nightmarish hours of trying to figure out who should get paid for what, because some of them had the same name. Then they had to start all over to negotiate with 15 more Sherpas to take them to upper base camp. Brad and his partner, Peter Carse, took the first 12. They had difficulty finding water and were then faced with another problem: having to melt glacier ice and the possibility of running out of kerosene.

The Brits were camped about 20 minutes from Brad's camp. They had every convenience you could imagine, including a telephone, fax, and a TV monitor. The generator didn't work at first, so they flew in a second one. There were about 16 media people and nine team members, all very friendly and generous with what they had. (This information came from Evie Nott, who was from Vail. She went into base camp with her daughter, who lived in Nepal.)

A postcard from Kathmandu arrived and a letter written at 11,000 feet was carried out by a sirdar (guide). It was then I learned about the fax and the Brits' overpayment of the Sherpas. Brad had said they would try for the summit the first week of May. The wait for a month and a half seemed endless. I tried to stay close to home the first week of May. May 4 was my 64th birthday, so I was hoping they would climb that day. Mother's Day fell on May 10, the other end of the week, so I was sure I'd hear something. I had been talking with a friend about what I would do on Mother's Day.

Makalu with base camp in the foreground.
Photo by Brad Johnson.

1990   1991   **1992**   1993   1994   1995   1996   1997   1998   1999

My feeling was that something was going to happen and I should stick close to home. I no sooner hung up after saying that and the phone rang. Brad's new housemate, Jack, said a fax had come from Brad. Needless to say, I was over there in less than five minutes! It'd come from the 17,700-foot base camp of Makalu, the fifth highest mountain in the world! Now, I didn't think anyone in Colorado had ever received a fax from that kind of elevation, let alone one that began, "Dear Mom, happy birthday and happy Mother's Day." I copied the article from Boulder's paper about it. Fun!

A fax had come from Brad from the 17,700-foot base camp of Makalu, the fifth highest mountain in the world! [It] began, "Dear Mom, happy birthday and happy Mother's Day."

So they were all set to go for the summit with all the camps set; now they just had to wait for the winds to die down. All week long, I expected another fax. Finally, on Tuesday, May 19, 10 days after the first one came, another fax arrived. Unfortunately, they didn't make it to the summit. After two months and two days, they had decided to quit. Brad tried on May 13 and 14, but a snowstorm ruined their chances. Again, on May 16 and 17, during a full moon, he tried with two of the Brits, but the winds were so intense that they had to turn back. He got as high as their camp IV at 25,600 feet. What a disappointment!

They had to leave base camp by Friday, May 22, because of their permit time and because it took about a week to walk to Tumlingtar, where a flight would take them back to Kathmandu. By May 27 and 28, they would be back in Kathmandu. I hoped to hear by phone from him when he got there.

At the end of the second fax he said I could fax him back, so I did, and according to his machine, it went through. I hope he got it. He sounded like he needed cheering up. He also gave me a fax number in Kathmandu where I planned to send another fax that night.

When he got back to Kathmandu, he planned to fly to the Philippines to stay with one of his wealthy Vail ski clients, who was going to pay for Brad to get his scuba certification. Brad was looking forward to time at the beach and in the sun. He and I would not see each other until July.

1990   1991   **1992**   1993   1994   1995   1996   1997   1998   1999

Spring into Summer

The annual Bolder Boulder foot race had 27,000 racers signed up. I took a 2½ year old and a 6½ year old to the stadium to watch their mom and dad come into the stadium and cross the finish line.

Then, on June 1, I had house sitters coming to stay in my home until my return on July 5. They were seniors from Sun City who wanted to get out of the heat. That relieved my mind, not having the house empty for over a month.

Flying was my first love. Here I am with my Cessna 206.

Rafting the San Juan

I left June 2 for an nine-day raft trip on the San Juan River. Nine of us put in at Sand Island near Bluff, Utah, and rafted 81 miles to Clay Hills, where we got out at Lake Powell. The San Juan was the fastest-flowing river in the U.S., and I'd never been on it. The following diary account of the trip was written by another rafter, Ann Phillips.

Dale Davidson, who worked for the BLM San Juan River Department, had given us a special river permit to thank us for our work on the Wetherill–Grand Gulch Research Project. Ken Evans gave each car a tape he had made of some of his favorite music to get us "in the mood" as we drove southwest to our launch spot. Ann and Russ Hayes came on the first part of the float from Sand Island to Mexican Hat, and Dave Phillips joined us on the second half down to Clay Hills Crossing. We saw Joe Pachak at the gas station in Bluff the morning we left, and he drove to Sand Island with his dog, Andy, to wish us well.

We were limited in space with just two rafts, the Quist's and ours. The guest list was: Julie, Ken Evans, Maddy and Tom Goldhawk, Marge and Fred Quist, Ann and Russ Hayes, and Dave and Ann Phillips. The trip was for at least 10 days with layovers at certain camps.

Day 1
We put in at Sand Island and floated to Upper Wash (river mile 4), where we camped and hiked.

Days 2 and 3
We stopped at Lower Butler Wash, saw the magnificent Kachina Panel, and floated to Comb Wash (river mile 6½), where we explored

Floating on the San Juan.

Rafts docking.

the Old Trading Post and the historic inscriptions. Others of us climbed the Mormon Trail to the top of the Comb. We stopped and photographed the 1880 Mormon inscription, "We thank Thee, O God," on a large boulder almost at the top of this steep section of San Juan Hill. Here, we spent a layover day.

Day 4
This was a very short float to Chinle Wash, where we made camp under a very large cottonwood tree near the river. We hiked from here, visited Navajo summer camps, and walked about a mile or so up the canyon to a ruin and the "baseball man" rock art. I believe we hiked up to the Mule's Ear Diatreme, a prominent geological feature which can be seen from the highway when approaching Mexican Hat.

Day 5
We swam in the river along the way. Ken Evans had brought a watermelon which we had for lunch, and we saw bighorn sheep along the left side of the river at about mile 18. We camped at Lime Creek, mile 20½.

Baseball Man, Chinle Wash.

The group studying a petroglyph block.

Examples of the many types of petroglyphs seen on this trip.

Below right; camp for the night.

A sampling of the structures we saw.

Interesting markings on a wall.

Monument Valley storm.

Day 6

We floated to Mexican Hat (mile 27½), arriving early in the afternoon. Dave met us there with Ann and Russ's car. He was hiding in the bushes when we arrived and squirted Ann with his water cannon. The Hayes drove home from Mexican Hat, and Dave came with us down the river. We camped at one of the spots in the Goosenecks (mile 33).

This was June 6, Fred and Marge's anniversary, and since they were married at West Point, we made an arch of tamarisk branches for them to walk through, a wreath of tamarisk flowers for Marge, and epaulets of beer cans for Fred's shoulders since he was a West Point graduate. We floated down to a campsite at the foot of Honaker Trail.

Day 7

I believe that we looked up at the visitor's center above the river with binoculars and

saw Fred Blackburn with a group. That evening, we camped at the base of the Honaker (mile 44) and walked out of the canyon on the old mining trail up to the top where it's quite flat.

Day 8

We floated from Honaker Trail to Slickhorn Canyon (mile 66), walked up Slickhorn, swam in the pools along the way, and enjoyed this magnificent canyon by exploring old oil

One of the group's two rafts.

drilling equipment and looking at the signatures at the base of the canyon. Dave described what this area was like in 1962 when he floated the river just before the dam at Page was completed, reporting that the hinges on their improvised raft came from the outhouse here that was by the old drill hole site.

Day 9
We floated from Slickhorn to Grand Gulch (mile 70) and spent time exploring and hiking up Grand Gulch. The water was high, and we camped on some wonderful flat

Moon rising over a butte.

rocks at the base of the canyon. The next morning, we walked up the canyon; water was surging out of a narrows, and we were afraid it might become a flash flood! We turned around and ran to our boats and left.

We floated on slowly to Clay Hills Crossing, unloaded our gear, hauled it up a steep bank, and packed it into the cars. We drove to the Sand Island Campground that night.

—written by Ann Phillips upon request

Another lovely camp sunset.

Bike Tour of France
with the Walkers

I got back on June 12 and had three days before I was off to Geneva with my bicycle and three friends, Ted, Barb, and Judy. The plan was to make our way south to Provence, which was to happen in a couple of days. First off, it took us three hours to put our four bikes together, because we had to box them up for shipping as baggage. Theoretically, it should have been a cinch to put them together, but two of the bikes had been put into boxes by bike shops. Cables were cut, odometer wires were yanked out, handlebar bags wouldn't go back on the way they had come off, the tires were completely flat, and brake cables were undone. Once the job was finished, we found ourselves in going-home, rush-hour traffic. No one at the airport could tell us where the bike path into the city was, so we decided to bike into France.

Before we could do anything, we needed to find a service station with air for our tires. The small hand pump couldn't bring the pressure up to 90 pounds. Soon, we discovered that not all service stations have air. Oh, well—France was just a stone's throw away, or so it seemed. A 14½-mile stone's throw against a 15 mph wind later, we found a service station. They had a strange air container: It was the size and shape of a volley ball with a base and had a cane-type handle on it from which the hose protruded. It was not long enough to reach the tire very easily. After struggling for some 10 minutes, a young girl who was wondering why we were having so much trouble came out of the station and showed us that it was very portable. All we needed to do was pick it up by the curved handle. How stupid of us! But after further struggle, and never being able to get more than 40 pounds into the tires, we surmised that this air container only had the capacity of filling auto tires, which take up to 40 pounds, and therefore would never fill our tires to 90 psi.

The next day, we found a bike shop of sorts where we were able to get most of our problems fixed and air in the tires. However, as we pedaled down the street, my front tire began to thump, so I had to return to the shop. I knew what the problem was, for it had happened once before. Because all the air had been let out of the tires for transport, when they were pumped back up again, the tire did not "seat" properly and was crooked. That would cause the tire to thump. It took forever for them to get it on properly before we were finally on our way.

Our next stop was the town of Bellegarde-sur-Valserine, where there was a railroad station. We hoped to hop on with our bikes and be in Avignon in a few hours. Our troubles with the trains began there and never ended, right to the bitter end of our three weeks. Despite what the French train system said—"You can take your bike on 2,000 trains all over France"—they LIED! There were only certain, very short trains that would take your bike. Long distance trains required that you box it up and ship it as baggage, which MIGHT get to your destination in six days! That was half of most people's vacation!

We decided to take a chance and gave them our bikes; they would go out late that night for Avignon. We took an early afternoon train, laid over a couple of hours in Lyon, then arrived in Avignon toward the end of the day. Next morning, as promised by the only ticket person who was willing to help us the entire time, the bikes were waiting for us.

However, the mistral (similar to our Chinook winds) had begun to blow. On inquiry, we were told it had just begun and usually blew for three days, six days, or nine days, and it was supposed to rain hard for the next two days. No way could we start biking in conditions like that. We decided to buck the train system and go on to the Dordogne region, which—as the crow flies—was directly west of Provence. To get there, we had to travel south along the Mediterranean and then swing back up north. It took us several days with

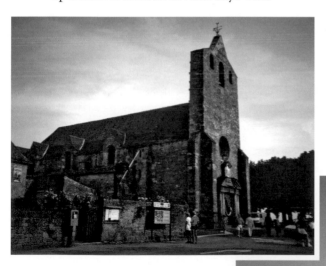

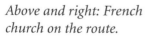

Above and right: French church on the route.

Top right: Stopping for snacks in Saint Genis.

an overnight or two, wrestling our bikes up and down stairs to change platforms, squeezing them into the area where you get on and off between cars, barely fitting, without tickets, possibly facing heavy fines for doing so, purchasing tickets for trains that went tomorrow instead of today, and on and on. You get the picture.

Finally, we started biking from Cahors. The 10 days we biked along the Dordogne River were lovely, with only one afternoon of really pouring-down rain on the way to Sarlat.

The problems we had in getting to the Dordogne area kept nagging us. We finally decided to start heading back. The best way was the way we had come, or so it would seem; but no, the problems were even worse. Now it was impossible to take our bikes. They wouldn't let us on with them, as we had illegally come, and we didn't have six days for them to go as baggage. While eating our bread, cheese, and fruit, and drinking our wine in the front

Cycling through the French countryside.

The Dordogne River.

Fitting two people and two bikes in this car was challenging!

Interesting stone masonry.

of the railroad station in Toulouse, I spied a Hertz Rent-a-Car across the street. How about renting a van? Good idea! Judy and I went to Hertz, the Eurocar, then to Budget around the corner, through the street repairs and in the rain, then on to Avis. None of them had a van, but it was our last hope for beating the system. "Do you have *two* cars that will take *two* people and *two* bikes each?" "Oh, yes, we have that."

We would have to check with our other two friends, so back in the rain and through the muddy street repairs we went to Ted and Barb. That sounded like a great idea to them. Let's do it! Back three blocks in the rain and mud to Avis. "Oh, we only have one car that will take two people and two bikes." "Since it's raining, would you mind calling Hertz to see if they have one?" She did, and they did. But wouldn't it be silly to rent one car from Avis and one car from Hertz? We'd better check to see if Hertz did, indeed, have one. Again, through the rain, pushing our bikes through the muddy street, we arrived at Hertz. Yes, they had two cars that would take two people and two bikes. "Since it's raining so hard, would you mind calling Avis and canceling the car they're holding for us?"

This whole experience took most of the afternoon, so by the time we had found two cars, it was four o'clock. We decided to stay overnight, pick up the cars when they opened at seven, and have a fresh start. Capital idea!

At 7:00 sharp the next morning, we arrived to pick up the cars and were given detailed maps with a lovely yellow line to follow on the auto route down to the Mediterranean, up to Avignon and Lyon, then east to Geneva. "You'll be there by 2:30 or three this afternoon!" "Marvelous! But mind you, we'll be back if we can't fit two bikes into the cars."

By 7:30, we were actually on the auto route. Certain that we could not stay together, we waved and said, "We'll see you at the airport in Geneva!"

Judy and I were ecstatic that we were in a nice, dry car as the rain poured down for several hours. Mid-morning, we pulled into one of those tourist stops for breakfast. Shortly after we pulled back onto the auto route, the skies cleared, but we soon came upon two large trucks stopped dead still in the oncoming two lanes across the median. Miles and miles of cars and people were piling up behind them, with people peering ahead to see what the problem was. I commented to Judy that it didn't seem to be an accident and hoped we wouldn't run into the same thing on our side of the highway.

It wasn't long before we were shunted down into one lane of traffic and, finally, onto an off-ramp. An orange-jacketed man approached each car with word of the problem. Of course, our almost non-existent French vocabulary made it impossible to understand him. However, I did catch two very important and worrisome words: "blockade" and "camion." Oh, well, there's been an accident involving a truck, we thought. I saw that some cars were coming down the ramp we were going up, getting back onto the highway. I asked the man if we could do the same. He said yes, but that we would be BLOCKED at Orange. After making an illegal turn onto the entrance ramp, we discussed what might be going on. It only

Quaint French homes with colorful flowers.

Ted, Barb, me and Judy taking a coffee break in Montignac.

1990   1991   **1992**   1993   1994   1995   1996   1997   1998   1999

Breakfast in Carennac.

When in France. . .

took another 10 minutes for us to discover that Orange was as far as we, and hundreds others, could go.

Still not fathoming the extent of the problem, we decided to try some of the small back roads indicated in white on our map. Unfortunately, we found ourselves on the west side of the Rhone River: Geneva was on the east side. It was noon now, and we were hungry. Approaching a restaurant with a lot of cars in front, we surmised it must have good food. It turned out to be a private party. The only waiter had a fit at our barging in, but he spoke very good English, and we finally discovered that we were in the middle of the French truckers' blockade. If we continued on we'd come to Pont-Saint-Esprit, where we would find many places for lunch.

Pont-Saint-Esprit was a tiny town with one main crossroad and minute plaza. We ate in a corner restaurant and watched the trucks pull in to completely block movement in any direction. It was obvious we would have difficulty if we kept the car. Through the waitress, we found out that the nearest Hertz was back in Orange, where we had just come from. But that seemed to be our only solution—turn in the car and go back to riding the trains.

By the time we finished lunch, our way was blocked except by driving down the sidewalk. I told Judy that it was probably illegal, but I was going to do it anyway. When we reached the turnoff to get out of town that, too, was now blocked. Continuing on another half-block, we came to the Rhone River, where there was a very narrow walkway right at the river's edge. It was just wide enough for our small car. Thinking that this, too, might be illegal but could get us out of town and onto the highway, I took the chance and drove along it until, perhaps several miles later, we found ourselves on the highway back to Orange. There, we turned in the car, used their bathroom

Biking around France was fun but logistically challenging.

to change into our biking clothes, and pedaled to the railroad station. Despite help from four people who spoke some English, it looked hopeless for us to get on any train with our bikes. Judy was in tears by now and said that if she cried a lot and I talked a lot, maybe we could get back to Avignon, where there were more trains and a better chance to find one that would take bikes.

Finally, the baggage man took pity on us. He helped us get our bikes down the stairs and up the stairs onto another platform. Then he told us to stay put until he gave us a signal. We watched as he searched for the head conductor. Just before the train was to pull out, he motioned to us to put the bikes on and then we, too, got on.

We visited Lascaux and saw the cave paintings.

A hurried shake of his hand and "thank you" didn't seem enough, but it was all we could do.

Just 15 minutes later, we were in Avignon. I decided not to haul my bike one more time up or down any more stairs and got on it to ride to the end of the track where they haul baggage across. Suddenly, I heard a crash and, wheeling around, saw Judy lying on the ground with her bike on top of her. I had only found out that she'd had a hip replacement at the beginning of the trip, and now she had landed on that hip. Visions of having to take her to the hospital flashed through my mind. But she was alright, just tired. When we finally reached the station across the tracks, a couple of young Americans approached us. Had we had any trouble with our bikes on the trains? We almost laughed in their faces. We couldn't even get ON the trains with our bikes. They showed us that there wasn't a train that would take bikes until the next day—and there was only one, AND it went at six. We made sure the timetable was correct, found a hotel, set the alarm for five, and tried not to think about what lay ahead tomorrow. There was a train, and we did get our bikes on, but we had to get off in Lyon and start all over again. We wondered where our friends were in the other car.

At the tourist office, we argued with the only man who spoke English. He said to take our bikes on a train to Geneva was IMPOSSIBLE! However, when I said that we would pay anything to get our bikes to there, he picked up the phone, called the baggage department, and discovered that in two hours there was a train we could put our bikes on in a box we had to buy. It would go on the same train we would be on and, by mid-afternoon, we and the bikes would be in Geneva. At last!

It was only 10:30 in the morning, so we had two hours to have lunch and relax. We both had a glass of WINE! After getting situated on the Lyon-to-Geneva train, I told Judy I was going to check to make sure our bikes were on our train. I watched the baggage man unload suitcases, but then he drove off with our bikes. I ran after him and asked where he was going—we were on *this* train, pointing to one end of a long line of cars which looked like one train. He pointed to the other end. When I said, "But we are on this one," he said, "No," that the two ends would separate and one train would go one way and the other end would go another way. Quickly, I ran back to where Judy was waiting. "Quick, Judy, we're on the wrong train!"

At last, we were on the right train and could relax. When we finally arrived in Switzerland, where there was some sanity, we shipped our bikes to the airport, not to see them again until Sunday, in three days, when we would fly back to Colorado. We became tourists and found an expensive hotel then took two boat trips, one around the lake and another one through the countryside. There, we visited a winery and discovered why American red wine gives me a headache, whereas French or European wine does not: It's the sulfites.

We arrived back in Denver July 5 in time for me to meet up with Brad.

After that, I'd planned on seeing some of Colorado's mountains and maybe some of Montana. I still wanted to get to Africa that fall. Brad and I had talked about it before he left, but we made no firm plans. He wanted to visit his other wealthy client who lived outside of Paris.

| 1990 | 1991 | **1992** | 1993 | 1994 | 1995 | 1996 | 1997 | 1998 | 1999 |

Above: Pagoda detail.
Above right: Guard dog statue at a temple we visited.

Above: Our group collecting their luggage.
Right: Elaborately detailed headdress and costume.

We were ushered down one flight and into a long line of Chinese carrying oversized carry-on parcels. One lady had three lampshades and a fan tucked under the top string. One of our people had labored over the purchase of a fan made of balsa with an intricate cut-out design.

After a short ride on a shuttle bus, people ran to the steps and ascended with jet engines screaming in our ears. I wished I'd been forewarned so I could have used the ear plugs United Air had provided. The wait took 10 minutes or more. The sun had decided to show its face, and sweat beaded on our foreheads.

At last, I reached the top and entered far enough to see into the economy section. A sea of black-haired, hot sweaty Chinese greeted me. I was immediately aware of being non-Chinese. Staring brown eyes scanned me top to bottom. The first seats were on row 15: I had to go back to 28F. I shuffled by others stowing their luggage down an aisle that seemed narrower than normal. A wave of heat overtook my body and I wondered if there would be air conditioning. Some people were raising their seats and placing their luggage underneath—not something done on other airlines.

After some squeezing through other hot, perspiring bodies, I reached 28F, a window on the right side of the plane. By doing as the Chinese—putting my bag under my seat—I had much-needed leg room.

Everyone fiddled with the air vents. A small stream came through but not enough to cool the air, or even one's face.

Even before the plane began to taxi out, and as soon as everyone was seated, the AC gradually came on in the form of handheld fans being passed out in ornately decorated boxes. It was so hysterical to see 200 seated passengers fanning themselves! Our section broke out in loud laughter.

As we taxied into position, the second surprise was doled out—cold wet towels. They were really helpful. Remembering my desert trick, I put mine around my neck.

Left: Woman weaving silk.
Below: A game of street pool awaits.
Bicycles are a main method of transportation,
moving wood panels and chickens.

Then the plane gave a shudder and inched forward, engines revving and becoming more powerful. It seemed we were on the runway a long time, but at last the nose was raised and we became airborne, fans flapping more rapidly than ever. Definitely a scene out of the dark ages!

We climbed through the steel grey blanket covering the city, breaking out above it into the sun and blue sky.

As we settled into our antique seats, cans of apricot juice were passed out. Announcements were made that we were unable to understand, but soon something new would be presented—a plastic tray with the following: one hard-boiled egg, one turkey thigh, one piece of crabmeat, one package of seaweed, one chocolate cookie, four sandwich cookies, one package of candy, one piece of cake, and one roll, followed by hot tea in small plastic cups that squeezed together when you held them. Then came one can of warm beer! The fans had to be put away but periodically came back out for a small bit of relief. Below, the grey sea was endless. Indeed, the plum season rains had begun.

An hour into flight, the plane gave a sudden up/down lurch that frightened its load; a wing came up sharply. Now I saw only blue sky as we banked to the left; perhaps we passed over some kind of navigation beacon. Clearly, the pilot was not smooth in his control changes.

Gradually, people began to doze off from the combination of altitude and warm beer. Occasionally, a fan fluttered.

Further westward, the clouds changed from long grey overcast to billowy white cumulus. It was impossible to see the ground.

Our Shanghai guide kept telling us not to expect hotel accommodations like those in Shanghai, nor would the transportation be as comfortable or efficient. As I rested for the first time in two days, I tried to imagine what lay ahead. I sipped the Beijing beer, official beer of state banquets. The people slept, the plane droned on.

Suddenly, on an unusually steep turn, I could see the ground: tree-covered hills and narrow yellow-ribbon roads twisting through the terrain. As suddenly as I could see it, it disappeared below the cloud cover. Periodically, the plane's power either surged or decreased. Now and again we would bank into a turn. I was relieved to observe the wings were relatively steady rather than flapping. The plane would hold together, but this was only the first of many such flights we'd make in the next 12 days. I could only imagine what the others would be like. I'd save my fan. When I could see the ground, I figured we were flying at about 30,000 feet. With only a third of the flight over, my cool wet towel still gave me some relief from the stifling heat.

Soon, the tree-covered hills gave way to desert sands, mostly flat, but occasionally a curving shadow would indicate small dunes. A patchwork of green fields dotted the endless sands now and again. Sometimes there was a river, a twisting road through low hills, a town, a double X airport, mountains with snow on the very tops, a lake, a reservoir.

The flight was long with only an occasional bit of bumpy air. Finally, 4¾ hours later, we arrived at Urumqi.

Urumqi

In town, we all took pictures in the marketplace: very dirty, but lots of good people pictures. We stopped at the museum. Roads were being rebuilt here: very bumpy rides. We traveled most of the day to Tian Shan Mountains and Heavenly Lake. The valley approach had many yurts. One on the side of the road was locked. A man came to

unlock it then sat off to the side. When everyone else was gone, I asked him if I could look inside. It had a blue door, colorful tapestries on the walls, and rugs on the floor. Two tiny goats were tied up behind the door. A 2X4 area was dug out to make an entry place to take your shoes off. A wooden frame was covered with thick felt; there was a hole in the roof. Some yurts had a stove and stack going out the roof hole. There seemed to be no grass here, only dirt, so when it rained, everything was muddy. The man's wife had gone to town, so the neighbor lady and two kids hurried over. One of my group, Delpha, took a Polaroid of them, and they were delighted. We wondered what his wife would say when she came home and found out what happened.

The road became very steep and winding, and each turn found one or two yurts. The doors were decorated differently—oranges, blue, yellow. On one promontory above the valley, there was a small gold-roofed pagoda. A stream rushed down the valley, forming waterfalls here and there. Once at the lake (Heavenly), the view across was of

Here I'm helping a family unload their possessions.

high snow-covered peaks, the highest being over 15,000 feet. The clouds came and went. We were mobbed by Kazakhs (not to be confused with Cossacks) from Kazakhstan with their horses. They offered people rides and several went, mounting strange saddles with two horns, some embellished with brass. The saddle blankets were splashes of color and sought after at the end of the ride. About six of us decided on a boat ride at 10 yuan ($2). There was a family on board—the woman, who was stoic, her husband, and two children, a boy and a girl. The little boy's eyes were like saucers (fear, maybe of the unknown). They didn't want us to take pictures. At the end of the lake, the boat was headed to the shore. The family's yurt and belongings were piled on the bow—the circular roof piece, the accordion-lattice walls, the felt, the tapestries, and rugs, plus three very large bags of flour. When all but the bags were unloaded, the lady helped the children inch along the foot-wide ramp from the cabin to the bow. Adults had a rail to hold on to, but the children had nothing. The boy had no coat and had to hunch his shoulders with the cold from the wind. The girl had a pink coat, but it lay back on her shoulders. Mom, on the other hand, was layered against the elements. She and the boatman attempted to lift the bags of flour over the rail and onto her husband's back, but couldn't. Quickly, I set my camera aside and helped, which broke the ice, and they all were grateful, showing it in smiles and waving, as we then took pictures.

Our dinner was in the local restaurant, and I thought if we were going to get sick it would be here, but we didn't.

Marcon, the lore babbler in the group, wanted to buy a saddle blanket. The haggling took us up a nearby hill past a large building, a dining hall, and further into a meadow dotted by yurts. Women shot out of them with arms filled with tapestries and rugs. The haggling continued, and Marcon finally made a purchase. We stopped to use the WC, which consisted of three very large rectangular holes in the floor over which one would squat. I had a flash of someone falling in.

Mr. Yung (Young) said he had arranged for us to sleep in two yurts. This was on our original schedule but had been changed, because they felt it would not please us. But our dismay and disappointment made them try to arrange it. An elder Kazak lady and grandson spoke to me and motioned that we could sleep in her yurt, and I could go in and look. There

There were rugs for sale inside this yurt.

were the gaily colored wall hangings and rugs and colored piles of bedding, neatly arranged around the circular wall. There was even a lone light bulb and boom box, neither of which we cared about having.

The 10 women shared one and the five men the other. The men had a stove, we didn't. We had a kitten fit! It was a big slumber party. I was going to read a story to them, but when it was discovered that the light didn't work, a great commotion began with men coming and going while I put on my pantyhose. They remade the lone electrical wire, did something then with a long pole and, with much hollering of directions, it was lowered through the hole. But, alas, once hooked up, it didn't work.

We had enough bedding to be comfortable. Some pads were body-wide for a mattress. The covers were heavy and thick, some covered with orange, blue, purple, or burgundy silk fabric. They were used but seemed clean. It was certainly something we could stand for one night. The pillows were strange, sounding as if they were filled with pebbles. Our guide told us that the beautiful coverlets came from the various yurts. They went around and got the nicest ones from each family.

On to Turpan

Shortly after six, we woke up, got dressed, and then it began to rain. The ground became a muddy skating rink. After a quick trip to a Chinese outhouse, we boarded

1990   1991   1992   **1993**   1994   1995   1996   1997   1998   1999

our mini-bus for the return to Holiday Inn just to pick up our bags. However, everyone took the opportunity to wash and change clothes. We also stopped in the coffee shop for a cup of coffee and a piece of walnut pie.

It was a long ride to Turpan and the Oasis Hotel, where they had a keeper of the keys. Every time we wanted to go into our room, a lady had to unlock it for us. The first time that happened, she couldn't get it open; then we wondered if we could get out once inside.

Once an important way-station on the ancient northern Silk Road, Turpan was a grape center located between two mountain ranges. It was very low, -154 feet at one spot. Because of the heat—with a summer temperature rising to as much as 104 degrees—many of their streets were completely covered with grapes, including the sidewalks. Very beautiful! The population here was largely Muslim with 60% Uighurs and 10% Hui. Food grown or made here included kabobs, bread, grapes, and melon. Locally, there were archaeological caves yet to be completely explored.

After dinner, we went to another hotel to see local minorities sing and dance. The food was exceptionally good at Oasis, again served at round tables, like Lazy Susans, in 14 to 16 dishes. We had been warned not to eat from the same dish because of the possibility of getting sick. Many used their own chopsticks, and I used my fork. I wish I had brought a cup, too.

High on the eastern outskirts of Turpan was the Suleiman Minaret at 144 feet tall. It was built by Duke Suleiman from 1776 to 1779 in Afghan style to honor his father, who had supported the Qing rulers against rebellious aristocrats. Its patterns of brickwork varied from bottom to top. It sat next to a large mosque that was still used by both Uighurs and Hui people on festival days.

The next day's events included a visit to the museum then on to a graveyard where, while digging for the irrigation system, they discovered 2,000-year-old tombs

with mummies and paintings on the walls. There were probably 500 burial mounds in the area. Travel a half hour east of Turpan by car to reach Bezeklik and the site of the Thousand Buddha Caves. The snowy Flaming Mountains were to the north and sand dunes were above.

The Thousand Buddha Caves.

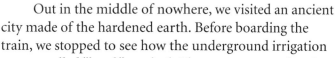
An ancient city in the middle of nowhere.

Out in the middle of nowhere, we visited an ancient city made of the hardened earth. Before boarding the train, we stopped to see how the underground irrigation system, called "kesel," worked. There were acres of underground tunnels through which water from the mountains ran to serve the towns and irrigate the desert oases.

To Dunhuang

The train was to leave Turpan at 2:40 p.m. As we unloaded our bags, I saw the sea of hot, dirty humanity waiting for the train and wondered if we had to share space with them. But we were ushered to the first-class area where it was quiet and clean, and had very comfortable upholstered furniture to rest in away from the others. We were to have "soft sleepers," which were tiny compartments for four with upper and lower bunks, similar to ours, off a long hallway. Once on the train, Mary, Mrs. Zhang, and I shared a compartment. The berths were sheeted with coarse cotton sheeting. The uppers had pleated flounce. There were lots of blankets and a pillow for each of us. A fan was overhead and running. Two large empty thermos jugs stood in a stand under a table by the window. A white cloth covered the table. A lace curtain was on the window, and monk-orange curtains hung on either side of the lace. A mirror hung on the back of the door, and when you closed the door, you could use it. Over the upper bunks and above the hall space was storage. On the table, a 6X10 porcelain tray with blue trim held two white-with-blue-design cups with lids.

Once settled, we watched the country go by. Later, I figured we had 400 miles to go, and if it took us 16 hours, we were traveling 25 mph. But others who didn't sleep so well said that during the night, we were only going 10 mph. Our dinner could have killed us with the fresh cucumbers and tomatoes, but somehow we survived the long night—except for Ellie, who ate something off the street before boarding. We were to arrive at eleven o'clock, but somewhere along the way, we were told because of flooding we would be late.

Breakfast was two eggs, bread, jam, and coffee—very non-Chinese, but good. Then when we hit Hami, the halfway stop, we discovered that we should have been there at three but, due to rain and floods, we were seven hours, plus or minus, behind. Now we'd be lucky to get to Liuyuan by six and then it was three to four hours' drive to our hotel in Dunhuang.

1990   1991   1992   **1993**   1994   1995   1996   1997   1998   1999

Below, rice field workers.

Dunhuang, located in the northwest desert corridor of Gansu Province, was an important caravan stop on the Silk Road for 2,000 years, linking Central Asia with China. Among its attractions were its priceless troves of Buddhist art and the Mogao Caves, also known as the Thousand Buddha Caves or grottoes. The city boasted a number of shops, a bank, and a cinema. Tourism there was still considered "new," and travelers would often see camels on the streets.

The Silu Hotel greeted us with hand claps from the staff of about one to two persons. Our rooms were wallpapered, had a TV (didn't even turn it on), dressing table, and heavy comforters on the bed with a coverlet that allowed the comforter to show through. The pillows were like those in the yurts: They made a rustling sound and felt like a grain. We were told that they were filled with hulls from rice or another grain. A thermos of hot water for the tea (or my coffee) with two covered cups was on the table. A large lace curtain with a lovely wooded scene covered the window. The bath was modern, except that the shower was the handheld kind.

The food all along, except for the Holiday Inn in Urumqi, had been served on a Lazy Susan with 14 plates: cabbage, bok choy, beans, radishes, mushrooms, eggplant, strange eggs with a gelatin, white eggs scrambled with tomatoes, cucumbers, sweet-and-sour pork, chicken and mushrooms, lamb shanks, and bean curd. The rice and egg-drop soup came last, so I mixed the two for a good soup. There was a fish dish and chicken, too. Their bread was very bland and looked like our butter rolls but was

Dune sunset.

more dense. There was also a sweetbread with sesame paste inside and a veggie dough ball called "mandu." The food had been good in most places.

We had a smaller bus than in Urumqi, so our luggage had to come behind us. Sometimes it was three hours behind. The group was very compatible, except for Marian, who drove me crazy. She made such a fool of herself and asked the most stupid questions. She had a 50mm lens and was constantly taking pictures from the moving van.

After dinner, we were taken to the sand dunes at sunset. I rode a camel with Mike, Sean, and Marian to the top of a high dune to take pictures. Sure was a beautiful sight.

Afterwards, I got to bed.

On Monday, we were taken to the Mogao Tombs (caves) a short drive southeast of town. These were the oldest Buddhist shrines in China with 492 grottoes still standing today. Eight dynastic periods were represented, dating from 366 AD. No photographing was allowed. We spent our entire morning there then had lunch.

Back in the p.m., we went to a silk/wool rug factory. A 6X9 rug (wool) I liked was $2,400 at 5.7 exchange rate (13,750 yuan). A 9X12 was 16,750 or $2,938. A smaller one, two-tone tan, was 400 yuan or $70.

Ellie had a birthday so I composed a poem. Mary and I recited it at a party for her on June 30. They ordered a cake, which traveled on the bus all day and was falling apart by the time we got there.

Here's the poem I wrote at the end of the trip:

Ellie in her quiet way
kept us all from going astray
Urumqi, Turpan, Heavenly Lake,
a yurt didn't even make her quake.
Collecting tickets and airport fee,
lending a hand to Mr. Gee
Arranging for a camel ride,
ordering potatoes—French fried.
Counting all "our every things,"
dealing with what the Silk Road brings.
Ever dauntless, ever knowing,
impatience or weariness never showing.
And now the tour is about to end,
with each one making a new friend
Our dreams will be of a thousand Buddha
and the variety of such strange fooda
Chopsticks, bikes and bright umbrella—
Ellie, we thank you, "one fine fella."

Other Areas Visited
Lanzhou

This capital of Gansu Province, located on the upper reaches of the Yellow River, occupies one of the oases dotted along the old Silk Road extending west across Central Asia to the Middle East and Europe. Since 1949, it's become one of the principal industrial bases in northwestern China in oil, petrochemical complexes, copper and aluminum, machine making, and textiles. Lanzhou is also the center of the atomic energy industry.

Lanzhou has a mixed population of over 2,000,000 consisting of Mongols, Tibetans, Uighurs, and Hui. The prize crop is honeydew melons.

From Lanzhou, one may visit the Bingling Temple, made up of Buddhist caves, by traveling 1½ hours via road then two hours by boat on the Yellow River. The temple has a seated Buddha that's 88½ feet tall, as well as statues and murals that date from the West Jin and Tang dynasties with inscriptions in Cave 169, the oldest dating from 420 AD.

Xi'an

One of the most popular tourist destinations in China along the eastern terminus of the Silk Road is Xi'an. It's a large city and the capital of Shaanxi Province in central China. In 1974, the burial site of Emperor Qin Shi Huang Di (3rd-century BC) was discovered here. The Weihe River flows through the rugged Western Hills just north of the city, where many ancient tombs can be found.

Dust storms and thunderstorms are not uncommon here, along with a rainy season that begins in July. The remains of a Neolithic village nearby indicate that this area was inhabited at least 8,000 years ago.

Xi'an currently has 15 universities and offers a thriving arts scene with theater, opera, music, and dance offered. Enamelware is an item that is plentiful.

Some highlights: The Giant Wild Goose Pagoda, built in 652, is so-called because it was built on a site where a wild goose fell from the sky in answer to the prayers of a group of starving Buddhist monks. They buried the goose instead of eating it and later built the temple. The Terracotta Army were found in 1974, marking one of the century's greatest archaeological discoveries. The thousands of life-size statues have stood guard over the tomb of Emperor Qin Shi Huang Di for 2,000 years. Three vaults containing an estimated 8,000 figures have thus far been identified.

Another recommendation is the Golden Flower Hotel, where we stayed. It boasts of a Scandinavian smorgasbord, piano bar, disco, cocktail lounge, health club with sauna, heated swimming pool, and Jacuzzi.

Guilin

Located on the west bank of the Li River, the landscape of Guilin is the image most Westerners have of China. The towers of stone suddenly spring from a lush, green plain

Terracotta warriors.

*The Great Wall
of China.*

that's laced with rivers and lakes. These karst formations appear to be battlements, or fade-in ranks, toward the horizon and are sometimes described as blue jade "hairpins." The stone forest creates a haunting atmosphere. The formations were thrust up from limestone seabeds 300 million years ago.

The climate: Most of Guilin's annual precipitation occurs in May and June, when it can pour for days on end. Overall, it's a pleasant place to visit during the summer, with warm days and cool evenings. The waterways and lakes around the city, kept full from the melting snow in nearby mountains, are sources of irrigation during the growing season.

1990   1991   1992   **1993**   1994   1995   1996   1997   1998   1999

By far, the best way to see and get around in Guilin is by bike. The town offers arts and crafts stores, bakeries, and a pharmacy.

The hotel where we stayed was the Guishan, which was built new in 1988. With 610 rooms, eight restaurants and lounges, and a swimming pool, the hotel overlooks the Li River.

Traveling by train to the east will take you near Jiayuguan and the westernmost part of the Great Wall. It's the oldest surviving segment, dating back to the Ming Dynasty and estimated to be built around the year 1372.

The city boasts of eight universities and two medical schools, even one that specializes in cancer. The local Uighur people have a high incidence of laryngeal cancer attributed to drinking hot liquids.

The religion practiced is largely Islam, with huge mosques still in use.

Some attractions: A camel ride (ha, ha) or perhaps a night in a Uighur tent. There are large carpet factories to tour, and the local artists make embroidered caps, leather boots, horn-handled knives, and jade carvings.

Gaochang (also Karakhoja or Khocho)
Southeast of modern-day Turpan lies this ancient-walled capital of the Uighurs. Its outer walls are 39 feet thick and 3.6 miles long.

Astana
Not far from Gaochang is Astana, which was used as a burial ground. Three tombs were open for viewing: one with painted figures (Tang), the second with a fresco of birds, and the third with two mummified bodies.

1990   1991   1992   **1993**   1994   1995   1996   1997   1998   1999

MY BROTHER PASSES

Although Colorado had a very dry snow year, I did quite a bit of skiing, both downhill and cross-country. In December I took a short trip to Fond du Lac for my brother, Tom's, 70th birthday. His wife, Gloria (63), was having major back surgery in March, so I planned a trip to Madison where friends of mine had pestered me to spend some time with them. I stayed with them while my brother and his middle daughter, Anne, drove back and forth from Fond du Lac daily to be with Gloria at Madison's University Hospital.

I arrived in Madison on March 9 and left on March 14. I was back in Boulder just over 24 hours when the phone rang at 4:30 a.m. and my niece, Anne, informed me that my brother was having a heart attack. They were putting him on a Flight for Life helicopter to Milwaukee. The details were many and long. I was back on a flight the morning of March 16. The entire family was scattered: His three children were in three different places, two of them going to Madison during their mother's surgery. Finally, all were in one place by the end of the day, Wednesday, just a week after my first arrival in Madison. Sunday, March 20, there was a funeral service for my brother in Fond du Lac. Over 325 people attended. I finally returned to Boulder on Monday, March 21.

Brad Prepares for a Climb

Brad was getting ready to leave for K2 on April 22. He'd be away for five months, so I would have to keep busy and be away a lot during that time so as not to worry. K2 was the steepest and hardest mountain in the world. Only 75 have ever reached the top, and 33 had fallen to their deaths. In 1986 alone, 13 lives were lost.

His expedition, sponsored by Reebok, was small. There were six—three Brits and three Americans. They would do it Alpine-style (no oxygen) and start in Kathmandu, where the last of the food was packed up and sent ahead by truck. They would fly to Lhasa then Chengdu, Urumqi, and finally Kashgar, where they would transfer to a truck that would take them to the end of the road. From there, it would be by camel to the north side of K2 and their 16,500-foot base camp. They would have only two Sherpas as far as the base camp. The camels would take them across a large river which, at that time of year, was low, but as they were there climbing in the spring, the runoff would get so high that they would have to wait until it receded so they could go back across it.

I thought of going with him as far as the camels go, or trying to meet him after he got out. Kashgar was a place I had hoped to visit after I enjoyed my China trip so much. I hoped to go to Budapest in the fall, so there was a possibility of my meeting Brad when he got back, then continuing on to Budapest, thereby going around the world.

My plans for the coming months included a week-long trip to Florida to see Steve Wittman, the man who taught me how to fly. He was very famous and was celebrating his 90th birthday, and my visit would be a surprise for him. I would also meet up with my nephew, Tom Osterman, in Atlanta and drive down to Ocala from there.

In early June, I hoped to raft the Chama River in New Mexico; late June, go on an archaeological trip; and late July, go off to Newfoundland to kayak and take an auto tour of the country.

Rafting the Chama River, Crow Canyon Archaeological Dig

My summer had flown by with many things to occupy my time so I wouldn't worry about Brad. That was an impossible endeavor, though, for as one lady friend who was also a climber (47) told me, "You can't not think about him. I wake up and there he is, in my head." She was from Spain and talked in a cute way. She also had been trying to climb all 8,000-meter peaks in the world, having succeeded in about six. She just returned from Pakistan where she tried Broad Peak but failed in three attempts: storm, wind, and exposure in the dark.

In early June, I rafted the Chama River which was so low that we had to push the raft the last mile. That was Friday noon, and by late afternoon, they had started to let the water out for the weekenders. We couldn't believe it! It rose before our eyes!

Toward the end of the month, Ann Hayes, my artist friend who did all the sketches in the Anasazi Basketmaker publication, and I went to Crow Canyon west of Cortez for a week of digging in an archaeological site. We would usually dig in pairs, but there was an odd number of us. When I heard that, I volunteered to dig a hole by myself. (They quake in their tennies when I call it a "hole," but that's what it was—three feet square—and they wanted me to go to BEDROCK!)

The gnats were out in full force, wriggling into our ears, behind our sunglasses, at the tops of our socks, inside our long-sleeve cuffs, and—worst of all—around our hairline. It was about 90 in the shade, of which there was none.

I never had been on a "dig" before and nearly fainted dead away when they handed me two pails and a trowel the size of a soup spoon to remove the dirt from my area marked off by yellow string. And I only had three days in which to do this! I had hoped to do it in one so I could get the heck out of the gnats. Once I began, I realized how foolish my volunteerism had been. But there was nothing to do but dig, and I dug, and I dug, and I dug. One of the "supers" came by and rammed a rod into the dirt to see how far down I had to go. It was over a foot! So I dug, and I dug, and I dug, spoonful after spoonful.

Apparently, they liked my progress and my even sides and floor, because they just left me there…digging, spoonful after spoonful. At one point, I muttered to my neighboring "hole" mates, "And we *paid* to do this?!"

Ann and I decided to do something else besides dig the last day, so on day two, I had to really get into gear, for they were eager to see bedrock in my "hole."

By lunchtime, I suggested that someone come help me empty the buckets (pails) to facilitate a faster digging pace. I dug handfuls until the two buckets were filled then— barely able to lift them—I carried them about 50 feet to the sifter. With every ounce of my 66-year-old strength, I'd hoist them up onto a 4X4-foot-square screen suspended between some teepee-type poles. With numerous shakings of the screen, I'd forget to

breathe in anticipation of finding some incredible artifact that would make all the sweat and gnat bites worth it. But alas, all I ever turned up were a few thumbnail-size rocks.

Finally, with only minutes to spare before our day was over and we'd leave, I hit bedrock with a cheer! The crew came running to peer into my neatly shaped three-foot-square "section" (note new and correct word). It was very inviting, as each handful of dirt had been very cool. So with no forethought or consequence of what might follow, I jumped in and curled up in the fetal position, just fitting cattywampus. Well, everyone grabbed a camera to record this highly unusual and frowned-upon behavior of a "hole" digger. (Had the heat gotten to me? Whatever was I doing?) And the head archaeologist held his cool, making no comment about my being in the "hole" but saying he was excited about

Edwin Bartholomew sifting for artifacts.

Me in the hole!

my reaching bedrock…wasn't I? I could have cared less because I had no idea what that was going to prove. I only knew tomorrow I wouldn't have to dig anymore.

Ann and I shared a modern-day hogan at Crow Canyon with two delightful ladies, one from California and one from Wisconsin. They were innocent greenhorns with no idea what lay beyond the dining hall. So we proposed they come with us at five the last morning when we would drive out to Hovenweep Indian Ruin to witness the end of the summer solstice. They did that. Their comments on what they saw along the way amused us. I reflected on the fact that we have a special life here in the West.

Having been given a map and directions, it only took about 10 minutes to discover the secret trail dropping off the rim down between some large rocks. Once to the canyon bottom and a few turns around even larger boulders, we found the overhang under which there were three 15-inch circles. The two on the left were only a foot apart and were actually spirals pecked into the rock five or more feet above our heads. The other was three concentric circles, one inside the other with a final large dot in the middle. It was about five feet to the right at the same level.

At approximately 7:00 a.m., the sun began to light up an area below the overhang. Gradually, the areas of light moved toward the center, passing directly through the middle of the spirals on the left and circles on the right until the two darts of sunlight met in the middle. It was an emotionally moving experience to watch while wondering about the artist who, centuries ago, discovered this panel among panels under an overhang where, only during this week of the year—June 19 to 25—a horizontal spear-shaped point of light appeared on the wall to quickly (in 10 minutes) pierce the center of the images and connect in the middle. How long did he watch it before he decided to peck in the spirals and the circles in precisely the right areas where the arrows of light would pierce their centers, year after year, during this particular week?

Suddenly, the phenomenon was over as quickly as it had occurred. With great reluctance, we quietly left that special place, each with her own thoughts as we headed

Ann Hayes and friends taking a well deserved rest.

1990   1991   1992   1993   **1994**   1995   1996   1997   1998   1999

back up and over the edge of the canyon, passing the ruins of Hovenweep along the way. Had the Indian artist lived in one of these dwellings? How long did it take to peck the spirals and circles into the rock? What tools were used? What was the significance of this event in that ancient culture? We could only guess.

So ended our week on an archaeological dig in western Colorado.

A brief flashback to 1993 and my 65th birthday.

Below, left to right: Ann Hayes, me, Anne Fenerty, and Rhoda Nozik. Anne hosted this party for me!

1990   1991   1992   1993   **1994**   1995   1996   1997   1998   1999

SEA KAYAKING IN NEWFOUNDLAND

Late July found me hopping from city to city (four in all) to get to St. John's, Newfoundland. Some friends of mine, Anne and Mike Fenerty, asked me to join them on a sea kayaking adventure. The first night we stayed in a lovely B&B, of which I found myself the proprietor before we left. We were on the third floor where three rooms shared a bath that was reached through the hallway. My friends had one room, I had another, and the third was vacant. I loved my room of two nights before we were picked up by a van pulling a trailer loaded with our kayaks. Before we left, Mike requested a room with a private bath for our return, and when he said "we," the proprietor thought we were all together (a Mormon with two wives).

The weather was miserable after weeks of cloudless skies, or so said everyone we met (a likely story). As we traveled to our point of departure, a Lance Cove fishing dock, I heard whispers of doubt from my soon-to-be kayak buddies regarding any future clearing skies. I detected little enthusiasm for donning parkas and spray skirts or camping out in the rain. No one wanted to be a wet blanket (pun).

At the dock, every conceivable item we might need for a two-night campout was stuffed into holes the size of a saucer up front and a rear baggage compartment 10X18 inches. There were only two things the guides failed to pressure through the holes: a steel fire grill and a four-foot saw. These were bungee-corded over the rear of the guide's kayak.

The drive, plus the packing, took most of the morning. Before we finally shoved off into the sea, lunch was served next to the van. Last-minute instructions were how to hold the paddle, where to put your feet on the rudder, and how to raise or lower it; these words gave us the nerve to push off from the sandy black beach to test our skills at paddling without tipping over.

Anne and Mike had a tandem boat, which was good for them because Anne never figured out how to paddle until the very last 10 minutes of the very last day. If Mike hadn't been in the back of her boat, she'd still be floating adrift somewhere out in the Atlantic.

There was a newlywed couple who had made their reservations through a travel agent who sent them to St. John, New Brunswick, rather than St. John, Newfoundland. That created somewhat of a glitch in the start of their honeymoon, but they finally arrived in time to join us. They were a delightful couple in separate boats, but Susan was not too sure about the whole thing. As it turned out, they both did beautifully.

Christine, a single engineer from Montreal, kept getting seasick but never complained. She was a great sport.

With grey skies and rough seas, we never strayed far from shore. Along our route, there would be an occasional stack of lobster traps on shore where the fishermen would leave them for the next "fish." Unfortunately, we saw little sea life such as whales, seals, sea lions, etc., but there were hundreds of seagulls and a few colorful puffins with large orange beaks.

Our two guides did everything except put up our tents. The campsite was in an abandoned town site which was situated on a hilltop—very exposed and waiting for a windy storm to happen, which did. I can't remember ever being in such a downpour with piercing flashes of lightning and booming crashes of thunder. I expected the tent to blow away and water to come pouring through the seams, but somehow it and we survived.

The food was delicious and plentiful, having been planned and carefully packaged by the loving wife of the lead guide. It just couldn't have been better. Although we didn't need to help with anything, Anne and Christine often did the dishes and we all located wood for the fire. Newfoundland was covered with trees that would never give out.

Our first full day of paddling took us to another abandoned town site perhaps 12 miles from camp. We entered a narrow inlet with cliffs on either side but with a sandy beach for docking the kayaks and having lunch. We climbed up through marshy meadows of blue iris and over a small pass onto the other side of the island, first

Mike and Anne Fenerty.

The group paddling off in their kayaks.

exploring a cemetery overgrown with weeds, trees, and underbrush. From the pass, we looked down upon another larger inlet where not too long ago there had been a small community. Their church was still standing but on close inspection, we discovered the roof and floor had been removed. Our guides told us they took it away to build it in another place, and some of the people actually floated their homes to their new location. It hardly seemed possible. How would they ever dry out?

After two nights out, one of them very rainy, we headed back. Upon reaching our starting point with the rain pelting upon us, the guides proceeded to set up a table under a very precarious awning which continued to fill up with water. Finally, someone had the idea that we didn't have to have lunch right then, and how about going to a restaurant? It was immediately unanimous that we pack up and head for civilization.

We were away from the B&B two nights and, upon returning, the three of us were in a new room—ONE room—and it was in the basement! Since Mike had requested a private bath for him and Anne and the proprietor thought it was for all three of us, my room and the bath were reached by going through their bedroom. I couldn't even leave my room without going through theirs! Needless to say, I was a bit put out. Besides that, my room had no lights for reading and no TV.

So…after having a shower and dinner, we went into the cozy sitting room for a while. It was this night that I suddenly found myself the proprietor of the B&B, with a parade of guests coming in with questions like "Where can I find some wood for the fireplace?" (It had become cold in the rain.) In fact, two different parties came with that question. Then an elderly couple arrived, saying that their room was in the house next door but the door was locked. The couples who wanted firewood were told to go out back and look under the deck. That's where I would have put it if I had owned the place. As for the couple who were locked out of their room, I rummaged through the two desks that were there for keys. One was labeled "19," which was the number of their house, so I presumed one of the many keys attached thereto would fit the front door, and it did! Anne and Mike got a tremendous kick out of this and said that I should go into the business.

In one corner of my basement bedroom, a door had been built on an angle to cover up some pipes that brought the bathroom water down from the room above. About midnight, the people in that room returned to it. First, one went in the bathroom and flushed the toilet. Down came the water in the pipes! Then that person took a shower. Down came the water in the pipes! Then whoever it was brushed his teeth. Down came the water in the pipes! There obviously was no getting any sleep that night, so I decided to write the proprietor a letter describing how I had helped two of her guests find wood and another get into their room by locating the keys. Best of all, though, was describing a night in this basement room where the water came down the pipes! And there it goes again. The second person flushed the toilet, took a shower, and brushed his teeth, and all the while the water came down the pipes. My friends in the next room were oblivious of my sleepless night.

The next morning, I delivered the letter to the proprietor, who showed up just as we were leaving for another day of kayaking. An excellent breakfast had already been served by her cook, and we would be back again that night.

Upon arrival around five that evening, we were greeted with large signs at each house indicating that the proprietor was available 24 hours a day, along with her telephone number, which no one had had before my letter of complaint. (My friends say, "Julie says it like it is!") My belongings were moved into house number 19 where that lovely elderly couple were the previous night. The "suite," as they called it, was spacious, but there was no door on the bathroom and, as you sat on the toilet, you could see the kitchen table and anyone who might be around. (The elderly couple had left after one night.) And the proprietor said that she had read the letter, and everything I had said was true. She now had her phone number posted at the front doors, and my room that night was on the house! Never mind that it faced a busy street and the traffic noise was as bad as the drain water!

So my sea kayak trip ended and, after two days in the rain on the other side of the island, I flew back to reality in Wisconsin, where there were corn roasts, barbecues, water skiing, and an ashes-scattering service for my brother.

BRAD'S ATTEMPT OF K2

I had kept myself busy with short trips over the summer in order to be near my fax machine. Brad left April 22 to climb the second highest mountain in the world, K2, in southwestern China. I could have cared less if he made it to the top: The important thing was for him to have the adventure of his life and to come home safe from the dangerous north face.

Reebok had put up $125,000 for food and equipment for this trip. Not many had succeeded in reaching the top via the north ridge, and only one in three who attempted the peak via any route survived. Just reaching the mountain was an experience in itself, and everyone said to go just for that. They were in Kathmandu for a week, putting the last of the food together and loading it into a truck. There, they all wore surgical masks in an effort to stay healthy but—alas—everyone had upper respiratory infections before they ever reached Urumqi in western China. Brad was also seriously ill in Lhasa, unable to raise his head off the pillow the two days they were there.

I had given him a going-away party the night before he left with about 40 of his friends in attendance. I wanted to give him something small to take with him on the trip, something that wouldn't take up too much room and, at the same time, would give him a boost when he was down. To make a micro-cassette tape with each of his friends saying something on it came to mind. Two of the people at the party left but, unbeknown to him, I did make the tape. When I gave it to him, I told him not to lose it and to take it all the way to base camp, which was to be at 16,600 feet. When he was cold and miserable and thinking "Why am I here?", he was to play it. Well, I found out that he played it way back in Lhasa, when he was in the hotel alone and so sick.

With the truck and five Sherpas on their way overland to an Army camp near the wide river they had to cross, the team flew to Lhasa, Chengdu (about halfway to Shanghai East rather than West, where they were going), Urumqi and, finally, Kashgar. I had grandiose plans to surprise Brad and meet him at Kashgar on his way back, but lack of reliable communication and an earlier return changed all that.

On May 17 from 12,550 feet, we got our first word via fax that they had arrived OK. They had with them a portable English telex machine and a solar-powered battery that had been loaned to them. We were supposed to be able to keep letters going in both directions but, for some as-yet unknown reason, they never received any of our communications; we received theirs about once a week. It began to wear on them because the conditions of the mountain were very dangerous, and with no word from home or any way of telling them we were hearing from them, morale quickly diminished.

From Kashgar, they piled into three Jeeps and traveled three days over bone-jarring roads across three 16,000-foot passes before they stiffly staggered out to begin seven days of walking with 47 camels and a few donkeys. Finally, they arrived at the Army camp of Maza in hopes of finding their truck and Sherpas. Much to their dismay and worry, they were not there. After worrying for two days and wondering if they had been hijacked or had had an accident, in they rumbled, totally covered with 12 days of dust, wearing huge grins and very dirty Reebok jackets with tales that would have to be told at a later date.

The river apparently was a snap to cross; they would have to worry about the return crossing when spring runoff would cause the water level to rise so high they might not get across until early September.

The previous winter had been mild, which left the mountain with little snow or ice to hold things together. They struggled to fix 10,000 feet of rope for safety reasons (all previous deaths were caused by falls), but weeks of sunshine melted out the metal hardware that "fixed" the rope. Mornings were spent chopping the ropes out of the ice that had thawed the previous afternoon and frozen again. Climbing with the hardware melting out became very dangerous.

By the end of May, they had reached base camp at 16,600 feet, exhausted from 13 straight days of nonstop load carrying by all six climbers and five Sherpas. Their loads,

K2's Chinese side, North Ridge.

Photo by Brad Johnson.

1990   1991   1992   1993   **1994**   1995   1996   1997   1998   1999

averaging 55 to 70 pounds, were carried twice a day for roughly four hours on glacial moraine, boulder slopes, and glaciers strewn with sharp rocks. Camp One, which took only two days to establish at 19,000 feet, faced the 12,000-foot wall of K2's North Ridge, thus demanding all their attention.

In just three days (on June 3), they reached a point halfway to Camp Two over the steepest terrain of the ridge, 55 to 70 degrees incline on hard, glassy ice that required front-point ice crampons. Because of the warm weather, large boulders and hotel-size, heart-stopping avalanches rumbled within a hundred feet of their route.

On June 6, a fax came in almost pleading with us to write letters, our first indication that none had ever reached them. Phone calls to London from whence the machine was loaned and calls across the U.S.

Climbers approach the North Ridge.

Photo by Brad Johnson.

to find someone who had telex capabilities mounted up. Our efforts seemed endless. The first place managed to get two short messages through, and we thought we had solved the problem. Unfortunately, the young man on night duty at that place had "gone around the system" (whatever that meant), and that was a no-no. They couldn't charge us for those two messages, and perhaps the young man lost his job. Several weeks later, we found another place in Boston that thought they could get through. My first bill for two one-page messages cost $129, and neither message got through.

The London folks decided that team members didn't know how to operate the machine, since no written instructions had been sent along with it. This was very frustrating for everyone.

It wasn't until the first of June that they had their first snowstorm of about six inches. By June 21, they had established Camp Two (21,800 feet) after watching an avalanche the size of a five-story building whiz by only a hundred yards away.

The route above Camp Two was described as winding their way through blocks balanced on blocks with various "grand pianos" tottering, waiting for their final chords.

Everything that avalanched went bounding down their route between Camp One and Two, loosening their ice screws and making their descent very precarious.

Their second snowstorm while they were at Camp Two caused the mountain to come apart with avalanches everywhere. One of them came down over Camp One while they were in their tents. One Brit managed to scramble out of his tent, dressed only in his underwear, just in time to be buried to his knees. This must have been a very close call!

Two teams—one Spanish and one Italian—arrived and, naturally, they wanted to take advantage of the work our team had done over the past two months, mainly to use the ropes. The Italians were not willing to help in any way, but the Spaniards were willing to help carry the ropes. That was good, because now they were high on the mountain and headed for Camp Three at 25,000 feet.

Around July 1, there was another big snowstorm, but they had an unusual 2½ weeks of sunshine prior to its arrival. Although climbers always welcome sunshine, our team welcomed the cold weather to freeze things in on their route where loose rock and avalanches had become a regular occurrence. The Italians were not helping matters any by sneaking over when our team wasn't around and using their ropes to fix their own, making the route even more dangerous with too many people using the ropes. And still, they weren't getting any messages from us.

On July 8, Brad and one Brit reached Camp Three. After spending five days fixing ropes to that level, they had returned to Camp Two to find that three of their team members had left! I don't know the particulars, but I'm sure Brad was extremely upset. Besides being poor sportsmanship, you never leave once you've committed—and they left without conferring with Brad and the Brit. The leader glossed over this to Reebok about 16 days later. Climbers get blackballed for doing something like that, and I'm sure he didn't want that to happen.

Now it was up to the three who were left. The leader had to go down to lower base camp to give the chief Sherpa orders for the three guys to leave. That de-acclimatized him, so he couldn't attempt a summit bid. Brad developed swollen glands and a sore throat, so he couldn't go, which left the Brit to try. Without a partner, he hooked up with some of the Spaniards to try for the summit. However, upon arrival at Camp Three, he found everything destroyed by an avalanche, which forced him to dig a small survival cave. The next day, while following the Spanish at 4:30 p.m. around 24,000 feet elevation, one of the Spaniards fell 250 feet without a helmet. The only reason he survived was that the rope became tangled around one of his legs. He broke a forearm and three ribs and had a possible lumbar fracture, plus all kinds of head wounds. Being in radio contact, Brad went up to help rescue him. At 1:30 a.m., they finally got him back to camp. At that point he was still alive, but they hadn't said any more about him. I'm sure they evacuated him.

That about did it for those who were left. Brad went the next day to Camp One to retrieve his belongings, and the one last attempt by the Brit was abandoned the next morning when a storm came in. So no one reached the top, but they were all alive and on the way home. Thank goodness!

August 1, they started across the river with water levels up to the camels' necks. I'm sure their tales were incredible!

Back to Life in Boulder

Things were pretty normal in town. I had a Swiss student, Veronique, with me for six weeks. She was studying UV rays at NOAA and was a lovely young lady whom I missed very much. I had replaced her with a 25-year-old Hungarian student from Budapest. His name was Gábor, and he was studying telecommunications. He was living in an undergraduate dorm and was forced to speak English, which he did very well. I wished my Hungarian was half as good as his English! I had spent quite a bit of time with him, including the entire Labor Day Weekend. He was fascinated with the mountains because he said there weren't any where he lived.

Veronique.

Gábor and his wife, Victória Zoller.

A Fall Hike

Not all CMCers spend their weekends climbing fourteeners, or even thirteeners. There are some who find it fun to do a destination hike during the fall, one of Colorado's nicest seasons. That's a hike that starts in one place and ends in another, not back at your car. Such was the path chosen by seven CMCers this fall.

On September 19, six friends and I walked from Aspen to Crested Butte. Ann Hayes, Elaine Hill, Libby Kohnen, Rhoda Nozik, and I met Ann and Mike Fenerty for mid-morning coffee at their mountain hideaway in the wilderness of Summit County. The drive over to Aspen via Independence Pass on that beautiful fall Colorado day was incredible, with the aspen ablaze in their orange-and-yellow coats. At the pass, we intended to have our lunch but it started to rain. Just down the west side, the sun reappeared long enough for us to hike up a side valley near a stream where we settled for a grassy lunch spot.

Once in Aspen, logistics of the hike required that we leave one car at the airport and the other at the East Maroon Portal Trailhead. I suggested we attend to that last aspect of the trip before doing anything else. After inquiring about where to park, we took a tour of Aspen's FAA control tower. Once permission to enter was given, we traipsed noisily up the metal spiral staircase but quietly asked a few questions and watched the comings and goings of several jets.

Some time was also spent in a lovely combination bookstore and coffee shop Rhoda knew about. There, we discovered Ann Hayes' book, *Meet the Orchestra!* Julie asked the receptionist if they would like to have some autographed copies, because the author was here! Of course, the book-browsing took precedence over eating or drinking, but eventually everyone gathered under the awning on the outdoor patio for tea, where the sound of rain on the canvas made us feel glad we were not yet out on the trail.

Our B&B in Snowmass turned out to be just a "B," as the second "B" was only coffee and a package of Rainbow sweet rolls. Good thing we took breakfast along! While waiting to go for dinner, I allowed the kid in me to come out by swinging on the kids' swings and sliding down the enclosed slides. As I was swinging as high as the short strong swing would go, a young man came over and asked if I would like him to give me a push. I was already going as high as I could and taking a short fall at the top, so I reasoned it was best to say, "No, thank you." Fun thought, though.

Rhoda had made reservations for us in an Italian restaurant called "Lucci's." It was a tiny basement restaurant with incredible food and reasonable prices. Before going to bed, a few of us soaked in the B&B hot tub, where two of the housekeepers were also soaking. The head housekeeper was bragging about how he and his wife cleaned the rooms in 2½ minutes! His wife changed the beds and vacuumed while he cleaned the bathrooms. I think she was getting the raw end of that deal!

Tuesday our trailhead deadline was 7:30 a.m., and we missed it by only 30 minutes. The weather was delightfully cool—high clouds interspersed with patches of blue sky. What weather the day would bring was questionable. Our trail up a glaciated valley called "East Maroon Pass Trail" was soaked with aspen trees in full yellow dress. Here and there, an occasional patch of brilliant orange, a sign of summer dryness, just had to be photographed.

An article we had read about this trip warned of several stream crossings along the way. Some required the help of walking sticks to maneuver across unsteady logs. I opted to remove my boots each time and wade, but soon discovered and used a pair of sneakers some hiker had discarded behind a tree. There were many stops for water, picture taking, or putting on and taking off rain parkas during short showers. Somewhere along the route, four mounted horses passed by. One of the local stables was guiding a couple to an overlook near the summit.

I knew I could walk about two miles an hour. Mentally, I noted that we would be at the pass by 2:00 p.m. after walking 10 gentle miles with a 3,000-foot elevation gain.

(We started at 8,640 feet; the pass was at 11,640 feet.) Sure enough, just before two, the pass was in sight. We stood briefly on the breezy saddle to take in the view and do pictures, then we scurried down a bit to get out of the wind before stopping for lunch. Repeatedly, we commented on how lucky we were to have perfect hiking weather. There were only occasional showers that added to the beauty of the day when the sun lit up the droplets.

The other side was five miles to the trailhead, where a previously arranged taxi would pick us up. We were to be there between 4:30 and 5:00 p.m. Again, we were right on target. Just as we had been told, we discovered a ski pole with a sign attached to it that said: "taxi will return." But, as Michael would say, "Yeah, but who knew when?" After only 10 minutes of waiting and more pictures, it arrived! Dark-skinned Ramon Burrell (possibly Crested Butte's lone black) met us with a 14-passenger white van. Once inside, just as the article had said, he wasted no time and handed out bottles of very welcome beer!

The ride into town from tiny, now-nonexistent Gothic was short. Along the way, Ramon told us that in mid-July, the surrounding hillsides would be covered with blue columbine. Just before reaching the ski area, the heavens dumped their load to create, just for us it seemed, the most beautifully intense rainbow over Mount Crested Butte that any of us had ever seen. Ramon stopped for us to photograph it and unknowingly almost dumped Rhoda out her door by pulling away with it open.

At our Crested Butte B&B, the Gothic Inn, the proprietress, Sonja, greeted us with an open mouth and the exclamation, "You came!" "Of course we came, why wouldn't we?" Seems there had been a blinding snowstorm most of the afternoon. The surrounding hills were covered with snow that had already melted. She assumed the weather would be so bad that we would cancel. As we had said, we were lucky to have had such beautiful hiking weather.

Sonja, a Czech, came here from California looking for a B&B after friends told her about the isolated town of Crested Butte. Her husband died of lung cancer at an early age and she needed to support herself and two sons. She stayed for several weeks in a B&B just behind the Gothic Inn. Every day, she peered through her tiny window at this large brown log house. She knew the owner was in financial trouble from the failure of his oil interests but thought there would be no hope of turning it into a B&B. However, friends encouraged her to buy it, which she finally did at quite a reduced price and with much haggling with the city fathers, mostly the mayor. She still had property in Czechoslovakia, where she went once a year and brought back a suitcase of favorite cooking items she couldn't find here.

The previous owner's wife was a ballerina, perhaps the reason for several piano curves one noticed immediately upon climbing the stairs to the dining area. The house was solar-heated with automatic thermostats that raised and lowered shades on a Trombe wall. A small enclosed greenhouse area housed a Jacuzzi. She proudly showed us the "bridal suite," which would be occupied the next night by a "lone" young man. Odd, you say? Isn't the world?

We occupied three rooms, two with twin beds and one with a single and a double.

Elaine and I shared the double which, compared to the cramped tent we had shared on so many camping trips, seemed palatial. Rhoda had the cot, which turned out to have a dirty pillowcase and sheets. Rather than making a fuss, she put her pile jacket over the pillow and slept in her long underwear.

Before dinner, we indulged ourselves by soaking in the hot tub. Ann Hayes lost her watch during this exercise (not in the hot tub). After taking a shower and washing her hair, it disappeared. Four of us joined in on the hunt but were unable to locate it. Then I heard somebody say, "Don't tell Julie where you found it." Well, it turned up on her RIGHT wrist where she never wore it! A good laugh was had by all.

Her story reminded me of something that had happened to my dad on the way to my wedding in 1954. My brother, Tom, Gloria, his wife, and my mom and dad were driving through one of the Dakotas on the way to Jackson, Wyoming. Dad had a terrible habit, which drove Mom up the wall, of spitting into a Kleenex. Thank goodness for Kleenex! Well, he spit into some Kleenex, threw it out the window (the thing everyone did in those days), and sat back to enjoy the scenery. Suddenly, after about 15 minutes, Dad said, "Oh, my goodness! I threw out my partial!" So around they turned to search for the Kleenex. When they found it, everyone got out to look for the partial, but it was nowhere to be found. Then, as suddenly as he had announced that

Our taxi driver, Ramon.

it was missing, Dad announced that he had it after all! It was in his mouth! Another round of laughter!

The next morning, we awoke to find the valley choked with clouds, not a good day to fly anywhere. After an unusual Czech breakfast, we "did the town." I spied a silver necklace and earrings I couldn't live without (had Kokopellis on them, and I love them). Mid-morning we needed to find a phone to check with Aspen aviation, our transportation back to Aspen. Mike, the lone male on the trip, had his cellular phone in his pocket (he couldn't be without it). This was a real plus for him, because we (mostly I) had kidded him about not being able to be without his phone. So there I was in the middle of Crested Butte's main street, calling Aspen on Mike's phone. It worked! The planes had been able to get into the airport south of town. Now all we had to do was call the taxi driver, Ramon, but a bakery and coffee shop distracted us. Ramon was supposed to be taking another group out to the trailhead, so I was taken aback to discover him in the bakery. I was so surprised to see him that I blurted out the stupid question, "Are you Ramon?" (Could there be two black men like Ramon in town?) His reply was, "None other!" An hour later, he delivered us to the airstrip south of town. We had a Cessna Turbo 206, which would take five of us, and a Cessna 182, a four-passenger plane, but because it wasn't turbocharged, only two of us could go with the pilot, who happened to be a woman. I elected to go on the 182, knowing the concern some had about a mountain flight in poor weather.

By noon, we were in the air flying right over the pass we had crossed and down the colorful valley we had hiked up. Partway down, we could look back and see the Maroon Bells glistening red in the sunshine. It took about 20 minutes to get back on the ground in Aspen. All went well and only one passenger felt queasy but made it. The trailhead car was retrieved and we headed home, again going over Independence Pass. Lunch was in Leadville. By late afternoon, we were almost back to Boulder when, just below Idaho Springs, it started to snow! Visibility was not too good, but the roads were only wet, not icy. How lucky we had been to have had such good weather. By five, we were back home after a great trip with some very special friends.

We thought maybe this destination hike would probably become an annual event, but—unfortunately—it never happened again.

Heli-Skiing in Canada, Off to Switzerland with Stella

After a New Year's trip to Mexico with a friend, it was ski, ski, ski. We didn't have much snow here in Boulder or in the mountains, so when I was in Boulder I did a lot of hiking and biking.

Brad and I left Friday, February 3, for Calgary and the Bugaboos for a week of heli-skiing. A young man I met there 14 years ago asked me to join him this year. We had helicopter-skied there through Canadian Mountain Holidays (CMH), which had about nine areas and lodges where people from around the world gathered to ski using a helicopter to get to the top of the mountain rather than a ski lift. All quite exhilarating and exciting! On that last trip, I met Richard, who—for some reason—had kept in touch with me over the years. I had never met his wife, and since I'm old enough to be his mother, it felt OK to continue the relationship.

Last October (1994), I got a letter from Richard saying that he and some of his friends were going heli-skiing in February, and since CMH was now using the new "Fat Skis," why didn't I join them? Not knowing that I owned a pair of these new skis, he went on to explain very politely that despite one's age, these skis allowed a person to ski perhaps 10 years longer than they would normally. Very kind.

So I felt honored that a young fellow would entertain inviting this "old broad" to go skiing with him. Well, heck—why not?

Now, Richard's invitation came about the time that Brad was to come out of the mountains from his K2 expedition and I thought maybe, just maybe, he would like to join me and this group of young studs. So I signed both of us up for the February trip, figuring if Brad didn't want to go, I could always cancel him out.

Well, we both went! However, just about the time we had to make the last payment, Richard called to say that he had had such a bad year (financial investments) for his clients that he felt guilty going and had cancelled. What could I say except that Brad was going with me and we would think about him slaving over his desk back in New York!

As it turned out, Brad was delighted to go, because Canadian Mountain Holidays gives a ski suit to those who ski a million feet. It's gotten the name of "the million-dollar suit," because it cost so much to go up there, and if you go enough times to ski a million vertical feet, that's about how much the suit would cost. So Brad would be getting his suit this year.

1990   1991   1992   1993   1994   **1995**   1996   1997   1998   1999

Pictures from our heli-skiing trip.

I shelled out so much for the two of us to go that I was anxious about one or the other of us getting sick or hurt so we couldn't go. Unless you take out insurance ($700 each), you don't get any money back. Well, who should get hurt but ME in a fluke ski accident! Wednesday, January 18, I fell and separated my left shoulder. Thank goodness it was my left arm! I immediately went for an x-ray and was grateful that I hadn't broken my collarbone. Then I started ultrasound and acupuncture treatments and got out my juicer, juicing carrots, broccoli, green peppers, celery, etc., plus all kinds of fresh fruits to hasten the healing. I was about back to normal, except—for no reason at all—I developed a very serious eye infection in both eyes. That, too, was about under control by the time we got on our skis. I also developed an upper respiratory infection and had been doctoring for that, but with lots of vitamins, minerals, ultrasound, acupuncture, etc., I recovered from all three very quickly.

We had a fantastic time skiing with Richard's friends, all about Brad's age and all looking down their noses at this "old lady" when we lined up in the morning for the first run. I know none of them wanted to have me in their group because I would either hold them up or they would be picking me up and waiting for me to catch up. Ha! Did I surprise them! By the end of the week, after jumping off cornices (six feet or more sheer drops) and dodging trees, they were inviting us (me included) to join them again next year.

Back in Boulder, the weather was so mild that I was even playing golf in late February. Brad and I visited Halifax and the ice fields where the seals give birth to their pups. We were gone into March sometime. Then I took a short trip to Santa Fe to visit a friend, and on April 12, I headed for Budapest for two weeks, followed by a week in Switzerland, for a three-week car tour with my Ft. Worth friend, Stella.

In planning the trip, we discovered Swiss rental cars cannot go into Eastern Europe, so I had to board a train and go to Freiburg, Germany, to rent a car. The trip revolved around mutual friends Betty Lou and Tom from Santa Fe who had been living and working in Budapest, Hungary.

In Switzerland, I planned to visit the parents of the Swiss student, Veronique, who had lived with me last summer for six weeks. As far as our Budapest trip, it was unfortunate that the friends who we were going to visit had already returned to Santa Fe. So it was lucky for us that their landlords urged us to come anyway, and they would give us a place to stay and show us their country, just as our friends would were they still there.

Stella couldn't drive a stick shift, so my job was to drive and she was to navigate. Her parents were from Croatia (or was it Bosnia?). Anyway, she wanted to go to Slovenia (different from Slovakia) just north of Croatia. Therefore, our first destination was Ljubljana (loo-blee-ahna), northeast of Trieste. If I were to tell you everything that happened you would still be reading this next Christmas, so I will just say that we were in the area three nights, then headed back north to Vienna.

The problem everywhere we went was where to park the car so it would be safe (i.e., not get hauled off by car thieves). After numerous trips around the city, I suggested that we find a place with an auto *platz*. As it turned out, the hotel we settled on was close enough to everything that we could walk or take a bus and never use the car during the three days we were there.

The next stop was Budapest, Hungary. When we reached the outskirts and a certain Agyp gas station, we were to stop and phone that we had arrived and Peter, our host, would come to show us the circuitous route to their lovely home on the Buda (and hilly) side of the city. Our place to stay was a garden apartment, and he would not hear of us doing our own cooking. We took all our meals, three times a day, with them either upstairs or wherever we were on the daily tours they had planned. Peter informed us right off that breakfast was between 7:30 and 8 a.m. Since our apartment was directly below the dining and living room, we waited and waited to hear that they were up. When it was finally ten to 8:00, we thought we better have a look. Well, Peter was fairly pacing the floor, wondering why we hadn't come up sooner. When we told him we were waiting to hear that they were up, he laughed and said we'd wait forever, because there was three feet of concrete between us. Their house was built out of the remains of a bunker and the walls and floor were three feet thick.

Our stay with them was certainly very special, and we can only repay them if they come to the United States and let us do for them what they did for us.

I had been hosting a Hungarian student, Gábor, at the University of Colorado since the previous September, so while we were in Budapest, we were also entertained by his family. The accent in Gábor indicates that the emphasis is on the "Ga," not the "bor" as we're used to pronouncing Gabor. His father and sister (who spoke better English than we could speak Hungarian) picked us up and drove us to the Franz Liszt

Me with friends.

Music Institute. There, Gábor's sister, Andrea, and we met her girlfriend, Sophie, who spoke beautiful English. She became our interpreter for the day. After a marvelous concert, we took a taxi to their apartment in "Pest." Buda was the hilly part of Budapest on one side of the river and "Pest" was on the other side of the river and very flat.

There, we met Gábor's Mom, Agnes, his brother-in-law, and aunt. I'm sure Gábor asked his mom to cook all his favorite dishes, because the spread of food she had prepared was incredible! And his father, Miklos (mik-losh), treated us to many Hungarian liquors. With Sophie as interpreter, we hardly noticed that we were speaking different languages!

I immediately fell in love with Gábor's family. His mom reminded me so much of him. All in all, it was a very warm, special event, one that will long be remembered.

From there, we headed for Prague. Everyone said we would love it if we liked Budapest. As it turned out, we didn't like it and left a day early. We felt that Prague was years behind Budapest in its recovery from communism. Forty years of domination had left a grim mark on everything and everybody. Faces and eyes were vacant and grey; buildings were still covered with 40 years of coal dust, whereas the buildings in Budapest fairly gleamed in their refurbishment. The one thing that impressed me the most was our visit to the Jewish cemetery, synagogue, and museum, with gravestone upon gravestone in the smallest areas between buildings. People were filing quietly by them, sometimes leaving a pebble, a piece of paper, or a memento on the top of a gravestone. This was an old tradition that was a symbol of someone remembering and caring. It was very moving. The synagogue had thousands of names carefully painted onto

Postcard from Chamonix, France.

1990   1991   1992   1993   1994   **1995**   1996   1997   1998   1999

the walls and ceilings. The museum was filled with paintings, done mostly by children who were incarcerated. They were done using any kind of paper, paints, or pencils obtained by a woman prisoner and artist. Again, a very stirring experience.

The two days back to Munich where Stella flew off to Ft. Worth were not without more adventure. In one of the places we stayed, I got locked in the underground parking garage of our hotel and, later, we both got locked in. A story too funny for me to put on paper, it had to be told out loud. Not only were we in stitches, but everyone who heard it ended up in stitches as well.

After returning the rental car, another experience on a holiday, I headed for Geneva. When Veronique, the Swiss student I had hosted, returned home from her stay in Boulder, her parents graciously wrote that should I ever be in Geneva, please do stay with them. Naturally, I took them up on their invitation at the end of my trip. I saw a different Geneva from the one I had known briefly years ago. The Red Cross Museum was another very impressive experience, and I celebrated my birthday while there with a sinful chocolate cake that Veronique made and which she, her mom—Jackie—and I devoured in one sitting.

Veronique took me to the Olympic Museum in Lausanne one day, and its incredible exhibit of animal sculptures (donated by Veronique's family, the Bugnions) gave me goosebumps. The final day trip I took was in Veronique's father, Jean Robert's, fire-engine red Audi to Chamonix, France. I had so many wonderful experiences and now have them as memories.

Peaks & Places Photography, Holiday Events

During 1995, Brad and I went into business together, calling it "Peaks and Places Photography." Since Brad's friend was killed last year on December 21, he'd taken a new direction in life and done well with photography. Basically, I provided the capital and he did all the work, but I'd been working on my own photography project—a coffee table picture book about Boulder—and wanted to complete it.

When I went to Hungary in the spring, I'd discovered that there wasn't anything like a coffee table book. So far all I had were winter scenes, but when spring arrived, then summer, there were lots of pictures.

I gave my annual Christmas tree decorating party for the fourth year. We made decorations with supplies provided by me, decorated cookies, worked on a picture puzzle—as we do every year—and played Jenga. It was all great fun for about 25 folks.

For a change, Brad was in Boulder for Christmas. He was here Christmas Eve and part of Christmas day before he had to go back to Vail.

Cusco canine.

MEXICO WITH RAINS

The year took off with a bang trying to get out of Denver International Airport for a New Year's weekend in Mexico.

I picked up my friend "Rains" at 4:30 a.m. in order to catch a 7:30 flight from our now-famous DIA. Without going into detail about lugging our suitcases up and down escalators and riding the train between concourses B and C several times, it can all be said in one sentence: We arrived in Mexico City at midnight when we were supposed to be at our destination at 2:30 that afternoon.

This time we visited Oaxaca for too few days, then went on to a new resort area called "Huatulco." We stayed on the oceanfront but it didn't fit our pocketbook, so we moved a block off the beach. We found a great restaurant where the tables and chairs were about 10 feet from the water washing up on the sand. How romantic, and here we were—two single women without any men!

On New Year's Eve we decided to eat "in town," which consisted of a tiny plaza around which there were four blocks of houses. A plaza restaurant had a crab special. As we watched the Mexican world go by on the plaza, I noticed a horse and carriage giving rides and suggested that after dinner, we take one. It couldn't be very expensive. And it wasn't—only 75 cents each.

The buggy held only two people. The owner was a very young man. As we left

the plaza to cruise the neighborhood streets, the horse began to trot. Suddenly, firecrackers exploded next to the horse. Jokingly, I said, "I can see it now in the hometown paper: 'Two female Boulderites feared for their lives as firecrackers cause horse to bolt!'" However, that never happened. Perhaps deaf with age, the horse kept up a steady trot through narrow, dark streets where we never would have walked on our own. Fifteen minutes later—and seeing lights ahead—we figured we must be coming back to the

Top: Observatory ruin. Above; Tidepool life.

plaza. *Whew*, I thought, *cheated death again!* But a sudden jolt caused the carriage to tilt in Rains' direction, and I was tossed on top of her. A wheel had come off! The poor young man immediately began to apologize and said, "No pay, no pay." At that moment I was in stitches, although it could have been serious. We got out of the buggy, surveyed our condition, and assured the young man we were OK. Off we went. "We should have paid him!" sez I. "When the buggy fell apart?! Not me," sez Rains.

As luck would have it, just above the accident scene was a new Catholic church. Rains was Catholic. We decided to go in and recover…or to give thanks, was more like it. On the way out, I gave the young carriage boy his pay…he needed it more than we did.

And so, life went on. We were back in Colorado in just four hours. I had bought a two-bedroom, two-bath townhome in Frisco—just 15 minutes from Copper Mountain—and I could now ski three to four times or more a week, and I did. I spent more time there than in Boulder! A new ski called the "Volant Chubb" contributed greatly to the most fabulous season of skiing I had ever had.

CAT'S IN THE CRADLE

by Brad Johnson

It was summer 1963, and I had been left with my grandparents while Mom and Dad went climbing in Peru. When they returned a whole month later, I pretended I didn't miss them; I even acted as if I didn't know them. I was eight years old, with two ascents of Boulder's Third Flatiron under my belt. My dad had even named a rock on Flagstaff Mountain after me. Surely I must be a seasoned climber, I thought. How dare I get left behind!

The following summer, when Dad left for the Alps, I was on the flight. Under his tutelage and tight rope, I climbed the Breithorn and Monte Rosa in Switzerland, the Civetta and the Cima Grande in Italy. These were my first alpine climbs, with glaciers, crevasses and early-morning starts. It didn't matter that all we did was walk-up routes. I was becoming an alpinist.

Over the next few years, I gradually lost interest in climbing. Baseball, basketball and sneaking over the fence on Saturday afternoons to watch University of Colorado football games seemed more fun. When Dad asked if I wanted to go climbing, I'd say, "Oh no, I'd rather play ball with the guys." So he'd go off to the crags with his buddies.

I came out of early retirement in 1969 to climb Mount Kilimanjaro with my parents. My first high peak. I can clearly remember lying on my back on the summit with a splitting headache, wondering why I had spent the last three days hiking to 19,340 feet just to spend 10 minutes on a cold, cloudy summit. Who's idea was this, anyway?

My interest in climbing was further eroded in 1970. I was 15, and Dad talked me into doing the Jackson/Johnson, a route he had pioneered on Hallett Peak in Rocky Mountain National Park. I tried my first lead. What a nightmare. I was scared to death on the sharp end, and it took me hours to complete the pitch. We got to the top in the dark and stumbled to the car without headlamps. I couldn't wait to get back to football.

Sometime during my sophomore year in high school, I began noticing a group of guys climbing on the flagstone walls of the school. Eventually, I decided to give it a try, and I managed a few traverses before my fingers gave out. This effort created some interest by a guy named Peter. He asked if I had ever climbed before, and I told him that I had gone with my dad a few times, but I wasn't really interested. When he learned that my dad was Dale Johnson, he was flabbergasted. Peter had read about the first ascents Dad had done around Boulder and in Rocky Mountain National Park, and he thought I was crazy not to follow in my father's footsteps. By the time the lunch bell sounded, I had agreed to go climbing with him the following Saturday.

Saturday was an exciting day — a new adventure with someone my own age. We climbed a steep wall with lots of air between our feet and the ground. I was hooked. Struggling, getting pumped and just barely making it up. The adventure! The exhilaration! I hadn't felt that before. From that Saturday on, I couldn't stop thinking about climbing. Every spare minute, I was out with Peter or

Brad and Dale Johnson in 1961; the Matterhorn is in the background.

JULIE JOHNSON

other climbers I had met.

Dad, in the meantime, had started a new business (Frostline Kits) and didn't have much time for climbing anymore. He had taken to backpacking, with the occasional peak that required a rope, crampons and ice axe. For the most part, his climbing gear was sitting in a box in the basement collecting dust. I couldn't get him to go out with me. He'd say, "Oh no, I couldn't do that. I'd be scared to death!" or, "I've got too much work to do on the business."

The following summer, when I was 17, we managed a climb together, the north face of the Grand Teton. We shared leads all the way, but this time, I got to lead the harder pitches. That was the first climb on which we were equal partners. Another year passed, and Mom, Dad and I returned to Europe to climb the normal route of the Matterhorn; Dad and I took turns acting as guide. My climbing skills had finally reached those of Dad's. But just as important, I was doing climbs Dad did back in the old days — both in Europe and home in Colorado.

Two years went by before we had the chance to climb together again, or, I should say, before I talked Dad into climbing. This time our destination was Mt. Kenya, and now it was clear that I was the lead climber. I was assuming the role Dad used to have.

After Mt. Kenya, Dad quit altogether, and I went on to work in a local climbing shop, teaching rock climbing and guiding. The progression of trips started: Yosemite, big walls, little walls, ice climbing, snow-covered rock, mixed climbing, Europe, Alaska, the Himalayas and Peru.

Peru. I had heard a lot about Peru, but it wasn't until I went there that I saw what a great place it was. Too bad I could not have shared this region with Dad during his climbing heyday and enthusiasm. My feelings reminded me of a song called "Cat's in the Cradle," by Harry Chapin, about a son who grows up to be just like his dad, and neither has the time to get together.

Now I'm 40, and Dad is 65. Last summer, I found myself looking for a partner to climb a few peaks in Peru. I asked Dad, and he accepted. Two weeks after arriving in Lima, we were enjoying the excitement of a new-found partnership. I felt proud to be leading Dad up a 6,000-meter peak in the Andes. I felt I was being given the chance to show him all the things I had learned from him, so many years ago. As we stood on the summit of Nevado Quitaraju, we shared the enthusiasm of being in our heyday.

Maybe I have finally grown up to be a climber, just like him.

Brad Johnson lives in Avon, Colorado, and guides treks and climbs in Asia and South America. Dale Johnson is enjoying his retirement in Boulder, Colorado, and in the surrounding back country. ▲

Reprinted with permission from Rock & Ice. *This article written by Brad ran in the January/February 1996 issue.*

SUMMIT PROFILE

Quality... Place

JULIE JOHNSON

By SYLVIA LOBATO

Some say you can't go home again, but Julie Johnson may be proving them wrong.

She was the "school ma'rm" in Old Dillon during the early 1950s, moved away for many years and is back again as a second homeowner in Frisco.

"We all have 20-20 hindsight, she says as she compares the price she paid for her Creekside Drive home to what she could have bought property for in Frisco in the '50s.

She could have bought a good piece of property for $3,000 and could have held onto her in-laws' property in Breckenridge, but did neither.

In addition, she and husband Dale were asked to put $3,000 into Vail a little later and didn't have the money. They could have borrowed it, but decided not to. The rest is history.

When it came time to look for a second home on The Summit, Julie looked all over, but centered on Frisco.

There are still some original buildings on Main Street and Frisco still feels like home. It feels like a community.

The old school site has long disappeared under Dillon Reservoir, but Julie's memories remain clear more than 40 years later.

After graduating from the University of Colorado with a degree in English and education, Julie began coming to Summit County to ski.

She was determined to stay in Colorado. She had come from Wisconsin in 1949 and fell in love with the state.

Besides, a season pass at Arapahoe Basin was selling for $35.

In 1952, Julie had been skiing at A-Basin and met several people who lived in Dillon, including the school principal, John Bailey.

One evening, she was in a local bar which boasted a jukebox and a back room for dancing when she told Bailey, "Boy, I envy you...I'd give my right arm to live up here and ski."

When Julie came up to go skiing, she slept in a mummy bag in the woodshed of the Frisco Hotel since she couldn't afford to rent a room. Money was scarce, but she still managed to ski.

As a beginning skier, she joined Ruth Wright on the A-Basin ski patrol, but she wanted to teach, so she was thrilled with Bailey's response.

Bailey was planning to leave and suggested she apply for his job.

Julie went to see Bob Roush at the Public Service substation. It was a cold day and he had his feet propped up against a pot-bellied stove.

"I told him why I was there," says Julie, "and he said, 'Well, I guess we'll have to have a school board meeting.'"

Roush told Julie to call Bernice Allen, since the meeting would have to be in her house, and the first die was cast.

The board told Julie she could have the job and they wanted a disciplinarian.

"I said I hadn't taught school before, but I'd see what I could do...they neglected to tell me I would also be principal," she recalls with a smile. "I was applying to teach seventh and eighth grades."

As she started to leave, someone added that information.

"I hadn't even taught school yet and they wanted me to be principal...I said I'd have to think about it," Julie adds.

She went back to talk with Bailey and learned that the principal's job wasn't all that difficult.

"He said, 'Ask for more money and take it,'" Julie says. She asked for, and received, a salary of $2,600 per year to start, with a second year raise boosting it up to $2,800.

Julie rented a residence from Bailey and settled down to work.

It wasn't long before she

Continued on page 11

The Ten Mile Times was a Frisco newspaper and is no longer in existence.

SUMMITFILE
Continued from page 5

discovered that being principal and teaching two grades wasn't all of it.

"There had to be all sorts of programs, the parents expected it," she says, "so I became the dramatics director."

Teachers included Kenny Caldwell, Maxine Caldwell and Ruby Lowe, all old enough to be the parents of 24-year-old Julie. All five teachers under her had experience, Julie had none.

Her classroom was on the second floor of the old school and she used a projection room over the gym as the principal's office. She called an assembly, introduced herself and let the students know what the rules were.

During the first week of school, Julie heard a knock on the door and found two little girls who had been sent there by Kenny Caldwell for using bad language.

She knew the girls were using language they had heard in town; she also knew they should be punished.

"What do you expect when every other business in town is a bar and the kids meet their dads in the bars after school?" Julie asks.

She had instituted girls physical education and took it away from the girls for a week. While their peers were playing, the two naughty little ladies were to study in the principal's room.

During lunch, Kenny asked, "What did you do to those little girls?"

They had returned to his classroom crying and continued weeping. Pressed for a reason, one pouted, "She was so nice..."

On into the year, Julie discovered that, though plays and programs were expected, there had never been scenery on stage. Students would put a sign on a chair designating it a tree and work around it.

Julie decided to build scenery and sent away through the grocery store to Denver for some mattress boxes.

When the boxes arrived, the only paint available was house paint and, despite repeated exposure to moving air and heat, it didn't dry well.

After the scenery was built, the stage was too shallow for it, so

Julie and her students hooked it onto pulleys, raising it to the ceiling when not in use.

It was used — a lot. Christmas and Easter programs were major productions and the whole town turned out. Mothers made costumes and the children got into their roles.

Basketball games were also big community events, especially after Julie decided to have the girls' team play the boys.

"I'm not lying," she says. "Everyone in the county was there. It was standing room only in the gym."

The first fall of Julie's Dillon career was beautiful, so she told her students to bring a lunch and show her their favorite places. She packed her seven students into her car and headed toward Keystone.

Along the Snake River, the students told her to stop and began pointing out the scenic beauty.

One of the children ran ahead and was getting ready to cross the stream, against Julie's better judgment. If someone fell in the water or got hurt, there'd be hell to pay.

She finally agreed to cross, with the warning, "Whatever you do, don't fall in."

Guess who fell in. That warning is the title of Julie's book in progress.

She was soaked up to her neck.

The group had their picnic anyway and Julie asked the students to keep her little pratfall to themselves.

She took them back to school, left them in their home room and rushed home to change clothes. The students must have behaved because nothing was said when she returned.

The next day, however, everyone in the grocery store knew the new school m'arm had fallen into the river.

After a time, Julie grew tired of having to carry oil to heat her place and found an apartment to rent from Millie and Earl Marsh in Frisco.

Marsh, mayor at the time, also wanted an "eddycated seccytary" and Julie became town secretary/treasurer, driving back and forth to Kremmling to do the banking.

Continued on page 14

Frisco naming story told from family perspective

Dale Johnson, former owner of Frostline Kits, had relatives who mined for gold here. In fact, his great-great grandmother was the first white woman here.

The surname Recen is recognizable, and the family lived on an Island on Ten Mile. One day, a scout came by, the family was gone, and he left his calling card. Scratched on a large beam across the door were the words, "Frisco City," not in honor of San Francisco, Calif., but in honor of a house of bawdy pleasure in Central City.

Originally from Recen, also known as Kokomo, five brothers prospected on the Gore Range. Today, a marker stands where their cabin was, and the legend continues that one brother didn't make it back after a prospecting trip and was found dead on the woodpile; another was found dead in bed, his dinner still on the table.

Apparently, the original Kokomo burned, so the people moved their post office to Recen, but kept its original name, so the town's name changed quickly.

SUMMITFILE
Continued from page 11

The apartment, above what is now the Daily Planet bookstore, had automatic heat as well as a garage. The Marshes lived in a house to the rear.

One winter, the snow was so deep that Julie could have walked out of her second floor window onto its surface.

The county snowplow driver lived in Frisco so she always got plowed out. "I never could close the school on account of weather," Julie observes.

Hank Emore, the school janitor, went out on big, wide wooden skis to check the power lines on the pass above Montezuma when the snow was particularly heavy.

While it may have been a bane for travel, all the snow proved to be a blessing for Julie's students.

She decided to start a skiing program and, with help from Bailey, put together a package which included a lesson at A-Basin and a half-day lift ticket for 50 cents.

Earl and Edina Ganong had children in the school and Julie was acquainted with Max and Edna Dercum, so she got Edna and Edina to help her take the students skiing every Wednesday.

Dale Johnson, a miner at Climax and third generation Summit County resident, won Julie's heart. The couple was married during her second and last year at Old Dillon.

After Dale went into the military, Julie went back to Wisconsin to give birth to son Brad, then followed her husband to his base in Georgia.

The couple returned to Colorado and, as the boy began to walk, his parents enjoyed the relaxed atmosphere at A-Basin, where they could leave their son in a sleeping bag in the car while they skied.

Brad had a pair of little plastic "drugstore" skis which came packaged with little poles and foot straps and skied on a nearby easy hill, then get back into the car to warm up.

One day, when the boy was about three, Julie looked up and saw him on the chairlift. "He got on there all by himself with his little drugstore skis," says his proud mom.

Brad is a ski instructor at Vail and has lived there for 17 years.

Dale, a geologist, didn't stay in his field, but went into business with Gerry Cunningham, originator of the Gerry, Inc., sports and outerwear business.

Later, Dale sold his half of the business back to Cunningham and began marketing Frostline Kits, enabling consumers to create quality outdoor items at home.

Julie went back to college and earned a masters degree in speech pathology while Dale ran his business out of the basement of their Boulder home.

That lasted until neighbors complained about huge delivery trucks pulling up to the house.

Dale stole Julie's cleaning lady away to work in the kit business.

She had previous mail-order experience and filled orders as they came in.

One day, she called Dale and complained that she couldn't fill all the 13 pending orders that day. He advised, "Call Julie."

From that small beginning, the company grew to employ more than 200 persons in the busy season, allowing the Johnsons to enjoy other activities.

They led mountain club expeditions to such places as the top of a 19,000-foot peak in Peru, up Kilimanjaro, almost to the top of Mt. Kenya, the top of Mt. Fuji in the winter, and up the Matterhorn.

Frostline was eventually sold to the Gillette Razor Company and Dale and Julie were divorced.

While Frostline may have worked for the Johnsons, it didn't work for Gillette. Within three years, the company had to sell to the walls and close all the stores and outlets.

A newspaper owner and his sons from Grand Junction picked up the pieces and it's still going.

Julie dedicated herself to intellectual pursuits and athletic adventures. She says skiing, biking and fishing are her passions, in that order.

She also became involved in an archaeological research project in the Four Corners area.

A Bureau of Land Management ranger planned a photographic exhibit of artifacts taken from Grand Gulch in the southeast corner of Utah and Julie put up the money, leading to the Wetherill-Grand Gulch Research Project.

Julie became the project director. With a couple of grants, it became a $150,000 research project.

The project ended after four years with The Basketmaker-Anasazi Symposium on Grand Gulch. Held in Blanding, Utah, it drew the largest attendance of any archaeological symposium anywhere.

"We called it reverse archaeology," she explains. The effort retraced the steps of 12 expeditions that had gone to Grand Gulch and taken artifacts out for museums and individuals back east, then looked for and catalogued the items.

Using Wetherill Journals and the names of explorers scratched on canyon walls along with the dates of their expeditions, the staff determined where the artifacts had been found.

The project won the highest award ever given by the Bureau of Land Management for historic preservation.

"I feel very fortunate that I don't have to work," says Julie, who spends as much time as possible on the slopes, either skiing alone or with the Over The Hill Gang at Copper Mountain.

As she talks, her voice fades and her eyes focus on a vision of some place she'd like to be.

Retire? Not as long as there's a mountain to climb, a slope to ski or a place to explore.

END

Seal Trip with Brad

Both Brad and I had always wanted to see the harp seals up close after having been up to Churchill to visit polar bear territory. The best time to take this trip was in mid-March for only a few weeks, when the seal babies were born.

Top: The fur of young pups is so white!

Upper right: I got to pet a pup!

Right: Brad photographing the seals.

Left: Mother and pup.

Photos by Brad and Julia Johnson.

Our first destination was Quebec City, where we stayed overnight in a place called "Peggy's Cove." With not much time there, we toured around the coast and visited Peggy's Point Lighthouse. What a spectacular place!

Then we were off to Magdalen Islands, a small archipelago out in the middle of the Gulf of St. Lawrence, to view the seals. We were taken out by helicopter to a large chunk of sea ice and given only an hour to take our pictures. The babies are pure white when they're born, which doesn't last long.

Since that trip, the business of flying helicopters to see harp seals had literally developed into a hunting expedition. The pilots had used their flying tours to locate where the seals gave birth. These locations lasted a very short time before the babies disappeared, so the pilots needed to make their trips short and quick to relay the information they had to those who wished to hunt the seals. A young lady who took one of the heli tours discovered what they were doing and contacted the right authorities to put a stop to the scheme.

The seals weren't usually close enough in to be able to take good pictures, but Brad and I tried! Here are some pictures of both Brad and me lying low and trying to get some good shots.

Sailing, Taking a Road Trip, Brad Leaves for Peru

About April 9, Rains and I flew to Grenada for a week of sailing. We started at St. George's and went all the way to the Tobago Cays in one direction and Tortuga Island in the other. We really didn't sail much as the winds were in the wrong direction, so we motored, but it was a great trip. La Tortuga Island was spectacular and the Cays were fabulously beautiful.

For six days in early May, I went on a driving tour in my new car, the Toyota Camry Wagon. I went to Cortez, Colorado, to visit friends with a new baby, then on to Halls Crossing to Bullfrog across Lake Powell to meet friends. We hiked on numerous drainages along the Burr Trail, which was a magnificent place! It goes through Waterpocket Fold and Capitol Reef, ending up at Boulder, Utah. I had a birthday celebration in the parking lot with horns, cards, and a lot of laughter! From then on, I was alone: Escalante, Bryce, Zion, Pink Coral Sand Dunes, and St. George, Utah, where I had friends and played golf before heading south to Las Vegas for an annual stockholders meeting. My Hungarian student-friend, Gábor, who had a job near San Jose, California, flew in after my meeting and we "did" the town. It was his first time in Las Vegas! He sure got an eyeful. Then I drove on to Sun City outside of Phoenix and Scottsdale, where I visited two other friends before heading home. I went through Montrose, Grand Junction, Glenwood, Eagle, Vail, Frisco, and finally reached Boulder.

The West was having a severe drought; everyone was burning up. While in Las Vegas, it was 115°! Just last evening, we had the first relief in weeks when it poured buckets for about an hour, even causing my phone to go out. And two days before the Fourth of July, 11 western states lost their electricity for two or more hours. Wait until the terrorists figure out how *that* happened! Can you imagine?! No stoplights, no computers, cellular phones out, refrigeration off, the whole country put out of commission. That's scary.

Brad left for Peru about the time I left on the driving tour. He was writing a climbing guidebook for an area outside Huaraz and spent two months there, hoping to climb and take pictures. But it was a whole month too early: The snow was in bad condition and it wasn't safe, so he didn't accomplish anything in May. The first two weeks of June, he guided a trek. After that, he had no climbing partner, as the one he had planned on fell off a ladder just before he was to join Brad and injured his back.

So he ended up getting together with some climbers from Salt Lake City and did a few things with them. Finally, he came back July 2, wishing he had stayed down there.

At the end of June, I was in Salt Lake City to attend and be part of the opening of the Wetherill-Grand Gulch Research Project's exhibit at the University of Utah's Museum of Natural History. It was the museum's centennial exhibit and was to be there until March 30, 1997.

I spent time playing lots of golf through the summer (even took lessons) and made many trips to what a friend called "La-la Land" in Frisco. I had a Fourth of July party in Boulder with a barbecue and 30 people attending. In a weak moment, I agreed to help a young friend drive to Madison with her three boys, ages 2½, 6, and 10!!! Need I say more? I made a quick visit to Fond du Lac then headed home.

La Tortuga Island and Tobago Cays sailing trip.

Lake Titicaca, Machu Picchu with the Wrights

It was August 3 when Brad and I left for Peru. Some old friends of mine—Ken and Ruth Wright of Wright Water Engineers (WWE)—had been doing a water geology research project at Machu Picchu. The source of water that had supplied the ruin hadn't run for many years, and the company was trying to locate it and get it to flow again. Ruth was also writing a guidebook and asked if I would do the photography for it (black and white). It had been 15 years since I had taken any black-and-white photographs, which worried me a lot. On such a trip, you have just one chance to get the picture. At the Utah Museum opening in June, our project photographer was there and I had drilled him on film, exposure, filters, etc. I hoped his recommendations would work.

The Wrights would be leading a research team from Boulder/Denver, so our group would have privileges the normal tourist didn't enjoy. Brad and I had been to the ruin before, but it would be great to take pictures of some areas we hadn't seen previously. He would be there just a few days then head back to Huaraz, where he would stay until September sometime.

Lake Titicaca, 12,500 feet—The Largest Navigable Lake in the World

Brad and I left the U.S. a few days early to go to Lake Titicaca to photograph the reed islands people, something we'd always wanted to do. We'd meet up with everyone else a day after they arrived in Cusco.

We flew from Miami to Lima where we stayed overnight in a private home in the Miraflores District. The next day we flew to Juliaca then took a *colectivo* to Puno, our base of operations, for 55 soles. In Puno, we stayed in Hotel Sillustani, one block off the main plaza where there was a walking mall and many restaurants.

The Uros people (Quechua), an ancient culture, lived on floating islands. One island in particular had nine families living there, and you could stay overnight if you wanted. It was very cold at night, so take a sleeping bag if you ever go! The toilet was like an outhouse in a blind of reeds at one edge of the island, and you walk to it on reeds of the *totora* plant. The lower portion of the *totora* could be eaten, just like sugar cane. The *totora* reed boats, called "balsas," were what they used to get around. Some natives had graduated to a larger motorboat.

Arriving by boat at an island on Lake Titcaca, where the Uros people lived.

Above: Typical island house.
Below. Uros woman grinding grain.

The natives' houses were square and had peaked roofs. The children went to school on the large island or in Puno five days a week. Fish, one of the staples, was caught with nets—a tiny fish that had an overly large front end. The natives' clothes were very colorful, and they didn't mind you taking photos.

We met one native who was 70 and claimed to have been born on the larger island. He and his wife had a reed-made *cocina* and a reed-made house where they slept. The wife knitted clothes. Women wove layers of ankle-length skirts that they wore with wool leggings. They had a small girl who went to school. She was nine and seemed to like drawing, so we bought a picture she made to be used as a postcard. The father sold us a very nice replica of the balsa for 5 soles. They had a tiny cat, two dogs, a couple of chickens, and a baby water bird. Life seemed to be satisfactory to them. We gave them some fruit and left.

There were many interesting things to do close to Puno. One may take a private boat tour of the islands for 120 soles, or $60, for four hours.

We took a taxi to the archaeological site of Sillustani where, on the surrounding hills, were unbelievable towers of large rocks similar to the rocks used to build Machu Picchu. Smaller rock ramps were used to get the much larger rocks up to next level, and the towers stood 30 feet high. The best light for photos was at sunrise at 6:00 a.m., and one could easily spend an hour or more seeing it all. The entrance fee was 55 soles each.

Another interesting place nearby was Chucuito, which had a fertility churchyard with a beautiful church next to it on a nearby hill. Puno itself was a bustling city of 20,000 to 30,000 people. Most residents appeared to be well dressed and we saw few, if any, beggars. It was a clean city with many street markets as well as sidewalk vendors, and there were many young women selling sweaters that were soft and beautiful for as little as $4.

Wright Water Engineers

We soon met up with the Wrights and got ready to travel from Cusco by train. We were up at 4:50 to be picked up at 5:50 for the 6:30 train. We had reserved seats on the first car for a four-hour trip, then we were to take the bus but had no bus tickets, so we bought them for $6.25 each. It was 20 minutes to the hotel via many switchbacks. Last year (1995) in early December before Christmas, there were signs of instability above the road because of water from the original spring. A boulder as large as one of the buses broke loose and thundered down the mountain, crossing and recrossing the road until it came to rest near one of the switchbacks. A landslide followed and it took several days for them to reopen the road.

For the first time, the Wrights couldn't get rooms in the Machu Picchu Hotel. Although they said the hotel was full, we thought some travel agencies blocked out rooms, and the hotel wouldn't double book them if no one was using a room. So we rode the bus back and forth from the village every day. We were fortunate to get rooms in the Peru Hotel in Aguas Calientes several blocks up the main street. There was no hot water, but at least there *was* water—*mucho frio*.

After two to three nights, we discovered if we paid the guard 5 soles and waited 30 minutes, there might be hot water. Sometimes there was no pressure and no hot

The road leading to Machu Picchu.

water, so it required two to three trips to the front desk to argue about the fact that there still was no hot water. The last night there, Brad got locked out. I woke about 11:15 to find his bed empty, but I dozed off again. *Not to worry,* I thought, *he'll be in by midnight.* At 12:10, I awoke again and remembered the guards were new and weren't going to give us our keys. They didn't know we were already guests there. After throwing on my fleece and tennies, I quietly went to the front desk; it was dark and no one was in sight. Then I saw Brad's shadow against the wall outside the front door. Sure enough, he was locked out, and the padlock held the door firmly shut. Opening doors behind the desk, I found no guard asleep. I rummaged through the drawers for a key that might fit the lock, otherwise it was obvious that

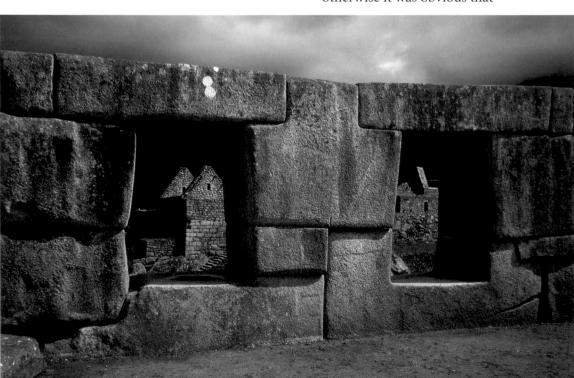

Some locals with their llamas.

Brad wouldn't get back in through the front door. Finally, he said I should try one of the windows that faced the street. With much relief, I was able to unlatch one and he could easily step from the sidewalk onto one of the padded seats that lined the wall of the windows.

Brad wondered if I had heard him banging on the doors and windows, even on up the hill, as the hotel covered about a block's distance beyond the front door. It was only a coincidence that I had a hunch from the previous confrontation at the desk and with the new guards that because of the late hour, I decided to see if there was a problem.

Ruth Wright, upper right, and a colleague, relaxing.

Perhaps once again our mutual ESP was at work. Morning came all too quickly, since we needed again to get up at 5:30 to catch a 6:15 to 6:30 bus.

So every morning, we were up quite early to catch the early light, and we would stay until six for the evening light. While photographing at the ruin, we stayed pretty close to Ken and Ruth, since they'd both been there several times. On Monday, August 12, Brad, Ruth, and I left at 10:15 and hiked to the Temple of the Moon way around Huayna Picchu. It was a very irregular trail, hugging a cliffside but not dangerous. It had many steps, man-made and steep, and in some places had a large roped handrail to help either get up or down because of the high rise of the steps. In some places, we were grateful to be in under the shade of the jungle vines, because it would otherwise have been extremely hot. The temple was built in several levels, similar to the buildings of Machu Picchu, constructed in niches and double-jam doors. One room was built around and under an overhang, which actually was a cave-like place. We stayed about an hour taking pictures there.

The return was all uphill with little relief of level stretches, which made it very slow going. We were gone four hours—three going and returning with one hour there.

The best weather was on August 13 and 14. Brad left early on the fourteenth but stayed in Peru for another month of climbing in the Cordillera Blanca, north of Lima about 200 miles, where climbers from around the world congregate that time of year. He was doing a climbing guidebook and would be photographing the various routes they took. It was the first English guidebook for that area.

And it was just as well that he left, because there were so many tourists at the ruin toward the end that trying to take photos with no people in them was almost impossible. It seemed that the mountain had far more people on it than it should've had.

On the thirteenth, Ruth and I were allowed into the arch dig with Elva. Two people climbed over the ropes when our backs were turned and were standing too close to the edge where it might cave in. It became too excitable, and Elva finally got rid of them. You can't believe what tourists will do.

On the last day there, Ruth and I went into the Royal Tomb and the Torreon, where a young aggressive Peru University student, who said she was also doing research, tried to follow us up the cordoned-off steps. Finally, Ruth told her we had a permit and she would have to get her own permit; neither the guard nor Elva had the authoritative right to let her stay. She finally left.

Ken, Gary, Dave, and Jan met on Monday with the COPESCO (an organization associated with UNESCO) people to discuss their problem with the rockfall and the water diversion. Peru mentality was to find a quick fix for today—no long-range thought. "We can do XXX mañana." One man named Freddy who had some authority realized their problem was long range—10 years. The most important thing, since rockfall closed the road for two months, was how to divert the water and stabilize the road, hotel, and ruins to keep tourism going. The spring was above the hotel and the system leaked, so the hotel might be in danger. They would probably divert some of the water down the west side. It was doubtful that water would ever run through the ruins and the 16 fountains, as it did during Incan times.

Did they figure out where they wanted to build and then find the spring, or was it the reverse? The 5% grade to deliver the water to the Royal Chambers first was a feat in itself.

No one knows how they got the rocks up there, how they cut them with no tools, and how they measured so accurately to get them fitted together, as they had no mortar. The many rocks that mimic various mountains or point to Salcantay (the highest peak in the Vilcabamba mountain range) certainly attest to the fact that they worshipped the mountains, the sun, and the moon.

The storage houses guard the present entrance; there's a long staircase to the original entrance.

Turkey, the Cradle of Civilization

What a trip! Old town Istanbul, congested with narrow, dirty streets, was located on a hilly landscape surrounded by water: the Golden Horn and Bosphorus waterways and the Black and Aegean Seas. Everyone here had a black mustache! Rugs were seen at every turn, and they were all irresistible. I bought a small one in the first outlying village. Hotels here were plain but adequate. At least they had hot water! Minarets popped up every direction we looked, and we heard five calls to prayer per day: I couldn't sleep past 6:00 a.m.! The dress code was very American with only a few female faces covered in the cities. There were many Turkish bathhouses, most of them for men. Only 30% of households had running water. The food was considered safe, and there were many window displays to help you decide what to eat. It was also very cheap, with our dinners usually under $5. Apple tea, available everywhere, was just hot apple juice. They served it in shot glasses on tiny saucers. We were sometimes enticed into a rug dealer's place for a cup of apple tea. While one could even plan to drop in mid-morning or mid-afternoon for a quick pick-me-up, we were never convinced we should buy a rug! And the tea just wasn't worth it.

On our fourth day in Istanbul, I had a car delivered to our hotel. I drove while Mary navigated. It turned out not to be a good idea! The map and roads didn't coincide, since the roads weren't marked. We got lost easily but finally found our way

Below: A sampling of the architecture in Istanbul, and a man carrying a tray of donuts on his head.

Above: Looking up at one of the minarets that were everywhere.

Upper left: A street apple tea server.

Left: Local group of women on the street.

after an hour. So we arrived at our first on-the-road hotel late in the day. We saw women sitting on the ground on a corner, making lace, and we stopped to take pictures. One of them left, running home to bring back rugs that she hoped to sell. We purchased one later in the village. The hotel, empty this time of year because it was off-season, was located on the beach by the Aegean Sea. Its waters were inviting but

Friendly villager.

Above: Pergamon ruins.
Below: Ephesus ruins.

Antalya harbor.

Amphitheater ruin.

chilly. While walking around, we saw a dog hobbled with a chain. I sometimes can't believe how cruel people can be. We saw a great sunset.

The second day driving was some easier, with our next stop the Pergamon ruins. When you see one ruin, you've seen them all! OK, not really. Ephesus was spectacular, and the port city of Kuşadasi was probably one of the greatest places we visited. Our hotel was next to the bus depot, however, with a very loud disco next door.

We visited two small villages, walked around to get culture-type photos, and were invited into a home by a man and woman. We were, of course, given apple tea! We used sign language to communicate; they let us take pictures. Their yard had an apple tree and grapevines. It was very private and very clean. I was sorry we couldn't talk with them.

In the next small village, yet another family invited us in. It was noon and they fed us: homemade

Typical rug shop exterior and interior. They were everywhere!

Rug on a loom.

1990 1991 1992 1993 1994 1995 **1996** 1997 1998 1999

Pumukkale. People shed their footwear to walk on the formations despite signs that say, "Please do not walk on the formations."

wine, grapes, homemade bread, and homemade goat cheese. The family consisted of the father, mother, a daughter, and a 15-year-old son. We didn't find out anything about the husband. We took pictures and exchanged addresses so we could send them a photo.

We headed inland to Pumukkale. Warm, mineral-rich waters flow down a hillside to create a white travertine-terraced area. Here, people shed their footwear to walk on the formations despite signs that say, "Please do not walk on the formations." Maybe they can't read?

Next was Antalya on the Mediterranean Sea. We stayed in the Ottoman Palace, which was a B&B. There were three minarets a stone's throw away, seemingly competing with one another for the best and loudest prayer at 6:00 a.m. There were a lot of fishing boats, too, and they all wanted to take us on a tour. Rug dealers were everywhere and all offered apple tea...no cost to look!

It was a long drive to the east and Cappadocia. Many thousands of years ago volcanoes erupted, and their deposits created strange formations like nothing we've ever seen. The shapes weren't really describable but were similar to pillars, or could be called "minaret-like." The deposits were called "tuff" geologically, a substance that was easily carved. Centuries ago, people fled war and carved out homes in the tuff, literally living in caves. One underground city had seven levels, and everything they needed was

in the ground. Large balls or 18"-wide wheels were rolled in front of their doors to keep enemies out. It was a pretty incredible scene. We were even spat at on a back road by a mother—she and her daughter were in a donkey-pulled cart. I guess she thought we were going to take pictures of them, but our cameras weren't in sight. Oh, well.

Finally, we took back roads toward Istanbul. The country

Cappadocia cave houses.

we had seen was very diverse with days of olive orchards, days of apple trees, and giant piles of apples on the roadside being loaded into trucks with front-end loaders (on their way to being apple tea, no doubt). There were other days where we saw nothing but potatoes being bagged. There was also something like a sugar beet and trucks that had towering loads of cotton bales. Once we went inland, we saw wheat fields as far as the eye could see, sometimes in front of low mountain ranges in various shades of purple with the setting sun behind.

In Istanbul, the finale was a Turkish bath in the only female Turkish bath in the city. We didn't know what we were getting into! We paid $9 for a bath and massage, disrobing in front of God and everyone. Shivering, we were finally handed a filmy, multicolored length of cloth to wrap up in. Shuffling to the next room, we shrugged our shoulders at the Turkish ladies: now what? They motioned toward the wooden door. Cautiously, we moved through a small passageway to a 60-foot-diameter domed room containing a round (about 30-foot-diameter) marble, sitting-level platform in the middle, covered with about 30 naked bodies, none over 25 years of age. Fortunately, all were female, and I decided that they were Scandinavian. All of them

Pottery shop and wares.

The night Brad arrived, his first comment was, "I thought I was leaving air pollution behind in Kathmandu, but this is 10 times as bad!" And it was. I handed him a mask purchased at the last minute, and we wore them in every city. Arriving at one of Delhi's five-star hotels that night, the Imperial Palace, the hallway was even polluted! We couldn't see the other end!

Why did we go there in the first place? And no, we'd never been there before, as many had

Left: Local man resting.

Below: Two views of the Taj Mahal.

Photos by Brad Johnson.

Right and bottom right: Locals bathing and doing laundry in the Yamuna River, Agra.
Bottom right photo by Brad Johnson.

Below: Brad contemplating a purchase.

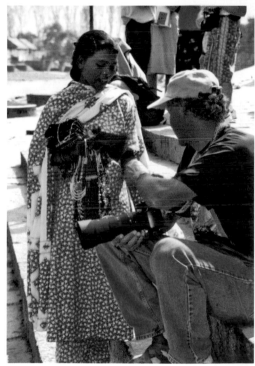

thought. For 10 or more years, I had wanted to go to the Pushkar Fair, which occurred every November during the full moon. That year it was taking place the middle of November.

But I'm getting ahead of our itinerary. From Delhi, we drove by

private car, with a driver, to Agra to see the Taj Mahal. Immediately, we were white-knuckled for the whole drive. Everyone was driving on the left side of the road and the traffic was suicidal. It was a game of endurance to see who would hold out the longest before giving way to the other guy by taking to the ditch. The roads were full of potholes and were so narrow that a car and a bus or lorry couldn't pass each other without someone having their tires in the ditch. Horns blared continually and there was nothing you could do except pray a lot. If you cautioned the driver, the response was a laugh. Their belief was such that what happens, happens: It was God's will.

Just as we arrived in Agra, our driver pulled into a repair shop. We were hoping to get to the Taj for evening light, and he said he would be only 15 minutes. One of the front brakes needed to be fixed, as it didn't work! OK—fix the brake! Fifty cents and almost an hour and a half later, we were on our way again. Muhan, our driver, dropped us at the west entrance where we shuffled in with the crowd. Elbow-to-elbow, we wondered if we would even get in before it became dark. Again, the sky was grey with pollution:

Top: Funeral barge preparing for departure.

Live statue.

Commuting via the river.

Below right: Something caught Brad's eye.

cars, trucks, buses, motorized rickshaws, and scooters—none had pollution controls and all belched fumes. After scoping the place out and deciding where we wanted to be in the morning, we had Muhan take us to our hotel.

It was not quite a hotel; it was a government guesthouse (hovel). Occasionally, the lights worked; there were no towels, TP, or soap. There was no window that could be opened or that would shed light into the room when the lights went out. I kept my head lamp handy. A non-functioning air conditioner in the only window had gaps around it. This allowed a tiny creature to come in during the night to chew on some food I had left on the table. The beds had only bottom sheets that had obviously been slept on before and were just straightened out for the next guest. The pillowcases were dirty. We had our sleeping bags, but Brad's was for 40 below, so I gave him my bottom sheet for something between him and the blanket. I had brought along two pillowcases that we used for the first, but not the last, time. My summer sleeping bag was OK. Brad's feet hung over the end of the bed. The bathroom shower was such that the entire bathroom got wet. Luckily, we stayed there only two nights.

Below: Peanut harvesting.
Photo by Brad Johnson.

Amber Fort in Jaipur.
Photos by Brad Johnson.

Next morning, a rented boat took us across the river behind the Taj. The early morning light created a magical scene. On our way there, we discovered a laundry on the edge of the river. The water was so thick that we wondered how on earth they could get anything clean. About six people, men and women, were up to their knees in the river. Each had a large stone slab for beating the clothes on. They wet the item, soaped it up, then beat it to death by flinging it over their heads onto the slab. Once clean (?), everything was laid out on the ground to dry. Several burros, loaded down with bags of laundry, came into the area. We were sure our sheets had been washed there.

As we watched this scene, another unfolded across the river. A man came down to the river, did his duty in it, then proceeded to wash his face and brush his teeth! That's India!

Emperor Shah Jahan completed the Taj for his wife in 1653, having employed 20,000 laborers over a 17-year period. He later built a smaller palace, known as the Agra Fort, on a bend in the Yamuna River. It was a perfect vantage point for viewing the Taj.

Aurangzeb, son of the emperor and self-proclaimed ruler, had a disagreement with his father, Shah Jahan, over religion. As a result, he put his father under house arrest in this smaller palace. The Shah spent the remainder of his life in a small room where he could see the Taj. Like many Indian monuments, the building was made of hand-carved marble which defies description.

Weavers and their products.

We tried to eat at American hotels so as not to get sick. At the Sheraton, we shared a table with a Belgian couple who were going to be turned away because all four restaurants were full. The gentleman said he had to be careful not to insult their guide, and when asked what they thought of India, they prudently replied, "India has a lot of potential."

Jaipur was our next destination. Again, the driving was frightening. We saw buses overturned carrying 60 people inside and on top; one ambulance was accorded. Many fields along the way were being harvested by groups of women in brightly colored saris, the typical Hindu woman's dress. The saffron, blue, orange, green, and red made for great photos. When we saw some close to the road, we stopped. Brad with his blonde hair and being so tall always made the ladies giggle in their shyness. We finally discovered they were digging peanuts, and they wanted me to try it. Squatting with a short-handled hoe-like instrument in hand, I gave it an honest try and came up with only one peanut, and not a very big one at that! The experience certainly made me appreciate peanuts much more.

When we arrived in Jaipur and found our driver leading us into what appeared to be the slums, my heart sank. Not another one of those dreadful government guesthouses! But much to our surprise and relief, we pulled into an alley and found ourselves at a beautiful *haveli* (house) owned by the Alsisar family (fifth generation). The owner greeted us and continued to be available to answer all questions. He had grown up in the house, now turned hotel, when there were four empty acres

The Pushkar Fair.

Photos by Brad Johnson.

surrounding it. In the '70s, the government demanded the return of three acres, and the city grew in around him. It was surrounded by filthy shops on a busy street, and nighttime found many homeless sleeping nearby. He recently completed a large two-story addition and was putting on a second story to the main part of the house. His mother lived with them. She had built a small temple at the front entrance, kind of like a small gazebo. Twice a day, morning and evening, she would go out, ring bells, and spend a short time praying. His ancestors all had just one son, but he had two who go to school in Ajmer near Pushkar. He had had an arranged marriage and, like everyone else, was married at home where his entire Army regiment plus friends and relatives gathered for the occasion. His ancestors were noblemen.

While in Jaipur, we visited the Amber (or Amer) Fort on the outskirts of town. Because of the constant warfare the ruling Rajputs indulged in, they heavily fortified their living quarters. The fort was built within the protective circle of the Aravalli hills with a wall running along the ridgeline, similar to that of the Great Wall of China. To visit the fort, most people had to ride an elephant to the top of the hill. Our experienced guide suggested we drive to the top, thereby missing the long wait to get on an elephant. After the tour, we rode an elephant down the hill. Again, this was another impressive structure built in marble by incredible craftsmen over the 15th, 16th, and 17th centuries.

Jaipur was the home of printed textiles. We were able to see some block prints being made and fabrics being dyed and hung to dry. Jaipur was also famous for blue pottery. "Pink City" was another name for Jaipur because, in 1876, the buildings were painted pink to welcome a dignitary and give the city a romantic, delicate appearance. Indeed, most of its buildings were deep pink.

We made our way west toward Ajmer, a relatively quiet town with some private schools just nine kilometers from Pushkar, our destination. During the full moon of November, this tiny village, normally with 12,000 population, came alive with thousands of decorated, bellowing camels in observance of the Camel Fair. One of India's most important and colorful festivals, the Camel Fair caused the small town's population to swell to 200,000. The streams of noisy camels descended upon the village from every direction, bringing with them camel traders and buyers, horsemen, snake charmers, thieves, performers, vendors, pilgrims, and tourists from around the world. The tourists were armed with cameras while the pilgrims came to bathe in the holy waters of Lake Pushkar and climb to the temples on the hilltop. It was an important pilgrimage center that devout Hindus visited at least once in their lifetime.

Because the village had few hotels, the Indian government erected a tent city to house several thousand visitors. It was a community unto itself with a giant dining hall (seating 2,000) and a government gift shop. Besides the tents, which seemed to stretch for miles across the desert, there were small "Baghdad" huts sporting such facilities as a temporary post office, a tent where you could make phone calls anywhere in the world, a fax machine, and a bank. The organization of the entire place was pretty upscale, considering what we saw elsewhere.

Loaded pack animals and locals carrying large wood panels crossing a rickety bridge.

Brad and our guide.

We never did see any buying or selling of camels, although I saw a man measuring one camel's girth. There were camel races, horse races, foot races, Ferris wheels, and booths selling bracelets, necklaces, and scarves. There were squatters making chapati, a flatbread consisting of flour, salt, and water rolled out very thin like a tortilla and fried in oil in a small wok-type pan. It all looked great, and I would've loved to have tried it, but after seeing what happens when they go to the (*ahem*) toilet, I shied away from street food.

Not knowing what to expect at a fair where as many as 50,000 camels were coming into town, I bought a pair of $14 tennis shoes that I could leave behind. I envisioned walking in camel and Brahma cow dung but, amazingly, there were women picking it up. I told Brad, "Look, the government has hired some women to pick up the droppings!" Well... dumb me, they were picking it up to dry and take home for fuel! It sounded terrible, but since the camels were staked out in the desert (sand), it was pretty clean. It would be kind of like picking up a sugared donut hole, ya know? So there they were, gathering all the donut holes and carrying them in large wok-shaped baskets on their heads to a place where they could lay them out in a single layer to dry in the sun. They did the same with the cow dung, which was like a six-inch pizza covered with sand.

Ten-year-old deaf boy who visited our camp. Look at those blue eyes!

The first night at the fair, we were in a "Standard" tent, which meant we had to walk to a communal bath tent for facilities. It wasn't bad, but not all the toilets flushed. The next two nights, we had a Deluxe or Swiss tent, which had the facilities at the back of the tent (and the toilet *did* flush).

On the day of the full moon, wagonloads of women—resplendent in their bright saris—streamed into the area. The wagons sometimes had as many as eight women and some children in them. I wondered why they came only that day, but that night was a big celebration (according to Brad, who couldn't sleep) with fireworks, loudspeaker announcements, and singing. I slept right through it.

Finally, we were on our way to Jaisalmer, our last adventure in this strange country. Jaisalmer lies on the eastern edge of the Sam Sand Dunes and Thar Desert,

which adjoins Pakistan on the west. Our hotel was on the outskirts of town, too far for us to walk anywhere. In the morning, we stood on a nearby hilltop that overlooked town. From that vantage point, we watched as many as six women, all carrying a bottle, walk to an empty field. Curious, we continued to watch as each squatted for their early morning elimination, whatever that might be. The sand and the water were for washing, no paper. Obviously, the women wore no panties, as they just squatted then flipped their long skirts aside.

Later, we were driven 40 kilometers to a tiny community (500) called "Khuri." What a surprise to see adobe walls similar to Santa Fe, New Mexico, surrounding an area with

Opposite page and right: Camel caravans traveling through desert, Western Rajasthan, India.
Photos by Brad Johnson.

two or three thatch-roofed rooms! The walls even had geometric designs like our American Indian designs painted on them. From there, we climbed onto camels covered with flies, and with an extra camel carrying the gear, our three camel drivers took us into the Thar Desert to spend a couple nights.

Nearby was a lake. As luck would have it—and as the sun was getting low in the sky—a stream of women in their colorful saris carrying jugs on their heads came from the village to get water. We heard an airplane but wondered where, in this desolate country, there would be a place to land. Then we saw it: an ultralight! As we approached the dune, it landed on a short strip of sand reasonably hard for a runway. Two men from Spain were on a filming mission for a Spanish TV travel program, and they had driven a large truck from Spain to make some travel films. The ultralight could be taken apart and put into the truck; they were living out of the truck.

Never having seen anything like this before, the tribal people came running from every direction. The next morning we saw the ultralight again, a speck in the sky. We couldn't understand what they would film from that height, then we saw one man jump out and paraglide. The tribal people were really amazed at that!

Our destination was a place on the dune where we could spend the night. Thick multicolored blankets were thrown down for us to sleep on. A tiny fire made with dead branches provided heat for cooking. With only two pots—one for a stew-type dish and one for frying chapati—they prepared dinner. They discovered that the flour had been left behind, so one of the camel drivers would get up at 3:30 and run back to the village for the flour. Chapati was part of every meal. By this time, neither Brad nor I could stomach Indian food, but...we had to eat.

Out of the darkness of night, a young boy of 10 appeared in the light of the campfire. Naturally, his hair was dead black, but this young boy had a shock of pure white hair right in the middle of his forehead and his eyes were sky blue! Never had we seen a more curious child. His eyes sparkled in the firelight. He was deaf, but he wasn't shy and made many gestures with his hands in hopes of communicating with us. Brad took some pictures using his flash. We asked him to come back in the morning for more picture taking. If I could have, I would have brought this child home with us.

In the village, we met another child—a girl—about the same age as the boy, and she was also deaf. Our camel drivers told us that it was unfortunate that they were not of the same caste, because if they were, they could marry. Could an exception be made in this case? No.

This camel safari and the Pushkar Fair were the cleanest places we had visited in

A deaf girl we met in a village.

India. There was no air pollution because there were few or no motorized vehicles. And because of the sand, things seemed to stay clean. There was a shortage of water, and the camel drivers didn't wash their hands. Therefore, that gave me some problems for a day or so. They claimed that sand was the cleanest thing around, but it certainly wasn't a sterilizing agent. Before leaving, when we were back in the village, we had some Indian tea called "chai." Brad said he wouldn't tell me how the dishes were being washed. "You'd better!" I replied. Well, the deaf child got 5 rupees for doing the dishes. She sat in the middle of the main street where everyone walked, camels included, and washed the dishes with sand! Oh, well. My father always told me if I had a dirty pan on a camping trip and didn't have a scouring pad, just use sand. It gets things really clean, but I don't know about the "bugs."

Back in Jaisalmer, we boarded a plane for Delhi. Thinking it would be non-stop, we were surprised at two stops they made. We did some heavy praying on three takeoffs and three landings. When we got to the second and last place, I said to Brad, "We only have 40 minutes to pray! If we make it back to Delhi in this 737 held together with bailing wire, I think we'll get home alive." I wasn't sure if we would be *well*, but we would be alive.

We made it to Delhi and caught our connecting flights. Brad flew to Thailand on Thai Airlines—a great airline—and I flew on United back to Denver. Never was I so glad to get on an American airline as I was then! And both of us continued to say we were so grateful to be back home. We were both well.

Hit from Behind

I did plenty of skiing during the winter and eagerly looked forward to 1998, because I would no longer need to buy a lift ticket in Colorado, or at least at most of the ski areas. The others would give me a hefty discount because I would reach the ripe old age of 70 in May. Surprised? No foolin'! It even surprised me.

In early March, Rhoda Nozik and I flew to San Francisco for the 90th birthday of Ann Hayes' mom. It was quite a fancy affair in the Ritz Carlton (we didn't stay there).

Toward the end of March, and very near the time that I quit skiing because I like the spring weather down in Boulder for hiking, some friends of mine who lived in Egypt came to Colorado and stayed in my Frisco townhouse to ski for a week. The very first day we were all together, we skied at Breckenridge, an area that's not on my ski area list. On the second run of the morning, I was hit from behind with no warning! According to witnesses, I flew into the air 10 feet (it was probably more like five). I came down on my right hip with tremendous force. The first thing out of my mouth was that I had broken my hip. However, I didn't just say, "I've broken my hip." First, there were a few nasty expletives I didn't even know I had in my vocabulary! Then I directed my attention 20 yards below me, with more expletives, to the young Texan who hit me. My friends were embarrassed by the language coming out of this old lady's mouth.

The result of being hit was that my pelvis was out of alignment. I was really sore and on crutches for about two weeks. A scheduled flight to Ireland the first part of April had to be canceled. However, with some quick wits on the part of myself and some friends, I found someone who could go in my place while I tried to figure out what my problem was and get off the crutches.

April 19, I was scheduled for a trip to Copper Canyon in northern Mexico. With that in mind, I was determined not to give up another trip, and I recovered enough to go with caution. Actually, we did several short hikes and my pelvis behaved itself. The most impressive thing about the Copper Canyon trip was the two privately owned hotels where we stayed. One was on top of the canyon, The Sierra Lodge; the other was in the town of Batopilas at the bottom of the canyon. We rode for 4½ hours in bucket seats mounted on top of a van down a twisting dirt road with spectacular views, having a picnic along the way in the shade of a huge tree.

What follows is the story of my trip to Copper Canyon.

Copper Canyon, Mexico

We flew Aeromexico to Chihuahua on a 20-passenger commuter. Once at our Holiday Inn Hotel, we checked out the place: indoor and outdoor pools and a hot tub along with exercise equipment. We took a walk after a snack.

We caught the 6:00 a.m. train the next morning for Posada Barrancas, our next overnight stop. We had just a short walk to our hotel, a quiet place on a hill with only four other guests. A 10-minute walk up another hill was the Hotel Mirador, sitting on the brink of a cliff overlooking the canyon far below. We took a walk along the rim overlooking the canyon then climbed a long ladder to the top of a huge rock, where we discovered dwellings under a couple of overhangs below the hotel.

Things were dried up this time of the year. Summer rains kept the tourists away until January or February when things were green. There were two large tours at the Hotel Mirador, which was where we were told to take all our meals because there were so few tourists. One Maupintour group of 22 had not come yet, and the rest of the tables were reserved for them. We decided to sit at the end of one of their tables, which was next to the window overlooking the canyon. After we were served our soup and had eaten it, the tour group came and was surprised to see us at "their" table. We told them the waiter had told us to sit there. Then one of their tour leaders came over and asked if we were with a tour. We repeated that one of the waiters had told us to sit there. Then a female tour leader came and asked us what tour we were with. We said we were on our own. She said the table was reserved for the Maupintour group and we'd have to leave. I said, "Are you prepared to physically remove us? We're staying here!" This didn't go over very well with the rest of the group and we listened to all kinds of grumblings—how unfair it was they couldn't all be together, the waiter needed to be reprimanded, etc. (*Ahhh*...togetherness!) Because we refused to move, the female tour leader made the comment, "*We* have more class than *that*!"

As we finished the rest of our meal and were getting ready to leave, my friend Lorraine walked over to the female tour leader and said, "If you had *any* class, you wouldn't have even mentioned it." So we both left laughing as we went down the path to our hotel across the tracks.

The Hotel Mirador seemed to be the only, or perhaps one of the few, hotels where all of the rooms had a view of the canyon. It was cantilevered over the edge of the rim. Several short walks could be taken from there, two on either side along the rim and one down into the canyon to some Tarahumara Indian dwellings. All were just a short 10-minute walk, in any case.

1990　1991　1992　1993　1994　1995　1996　1997　**1998**　1999

In the morning, the train was late by more than an hour, so we missed lunch at our next stop and just ate snacks. At Creel, we wondered who was going to meet us, but the lodge people were there. They used a Suburban with two seats on the roof for transportation.

We drove out of town about 30 minutes to a dry valley and toward the village of Cusárare, arriving at an old motel that had been turned into Copper Canyon Sierra Lodge. It had been purchased by an American, Skip McWilliams, who was from Michigan. He had made it into a lovely ranch-type lodge. There were no phones or electricity; all the rooms had oil lamps, including the bathrooms. There were propane refrigerators in the kitchen areas, which were spotless. The lodge was nestled among the trees and surrounding cliffs with a small lake in the lower valley. Several log houses dotted the edges of the valley where the local Tarahumaras lived. One such house had a family with 12 children. Our bathroom in the lodge had black-and-white tiles and big showers. The towels were so large and heavy that one could hardly lift them to dry off! Pink flower blossoms and green leaves were placed on the washcloths and bedspreads, which matched the curtains. Every detail was taken care of, including battery-operated reading lights that fastened to your book. Mexican Indian-designed wool rugs covered the Mediterranean tiled floors. The gorgeous wall murals in many of the rooms were done by artists from Creel or Chihuahua. Century plants lined the edge of the long porch outside each room. Chickens crowed in the distance. Piglets nursed in the

backyard. Children played in the stream. The porch railing was made of rough-hewn logs and log furniture invited resting and reading a book or enjoying the view. Guides were available for horse rides, hikes, or trips to town or to the nearby horseshoe-shaped Lake of Arareko, where you could rent boats or fish. Alcoholic drinks or soft drinks were "on the house." Fresh, pure water was on the table in your room. A pot-bellied stove warmed you on cold mornings. Coffee, tea, or hot chocolate was brought to you before you even got out of bed and, if you wanted, the fire was lit. Fresh fruit was always available—pineapples, bananas, oranges, apples, avocados. Margarita time was before the 7:30 dinner hour; breakfast was early. If you were on the trail at lunchtime, it was cooked before your eyes: fajitas and fresh tortillas with beer, pop, and fruit.

Our first day trip was to the Continental Divide for a short hike and then to Creel to shop or sightsee. Our guide, Ray, was from Arkansas. He knew the owner, Skip, and periodically helped out when the regulars were off. Our Mexican guide was Rene, who was from Chihuahua, 26, and just married. He loved singing but said his friends told him he couldn't sing! Just talking made him think of something, and he started singing.

Every night, there was a large bonfire nearby where people gathered for tall tales and to see the stars. We saw satellites both nights we sat around the fire. The second night, we saw at least five, one going south and the others west. Another guest was Cooper Young from Texas. He grew hydroponic Bibb lettuce; his wife didn't like this kind of trip.

Our new guide, Marcos, drove us to Batopilas at the bottom of Copper Canyon for our next trip. It took 4½ hours! We ate fajitas on the road, but they forgot the tortillas! They used a wok to cook the beef, onions, and red and green peppers. We drank beer and ate fajitas, avocados, and apples. Many cactus of various kinds were blooming, with others along the way just about to.

Batopilas stretched along the river several miles with two or three hanging (suspension) bridges for crossing to the shady side. There was a town square, police station, school, church, a couple other hotels, and many small businesses. The Riverside Hotel, dating over 100 years, was fully restored with stencil paintings everywhere. Each room had a name—Mary, Gloria, Ana, Noel, Elena. Ours, Mary, was on the back wall of the building, so just on the other side of the wall was a street and we could hear people talking and walking. The front-side rooms faced the main traffic street. Outside our room, in the center of the patio, was a light-blue, round tower with a deep-blue dome. One of the other rooms down a stairs around the tower also had a deep-blue tiled dome. Flowers were growing everywhere: bougainvillea, gardenia, palm trees, and roses large and small. Wrought-iron chairs and benches were scattered throughout the walkways. They were painted in colors to match the designs, i.e., roses. A covered sitting room was furnished with a table and wicker furniture with cushions. Each room was different in shape, and the bridal suite had steps leading down into it. The iron bedsteads were painted colonial-white with marble-covered settees and paintings of nude women in large frames on the walls. The ceiling in the sitting room (red) told a story in pictures. Some rooms had inlaid tile floors. The hotel had an open kitchen, and you were welcome in anytime. The staff was made up of 17 young people. The manager while we were there was Oscar Ortega, who had studied voice for 10 years in Spain. He made his home in New York. On September 28 he would sing at Carnegie Hall, then in Washington, D.C. We told him we would go to hear him.

In an hour and 34 minutes, we walked to the Lost Mission of Satevo to hear Oscar sing six songs: "Ave Maria" and "Amazing Grace" were two that I recognized. They were simply beautiful. The church was being renovated...slowly. Oscar had driven down so we didn't have to walk back up. We sat in the back of the pickup truck on old auto seats. Before heading back to town, we were driven up the road toward San Ignacio just to see the view.

Meals at the hotel were served on a damask, pure white tablecloth with pink-rose China and elegant silver. The main red living room had an unbelievable crystal chandelier which was electrified, and they turned it on in the evening while we had margaritas. Because there wasn't constant electricity, there were oil lamps everywhere.

There were old pictures on the walls taken a hundred years ago. One large framed piece had a collection of keys in it with a description of them, which said the building used to have buried treasure in it, and because there was so much silver hidden or stored there all the doors were double locked. Three hidden treasures were removed by the former owners.

One day, we walked to a high mountain home of four families. The trail was very rocky and uneven—not easy walking. We got there in a little over two hours. If we had taken fewer rests, it would've been less time. Dave Del Villa came with us (67) and Lido was our guide. We passed a garden with beans and corn, then an old mine with a large cement tank which had been for water but was dry. A long, long hose snaked from some water source above and provided enough pressure for a "Rain Bird" sprinkler to operate. In this dry, hot desert canyon, it was incredible to come into a green oasis-like area scattered around the hillsides. Acacia trees in all their glorious green cover dotted the hills; there were organ pipe cactus and other kinds, some in bloom (yellow), and hibiscus.

Chickens came and went from the house. A tiny boy caught one chicken and carried it to his mother by the legs, upside down. We thought she was going to kill it, but it was a sick chicken, so she tied one leg to a fence and put out crumbled tortillas. The sick chicken kept getting pecked to death.

Grandmom was over 100 and was gumming lunch when we arrived. Finally, she finished and moved out into the sun. She appeared to not see well and we thought she couldn't talk until Lido went over to her. Then she talked up a storm.

The yard was bare dirt as was the living room, with white plastic chairs around the perimeter. We moved them out into the yard in the shade of the largest grape arbor I've ever seen. It must've covered a 30X30 area, and it provided cool shade. They had a shower behind a rock where a hose from somewhere above brought water down when needed. Many kinds of flowers were growing and fenced so the animals wouldn't destroy them.

On the way down, we passed some caballeros with burros on their way up and, of course, we had to stop and chat a bit. Lido showed us where a huge rock had come down in 1995 and killed an entire family of seven.

1990   1991   1992   1993   1994   1995   1996   1997   **1998**   1999

By the time we got back to the hotel, around 1:30, I was in need of some Aleve. Everyone else was still eating lunch, and they were surprised we had gotten back so soon.

In the mid-to-late afternoon, we walked to the suspension bridge on the upstream end of town, crossed it, and walked to the ruins of Alexander Robey Shepherd's home across the river. It had been a huge mansion in its day where they raised seven children. Shepherd, the last governor of Washington, D.C., had come to Batopilas to start anew after having lost a fortune in real estate. They came in the late 1800s and when he died in the early 1900s, he was worth about $6 million.

The ceiling of the Riverside Hotel in Batopilas told the story of the Shepherd's move to the valley, showing a piano being hauled down the steep mountain road. The living room had a wide stencil band on the lower part, elaborate sideboard, fancy lamps, old radio and piano, and huge nude photos. The entire place was very open—no locks on the doors. They used horseshoes to keep them latched. The smell of gardenias filled the living room and hallways.

The last full day we were there, we went in a pickup truck for three hours up a twisting, dusty narrow road to have a picnic. The views were spectacular until smoke filled the valleys and caused a series of purple ridges. The picnic was brought up in another truck. By the time it arrived, we were all famished. They built a charcoal fire, so I saw several hours passing before we would eat. It was about 1:30. While the fire began to get hot, they peeled 12 avocados, sliced six tomatoes, and diced them all; cut and diced three medium chilies; diced one onion; squeezed several limes onto the mixture, and we had guacamole—a whole dishpan full!

Seventeen onions were peeled and placed in aluminum foil. They gave them a dash of seasoned salt, regular salt, and Worcestershire sauce, plus a sauce used on steak. The foil was closed up and put on the coals. Four chickens appeared. The breasts were split and the wings twisted so the whole thing could be flattened to cook quicker. They were salted and dipped in a tomato sauce, then plunked on the grill after the tortillas were cooked...enough for 17 people! We thought that was the end when out came not one, but two fillets about two feet long. The chef, Antonio, sliced each lengthwise, but not all the way through, and laid it out so it, too, would cook quickly. He waited to put them on until the chickens were almost done, which he tested by sticking a knife into the fatter part of the chicken and squeezing it. If it was red it wasn't done; if it was clear juice, it was done. We couldn't believe the feast!!!

Lorraine and I got lost on a short hike while we waited for the cook truck to come. As I saw it coming, they saw us and helped Lorraine get down the slippery hillside which was covered with large brown leaves and pine needles. It made it almost impossible to walk. They gave us a ride around the corner and up the hill a short distance.

After we ate, they cleaned everything up and poured water on the fire. Antonio went with them and they were off to the next town. We returned to the hotel to clean up and eat again around 7:30, just soup and salad. We were gone the day a funeral was held for a 16-year-old girl who took her life by drinking pesticide. She had been dating a boy her mother didn't like, and the mother told the girl she couldn't see him anymore about two weeks ago. The entire town showed up at the church, right about when we were trying to get back to the hotel on the one-way street. We were showering when they finished the service and carried the casket down the street to the cemetery.

Our last day was spent driving back to the lodge on the rim. When we arrived, lunch was waiting for us: a delicious soup—tomato base—carrots, zucchini, onions, spaghetti, individual veggie tortillas, and mixed veggies.

We walked 35 minutes to the mission, bought two baskets, were unable to get into the school, but we got a lady to unlock the church, which was really beautiful. The trail followed the stream, where we saw women doing wash late in the day, which seemed odd to me. Then we hiked to the falls another 35 minutes and sat with Juanita and Maria for a short time, then decided to head back so we didn't miss margarita time.

We sat around the fire again that evening, but we only saw one satellite. The final day there, we arrived back at Chihuahua for the 1:00 p.m. flight to El Paso, then on to home.

70TH BIRTHDAY, GRAND GULCH TRIP

In early May, some of my friends and Brad sprung a huge birthday party for me. I laughed so hard at some of the skits, songs, and poems people wrote that tears streamed down my cheeks. I was planning to have foot surgery mid-summer, and my young friend, Cari Minor, wrote and sang a song called, "Sensible Shoes." It was all great fun.

On May 9, I left with four friends for a week in Grand Gulch. (Remember?

My 70th birthday party.
Photos by Brad Johnson.

The Wetherill–Grand Gulch Research Project?) That was a real test to see how my map reading skills were, because every other time I had been in Grand Gulch, someone else was leading and I was just a follower. I surprised myself by remembering where the cliff dwellings were. The story of this trip follows.

Grand Gulch with the Ladies

It was early May in Boulder. After everyone gathered, we broke into two driving groups. We'd decided to drive two hours and then switch cars, and the first switch was at Brad's in Vail to pick up some film. Then it was on to Grand Junction and lunch at Wendy's; at Moab we made the last switch then drove on to reach Blanding by five. We had two rooms, one for three and one for two, so Marge and I shared. Dinner was at the Old Timers Restaurant where we discovered that Fred Blackburn was giving a show at the Edge of the Cedars Museum. So we went there and caught the last 20 minutes. Winston and Kathy Hurst were there, along with Victoria Blackburn and both kids. They were all surprised to see us, of course.

We needed a weather report, so we stopped at Winston's. Then Marge needed help with her pack, so were up until after eleven deciding what she should take and what to leave behind to lighten her load. Fred called her, saying she had left all her important pills at home; she decided to take a vacation from all her pills.

We arrived at the trailhead about 11:30. As we went into Bullet Canyon, I was able to spot dwellings and a tower ruin on the rim. There were so many pictographs and petroglyphs. Above one, we found a spot in the shade for lunch, then pressed on to Perfect Kiva, dropped our packs, and hiked up. French's name was barely discernable. In the kiva, "CHG" could still be seen on the back wall.

Here we are at the trailhead. From left to right: Marge Quist, Maddie Goldhawk, Rosie Hauge, Elaine Hill.

1990   1991   1992   1993   1994   1995   1996   1997   **1998**   1999

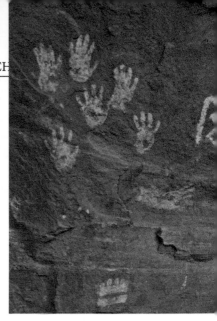

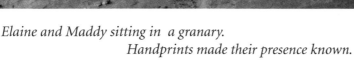

Elaine and Maddy sitting in a granary.
Handprints made their presence known.

It seemed that more and more signatures had disappeared. Wetherill's name on the rock with all the metates was completely gone, and all the metates had recently been scoured clean and smooth, revealing fresh sandstone. We took pictures.

Inside the kiva, at least two beams were cracked from the weight of people walking on them, or more likely it was Utah kids jumping on them.

Shortly after we packed up, around the corner, Jailhouse came into view. On the tree-shaded bench across from it, we came upon a very nice young fellow resting. He was Jan Kliewer from N.W. College in Powell, Montana. We had a long conversation with him about the Wetherill–Grand Gulch Research Project. He was delighted to have run into us and then proceeded to say he'd move on, because that spot was good for a large party. There was a good spring just over the hill, just as Dale Davidson had said.

It was my turn for dinner, which took forever, it seemed, and it was dark before we finished. In the morning, Jan came back and overheard Maddy Goldhawk complaining about her pad going flat. He gave her his to use, and to return to him by mail.

We pushed on to the junction, then decided to pitch tents and go without packs that afternoon at about 3:30 to see if we could find Green House. At 5:15 we found the drainage, but it was not the right one; a small dwelling appeared under the Kissing Rocks and Maddy hiked up there. She discovered campers on the other side who said Green House was in the next drainage, but it was too late to continue. So we figured it would be an hour and 20 minutes from the junction with no pack and no stopping. When Kissing Rock appeared, it was around the next corner.

Back at camp, Marge's dinner was couscous and dehydrated veggies. Really good and lots of it.

Above camp were two storage rooms, a good landmark to see when coming from downstream. After breakfast, we decided to try for Green House again, since we knew where it was. One hour from camp to Kissing Rock, then through the camp spot under a dwelling and one lone tree. The drainage was full of brush all the way down into the main gulch, making it hard going. My legs and arms got all scratched up. Once into the canyon, if you kept a sharp eye, you could see it. I remembered having to go beyond it, where a pile of rocks leaning against the cliff allowed me to climb a wide space and make my way up into the ruin. It was exposed, and Rosie Haugie had difficulty with it, but we helped her get up. Then we discovered that the area just before the doorway was even more exposed. She waited for us to go into the area where the Green House was, then we helped her. The Green design was still well preserved, amazingly, probably because not many folks can get up into it. Forty minutes later, we started back. It took about 20 minutes to make our way into the canyon and another 20 to go out. On the way in, I guess I stepped over a snake, which Elaine was petrified over. I never saw it.

We got back to camp around 12:30 for lunch. While packing up, four men came down from Bullet. We said the place was perfect for camping—shade and water. We actually didn't get on our way until 2:30. As we went up Kane, there were several ruins. The first one had a moon and lots of art—a large man and woman on the left. One had a strange headpiece, and there were green handprints and a geometric design. The way up was difficult, and after I gave up and said Brad or Vaughn would waltz up it, Elaine decided to go for it and made it. Coming down was more difficult, but she did it.

At right about the time I figured we'd be at Green Mask, there we were. However, on the way we had to hike a deep sandy drainage lined with debris and go through some deep eroded areas until we got where we saw the landmark, the campsite, then the overhang, and finally the archaic art—Green Mask and the princess with nipples. Maybe the Prince had a penis with a ball on the end?

Someone was already at the campsite, so we decided to look for another place. At the mouth of the canyon, five feet back downstream, was a sandy spot with water. We decided to camp there when four men appeared, saying six more groups came through the Bullet campsite, and they saw so much toilet paper that they decided to move on. They were of a mind that under the present circumstances, the couple at Green Mask was going to have to share, since water was at a premium.

Our site became so windy that sand filled Rosie's new tent because of all the netting. We finally broke branches off the tamarisks and put them along the lowered sides of the fly, then leaned our packs up against them to keep sand out. We must have given our sleeping bags three shakes before we thought we had the problem solved. Everything was covered with sand, inside and out: clothes, eyes, hair, supper, dinner, drinks, our mouths, eyes. Rosie got the idea to put more branches around as more of a barrier and hope for the best. What a windy, sandy night.

Somehow, we got an early start. It was May 13, and our destinations were Lion Tracks and Split Level. Of course, we saw lots of rock art and dwellings along the way, so it seemed to take a long time. At 11:30, my feet were killing me. We stopped by some water to soak sore feet and have lunch.

By 1:00, we suddenly found ourselves at Split Level and camp! Hooray! We set up the tents, picked a site for cooking, then went exploring to find Lion Tracks. On the way back we met Ken Sleight, who was brewing coffee for six people who were still on the way in. When we were on our way to Split Level, we met five guys with horses who offered us their beer, wine, and coke. They were cooking with wood they'd chopped. Ken Sleight said that they needed to so some things differently, and he had brought in

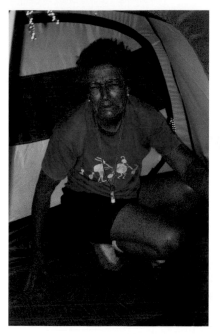

One of the many ruins we saw on this trip.

Sand everywhere! I was not happy.

a fire pan and his own wood. The five guys were boozers and said they were going 26 miles that day, from Kane to Jailhouse and back to Split Level.

When the horse fellows returned, the canyon was filled with raucous laughter, chopping wood, and the horses baying. The chopping went on for two hours, and after dark it started again. Ken went over to see the wood fire for himself and talk to them. The next day, he said they'd been coming here for seven years and didn't know of any fire restrictions. Poor Sleight carried in wood logs and his guests had to stand around in the evening to keep warm! The noise continued for hours, and just as I was about to drop off, the wood cutting started again. They had no respect or consideration for anyone else, and there were three parties camped there.

The next morning, we packed up early. It had rained off and on all night and things were cold and damp. We stopped at Ken's again and he said the horse guys were going to be camping there two to three days, so hopefully we could get in touch with Dale Davidson in Monticello about them. One of Ken's guests suggested we let the air out of their tires! And we might. They were from Salt Lake...unfortunately typical.

Now we were on our way to Todie, where the big panel was up high. I knew as soon as we hit the barn and saw the junction that this was where Bruce and I took photos. Rosie and Marge couldn't get up the slick rock, but after lunch around 11:30, I took Rosie up a different and easier access on the left in the main valley. Elaine and Maddy went further up Todie, where they saw more granaries.

We continued on about 1:15, and by 3:30 we arrived at Turkey Pen. Too much had changed in eight years. Every dwelling and all the rock art was different. The heavy growth of trees, sage, grass, and tamarisk made it almost impossible to see some of the sites we had been able to see years ago.

At Turkey Pen, the square kiva was now a great reconstruction project. The horse situation and toilet paper problem had to change. Ken had said he would carry an ammo can and toilet seat, like what was required now on river trips. As for the horses, we agreed that ALL horses needed to have a permit and had to get a key to the gate.

SUMMER TO WINTER

I spent the July 4 weekend in San Jose, California, with my Hungarian student/friend Gábor, who was living and working in the computer business there. We drove to Monterey instead of staying in San Francisco, therefore missing the greatest fireworks show of the year. In Monterey, it was trying to rain and the clouds were so low that the fireworks disappeared up into them, creating some very colorful clouds. We sought out a coffee shop and played Scrabble.

July 17 saw me having surgery to correct a bunion and hammer toe. (You see, I'm OLD!) I was on crutches for four weeks, the most difficult thing I've ever had to do in my entire life. I had gathered up all my area rugs, borrowed a wheelchair from the senior center (since I was a senior now), and figured out ways of doing all sorts of things like change the bedding, manage stairs, drive, and grocery shop in one of those motorized shopping carts. Can you just imagine me in one of those carts, roaring around the grocery store, dodging people and stacks of cans? People were running for their lives!

By August, I was getting around on crutches pretty well, so we took in the ballet at Vail. With my crutches, we were given far better seats than we had ever had on the lawn, so I'll have to remember to take my crutches with me in future.

My recovery from surgery seemed very slow, so I saw every kind of therapist I could to try to get my foot and body feeling better. The surgeon apparently had on blinders that allowed him to see only a 3X5-inch area, which was where the surgery was. What happened as a result of that was not part of his fee. While I was on crutches, not much happened; my shoulders needed to be replaced but, overall, that was minor compared to what followed. When I could finally start to put weight on my foot, my pelvis objected. Well, yours would, too, if you had a normal-soled shoe on one foot and a four-inch-high, slanted foam-soled boot on the other! As I went about my up-and-down routine, my pelvis and my back talked to me. When I called the surgeon about this, his reply was, "That IS a problem." I was speechless. *Me*...can you imagine that? I wanted to say, "Well, of course it's a problem. What do you suggest I do?" I mean, *really*!

> *Can you just imagine me in one of those carts, roaring around the grocery store, dodging people and stacks of cans? People were running for their lives!*

However, that was my clue: I would have to take my recovery into my own hands. So I kept the chiropractor, the acupuncturist, the massage therapist, the second-opinion orthopedic surgeon, and the rec center in business for weeks.

In late September, Lorraine and I flew to New York where we stayed with my old friend from the Wetherill Project, Linda Asher. We wanted to make the trip especially to see the Mexican tenor, Oscar Ortega, in the Carnegie Weill Recital Hall. Oscar managed the Batopilas hotel in the bottom of Copper Canyon when we were there. We had been told to be sure to have him sing for us in the Lost Mission, about four miles from the hotel along the riverbank. He did just that, which so inspired us that we told him we would fly to New York just to hear him. Both events were spectacular. Afterward, we saw him at a reception where he expressed his surprise at our coming just to hear him. If you ever see his name at a venue where he's singing, don't miss it. I was glad it was at night so people didn't notice my black clodhopper "sensible" tennis shoes!

Sometime, perhaps in October, I had an e-mail from Veronique Bugnion, the young MIT student who had spent a summer here at my house in Boulder while she studied the effects of the Colorado sun. She asked if I would care to spend the Christmas holidays with her and her family (I had met her mom and dad, but not her brother, in Geneva, Switzerland). Well, I could hardly say no, but I didn't know if I would be able to ski. Actually, I'd been trying to get my foot into my ski boot for several weeks when the invitation came. I decided to go, even if I couldn't ski. It would be fun, and I'd heard that Verbier was an absolutely spectacular place.

In late October, I went over to Cortez, Colorado, and on to Bluff and Blanding, Utah, where Fred Blackburn had brought about 14 of the Wetherill heirs together for a symposium directed at getting them to gift the artifacts and historical documents to a museum. That week was such an inspiration and so heartwarming that I'd gotten myself involved again. This time I was going to try raising enough money to pay the salary of a curator at the Anasazi Heritage Center in Dolores, Colorado. It would take $30,000 annually for them to accept the Wetherill collection and pay another curator to look after it.

Ski season arrived but it forgot to snow. I now could get my foot into my ski boot and I needed to see if my foot remembered how to ski. Lorraine and I drove six hours to Wolf Creek Pass, where they had 77 inches of base and had just had 22 inches of new powder. The areas within a couple hours of Boulder had only six inches of base. My foot remembered what to do, so I was set to ski at Verbier.

VERBIER, SWITZERLAND

I left December 17 and returned December 29. The trip over couldn't have been worse: I counted 15 croupy children around me. When Brad and I went to India in '97, I had taken nose and mouth masks you buy at the pharmacy. I had put one in at the last minute and wore that mask the entire way except while I was eating. And I didn't get sick.

The Bugnion's chalet was a 1½-hour drive from Geneva. It wasn't possible to actually drive to the chalet, but there was a beer pub about a hundred steps from it where we could park long enough to unload and carry everything up the stairs. With four bedrooms upstairs and bunks in a basement rec room, the place slept 10. What used to be a storage room across the yard among some pines was now an extra room which slept two. Off and on, there were anywhere from five to 12 of us. We took turns

Veronique's father, JR, and me.

Above: Veronique's parents, Jackie and JR.

Left: Veronique.

cooking, which was a real challenge for me because grocery shopping in Switzerland was nothing like shopping at King Soopers or Safeway. We played some board games—I tried my hand at bridge—and we put up and decorated a small tree with real candles. The snow up high was good, so we skied almost every day. And I have never eaten so much cheese in all my life! (Even being from Wisconsin.)

What a place the area was: miles and miles of every kind of terrain. Had there been enough snow, we could have skied to three different villages. Transportation was everything from T-bars, two-person chairs, and four-person chairs to *teleferiques* for either four, 35, or even a 150!! You have to have a lot of faith in the cables.

Interestingly, there were few employees. Once you purchased a ticket (mine cost only $20/day), you put it in your pocket and might get spot-checked. There was a chip in the card, and as you went through the stylus, it checked for the chip and they knew whether or not you had a ticket. Those Swiss folks were *very* clever.

The last day and practically the last hour I was there, I took a *parapente* (parasail) ride on skis. As I stood at the top of a steep drop, getting ready to ski down, I told my pilot I hoped I wouldn't fall before we took off. He assured me that if I pointed my skis straight down and held onto the strap he handed me, all would be well. It took only about 30 feet before we were airborne. I instructed him to fly over my friends' chalet, as they would be watching for me. I whistled and cried out and waved, as did they. Then I had a chance to steer the wing, and after about 25 minutes, we were spiraling down at a tremendous ear-popping G-rate to land gently on a partially snow-covered field near the lower *teleferique*, which I took back up the mountain to the chalet. As I thanked my pilot and said good-bye, he told me to wait, he had something for me. Out of the depths of his pack came a tee-shirt, which had two people with skis *parapenting*, and it says, "I DID IT!" Verbier.

And so ended 1998. I wondered what was in store for me in 1999.

The pilot and me.

Here we are, taking off.

Flying over the valley.

Mission accomplished!

Miss You Poem

Just a little line to say I'm living
That I'm not among the dead
Though I'm getting more forgetful
And more mixed up in the head.

For sometimes I can't remember
When I stand at the foot of the stair
If I must go up for something
Or I've just come down from there.

And before the refrigerator so often
My poor mind is filled with doubt
Have I just put food away — or
Have I come to take it out?

And there's times when it is dark out
With my night cap on my head
I don't know if I'm retiring
Or just getting out of bed.

So, if it's my turn to write you
There's no need in getting sore
I may think that I have written
And don't want to be a bore.

So remember, I do love you,
And I wish that you were here —
But now it's nearly mail time
So I must say Good-bye, dear

There I stood beside the mail box
With a face so very red
Instead of mailing you my letter
I had opened it instead.

— Author unknown

THE YEAR IN REVIEW

It had been almost a year since I had my eyes lasiked. It was marvelous to see the clock, the outside of my window, and the night sky, and to travel without worry of an eye infection using contact lenses.

In February, I traveled to Salt Lake City with family and friends. Late March found me in New York to attend the 95th Explorers Club annual dinner and meeting, held in the Waldorf Astoria Hotel. My directorship of the Wetherill–Grand Gulch Research Project between 1986 and 1990 seemed to have been significant enough for me to become a member of this illustrious international professional society. Whew! That was a mouthful! The Explorers Club was founded in 1904 by five of the world's leading explorers. The organization was dedicated to the advancement of field research and scientific exploration, and to the belief that it was vital to preserve the instinct to explore. The list of members was impressive: Richard Byrd, Charles Lindbergh, Chuck Yeager, Jacques Piccard, John Glenn, Buzz Aldrin, Sir Edmund P. Hillary, Barry

From left: Hugh Downs, me, Jim Fowler, Brad.

Brad and me at the 95th Explorers Club annual dinner.

Bishop, Tenzing Norgay, Theodore Roosevelt, Lowell Thomas, Jane Goodall, and Jim Fowler of *Mutual of Omaha's Wild Kingdom*. There were 30 chapters worldwide. Can you believe someone you know is a member? That's me!

I decided to take Brad with me, IF he would go. He would have to wear a tuxedo—his first. As we were getting him suited up at the rental place, I said I didn't have a daughter, but I sure was having a ball outfitting my son. And he was handsome! We rubbed elbows and shook hands with some VIPs, including John Glenn, Hugh Downs, and Jim Fowler. Jim and his animal friends on *Mutual of Omaha's Wild Kingdom* captivated us. At the meeting, dogs pulled Norman Vaughan in a dogsled across the stage. He was the last surviving member of Admiral Richard E. Byrd's 1928 Antarctic expedition. F. Story Musgrave kept us mesmerized with his photographs taken from the first Skylab mission. Besides working in the space program, Musgrave held degrees in physiology, biophysics, and literature, just to name a few. The highlight of the evening was the introduction of Brian Jones and Bertrand Piccard who, just days before, had completed their balloon world circuit. They received a standing ovation.

The end of May I visited Ireland, where my friend Lorraine drove us in a rented car around the southern part of the country. My left hand was still recovering from the white-knuckled "clutched" position, and I was sure the rental car agency had to replace both left tires after we returned the car. The highlight for me was visiting the Waterford Crystal factory. I ended my journey by going to England to see friends who were about to embark on a barge trip down the Severn and back via the Avon. Two of the women were senior citizens and not sure they really wanted to do this, i.e., maneuver the barge themselves. They had been given instructions which they were trying to memorize when I met them. One blast on the whistle meant "we're coming straight through," two blasts meant "we're turning left," and three blasts were "we're turning right." The fourth blast meant "we're coming around the corner"! I found out later that one of the ladies had fallen overboard, and people had been killed doing the same thing when they didn't get far enough through the lock before the water changed levels. The rear of the barge caught on the lock, allowing the front to lower and thus spilling everyone and everything overboard!! I was glad I wasn't with them.

I also surprised some very longtime friends who lived in Droitwich by calling and having lunch with them after not seeing them for about eight years.

From mid-June until mid-October, I directed the completion of an attic space into an office in the house Brad had recently purchased. It was situated on an escarpment on the north side of the east-west running San Juan Mountain range in southwestern Colorado. On six acres, it was quite isolated, 10 minutes from the tiny mountain town of Ridgway (no "e" because it was named after a man with that name). I helped in many ways, being on the sawdust receiving end of a plainer making the staircase uprights, filling nail holes, sanding, staining, and finishing. It was a small two-month job which took until the first week of October, probably because I kept feeding the workers cookies.

Two dear Swiss friends visited me there in early October. We did a whirlwind trip through the southeastern corner of Utah and the southwestern corner of Colorado—Hovenweep, Bridges National Park, Monument Valley, Goosenecks of the San Juan River, and Aztec Kiva. Then I quickly moved a couple carloads of household items back to Boulder, packed my bags, and headed for Nepal.

After having been in Peru for a couple months, Brad left Colorado in September for Nepal. He and a friend intended to climb two 8,000-meter peaks in the Himalayas, Cho Oyu and Shishapangma. Despite terrible avalanche conditions, he reached the summit of Cho Oyu, but while there, a world-renowned climber and friend, Alex Lowe, was swept away by a sudden unexpected avalanche on Shishapangma and killed. Needless to say, they did not continue with their plans.

Brad and me at the Statue of Liberty.

Nepal with Brad and Annette

Now for the real adventure of the year. In all my travels to a total of 64 countries, I had never been sick and never had as bad a trip as these two (Nepal and India) turned out to be. Brad's present companion, Annette, and I met Brad in Kathmandu, Nepal, mid-October. Besides acting as a carpenter in Ridgway, I had been exercising daily, so I felt I was in great shape and actually had lost 12 pounds I didn't have to carry up the mountain trail. My objective was a place called "Kala Patthar" at 18,000 feet, from which vantage point you can see Everest and the surrounding peaks. Brad had wanted to get up there, for no reason other than to enjoy the spectacular vista.

Long before agreeing to this trip, I had concerns: Could I do such a strenuous trip? After all, I wasn't as young as I used to be, and bodies change with age (as we all know). Were we going to have a hyperbaric chamber along? I was assured by friends who had done the trip years before that I wouldn't have any problem. There was only one day where the trail was very steep! Ha, ha, ha! Not only was the trail full of dung goo, it was also very rocky, to the point of having to judge carefully where each foot would be planted. And steep? That was putting it mildly!

Mt. Everest.

Right off the bat, after landing uphill headed for a sheer cliff we undoubtedly would run into, the trail lost 2,000 feet from 9,000 feet. Then we crossed a raging river on a swinging, suspended bridge with frayed cables, the rotted planking filled with gaping holes (one false step would land you facedown in a newly dropped dung pile). But as my friends and dear son, Brad, had assured me, I could do it: no problem.

The monsoon was still raging in Nepal, so the higher mountains had two-plus meters of snow (unusual for this time of year); at the lower elevations it was still raining. People below were counting on the monsoon ending and people above were eager to get out of the snow. Everyone met in the middle at a gathering place called "Namche Bazaar" (11,300 feet). We arrived there after hiking in the rain for three days. There were elbow-to-elbow people, and I'm not exaggerating—there was no room in the inn. We, fortunately, had a friend who lived there who let us sleep on the floor of his religious room—altar, candles, and all. Besides that, everyone seemed to be sick. Cots were everywhere, and I wished that I had taken my own cup, bowl, and spoon. Needless to say, on the third day I started with a cold that settled in my chest—not good. I went through six rolls of TP (thank goodness I found some that wasn't sandpaper) and coughed so hard I was surprised I didn't crack a rib. None of this held us back, although we did change plans and spent three days in the Sherpa village of Thame, hoping my cold would get better.

Because of the rains below and the snow above, the trails were muuuuudddddddd! And the water was mixed with yak dung, cow dung, and every other kind of dung. It was not pleasant. I used a pair of ski poles to balance so I wouldn't slip (not wishing to be covered with wet dung). I also carried an umbrella while it was raining. Can you see me? I was quite a sight.

After the initial three days of rain, the monsoon finally decided to stop, the sun came out, and we had fairly decent weather the rest of the time. Before we would reach Kala Patthar, an early objective was the Mani Rimdu Festival observed in the Tengboche region (12,500 feet), a high ridge looking out across the Himalayan range of mountains that approach the Everest area.

Where we stayed was different, but the constant was the difficulty of the trail, which was either steep going up or steep going down, or both. At Tengboche, there were so many people we decided to leave and return the next day in hopes things would be more normal. I guess it was, but I became very irate when a helicopter came in and out jumped a smartly dressed and coiffured female with her handsome companion in street shoes, obviously just flying in for an hour or two see the festival. I had hiked five long days to get there, and for someone to be able to fly in just didn't seem right. The effort it took to get there wasn't worth almost suffocating in the night from a poorly ventilated woodstove just outside our door, or the muddy climb back up the next morning to see the monks either blowing their off-key horns or waving their brass ornaments as they clumped in their felt shoes to the less-than-melodic music.

We plodded on and upward (unfortunately taking the long route) to a place called "Dingboche" (over 14,000 feet) where another friend of Brad's owned a teahouse (a sod floor building with rooms just big enough to hold one or two beds and turn around between them). There was a community room where you ordered your meals and sat at tables around a centrally located woodstove fired with dung. The unseasonably cold weather forced those of us who were tenting into the small rooms in an effort to keep warm. Consequently, those of us who were actually paying to stay inside were pushed off into a corner farther from what heat the tiny stove could generate.

The menus in these teahouses were all the same—grease-laden omelets, grease-dripping fried potatoes, grease-soaked fried rice...you get the picture. We didn't have any fruit or vegetables for an entire month! I was thankful for "porridge," which I managed to swallow each morning. A friend back home had suggested taking a small container of cinnamon and sugar so I could at least stomach breakfast.

From Dingboche we trekked over a vast plateau, always gaining altitude while crossing silt-filled rivers and slipping in the snow, which now covered the scene. Long after passing Lobuche, we arrived at 16,700 feet and a place called "8000 Inn," where Brad and Annette had been waiting for me. I was not feeling well at all. Food of any kind made me sick to my stomach, I was short of breath, and I wished that they had a hyperbaric chamber. Much to our surprise, they *did* have a French-made one. This was a big plastic bag inflated by a pump, thus changing the atmospheric pressure inside it to make the air that of 7,000 feet instead of 16,700 feet. Within an hour or two, the patient recovered.

Fortunately, the researcher (Italian) who was in charge of the chamber had an oximeter to check my oxygen assimilation. At that elevation, oxygen assimilation

should have been 85 or above, but mine was only 60. That meant that I really needed to either get into a chamber or get to a lower elevation, which at that point (eight in the evening) was not possible.

Two porters were brought in to pump the bag, something that had to be done every few minutes to keep the pressure constant. The Italian, Brad, and Annette were there. They could talk to me and with a flashlight check through the tiny window above my head to see how I was by looking. I can't say that I was fearful at this point, for I

The main walkway through the village of Lukla.

Above and below: Near Lukla, where all the planes and helicopters must land and take off.
Here, they deliver trekkers and climbers who begin their hike up Mount Everest.

knew that I would recover. However, I'm sure Brad was frightened. Months before we left home, I had asked him if we were going to have a "bag" with us, as he used to own one. Again, I was assured that I would be OK, and that there was a bag at a village on the way. But we had passed the village earlier that day, so now it was a day away. Each time they pumped, there was a very high-pitched loud "hissing," which really bothered my ears. As the pressure increased, I had to hold my nose and blow to clear my ears, just like when a plane descended too quickly.

By 10:00 p.m., I had been in the bag an hour and the Italian felt I would be OK. I was able to sleep that night, and the next day, they checked my oxygen periodically. Unfortunately, I wasn't stabilizing, and it was obvious that I wouldn't be able to go to the 18,000-foot hill but should descend instead. That night, Annette had food poisoning and was sick all night. I thought none of us would get there. I went down with my porter to a lower village but Annette and Brad stayed on. Annette recovered enough to get to Kala Patthar the following day plus descend to where I was waiting in another teahouse, 14 hours later.

On my descent, I also had a bladder infection and was constantly squatting behind a boulder. I was having a dreadful day!!! I kept telling my porter that I had a BIG problem. My medicine was in the duffel he was carrying, and I didn't have the heart to have him untie everything so I could get at it. So I suffered!

When Brad and Annette finally caught up with me, we discovered that we were behind a day. Instead of having three days to get to the airstrip for the flight back to Kathmandu, we had only two. This meant that we really had to move. Actually, I enjoyed the very last day. It was sunny, and back at lower elevation, my cough was getting better. I could breathe and the surroundings were green. We really didn't have to hurry, as we would easily get to Lukla where we would stay the night before our flight the next morning.

After two days in Kathmandu, with last-minute shopping, pictures, and dinner with friends, we flew to India. Varanasi (or as those who have been there call it, "Very Nasty") was the most holy place in all of India, where death means cremation and ashes being dumped into the Ganges. People wash, brush their teeth, drink, defecate—you name it—in the Ganges.

By this time, the filth of Nepal and now even more filth in India was getting to both Annette and me. I knew we had to drive for six hours to get to the park where we hoped to see tigers. However, after a short flight from Varanasi to Khajuraho, we drove for 7½ hours on what used to be a highway but was now worse than a Colorado four-wheel-drive road. By the time we reached the park—which was after dark—we were exhausted, to say the least. Our bodies had been shaken almost to death! We were awakened at 5:30 a.m. for our first drive in search of the elusive tigers. That day I was OK, but the following day, my body just gave out and I slept for a day and a half. I had no symptoms other than the fact that I just didn't feel well. Again, the food was so bad I couldn't eat anything but bananas, biscuits, tea, and porridge.

After six days, we had to do that terrible drive again, but we had a better vehicle and driver who drove like a kamikaze, cutting the 7½-hour drive down to 5½ hours. In order to leave the country, we had to fly to Delhi. We were to stay in a hotel 45 minutes from the airport, but we were only going to be there five hours, so eating up 1½ hours driving made no sense. We were met by a travel representative and I told him to take us to an American hotel that was very near the international airport. It turned out to be a Radisson, and for $115, we had a day room which had a shower with hot and cold running water, a toilet that flushed, a health club with a hot tub, and an incredible buffet with food we could stomach before we had to catch our midnight flight home.

Annette and I said good-bye to Brad in Bangkok. He went to some remote island off the coast for some R&R, but Annette and I continued (three days) back to Denver. That night, we slept from ten until two the next afternoon. It took me a month to recover.

Need I say how good it was to be HOME! So there you have it! Another year with Julie. Enjoy your rockin' chairs.

Monks from a nearby monastery entertaining the visitors.

Rainbow in the San Juans.

2000-2009

Morocco/Tunis, May

My friend, Rosie Hauge, and I decided to take a trip to Morocco. Getting there was an adventure in itself, but we arrived safely and were ready for whatever confronted us.

Some Background on Morocco

The country had grown to four million people at the time of our visit, and many new roads were being put in. Berbers, Moroccan natives made up of three distinct groups with their own language in three dialects, were 90% Muslim and 1½% Christian. Their origin was unknown but was possibly Euro-Asian.

Seventy-six TV channels were beginning to change the country, but it was still mostly men who ran the businesses, whether it was a doctor with his patients or a lawyer with his clients. Only four years ago, absolutely no woman could be in business.

At the turn of the 20th century, the French took over Morocco and began colonization. This was when wine was introduced to the country. About 50% of

Casablanca's Hassan II Mosque.

their agriculture was in olives, but the main trade was in honey, eggs, wheat, barley, mushrooms, and whole lamb. The seniors often picked the olives. Only three rivers in the country were used for irrigation: Two emptied into the Atlantic and one into the Mediterranean.

Summer temperatures equaled 30°C with 20°C as an average. Desert temperatures were 110°F. Mild winters averaged at 12°C, but it could be below zero in the mountains.

The country's eucalyptus trees were used for charcoal, but many had been cut down to heat water for Turkish baths. A number of palm trees made it look like California, and the climate was similar to California's.

Many North African cities had an area known as a "medina," where the non-European population lived. The medinas were walled-off, each becoming a city within a city.

The country's capital—named Rabat, meaning "fortified monastery of victory"—had 2,000 employees in the Dar al-Makhzen Palace, built in 1865. A special school in Rabat taught the entire Koran to 150 boys over a six-month period.

Our Tour Begins

Casablanca

Originally founded by the Berbers as Anfa, the Portuguese renamed the settlement "Casa Branca"—literally White House—in the 15th century. It became known as the White City at that time. The name was changed to the Spanish version, "Casablanca," in the late 1500s.

Dyeing leather on the rooftops.

2000   2001   2002   2003   2004   2005   2006   2007   2008   2009

Casablanca had the largest port in Africa because Rabat had a huge sandbar in its harbor, preventing it from being widely trafficked. Casablanca's Medina abutted the ocean, and when the French took over and the city began to change, everyone agreed to preserve the Medina as it was.

A big home here could cost as much as $400,000. There were absolutely no photos of buildings, flags, or soldiers allowed, or you may be fined 50 to 60 dirham (DH).

The city had the most beautiful mosque, the largest in the country, where over 100,000 people prayed. The roof of the Hassan II Mosque opened up and accommodated 20,000 worshippers inside and 80,000 outside. Some of the mosque was built over the sea and offered a glass floor so, while they prayed, they could see water. On one minaret were three balls to represent three major religions: Judaism, Christianity, and Islam.

DAY 3

Our hotel looked out to the ocean. We had lunch on a deck overlooking the city and a pool. Low tables held many plates of great food: tiny hamburger patties, chicken on a stick, and fish. At night, we had a mixed salad that we thought was large enough to be dinner, then we were served a plate with a lamb bone and prunes done to a turn and tender. There were ice cold drinks plus fruit piled high on a large platter.

We would be off to Fes the next day.

DAY 4

Fes

Volubilis was the seat of power until the 11th century, when it was abandoned in favor of relocation to Fes. Volubilis was now a partially excavated Berber town dating from 3rd century BC. The Romans took it over in the 1st century AD but later abandoned it to the local tribes. During the French rule of Morocco, an arch was built in Volubilis dating to the 3rd century AD.

Seventy percent of the population in Fes was 25 or under. Even though many Jews emigrated from Morocco to Israel in the seventies, there was still a large population here. Their trade had been in salt or gold, which made them very rich. Those who remained were the poorest with an economy in agriculture. Tourism had taken over, and oil was just discovered.

The Fes Medina was large, 60 square miles, with half a million people living in it. In the 5th century, there were 5,000 mules/donkeys in the Medina, and this form of transport—especially for moving goods—was still widely used. If you heard "*ba lec,*" it meant get out of the way of the mules. On the hills you saw occasional herds of sheep in tan colors, deep to dark. Olive groves and palm trees dotted the countryside; pomegranates were sold along the road.

There were 900 streets and over 600 shops, with 350,000 people involved in making craft items. The government-fixed pricing was part of the culture, with Fes's popular blue ceramics and other items for sale at a set rate.

We were taken on a walking tour, ending up at our guide, Aziz's, home which belonged to his sister-in-law. She went to France to earn money then never returned,

2000   2001   2002   2003   2004   2005   2006   2007   2008   2009

but she had bought the flat planning to use it and, in the end, never did. She let Aziz and his family move in. Aziz's wife was a teacher working 20 hours a week, teaching Arabic. There was a large parlor, done in a striking blue, used only for guests. We saw their 3½-year-old daughter and six-month-old son who had very large eyes. I felt he could not see well. We had tea and cakes.

That evening, we had dinner in what used to be a private home on a backstreet. We sat at round tables in a garden area that had a Plexiglas roof that opened automatically. We were served various salads then three large covered, round platters of chicken, lamb, and veal. Too much to eat!

DAY 5

The next day, we were shown the Jewish area of Fes. We also looked at the Medina from a hilltop across one of the rivers running on either side of it. We were told the cemetery was always across from the door to a Medina so they didn't need to carry the dead very far. We then visited the royal palace where the bronze front doors were being cleaned with lemon juice, soap, and water. Then we spent the rest of the day in the Medina, where

Above: Royal Palace door cleaners.
Below: Royal Place.

people and working animals went about their daily chores. The streets were very narrow, so when a burro came you'd hear a loud *ba lec!* We saw leather being tanned and flatbread being baked. Each household would bring their unbaked bread to a communal oven—sometimes the children would be carrying it—where baking took about 30 minutes.

There were stores for everything: shoemakers, clothes, galabias (tunics), leather crafts. A bronze star and a carpet shop were big attractions. I bought a 9X12 rug for $3,800. After spending hours in the 9th century, we hurried to send e-mails back home.

Next, we were off to the desert, at first barren, then rocky and volcanic, and finally some apple trees, delicious and green. This was Imouzzer Kandar, an area just south of Fes. People here used to live in caves in the mountains. There were green forests with pink-roofed homes built by the French. In the country, where terrain was very rocky, fences were made of rocks, and elaborate irrigation systems had been built. There were two dams holding back waters which now were all mostly dry due to a 10-year drought. In two more years, they would be completely dry. We went through areas of cork oak trees. The mountains had no problem with lack of water.

From here, we passed a large oak forest. There were hills with ribbons of rock walls, sheep the color of dirt (red), and white rock walls that were snow fences. Some places were snowbound for two to three months at a time.

Ifrane was a very clean city, which was unusual for Africa. The royal palace here with a red flag in front of it meant you couldn't take pictures. The red tile roofs, peaked rather than flat, with beige stucco walls were very attractive. The Spanish-Moorish architecture made use of soft cedar wood.

DAY 6

We went across the middle of the Atlas Mountains today, passing two ski areas along the way. One sign said "teleske." The Middle Atlas Mountains were 6,000 feet in elevation.

Went through the Ziz Gorges and Valley where the geologic terrain with anticlines and synclines was incredible. We lunched at a hotel chain, Asma, in Midelt. In Erfoud,

Ziz Gorges.

we transferred to Land Rovers. We were very cramped, and to see out you needed to bend over. I was in the back and couldn't straighten out my legs. It held seven but we had only four or five. After a very rough road and a nine-hour drive, we arrived at camp: four showers, three johns, and plenty of double tents, a cook tent, and dining tent. A diner was nearby.

Our camp area was in a sand dune called "Erg Chebbi," the highest in Morocco at 3,800 feet. Camp was at 2,900, so we climbed 900 feet at sunrise with the help of the Berbers. Rosie and I took our cots outside and slept under the stars in a cool, comfortable breeze. A group of men came after dinner to play and dance around the campfire. Actually, they were nomads!

DAY 7

After climbing the dune for sunrise photos, we rode camels (dromedary) for an hour, then drove again over a bumpy road to Rissani, where we visited a fossil factory after a short stop at a rundown royal palace (could have eliminated it). Then we had a very short stop in a school for boys only that was funded charitably. The afternoon drive was way too long and bumpy—my butt really hurt and I needed to be able to put my legs out straight, but couldn't in the back of the vehicle.

Camp was truly in the middle of nowhere. No Frenchmen, no nomads, no planes, no people (other than our group). We had a Moroccan meal demonstration with half an onion, tomato, saffron, ginger, cumin, paprika, black pepper, garlic, parsley, olive oil, and chicken. Mix all and stuff the chicken, cook 20 minutes. Then add a potato, other half of the onion, another tomato. Cook half an hour. Cut pickled lemon and pickled olives over top (pickle lemon with a half cup vinegar in one-half kilo water for one week in the fridge). Add water if needed. Food was served piled in pyramid fashion.

DAY 8

Leaving camp on foot, we walked an hour, picked up fossils, and visited oases. We were held up by Bill, who insisted on walking the entire way, so 20 minutes were lost. A very inconsiderate man. Of course, he was looking for the cheers and applause that greeted him.

We saw camels, bought scarves, danced, drove back, and had salad for lunch. The afternoon heat was unbearable, even in the shade. The flies were incredible.

An Islamic lesson: The Berber bury their dead ASAP by saying a prayer, putting them in a grave one meter deep by 20 inches wide, and laying them on their right side, facing Mecca. There was no coffin.

We drove toward Tinerhir with stops along the way. The first was the Berber cemetery. Again, I was embarrassed to be American when Bill, once more the center of attention, lay down as if dead, positioning himself like we were told was the Berber burial custom.

Our second stop was at a 40-acre farm run by a Berber unit of 26 people. They had three wells with pumps run by diesel and could only keep half of the acreage growing. The price of a generator and diesel fuel, etc., was too expensive. Soon, the life of these people would disappear if they didn't get help. One very young girl was

Above: The tour group mobilizing via camel.

Right: Our desert camp. We really are in the middle of nowhere!

carrying a baby whose head was flopping and whose eyes were shut. Before leaving, one man pointed to the baby's eyes and indicated she had a problem. Rosie took this badly.

Back in the vehicles, we made another stop on a small pass where Rosie discovered a viper four feet long and many frogs in a well. Back on the road, similar to a jeep road, the others were impressed with the exposure and narrowness of the road. We stopped on a 5,000-foot pass and could see the High Atlas in the distance.

Several small villages later, we were nearly at our destination, Tinerhir, a town that had prospered on silver and gold. We stopped on the way to look over the fields and many adobe-type homes. Our guide said it was a mistake for Moroccans to make homes of cement, which were cold and miserable in the winter. The adobe was warm in the winter but cooked in the summer.

In the Todgha Gorge at Tinerhir, one man had settled in the caves before the hotel was built. He started serving tea to tourists and gradually made enough to build

Above: Here I am, taking in the desert sunset with our guide, Aziz.
Below: Dune sunset.

the hotel. The carpet shop, Maison Berber, was owned by people who moved into the city when they were still Tuareg, or "blue people," called so because of the indigo-dye colored clothes they traditionally wore and which stained their skin. They had to sell everything to do this. They bought a piece of land then built a shop and a home. This happened 25 years ago. Today, they were some of the richest people in Tinerhir.

DAY 9
This hotel was the poorest one we'd been in. The bathroom was one that got the entire place wet. On the upside was that the food was great.

We went to the Maison Berber carpet shop, where 25-plus rugs were thrown out for us to look at. There was a beautiful light-blue one with a white center and the same price as mine—$7,800—but it wasn't old. The owner, in blue over which he wore a white galabia, sprinkled all of us with rose water which was the traditional greeting. We were there too long. Rosie, Sophia, and Joan all bought rugs.

For lunch, they served an omelet of onions, green peppers, tomatoes, saffron, eggs, parsley, then a two-inch ground beef patty and French fries. There were two kinds of mustard and ketchup. Oh—we started off with soup, salt, pepper, and cumin.

After lunch, we drove up a gorge where we stopped at a trading post, then at a strange eroded rocky area similar to the Flatirons. Bell bought a green and gold dress for $10. Back in town, we stopped at a school where we were told not to take pictures. Aziz told Rosie to take one when the teacher wasn't looking. Her flash went off so everyone knew that she had taken a picture. A man ushered her out and read her out, calling her "an ugly American." It wasn't planned and Rosie was really upset, going on and on, over and over every detail. Our hotel was a block away and we walked there after giving a donation to the school.

After dinner, drummers came in. There was a wedding on somewhere, so I decided to try to find it. I ran into a few people who wanted to join me, and we walked until we found the party. There were three large rooms with no furniture. I was invited into the room with the married women, young girls, and children, all sitting on the floor. One room was only for men. Some girls were playing drums and little girls wiggling. Four Swiss girls were also there, invited by the hotel owner, all in borrowed clothes. We listened, clapped, tapped, danced, and I trilled, to the delight of the married women. Finally, the fellows called me out. Abraham put an arm around me and got too friendly. I finally told him I was 72, and that kind of put a damper on his advances.

DAY 10

We drove up the Gorges du Dades, full of incredible geologic formations, to the pass then returned. The pass and gorge were like nothing we'd seen anywhere. The Berber homes were so similar to the Anasazi that we couldn't believe it. I would have loved to have had Winston from the Wetherill–Grand Gulch Research Project here. The way they built their homes, kiva-like structures, cliff towers, the overhangs and rock dwellings—the adobe, how they grew corn, etc., in the valleys—it was all too similar not to be connected. Women did all the work; marriages were arranged. We went to a private home where the kitchen had a corner fireplace, like in Peru. The ceiling was black with smoke. We took our shoes off, ate fry bread with honey and nuts (almonds, walnuts), and drank tea.

On to the next town where we had lunch in a private home and a demonstration of a wedding headdress (which Rosie modeled), and Aziz told us of their customs. Bill and Caroline were the bride and groom. The galabia for Bill almost didn't fit. Caroline's outfit was all sparkles covered with white lace pieces. Close friends were the ministress to the bride and the minister to the groom. They were confided in as to whether the marriage was consummated or not. The pair was in one room together

Gorges du Dades.

for seven days. If it wasn't consummated, one or the other was humiliated; some committed suicide. Aziz had friends who had killed a chicken to get blood to bloody the sheets and prove to the world that the marriage was consummated. Geo and Bill and Maurice asked dumb questions.

In the afternoon, we headed across country similar to the area near Monument Valley. The terrain was incredibly beautiful. The face makeup on Rosie (when modeling the headdress) wouldn't come off. When we got in the next town and were just walking down the street, Rosie with the Berber headdress and shorts on gave the locals the giggles. We had lunch upstairs in a lovely place.

Aziz had shown us Moroccan culture with much pride and did it well. The Berber culture was dying out; there were more girls than boys.

In Ouarzazate, our hotel, where many movie stars stayed, was gorgeous. There was a pool in the garden with a buffet next to it. Our room had a living room and 1½ baths. Abdue called and wanted Rosie to go out on a scooter. We saw one casbah.

DAY 11

The next day, on our way to Marrakesh, we saw a casbah where movies were made, then drove far off-road to Telouet to see one that was falling apart because a pasha (a man of high rank in the village) said not to restore it. In Marrakesh, horse carriages took us on a city tour. We saw the ornate palace and a mausoleum closed for 300 years until the French came. There were tourists galore and belly dancer men with twirling tassels on their hats. By this time, we'd had enough. We had a farewell dinner in the Medina in a

2000   2001   2002   2003   2004   2005   2006   2007   2008   2009

garden area where candles burned along a narrow walkway and the ceiling was rolled back.

DAY 12

The last day was a long one, one until eleven. We walked to the square for photos and I tried in vain to find a cyber cafe. Aziz took us to the airport, where I had to pay $57 over-baggage for the rug. Rosie got away with no extra, but Joan paid more than I did.

Three men met us in Tunis and took us through heavy traffic to a dump of a hotel, two-star. Our female guide met us at 10:30. We had a short city tour, walked in the Medina, then lunched in a small cafe. In the afternoon, we saw incredible mosaics in the Bardo National Museum. They were larger than room-size and depicted life in Tunisia over time. We were dropped off late that night at the hotel with no suggestion as to where to eat dinner. At the hotel, our dinner was soup, fruit, and bread for two for $5. A double there was under $50 with three meals.

DAY 13

Cities we visited: Dougga and Thuburbo Majus, from which some of the mosaics in the Bardo National Museum had originated. The Dougga ruins dated from the 2nd to the 7th century AD and were made up of a complex of temples and bathhouses. As many as 10,000 people had lived here. The Berbers of Tunis, the Romans, and the Phoenicians were involved in building the town, and the Arabs destroyed it. The very large statue of Jupiter (Zeus) we saw in the Bardo museum came from Dougga.

Home the next day.

Tanzania: A Trip with Brad and Bunker Sands, June

Years ago, when Brad was a ski instructor at Vail, he'd met a Texan by the name of Bunker Sands who asked Brad to guide him and his family on an African tour, including Mt. Kilimanjaro. This ended up being a trip that I joined in on.

Bunker's group consisted of his three children—all boys—and their girlfriends. One of the gals didn't want to do the Kilimanjaro climb but was afraid to wait in Nairobi by herself, so I volunteered to meet her there and get her back together with the group afterward. Following that, they would continue on to do a safari tour of other parts of Africa.

We met the rest of the group at the Mt. Meru Hotel in Moshi, where we all took some time to exercise in the pool. The troops all seemed to be in good shape, despite the long descent down Kilimanjaro. Bunker, however, had had a hard time and was very tired. We had dinner late—7:30—and went to bed soon after.

An afternoon game drive.

Another gorgeous African sunset.

Up at 6:30 the next morning, we readied ourselves to leave for Ngorongoro Crater and the first safari tour. The road was just like the roads in India—very bumpy, which made the trip tiring. Our lodging at Ngorongoro Sopa Lodge was incredible, situated as it was on the rim of the crater. By the time we were all settled in our rooms, it was time for lunch. Afterward, we went on an afternoon game drive until six and saw an elephant, hyena, many Thomson's gazelles and Grant's gazelles, a mother and two baby cheetahs, warthogs, zebras, red bill and yellow bill ducks, Egyptian geese, secretary birds, and kori bustards. We had good light with a gorgeous sunset. Later, dinner was at 7:30.

The next day saw another early call for breakfast, and we would have yet another long bumpy, dusty ride from Ngorongoro to Serengeti Sopa Lodge. On the way, we would go down into the crater. After transferring our belongings, we started down into the crater at about 7:30 to 7:45. The scene was incredible, with herds of wildebeest and zebra, foxes, hyenas, an elephant and baby, and we just missed a lion kill—a Cape buffalo. The other buffaloes chased the lions away and crowded around the dead one so the lions couldn't eat it. Not wanting a confrontation with the herd, the lions worked their way toward us, where a small pond had hippos in it. We expected some action between the two groups, but the lions just drank and lay down.

Tours into the crater were only allowed until just before dusk, and the time we'd taken to view the animals and have lunch was about to make us late. We had to rush to leave the crater and reach the exit of the park boundary, two hours away. Our drivers ripped up the gravel road like maniacs as we left, narrowly missing game and people. When we reached the park border, we saw lots of starlings, storks, baboons, lions, elephants, and hippos. Our driver was getting eaten by biting flies and chose to head straight for the Serengeti Lodge. Our bags were in another vehicle, so we waited a half hour for it to arrive. After that, we watched dik-dik drinking at a nearby pool while

THE CURIOUS
CHEETAH

*Heading back to his friends on
the anthill to report.*

"I have this feeling we're being watched," said the mother elephant to her baby.
Photo by Brad Johnson.

having drinks before dinner. At sunset, it began to cool off just as a dinner of fish, potatoes, vegetables, chocolate, and éclairs was served.

Up at 5:30 the next a.m., we headed out at 6:30 sharp for Serena Lodge. The first couple of hours on the road, nothing happened, then—finally—we saw lions on the hunt. We watched for a long time and eventually lost sight of them, so continued on our way to Serena. Saw three cheetahs on an anthill and stopped to watch them. One came over and hopped up on the hood, then went up on the cab, peering in under the canvas to look at us. It appeared that he wanted to jump into the vehicle. The two young students inside with me were terrified! Had there not been rows of seats, or if there had been a flat place for him to land, I'm sure he would've jumped inside. He lay down on the hood for a time then finally climbed up on the cab again, jumped down, and went back to the anthill. All three cheetahs came over to lay down in the shade of a tree, which put them in the middle of the road. By then, our driver had alerted other sightseeing tours that there were three cheetahs in the road, and the line of travelers and vans began to arrive to get

An impala with her baby.

pictures. We were fortunate to be the first on the scene, for what had just happened wouldn't have taken place with all the crowds of vehicles, people talking, and cameras clicking. What an event!

Not long after that, we watched an elephant herd with babies for a long time. A baby attempted to tear down a small tree. We left that spot only to learn that a leopard had been in the grass near the elephants, and it was now in a tree. We returned for shots, and droves of cars came by. Finally, we left for the lodge and got there around noon in time for lunch. I swam first, had lunch, then went back to the pool. We had another game drive at 3:30, when Brad and Bunker saw three lions on the side of the waterway, as well as a saddle-billed stork.

Next, we were off to Manyara, which would be a long drive on yet another very bumpy road. We stopped at a Masai village with 86 people. Each man there could marry 10 women, and each woman had her own house of sticks and cow dung. These structures were built very much like the daub and wattle of our Southwest Indians.

The village children's eyes were covered with flies. I'm sure one small child was blind. One of the men went to another house, where we were told one of his wives was pregnant. Women stayed in the village while the young men left to learn about life and what was required of them as they grew into men. The village men looked after the cattle and the women carried wood, water, and the children.

Their houses had an entrance then two rooms, one for children and one for adults. Behind a stick wall was a place for calves to stay after they were born. The floors

Photo by Brad Johnson.

2000   2001   2002   2003   2004   2005   2006   2007   2008   2009

of the bed area were raised about eight inches. A fire in the center of a larger room heated the entire house, with smoke filling all the rooms. Very small peepholes, the size of saucers, allowed light into the room.

The average age of a Masai was mid-fifties. After the young men went through circumcision, they wore black and painted their faces white to look like masks. Supposedly, they had to kill a lion with a spear to become a man, but the nature-to-tour fellow said not—there weren't enough lions now. In the early eighties, the Masai dogs transferred rabies and something else to the wild dogs—all were killed off and the lions got it also, with 75% of the population gone in a short time. Now, the lions were coming back, mainly because of aid that came in to rid the Serengeti of rabies. A lady named Clare Cleveland had decided to vaccinate all Masai dogs to rid the country of rabies. It was a huge undertaking.

On the way to the Manyara lodge, we saw lions in a tree. Two came down while we watched and a third stayed. The lodge sat on a rim above Lake Manyara. In 1996, the lake had no water, and the bed was so dry that you could actually drive across it.

The next morning, the naturalist took us on an early walk full of interesting things. We saw a thorn tree with two kinds of thorns—hooked (tiny), and long and straight. Giraffes got all the thorns going straight and ate them with the leaves. The trees adapted to the habits of the animals so they could survive. Some were seeded when the animals ate them and the seed went through their digestive tracts.

The naturalist talked about termite hills. The king/queen are both the workers and the warriors. They bring in food to grow tiny mushrooms that they feed on. When there are too many workers, the warriors kill some off. The temperature was

2000   2001   2002   2003   2004   2005   2006   2007   2008   2009

kept constant by bringing drops of water into the nest from underground. This was very much like air-conditioning, with air coming in around the drops of water in the bottom and going out holes above.

After a day or two at Manyara, we took another long drive to Tarangire Lodge in Tarangire National Park. We came onto five to eight lions near the road, and there were elephants everywhere. Later, an afternoon drive brought only birds. The first sighting was at a zebra kill where dozens of buzzards were feeding on the carcass. At a green swamp, there were more birds and some elephants were eating. The baobab tree, an icon of the African savannah, lived for thousands of years. Those we saw in Tarangire were here long before the elephants came, because the elephants ate them when they were young. There were no new baobab trees here because of this.

The Tarangire Lodge was huge!!! And there were lots of elephants, zebra, and wildebeests to view. However, I didn't think the meals were as good as at the other lodges.

In bygone days, people who got malaria thought it was contracted from the acacia tree that had green bark, and it came to be called the "yellow fever" acacia. It was later proven that mosquitoes were the cause of malaria. Another type of growth we saw was a bush that had very rough hairs on it, which the Masai actually used to sand and sharpen their spears.

The cheetahs we saw wouldn't jump into the car, but it was scary just the same. We saw a leopard kill in a tree.

Tarangire National Park was the final leg of our tour in Tanzania. Bunker, his family, and their friends all went home with tales of their Kilimanjaro climb and the wild African animals.

The next three pictures were taken by Brad when he was guiding Bunker's party up Kilimanjaro. Below: The group on the Machame Route.

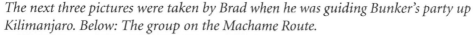

251

Above: A view of mountains from a camp on the Shira Plateau.
Below: Mawenzi, Kilimanjaro's second-highest volcanic cone at 5,149 meters, and the ice cap as seen from the summit.

2000   2001   2002   2003   2004   2005   2006   2007   2008   2009

I Play the Slots in Wendover, NV

2001 had not been the most exciting year of my life. There were no great out-of-country adventures. Can you believe that? I visited my birthplace, Fond du Lac, Wisconsin, not once, but twice! I spent the Fourth of July with my sister-in-law, Gloria, and her family on Lake de Neveu where I spent my childhood. They always have what I call a "down home" parade, where the kids decorate their bikes and wagons and the adults wear their Army, Navy, or Marine uniforms. The rest of the day was spent in the lake or eating, followed by the FIREWORKS! I think there was a competition to see who could spend and shoot off the most money. I never saw so many lights in the sky!

The rest of the year was filled with skiing (with a brace on my bad knee). Like last year, I skied at Lake Tahoe with friends and found the snow no better than the year before. It was just too low in elevation to be light and fluffy like we have in Colorado. But there were other things to do when in Lake Tahoe, like gambling!

Bet you didn't know that I liked playing the dollar slots. I did one year on the way back from picking up a car in San Francisco. Stopping in Reno, I lost all but $40 of what I was willing to lose. We made a second stop in Wendover, Nevada, just west of Salt Lake. There, we watched a young gal as she played two machines at once, both buckets brimming with dollar pieces. I told her we had lost all but $40 in Reno: Was that enough to play the dollar slots?

She assured me that it was, so I changed my cash into casino dollars and then asked which machine I should lose it in. Mulling it over—looking first at one machine, then another—she pointed to a nearby one and said, "Play that one." Not yet convinced, I attended the machine, only to be shocked that I had to play three coins each time. But this gal insisted that I play three coins. Three went in, then another three with nothing happening. My suspicions were coming true—I soon would be broke! But with the third three, the bells jangled, the lights flashed, and the place went wild! Still, I wasn't sure what had happened. A perfect stranger patted me on the back, yelling, "You've won, you've won!" "What did I win?" I shouted back. "You've won $1,000!" Stunned, I watched as dollar pieces clanged into my bucket. The casino rep came to gather the numbers and tell me that he would have to get the rest of the money because the bucket only held $500! My naiveté prompted me to say, "Oh, that's all right. Just write me a check!" The entire audience broke into laughter. My gambling mentor said, "I've never heard anyone say that!"

So began my frequenting certain casinos and playing the dollar slots. While at Lake Tahoe late one February, when—again—the snow was not to my liking, I informed my friends they could find me wherever the dollar slots were at Harvey's. About a half-hour later, they arrived to find not one, but two machines spitting out dollars, lights flashing, bells ringing, and me wondering how I would get all my money over to the cashier for exchange. In all, I had won $1,035 above the $200 I started with. Then this spring, on my way to visit a friend in Santa Fe, New Mexico, I arrived a couple hours before I was expected. I wasn't sure it was wise to play in a new and unfamiliar casino owned by the local Indians, but—after browsing through the dollar slot area—I took a deep breath, got some coins, and started playing. I always played the same machine, even if it wasn't paying. After 1½ hours, I walked away $480 ahead!

OTHER HAPPENINGS

In April, I visited the Mayo Clinic in Scottsdale for a complete physical. That, in itself, was quite an experience. They pronounced me fit as a fiddle, and then some. Then Rosie Hauge, the gal who joined me last year in Morocco, and I decided to get 10 other friends and go back to Morocco that October. A lot of time was spent getting the trip organized, then September 11 caused a couple to drop out and another needed surgery, so we had to put that trip on hold. Perhaps in the spring we'll give it a go.

Temporarily, I'd had a friend living with me while she got herself divorced. Keeping her mind off her problems had turned out to be a full-time job. We did many things together, but we also did many things with other friends. It was her brother who we'd visited in Tahoe for skiing. In late summer, we drove there, this time to fish, one of my passions. Catching a fish this large was another new experience! And you see the results pictured here. Wow! A 20-inch lake trout. Yes, we ate it!

Brad had moved to Ridgway, Colorado, north of Ouray, Colorado, and about a six-hour drive from Boulder. He hadn't yet said if that would be permanent. With his moving, the duplex at Vail needed to be rented, which I accomplished June 1. I

My 20-inch lake trout.

had been anything but idle without foreign travels. Lots of golf had been played and friends within a day's drive from home visited.

Speaking of home, if you and your loved ones gathered this Christmas, I'm sure your time together was even more pressured after September 11. We had such an abundance of "things" while so many in the world didn't even have a place to lie down for the night, nor food to eat. We're all so blessed. Over the years, as I have traveled to countries such as India, Peru, and places in Africa very much like Afghanistan and Pakistan, I had always returned feeling more blessed to be an American, to have my freedom, to have far more material things than I needed. It seemed that our lives would never be the same again. However, I had faith that our country would continue to be a free society where women have a place, aren't required to stay indoors or cover themselves from head to toe when they go out. Daily, I counted my blessings. One of them was in having great friends like you!

Visited the Czech Republic, Hungary, and Switzerland

It was strange how this trip came to be. Lorraine, my traveling companion, interior decorator, and friend, introduced me to Don Prikryl, a house painter she thought was Polish. At any rate, after Don did some painting for me and I discovered his mother was visiting, I invited them over for coffee and to see my home. Later, his mother left for a short time, then an aunt came. I had her over for coffee. Neither woman could speak English, but Don acted as interpreter.

Periodically, Don would call me or I would call him to see if he had found a girlfriend. Invariably, he hadn't found the right mate. I told him he was trying too hard.

Several months later, he and his mother had to go home in the spring so his mom could obtain some medical exams needed to get some kind of U.S. citizenship. This would give her Medicare! I couldn't figure out how—she didn't speak English and had never worked or lived here, so how could she sign up for Medicare? But so be it. They wanted me to visit them at their home, and how could I turn down an opportunity to see the Czech Republic or Poland with people who lived there?

Don and me.

They had their tickets on Lufthansa when I returned from a ski trip and thought there were no more seats. But I had many miles I needed to use, and in calling United, I found I could get a seat in business class on THEIR flight using 110,000 miles I'd saved for a couple of years. So I was on Flight 447 in business class with no one ahead of me and no one next to me. I'd say they weren't making any money on that flight!

The plane was an Airbus, and I'd never been on one of those before. I hoped it stayed in the air! There were six seats across—two, two, and two. Lots of room. Forty-two business-class seats, and there were only about 10 to 12 people. Surprisingly, we left only 10 minutes late. The flight time was nine hours, five minutes, and by 6:00, we were being served drinks and nuts (tomato juice and almonds). The movie was *Domestic Disturbance* with John Travolta.

After a terrible veggie dinner, I noticed that most of business class was asleep. I took a quarter of a sleeping pill and melatonin, put my blinders on, covered up with two blankets, and slept from about 7:00 p.m. until 12:30, about 5½ hours. Breakfast was served before landing around nine European time.

Looking out the window, the fields were green, and the sun was low and shining through thin clouds. I could see many small scattered villages, twisting rivers and valleys, highways, red commuter trains, castles, cultivated fields, red tile roofs, canals, barges, and autobahns. Busy busy. Smoggy forests, gravel pits. Smokestacks.

Don's friend who picked us up was driving a VW rental wagon with plenty of room for all of our bags. We drove on the eastern highway through Slovakia, which used to be part of Czechoslovakia when, in 1993, they chose to split with the Czechs. The fellows were afraid I might need a visa at the border, but I didn't. Going through the open farmland through Bratislava was the shorter way to go. At the border, we encountered miles of semis lined up to get through customs. Some stayed all night—24 or more hours, waiting to get through. According to Don, there was no reason for it, it was just the way those in power chose to deal with it.

We were more than three hours getting to Don's home, owned by his sister. Don's father had committed suicide when Don was young, and Don's sister, being older, got the house. Don and his sister grew up in the house, and it would stay in the family. That's the way it was. He and his mom stayed in the house when the sister married, and now she lived an hour away; an aunt lived next door.

The houses here were very close to the street but, once in the house, they all seemed to have lovely quiet backyard gardens. Their house was brick, sturdy and re-plastered every 15 to 20 years. Across the street was a factory, so it was not in the best of areas. Typical of homes here, the back room was heated separately; only rooms that were used were heated. Mom slept in the warm kitchen and Don slept in a tiny room off the front entry hall. A large back room was not heated well, so it wasn't used much. The bath was cold. The toilet, off the front hall, was cold to sit down on.

Their TV and radios were covered with a pretty napkin-type cloth. The beds were single, except the one in the back room that had a mattress about six inches thick on a board. My bed, the width of a single bed, had very stiff laundered sheets, a very large pillow, and a cover with sheepskin on one side and wool plaid on the other. The down cover looked like it had a brand-new, stiff cover on it with a blue water lily pattern. I felt like it was purchased for my coming, as well as the sheets being starched and pressed.

On one wall of the room was a bed running the length of the wall. There was walking space in the middle of the room. On the other wall were a narrow desk and shelves and cupboards. A few pictures were on the wall. Above the bed was a narrow shelf with a radio/CD player and a bunch of tapes lined up. The carpet on the floor was a gaudy red, tan, black-and-white hotel lobby pattern. There was a light for reading. The end of the room was filled with a window that looked out onto the street, just a car-length away, across to the factory chimneys.

My room was actually Don's room. He was sleeping in the living room on a bed similar to mine—narrow and along one wall. One wall of the living room had a glass cupboard containing all the prized possessions—crystal, mementos, pictures of family. One corner had a desk where Don had his computer. The TV, in another corner, was covered. There was a large table in the middle of the room and one easy chair. The kitchen had a table in the middle. One corner had a small gas two-burner stove. An on-demand water heater and tiny sink were next to the door from the hallway. One door led to the living room, one to the hall, one to the back bedroom, bath and pantry, and one to the head of mom's bed which was next to an old-fashioned wall hot water radiator under a window.

Everyone had house slippers. I was glad I'd brought my own. I wasn't looking forward to taking a bath. It was so cold in the rooms that weren't used.

Don's sister made us dinner in a matter of minutes: French-fried cauliflower, fried potatoes, and mom's canned pears with bits of pineapple. We had a very strong, welcoming drink in tiny glasses—potent enough to either kill you or any germs you may have picked up along the way.

His sister was limping. It turned out that she'd injured her knee getting the house ready for us. She had a friendly husband. The aunt, whom I had met, came over from next door. After dinner, I sent Brad an e-mail—also my Hungarian friend, Gábor. We all went to bed about nine. I slept well and was warm. I wore my wool footies.

Breakfast was coffee with lots of bread and cheese. No fruit! I was given a tour of the house, which had a nice enclosed garden with the warm morning sun shining on the fruit trees and some flowers. We went to the neighboring house where Aunt Ludmilea lived. She had married for one year, divorced, then never married again. She was a schoolteacher. Being alone, she had saved enough to take care of herself and do some traveling. She had a new small refrigerator and freezer, so now she could have

Don with his mom (left) and Aunt Ludmilea.

2000   2001   **2002**   2003   2004   2005   2006   2007   2008   2009

ice cream and fruit. In the back was a very narrow, long strip of land where there were strawberry plants, raspberry bushes, and some fruit trees. She was younger by four years than Don's mom, who was 74.

Don and I got on some ancient bikes. Mine had mountain bike tires with pedal brakes for the rear, hand brakes for the front. We cycled across a busy byway and railroad track to the cemetery where Don's father and maternal ancestors were buried. He had been close to his dad, learning much from him about fixing cars and houses, etc. When he went home, he always visited the cemetery to say hello to him. His father became an alcoholic and there had been constant arguments between his parents about drinking.

We rode back to an area where the family owned a narrow strip of land with fruit trees and strawberries, some potatoes, too. The land was crossed by a narrow canal where a shoe factory used to ship out shoes on a barge to a river. There was more land on the other side of the river. This land had been in the family for hundreds of years.

We continued biking down a rutted dirt road and along a row of houses that Don designed (his background was in civil engineering). All the roofs were flat and the houses were three-story, all alike. We saw the elementary school from a distance where he had played soccer.

When we got back, Don was frozen from the wind on the bike ride, so we had a drink and a cookie (not sweet). His mom was watching a morning soap opera with American actors whose words were dubbed in Czech.

We had to go to another village for pictures of Don's mom for her passport. While he had all his hair cut off, Mom and I had chocolate cake and coffee, bought some oranges and bananas, and I took photos of the square and the people. We toured a couple blocks before driving back home. The exchange rate was $1 = 35 koruna (Sk).

After a lunch of soup, dumplings, and a piece of pork stuffed with sausage and wrapped in bacon (too much to eat), we drove to three other towns. The first was a spot where we drank mineral water from a strange cup Mom gave us. We sucked on the spout. Different places had different minerals in the water, so it tasted different. Don's sister went to this town for an entire month every summer and got it all paid for by the government. She had something wrong with her back. She and her husband lived in a three-bedroom apartment on the fourth floor of a high-rise. There were two toilets and one shower. They had every convenience one would want. Don said he couldn't do that.

We went to another town to visit a travel agency called "Fischer." They had expensive trips. Don wanted to take a gal he met on the Internet somewhere warm to get acquainted. She lived west of Vienna and was also Czech. She was 15 years younger, though. We also went to a climbing store to get a magazine with climbing stories.

Finally, we stopped at a very large shopping center where there was a McDonald's plus other stores. Don paid for phone call time there. On the way home, the sun was full with orange and red. I never saw it that way except in Africa. Then the moon was full and pink.

We went out to dinner very late, and Auntie came along. We met Don's best climbing friend and the friend's wife, Donna. We ate in a restaurant with an oval wine cellar ceiling. Very nice. I ordered a Cobb salad that came on a plate with two pieces of chicken in the middle of some lettuce. Tomato slices and cucumber slices sprinkled with Roquefort cheese and bacon bits, all covered with creamy dill dressing. Very rich and not what I expected. Everyone ordered what they wanted. Donna had hot red wine and the fellows had beer. All had wine, apple strudels, and coffee for a total of $15!

The Friday before Easter, we slept late. Mom went to the doctor at 7:00 a.m. After breakfast, we drove to a winery owned by a family friend. We drank samples of perhaps five to six white wines as we stood among the oak barrels. There were also some steel barrels standing upright. The friend had a long glass pipet to draw some wine from different barrels. We switched to red wine as time passed, and now we were in the middle of morning. I was beginning to reel. Mom didn't want any more, either! The friend insisted. By the time we finished, I could barely see or stand. We went to town and had something to eat, onion soup and bread for me. I had a hard time keeping everything down. We went home where I took a nap and finally felt better. Don wanted to take an hour to run, so we drove out into the country as the sun was setting. The countryside was beautiful. While Don ran, I walked up a mountain path to some large climbing rocks. The flowers and moss were gorgeous in the low sunlight. I read a book while waiting for him to return.

We drove up another hill with a narrow street, one car wide, to see where his grandfather used to live. Then on up a country path to see a small strip of land his grandfather left him. He didn't know what to do with it. It had a falling-down shed where he spent many nights with his grandfather. Plum trees were growing, ones he had planted three years ago to work off a breakup with his girlfriend. The land used to be planted with grapes, but no one took care of them anymore.

It was now Friday evening. We drove an hour to Don's sister's and stayed for dinner and overnight. His sister made dinner—a cold pasta salad. It was very good! She bought four swan desserts filled with pudding and a lot of cream. Then we walked up a couple blocks to a bar for a beer and coffee. There was a beautiful full moon again.

Don had made a movie on climbing Kangchenjunga in Nepal. His Czech friend was killed on the trek around Annapurna. He had left the group to climb a 6,000-meter peak and an avalanche came down and killed him while the trekkers watched. They even took photos as it happened. The movie was a lot like the one Brad and I had watched before my trip.

We left his sister's and took turns driving for the next four hours toward the Tatra Mountains. We had lunch along the highway at a place called "Dechtáre," a quaint wooden chalet-type place on the lake. Then continuing on, we stopped to hike the Štrbské Pleso Trail to Popradské Pleso, which took us on an icy snow-covered trail that slanted so much that we couldn't stand up. I needed ski poles because my boot soles wouldn't hold. The trail went through a forest across several avalanche paths, some very steep. We had tea at a lodge on a frozen lake. Some cross-country skiers were there who had shaped skis and a different style of toe piece. Two pins came from each side of the front toe piece and went into holes, one on either side of the boot's toe.

Returning to the car, my hip had about had enough from slipping on the icy trail. The total round-trip time was about 3½ hours. Driving on, we stopped to eat dinner in a small charming, privately owned restaurant. The entrée I chose was a surprise. It was a plate of inch-long pasta with mushrooms, accompanied by cheese and wine. Very good, and there was plenty to eat. A raw salad came with it that was more than I could eat.

The pension we stayed in was newly decorated. Don had stayed here before, but in a separate chalet across the road. He slept "like a stone," in his words, so by 11:00, he was in la-la land and never heard a little girl screaming and running through the halls. For two hours, the noise went on. I finally drifted off at one.

Surprisingly, Don was awake around seven. After a plentiful buffet breakfast, we headed for Krakow with me in the driver's seat. It was Easter Sunday. Along the way, we passed many uniquely Polish churches with people standing outside because there wasn't room inside. There were perhaps 12 privately owned small Poma lifts, and there was enough snow that people were skiing. The latest equipment and clothes were being used. In Krakow, we somehow drove right to the old part of the city where there was a wall surrounding a large castle. We also found the central plaza where everyone gathered—men, women, children. Balloons and flowers were everywhere. Barbecue stands sold shish kebab, brats and kraut, beans, and potatoes. A group of young monks was playing real swing-type music, praising God, clapping their hands over their heads, swaying to the beat and grabbing people from the gathering crowd to do a conga line. Everyone was singing, clapping, and swaying. Even a small group of Sisters took part. Benches around the square were filled with people watchers, mostly elderly folks. There were baby buggies, babies feeding pigeons, horse and carriage men giving rides around the square. The stores were closed; only craft stalls were open. People were wandering

Known locally as Brncalova Chata, this is a lodge we saw while driving through the Tatra Mountains. "Chata" means cottage. What a cottage!

2000   2001   **2002**   2003   2004   2005   2006   2007   2008   2009

aimlessly along a walk next to a river; some people were asleep in the first sun of spring. Tour buses were parked and there were Germans wandering about. Unfortunately, there were few Polish people in the Slovakian area where we were staying.

The Slovakian government proclaimed that every Pole crossing the border into Slovakia had to exchange $50/person in Slovakian money. If you earned only $400 to $500 per month, this would be impossible. So forty million Poles had to stay out of Slovakia. It was a dumb move on Slovakia's part, because the hotels and pensions were empty. In 1976 in Štrbské Pleso, the Olympics were held, and we were in that area. We decided to eat back where we stayed, the Tatranska Kotlina "Koliba Pension."

Our second hike was to the Tatras. I slept better and was up early. We hit the trail at nine for this two-hour, 45-minute hike. We did it in two hours and 20 minutes. The trail on the lower part was icy again. We should have done it on snowshoes or cross-country skis. Some cross-country folks were on it. The trail wound through heavy forest, finally opening up with the mountains all around. In a large snowfield, there was even a lift. Some rock outcroppings looked interesting, and Don said they were great for climbing.

There was a large hut that you could stay in and get meals. A generator provided electricity, and there were even hot showers and clean flush toilets. There were lots of young people and loud music. A small lake below was enticing to throw ladies in, clothes and all. For some reason, the men got a great kick out of that. Some threw buckets of water on girls who complained because they had no other dry clothes and it was cold out.

After lunch, we continued, and the hike out went faster, just two hours. On the drive back, we ate in a very nice restaurant where four Americans were also having dinner. I asked where they were from, and they replied that they were from a San Diego electronics company.

We stopped to pick up a book about New Guinea and the same movie that Brad and I had seen last weekend.

We decided to get massages—it turned out that Don only wanted an hour in the sauna. But a very handsome, tall fellow had enough time to give me a 30-minute massage that cost $4. I was handed a towel barely large enough to cover me. The ladies undressed on one side of a curtain which hung in the middle. Men were on the other side. It was all hanging out! Rhoda would have died! Communal shower. Then I had to wait while the men undressed.

I was finally told to go to a room and lie on my stomach, thank goodness. He did only my back from my butt up. Then he said "sit up." Oops! What next? But he continued to do my upper back. I would really have welcomed some leg and foot work, but it felt good just the same. I survived and even had a shower to myself when I finished.

Tuesday, April 2

It was a lazy day. I washed my hair, got my clothes washed, and packed for Prague. We shopped in a neighboring village and lunched at the same place we had eaten last night.

2000   2001   **2002**   2003   2004   2005   2006   2007   2008   2009

Don took me to a castle. They were so busy over the weekend that they were closed today, so we couldn't get in. We walked to a church on a nearby hill. When Don was 16 to 18, a building behind the church was given to the local climbers. There were some large bouldering rocks below it and Don wanted me to see them. We had to scramble through leaves covering a faint path. It wasn't easy in my shoes, but I managed. Then we walked back to the castle and to the car.

In the evening, we left at five for a two-hour, 20-minute drive to Prague. It was a great highway—four lane. We got wrong directions from a friend and ended up downtown, then had a nice dinner at Mimosa Restaurant. I forgot to mention the spectacular red-orange sunset.

Don got us to his friend, George's, house in a residential area corner lot. George's father left him the house and he was gradually upgrading it. It had a new bath with all the conveniences—Jacuzzi, shower, marble counter, fancy sink, mirrors, and large two-toilet closets, separated, in upper and lower halls. The toilets had tanks with a pull chain—one-third pull for peeing, a full pull for BMs. The kitchen refrigerator, freezer, dishwasher—everything was new and modern. The house was very male in style. The living room had a Bose sound system and a big-screen TV with 35-or-more channels. The only furniture was a round table with four chairs, an L-shaped leather sofa, one leather easy chair, and the TV. The place had cherry cupboards with Swedish brass hardware. He drove an Audi wagon with a stick shift, 185 hp. In his two-car garage was a bright lemon-yellow Porsche "Boxster." Its roof opened in 12 seconds. George was very proud of everything.

One wall of the living/dining room was all wine and liquor with backlighting. He was proud that he had chosen everything. Obviously, he had money. He'd been divorced for three years and had a 10-year-old boy. He had a new girlfriend, a young blonde, with an 11-year-old boy, and they would soon be moving in together to see how it would work. Don thought George was one "sharp" man. He was a big guy with no hair except for a mustache. He talked loudly.

As we sat at the round table, we talked about the wall that was covered with bottles of unopened liquor. The shelf was just wide enough for the width of a bottle. The lights came down from above. The two stayed up until after midnight, drinking two bottles of wine.

Wednesday, April 3

We needed to take the "tube" downtown by nine the next morning to meet Don's English teacher, Marcila, who would be our guide. We arrived at a metro station where she had her four-year-old son, Andy, with her in a stroller. We went on cobblestone streets into the metro and on to Prague Castle, seat of the president, which had a thousand-year history. Like England, there were two guards at the entrance. We could go into the courtyard. We knew the president was there because the flag was up, so it was amazing that we could just walk around the grounds.

Prague was known as the "city of a hundred spires." There were 1,200,000 inhabitants. Prague was the capital of the Czech Republic and the historical capital of

The Charles Bridge spanning the Vltava River.

Bohemia. Life at one time was governed by religion, and many giant churches were built. This was the birthplace of Einstein, Mozart, and Dvorak. The city was dominated by Nazism from 1939 to 1945 and liberated by the Russians and Americans. In 1993, the Federal Republic of Czechoslovakia broke up into the Czech and Slovak Republics with Prague and Bratislava as the capitals.

The Vltava River ran through the city, which was surrounded by the rolling green hills of Bohemia. Prague had elegant shops and first-class restaurants and hotels, including the intercontinental Radisson and other five-stars. The streets and toilets were clean. Fifty years of communism had left the economy rebuilding itself to keep up with its European counterparts. There was a Jewish area, called the "Josefov Quarter," which had been the Jewish ghetto during the Nazi occupation.

The most charming parts of the city were the museum, the synagogues, and the cemetery where 12,000-plus were buried at different levels because there wasn't enough room. The buildings were ornamentally detailed. One tower was black and was called the "Powder Tower" because the gunpowder was stored there in the 13th century. At the entrance to the castle were two fighting giants. The black tower served as a prison. Legend had it that a man was imprisoned there. They gave him no food, so he played music to get food to survive.

After Marcila ended our tour, we went back to the house, watched TV, and waited for George. At 8:30 George's brother, Vladimir, showed up. He told us that George had an unexpected problem at his company (which made brakes, filters, etc., car parts). Seems the union was attempting to unionize his 100 workers. Big headache! Later, we met George and a colleague in a nearby Chinese restaurant. Vladimir and I enjoyed talking about flying. He was a top OB/GYN doctor, operating and teaching. He said he only worked two days a week, but I doubt that. It turned out he was learning to fly and had flown into the Prague airport to see how it was that day. He needed to do that

Above: A cemetery in Prague.
Right: The famous Prague clock.

to pass his exams. He had waited for months to take the exam. Seemed there were few examiners here! He laughed when he said he could fly all over his tiny country in one day.

Thursday, April 4

The next day, Don took his mother to the doctor again, then he took off at noon to see the Internet girlfriend. His mother knew Marcila's mother and had stayed there the night before. In the morning, it was off to the American Embassy for papers.

But for me, a 26-year-old neighbor from across the street, Ramona, was my tour guide. She studied English three times a week, so I was practice. She showed me the old town, the clock, and more. I bought crystal for T.O. (my nephew), Jackie, and Gábor. We got back about four. I gave her $20 for being my guide. We took photos, exchanged addresses, then we met up with Mom. Later, Ramona came and asked Mom and me to come to her house for coffee and Bailey's. It was nice to see another house not so grand as George's! Ramona's mom had worked in a hotel for 25 years. Her father, too, for 10, then he bought a pension 100 kilometers from here. He'd had the business for 10 years and came home Sundays and Mondays only, but he'd decided to sell it. Her parents were in their late sixties.

Ramona's boyfriend also worked in the hotel as a waiter. She was a waitress and bartender. She had taken the day off to be my tour guide.

Back at George's, I started writing in my journal and heard someone cough and a thump. After looking everywhere, I decided not to worry: George would be back soon. Around six, I saw a shadow in the hallway and called out, "Is that you,

Right: A cathedral; below: a Prague marketplace.

This bog was developed by a group of DuPont men who used it as a place to hunt and fish in Canada. They were able to obtain about 2,000 acres with the help of a couple of Canadian men. They formed a corporation, made bylaws, and had a membership limited to 30. Each paid a certain amount each year to cover expenses. Early in the year, they each designated what week they wanted when they could get off work. The "camp" had three cabins. One was old and had two uncomfortable beds and an ancient kitchen. It used to be the caretaker's place. Another old one was called "the honeymoon cabin." It was about to fall down. Another, new and built of logs with an open beam ceiling, was where the main kitchen and dining room were located. Anything electrical was run off of propane. They had a freezer, and the lights were propane with mantles. The main living room had a pool table, lounge area, a small kitchen, and bathroom. Its porch overlooked the lake to the south.

A new house, also log, was where Suzanne and Girard, the caretakers, lived. Suzanne was a great cook!

Furthest away was a duplex cabin where Jackie and I were. It had twin beds high enough

Looking out on the lake and dock.

Veronique and Andy.

Some of our group relaxing on the porch.

Early morning mist on the lake.

to put luggage under, a bathroom, and shower. Too small. The room was lit by propane.

They were going to build another log cabin to replace the honeymoon cabin. However, new regulations required a 50-foot setback from the water, so they couldn't just level the old log building and build another. The new one would be further east and overlook the bay inlet.

Lunch today: fish, pizza, lasagna, French toast, fruit, coffee.

I was actually up and out of the cabin a little after six. There was lots of mist on the lake. The water was warm, the air was cool. In 10 minutes, I caught four good trout on a Double Humpy. Then they quit. I decided to try another area.

The lake was so beautiful—the trees were pretty and the grass was very much like Wisconsin's. Lots of clover, too. June was said to be cold and buggy with black flies, so August was the best time to be here. Dick thought September was best, but I found the temperature to be very comfortable right now. It was quite a place.

There were five canoes at the dock on the lake, all flat-back ends with weights in front in case you wanted to paddle alone. The dock had a T for getting in and out and for tying boats up.

In the evening, I caught five trout. Girard helped you in and out of the canoe and cleaned everything we caught. I decided to watch him to see how he did it. He started at the tail with a very sharp knife, went up to just behind the Adam's apple, then cut across the jaw. Then, with thumb and finger, he grabbed the jaw and pulled all the guts out. I had a hard time doing it.

Our menu was: Saturday, late arrival—sandwiches and beer; Sunday, pork chops; Monday, roast beef.

Last night I went out right after dinner and caught nine in about 10 minutes on a Double Humpy.

Sunday night it poured rain, so we got a ride to our cabin. Monday night also rained hard. Monday, after lunch, we got the mountain bikes fixed up and we all rode to the Maine border. Andy had done this many times and said the view was pretty great. Well, when we got to the barrier, out popped a uniformed U.S. Game Warden on the Maine side. Fortunately, he was friendly. In all the years he had been on that trail, no

one had ever been on it. He asked if we were Americans and if we had IDs. He also went through Jackie's pack. Jackie had just said "it looks like a Third World country," meaning the barrier which had no sign to indicate a border, U.S. or Maine. It didn't have a Keep Out sign or anything.

We had eaten so much food! Not just pizza at one meal, but pizza, lasagna, French toast, fruit, chicken, crepes, roast beef with onions, veggies, eggs, bacon, and trout sushi. Groan!

There was a fly-tying area in front of the windows, which gave lots of light. That was a great idea for tying flies.

This was an especially great trip. I loved to fish! I knew how to handle a canoe, having grown up on a lake in Wisconsin. I was really grateful for having been invited.

Above: The whole group. Below: The cabins from the lake.

Antarctica with Brad, November

The shuttle came about five minutes early so, again, we were rushing. After we were finally onboard, Brad's comment was, "I can't believe we made it!"

It was a good thing we arrived at the airport with plenty of time, and it wasn't busy at American. Three girls opened all 200 cans of our film, took each roll out, looked into each end, and replaced them. Fortunately, at Dallas, we didn't have to repeat that, nor did we in Santiago, Chile.

There appeared to be about 27 people doing this "pre-trip" with several groups sharing the ship. One couple from California had camera gear that wouldn't end, taking only four or six shots per roll. They did their own developing and printing. I hadn't met them yet, but there was a couple who were members of the Explorers Club. Sandra and Marie seemed to be together and were taking a Muench workshop on landscape and wildlife photography. We knew nothing about it.

I didn't see much of Santiago. I went to bed early, but Brad went to the main plaza where there were magicians and entertainers. He was told they only perform on Sunday nights, so they wouldn't be there when we came back.

Our Hotel de San Francisco was right downtown and very nice. The only problem was we had one key, so when Brad came in at midnight, I had to let him in. There was free Internet in the hotel and a fitness center where nothing worked except the bike. They had bottled water there, so I filled our bottles for free.

The meals were elegant—lots of fruits and veggies and, of course, lamb. Everywhere you looked, there were sheep.

Next morning, we had a huge breakfast in the hotel, then boarded the bus for Punta Arenas to head to Puerto Natales. The land was really variable. Besides the mountains in the distance, some places were altiplano—flat and windy with nothing growing. The lake area had many sizes and shapes of lakes and fjords. We drove through large areas of moraines. I had to look at our bird book to list all the varieties we saw, plus a fox.

We stopped at a lovely place for lunch, arriving at our destination late in the afternoon. At the typically late hour of 8:30, we had dinner.

Puerto Natales to Torres del Paine

The next day, we left at 9:30 for another all-day drive to the granite towers of Torres del Paine. We had lunch at Pehoe Lake and later changed buses to cross a stream to reach Hosteria Las Torres, which was situated so you couldn't get a view of the Towers.

We made many stops along the way for pictures of guanaco (like llama). We saw many birds: rhea, great crested grebe, black-faced ibis, speckled teal, Chiloé wigeon, yellow-billed pintail, Andean condor, cinereous harrier, chimango caracara, crested caracara, white-winged coot, Magellanic oystercatcher, southern lapwing, Patagonian negrito, long-tailed meadowlark, great grebe, and the black-chested buzzard.

The Hosteria Las Torres was relatively new. Our rooms were so new that the shower curtain still had fold lines from the packaging. The shower curtain also had satin trim and lace. The bedsteads were crafted of beautiful blonde wood with head posts on either side of a high rounded top. The beds were twin in our room and were covered with blankets that had a lovely two-inch black plaid pattern in red, yellow, green, blue, and white—very cheery. The heavy lined, light-green drapes were gathered at the top and tied back with a plaid (matching) wide pull back. The light fixtures were matching wood (blonde) and swiveled at each bed for reading. The room had a three-piece chandelier and was carpeted in dark blue. The dried flower arrangements on the walls added a nice effect; one of them surrounded a straw hat. A very large mirror was the centerpiece of the bathroom with a frame of 8X11 tiny, diamond-shaped tiles in light blue, tan, and white, then surrounded by 10X10 tiles in a mottled light blue and white.

We watched slides at 7:30 and had dinner (a buffet) at 8:15. After the slide show, the huge buffet consisted of turkey, lamb, beef, salmon, and many veggies and more desserts than we needed. Wine and other drinks followed.

The auditorium where the slide show was held had three to four small windows very high up that shined into your face as you looked at the screen. As usual, there was no place to put the projector, so the slides didn't have a keystone effect. The projector was ancient, one of those push-in/pull-out kind. The gal doing the show needed someone to operate it, and Geoff did an OK job. One upper light was a real problem, but Brad finally turned it off just as a girl from the office came. She turned it back on! Laugh!

November 13

Our first destination in was a lake in Parque Nacional Torres del Paine. We had to change buses and get into a smaller bus after walking across a bridge that looked OK but wasn't. The bus we got into had been winched across.

We drove to where we could walk across some grey gravel to where beautiful icebergs were pushing their way downstream. We had a short walk right after getting to the bridge—a flat tire—so we walked up the road until they picked us up. Along the way, we were able to photograph a guanaco behind some rocks.

After 30 feet of icebergs, we arrived too late for lunch so had to wait until 2:30. At the park office, there was an observation platform above the lake, so we watched different birds—a coot (duck) feeding its baby.

Finally, we arrived at the falls. With the light getting low and the sun on the spires, we all had great fun photographing.

On the drive back, Brad spotted a puma—a lion—and that made our day!

November 14

We had choices today. I decided to go to a tiny lake at the foot of the Tres Torres. It was supposed to be four miles, but I think it was farther through the up-and-down terrain. The map said it was 4½ hours. I was on my way at 7:20. Brad had left earlier to go up a big hill where the view across would be good. I don't know when he left, but it was still dark out.

I reached the foot of the rockfall a little after ten, so their time of 4½ hours could have been OK. At eleven, a storm blew in: Since I was alone and had no idea if it would continue or clear up— and because of my knee (I was wearing my new brace)—I decided to turn back only 10 to 15 minutes from the lake. Going down wasn't easy. There were a lot of very steep places covered with roller ball bearing-type rocks, and I did badly in those spots, as did my knee.

I stopped at the *refugio* around one. I only had a $10 bill, which they wouldn't take, but the fellow behind the bar gave me a hot chocolate anyway. That was really nice of him. It was three before I arrived back at the Hosteria, where I got a cup of tea. Two of our group were headed my way as I went into my room. They informed me that Brad had come back for lunch then went hiking with some of the group, who had seen a puma with two babies.

I took a much-needed shower, letting the water stay in the tub to warm my aching feet. I washed clothes and turned up the heat to dry them. Then I turned my attention to packing, because we'd leave tomorrow, and I wrote a postcard.

November 15

We were taken northeast of the park area, where we saw a very interesting waterfall. Then we were taken to a huge cave that was extremely deep where, 1,000 to 1,200 years ago, Indians lived. Once it was discovered by a local farmer and word got out, the locals scavenged so much that archaeologists couldn't determine what had happened there. There were pieces of a huge beast that were found. From 1895 to 1897, Otto Nordenskjöld visited there and took some artifacts back to Sweden.

In this part of Chile, Indians who came from the sea were called "canoe" Indians. In the 1880s, the ruler commanded his army to exterminate all the Canoe Indians. A few survived, ending up being helpers on the farms. There was no written history, just handprints and guanaco paintings.

November 16

After a three-plus-hour drive to Punta Arenas, we spent some time at the airport (new and modern) where we didn't need to worry about our large duffels, only our carry-on bags. We had to send one bag of film through the "new x-ray" that was called "Proscan." I'd hoped it would be OK, and for some reason it was. We were an hour late taking off, so we had no time in Port Stanley, Falkland Islands, for more than a huge buffet lunch and tea. Then we were off to the ship and boarding. The cabin was #201 near the engines, several floors down in the middle of the ship and next to the reception desk. It was a good place to be in rough seas because it rolled less.

We had a mandatory lifeboat drill, as well as instruction on how to put on the life jackets. A meeting in the lounge introduced Captain Leif Skog, commander, and the crew, all of whom were very interesting folks. We heard about some of them over the next few days.

The ship, the *Endeavour*, was newly outfitted, and someone who had been on it before said it was like revisiting an old girlfriend and enjoying how she had grown and changed. The library was a quiet place, off which were the fitness center, sauna, and Internet access. The exercise room opened onto a back deck and included several treadmills, a bike, weights, an arm strengthening machine, sauna, and showers. The Internet area had two computer stations, so I sent a message to a friend, although I don't know if it went through. One could get a drink of coffee, tea, cocoa, or juice and eat cookies anytime during the day.

We had two days at sea to reach our ultimate goal, South Georgia Island. The seas were very high and many never left their cabins. David Muench and his companion were right across from us and sick for days.

There was an open-door policy onboard, so our cabin was never locked. We never needed to make our bed and were delivered clean towels every day.

November 17
We were on the ship all day and had rough seas. Our entire day consisted of various seminars, classes, a video presentation, and—of course—our meals with an afternoon tea. In the evening, Captain Leif and the crew welcomed us. Last, before bedtime, we had an 11:15 lecture and slide show from Conrad Field on the whales of the Southern Ocean.

November 18
On ship again all day and were entertained by the following:

Conrad Field showed slides of pitbull and blubber slug seals; Peter Harrison presented slides on "The Birds of South Georgia"; Morton Beebe, representing the Explorers Club and National Geographic, showed slides of Ernest Shackleton's crossing

Our ship, the Endeavour.

Places I visited in Grytviken. Clockwise: Shackleton's grave, a museum, and a church.

of the Antarctic, 1914-1917, plus the company's first year at the South Pole base.

November 19

We reached South Georgia Island today. It spanned 105 miles from northwest to southeast, and just over half of the island was permanently covered by snow and ice.

We had our first "wet" landing at Grytviken, established in 1904. We visited Ernest Shackleton's final resting place, the whales' graveyard, and made a toast to him. He was buried there at his wife's request in 1922. We also visited a museum and church before sailing on to Fortuna Bay north of Grytviken.

November 20: Stromness

It was a grey and nasty day when 36 of our group decided to hike on a trail of deep snow, from Fortuna Bay to Stromness, to experience the last four miles of Ernest Shackleton's desperate trek. Visibility was very bad until they reached the summit, where they could see the whole village of Stromness below.

Neither Brad nor I wanted to get cold and wet, so we didn't go. The ship motored back to Stromness, another former whaling station. Shackleton arrived here after a 36-hour traverse of South Georgia Island in an attempt to save his men, who were left behind on Elephant Island. He had been to Stromness before and, upon arriving,

Curious gentoo penguins.

the manager of the whaling station asked, "Who the hell are you?" Shackleton and two of his men were tired, frostbitten, bedraggled, and dirty.

There were thousands of gentoo penguins here. I sat on the beach and was soon surrounded by hundreds of them, all quite curious. This was on a long, black sandy beach. We also saw elephant seals and reindeer. Afterward, we stopped at Hercules Bay, home to large macaroni penguins.

November 21
We had an early wake up at 5:45, and our group loaded into Zodiacs at 6:30 a.m. Our destination, Prion Island, was named for the tiny prion seabird and breeding grounds to the very albatross we had seen slide

shows on. The island terrain was hard to walk on, with lots of hummocks and holes that were difficult not to fall into. We had to walk up a small hill where thousands of albatrosses had gathered on its edge and were laying eggs.

After lunch we stopped at Right Whale Bay where the shore was covered with fur seals that were the most vicious kind—very aggressive. Away from the shore were millions of king penguins, some marching in line and others prancing. They were very curious and came right up to us.

Word came that a German ship would rendezvous with us during dinner to bring us supplies and luggage that had been left behind. This meeting took place after dark and before leaving King Haakon Bay.

During dinner, several three- to four-story icebergs floated by. Then the captain announced that he would show us the cave where Shackleton and his crew landed before they began the trip to Stromness. It was dark, so the huge spotlights ran and were directed to a small bay where there was a brass

Below: Zodiac boat en route to Prion Island.

plaque an Irish group put up while doing a reenactment of Shackleton's journey. In the beam of the light we could see hundreds of blue petrels. Two landed on the deck, and one of the guys picked one up and showed us its coloring before letting it go.

Friday, November 22
We were on the sea for two more days, now on our way to Elephant Island. Icebergs became quite common, some very tall and others just small ones.

Geoff Renner gave an excellent talk on the geology of Antarctica. The second lecture by Explorers Club member Morton Beebe was extremely bad!

Chinstrap penguins surrounding a bust of Captain Luis Pardo on Elephant Island. It was Pardo's ship, the Chilean naval steamer, Yelcho, *that rescued Shackleton's crew.*

After lunch, they showed part one of *Shackleton*, a TV show starring Kenneth Branagh. It was excellent!

Rob McCall talked about the greenhouse effect and the changes of the climate and Antarctica.

Just before dinner, Peter Harrison presented slides called "Penguins 101."

November 24

We woke up at about 3:00 a.m., surrounded by blue icebergs. Around 5:30, we dropped anchor close to Elephant Island, where Shackleton and his 22 men had landed after drifting and floating on ice for three months after their ship was destroyed by sea ice. It was from this place that Shackleton and five others set out for South Georgia Island 800 miles away with only a sextant to navigate by in cloudy weather. It was 137 days before rescue arrived for the crew in the form of the Chilean naval steamer, *Yelcho*, captained by Luis Pardo. According to one of our guides, Peter Harrison, Shackleton had been there from 1914 to 1917.

We were lucky that the waves weren't so high that we couldn't disembark. The guides cut steps in the ice and put down a rubber pad for us to step on so we wouldn't slip and fall. We could stay only long enough to take a picture and say we had been there. The actual landing place was farther to our right.

According to Peter Harrison, the seas had always been so rough that it had been five years since anyone was able to set foot on the landing site. We surely had been lucky.

Brad and me kayaking.

We had a mandatory kayak briefing, then saw the last part of *Shackleton*. Still excellent!

November 25

We navigated through Gerlache Strait, a wide channel separating Anvers Island and Brabant Island from the Antarctic Peninsula. We were able to kayak and go ashore onto Antarctica, the fifth largest and southernmost continent on our beautiful planet. We cheered and toasted everyone who had ever stepped foot on it.

Brad and me, bundled up against the cold.

2000   2001   **2002**   2003   2004   2005   2006   2007   2008   2009

Australia with Liz in June

After my trip to Europe in 1950 when I was a college student, I made up my mind that I would take my nieces and nephews wherever they wanted to go after they graduated. I felt everyone needed to see another part of the world. My oldest grandniece, Liz Faris, chose Australia, so off we went.

The flight from California was LONG—14½ hours! We arrived in Sydney at 6:30 in the morning and were met by Tessa and taken to our hotel, the Sebel Pier One near the Sydney Harbour Bridge. Our rooms weren't ready, so we ended up meeting in a freezing business center for orientation. When our room was ready, we freshened up then went out for a walk and lunched at the Hero of Waterloo Dungeon. We had dinner on the waterfront at Circular Quay, the main ferry dock in Sydney. I was in bed by 8:30.

Sydney, Australia.

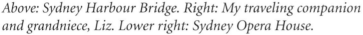

Above: Sydney Harbour Bridge. Right: My traveling companion and grandniece, Liz. Lower right: Sydney Opera House.

June 18

I slept pretty well and woke just two times, once at 1:30 and again at 5:30. I decided to go to the exercise room and work out there.

We took a half-day bus tour and saw many sights: The Rocks, Bondi Beach, Mrs Macquarie's Chair, and Darling Harbour. We had lunch at the Blackbird in Darling Harbor, then visited the Sydney Aquarium. Fantastic aquarium! We took the monorail and rocketed back to Circular Quay; had dinner out later by taking a taxi to a Thai restaurant. Got back by 8:30 and hit the sack.

June 19

We walked to Costello's, the opal store. Liz bought a lovely necklace and ring for Anne, her mom, and for herself; I bought a necklace for Brad's gal, Rosmery. We then had a long cruise that included breakfast onboard and saw all the expensive homes on the bay, including Russell Crowe's mansion, the top floor of which had been transformed from a deckhouse to an apartment on the waterfront. We then had a lovely tour of the Sydney Opera House. Last year, an English fellow and friend climbed the tallest spire and painted "NO WAR" in red. They had their lawyer there, anticipating trouble. Up to then, there had been no security around the opera house, so by the time the police came, it was done. Now there was security around the entire place. We had the afternoon free and went shopping, and Liz bought a jacket and blouse. We walked forever up Pitt Street to the mall, where we had something to eat in the food court then walked back to our hotel the long way, winding up at the Sydney Tower, the second-tallest observation tower in the Southern Hemisphere at 1,014 feet. It was sunset, and it was really unbelievable how tall it was. Sydney was such a beautiful city there on the water's edge.

June 20

This was our last day in Sydney, and Liz and I slept in. After breakfast, we walked to the cruise dock and took a ferry to Taronga Zoo. The zoo was exceptionally well done and took us four hours to see everything. Back at Sydney, we walked up George Street looking for a bank and opals. We both changed money. I used a credit card but didn't get a receipt for a $200 debit, which worried me. We finally took the monorail partway back, then got on the bus, stopping and eating at Rossini's. The waiters there were funny! We arrived back at the hotel by six, watched a bad movie, and packed. We had to be up at six and gone by seven.

June 21

Had the suitcases out the door by 6:30 and took the bus at seven to the airport. Our flight, three hours long, was to Cairns (pronounced "Cans"), a settlement that began as a collection of tents housing 300. Here, we boarded a bus and drove for two to three hours to the resort.

After Captain Cook landed at Botany Bay (Sydney) in April 1770, he sailed up the coast and struck the reef off Daintree, and had a terrible time getting the ship off of it. Subsequently called "Cape Tribulation"—our destination—Cook and his crew collected over 200 plant species, many of which they'd never seen before. They also saw their first fruit-eating "flying red fox," the local bat. They counted 170 species of birds.

We arrived at a resort at Coconut Beach in the rain forest. The individual cabins were screened in on all sides and had movable shutters and fans. The furniture was rattan with a king bed and could be made into two smaller beds. You could hear what everyone was saying because the cabins were open and so close together.

The beach was sandy and there were warning signs regarding three crocodiles and the jellyfish. A bottle of red vinegar was sitting by the sign, and you were to pour it on a sting if one of them got you. This time of year, they were mostly gone, but diving and snorkeling were done way out on the other side of the reef because of them.

June 22

We didn't have a wake-up call, but Liz wanted to do yoga ($20) at seven, so we got up at six. After eight, we ate breakfast then were taken on a bus by Siggy, a German

2000   2001   2002   **2003**   2004   2005   2006   2007   2008   2009

guide, to the rain forest. She was so full of info that I couldn't possibly remember all of it, starting with the poo of birds: It has seeds in it that are deposited high in the forest. After all the sun and moisture, the seeds sprout and the plants grow down to the ground. In particular, the tentacles on ferns have barbs that allow them to latch onto other vegetation, so they can climb trees and reach for the light. Every plant seemed to have a job in keeping the other plants growing. While on the tour, we spotted flying red foxes that looked like large bats, and also cockatoos.

Afterward, on the river, we saw a baby crocodile and two large ones. On the drive back we saw a cassowary—Australia's largest flightless rain forest bird—cross the road and disappear into the forest.

We were in Daintree National Park, but there was no such thing as a "dain" tree. There was, however, marvelous Daintree tea that we hoped to buy in the supermarket. After lunch, we sat by the pool and read. It was our first lazy day.

There were 14 world heritage sites in Australia, including the Great Barrier Reef and several tropical rain forests. The forest at Cape Tribulation was estimated to be 100 million years old.

The GBR was 38 kilometers offshore; the Cassowary Coast, south of Cairns, had as many as 25 offshore islands, including the resort islands of Dunk, Bedarra, and one of the world's largest island national parks, Hinchinbrook.

Australian road sign. Don't see this one in the U.S.!

Some Aussie terms: Banana Bender = Queenslander; barbie = barbecue; fair dinkum = real deal; sheila = woman; ocker = a simple breed of man; snag = a sausage; bonzer = something pleasing, i.e., It's a bonzer day, isn't it?

Winter was the dry, hot season; May to October was warm with low rainfall, sunshine, and breezes. You could only swim from April to October because, from November to March, the box jellyfish—"stingers," as they called them—were in the coastal waters. The venom of this jellyfish was one of the most deadly in the world. Seawater temperatures ranged from 23°C in July to 29°C in February. Average rainfall was 186 mm per month, or 2,010 mm per year.

Monday, June 23

After a drive, we stopped at Port Douglas where we boarded a catamaran and cruised out to an island reef to snorkel. We actually saw more while on the glass bottom boat than when we were snorkeling! Liz wasn't comfortable until she had a "snake," a long rubber tube. I held her hand and took her around. Afterward, we drove on to

Cairns, where we stayed in small apartments. A washer and dryer were supplied, but Liz's clothes were all heavy cotton that took forever to dry. It was very humid here.

June 24

We traveled up a steep railroad grade to Kuranda, where we visited a butterfly museum. It wasn't as good as ours, but the guided tour made it worth the $10. We shopped, and I bought a boomerang while Liz bought a didgeridoo, boomerang, and clap sticks. It poured most of the day.

I left my luggage wheelie in Daintree, which was too bad, for it was so lightweight. Tess was going to try to get it sent down.

We bought chicken and coleslaw at a Woolworths for dinner, while the others went to Tjapukai Aboriginal Cultural Park for dinner and a show. Tjapukai was intelligently presented and a culturally fair presentation of Aboriginal myths, customs, and history. It was the top attraction in Cairns.

All these extras were costing $50 to $100, and with me paying for Liz, it had been adding up.

It would be good to move on in the morning to Alice Springs.

June 25

The flight across the central area of Australia to Alice Springs was very much like our Four Corners. There were long, long stretches like washes, some larger and some smaller. Dry riverbeds cut through some of them. I would've liked to take a flight around it to see it from the air.

After leaving our bags at the hotel, we were bused to the Ayers Rock and Cultural Centre. Then we drove around it and went to another rock outcropping. After spending

Ayers Rock at sunset.

2000   2001   2002   **2003**   2004   2005   2006   2007   2008   2009

a short time there, we returned to Ayers Rock, where Tessa and John (the driver) spread out chips and salsa, cheese and crackers, and champagne—orange juice, too, if you wanted a mimosa. We spent about an hour there with 10 or more other busloads of mostly Japanese tourists. Everyone was eating and having champagne. The entire idea was to watch the changing color of Ayers Rock as the sun set.

When we got back to the hotel, we did a bit of shopping and then went to our room.

June 26

We had a five o'clock wake-up call and made it to the bus by 6:15 to travel to the trailhead. We walked around Ayers Rock for two hours.

By bus, we stopped at Camel Place, where Liz rode a camel. We had lunch at the station and went next to School of the Air, which covered 700,000 acres and had 7,000 head of cattle. The kids there learned by using the computer and radio. The 10-day lessons came in the mail and were sent back to the teacher. Solahart solar panels were used for heating. Their water was domestic; they had diesel for vehicles and electricity. One year's supply of diesel was $70,000.

When we returned, we went out to dinner and Tess had a great kangaroo dish.

June 27

We were up at the crack of dawn to go ballooning. The basket was twice as large as usual—it held 12 plus the pilot. We had enough propane for one hour, and an FAA inspector was with us. We all helped to get the balloon filled then climbed in before takeoff with the basket on its side. Each of four sections held three people, and there were ropes to hang onto while it was on its side. When we were upright, we could stand up. We were only 40 feet above the ground for a long time, due to wind direction. Later, we were 350 feet above the ground. We saw a large group of kangaroos just before we landed. Great fun! Helped pack up the balloon, got it flat on the trailer, then drove off to a place for breakfast—really good. We met a retired couple who were from Brisbane.

Tess met us and took us to the Aboriginal tour. The guide, who was an Aboriginal, wasn't very good. We saw some rock art after wading a pond near where the guide grew up, then went to another station where we had tea and bread with molasses. We ended up riding a scooter back to town.

Liz riding a camel.

Finding ourselves with a free afternoon, I decided to wash my hair, use the Internet, and shop. At 5:30, we went to the telegraph station where Alice Springs started. There was a demonstration of boomerang throwing by Alex, also whip cracking, then we saw what was supposed to be the spring.

For dinner, we went out to a steak house, which was terrible! Entertainment was a single singer, who was too loud.

June 28: The Ghan Train

After seeing the Royal Flying Doctor Service, the Central Australian Aviation Museum, and the local art, we had to go back to town because the train we were taking to Adelaide was late. I checked e-mail, bought subs for lunch, had a Basket of Robins, and roamed town where the Aboriginals had rioted the night before, breaking shop windows and bending steel mesh grids over store windows. This was a continual problem, along with drugs and alcohol.

Finally, we boarded The Ghan train in mid-afternoon, two hours late because of water on the tracks up north. Like others in the tour, we had a sleeping compartment with upper and lower bunks, a shower, toilet, and sink. The room was so tiny that there was no using the toilet! On our car were a smoking room, lounge, and dining room. We had a really nice dinner with great dark chocolates for dessert following. We watched for camels and kangaroos but saw none.

Here I am having dinner on The Ghan.

One of the gals in our group, Dee, had an Uno deck, so we played until eleven then both went to bed. I slept well and only woke once when the train stopped. The stars were spectacular.

June 29

Up by 6:10 with an offering of coffee or tea. There was no time to shower and we had to hurry eating to make the tour.

It was cloudy and beginning to rain. We traveled through farm country where we could see an abundance of things growing. Road signs along the way included "Overtaking Lane" and "End of Take Away." Dee had eaten a chicken sandwich the night before and got food poisoning. She was up sick all night on the train. They took her to the hospital for a half day while we toured Adelaide.

A lot of the buildings were very much like what one would see in New Orleans, where the steel decorative fences that served as ballast on the early ships were used.

2000   2001   2002   **2003**   2004   2005   2006   2007   2008   2009

Otherwise, we visited a winery and tasted a bunch of wine. My camera bumped the wall in the toilet and popped open. I had to quickly find some duct tape to hold it shut. Fortunately, a Shell station was nearby and I found some there. That roll would be partially ruined.

After a dinner of whitefish, we walked to a nearby penguin sanctuary/park. Using colored flashlights, we walked through an area where the penguins had burrows. These were called "little" penguins rather than fairy penguins. They had their fuzzy brown babies and made a lot of noise. Fun! Liz really got a kick out of it.

As we drove to the ferry in Adelaide, we saw a gang of grey kangaroos. The four of us—Kathleen, Liz, Dee, and I—who had played Uno last night played again while on the ferry. By that time it was dark, so we couldn't see anything anyway.

Koala head.

The temperature here was very much like our fall weather. We had been lucky with the weather, as it rained while we were on the train and rained while we were having dinner. Because it got dark early, it would've been better if I'd had 400 speed film instead of 100 and 200.

There were two couples in our tour group: Tim and Mary and JoAnn and Jim. JoAnn and

Liz feeding a kangaroo.

Jim had hearing problems—for that matter, several others did also—so the first pitch of conversation was usually high. It didn't help that JoAnn didn't listen. Kathleen and Mary were sisters. Mary was the only smoker among us. She smoked outside, but when she came back in, her breath was so bad I couldn't stand to be near her. One morning, I had to get up and leave the breakfast table.

Cindy and Donna lived in Oregon, Wisconsin. Donna was a radiologist and Cindy was into health, but she was so thin that she looked anorexic. Donna wasn't so bad. They obviously were a "couple." Cindy wore a wedding ring and Donna had a baby ring on her left little finger. They had a lot of money and traveled four months out of the year. They had recently bought a small Mercedes, so small that golf clubs wouldn't fit inside. Another gal in the group, Annette, taught school in Minnesota.

Monday, June 30

We departed at 8:45 for an all-day bus tour on Kangaroo Island. Located on the south of the island, Seal Bay was covered with seals. A wooden walkway wound around the beach, and we hiked along it, staying at least nine to 10 feet from the Australian

sea lions there. The lion was so-called because of the light hair on the back of its neck, which the sailors thought made it look like a lion with a male ruff. Lunch was at Beckwith Farm and while there, we wandered through the gum trees where the koalas were munching high in the trees. We were able to take pictures of small kangaroos also.

Next stop was Flinders Chase National Park, where we looked for kangaroos but only saw koalas. The rocks there were remarkable with very unusual carved-out formations, and the whole area was pretty spectacular. I didn't take any pictures.

Next, at Cape du Couedic Lighthouse, we wandered down a wooden path to the cliffs where the New Zealand fur seals were frolicking in the rocks and sea spray. We visited a eucalyptus oil distillery and saw how the leaves were crushed to get the oil out of them, then it was sent to various places to be used in a variety of products— soap, disinfectant, insect repellent, decongestant, stain remover, cleaner, penetrating oil, and to soothe bites and stings. We were all given a sample.

Finally, we drove to dinner then went on to the hotel, where we once again played Uno before bed.

Australian sea lions.

Tuesday, July 1

We were up early to fly to Adelaide then to Melbourne and, finally, Hobart in Tasmania. Hobart was an excellent city situated on a large bay with a bridge very much like the Golden Gate in San Francisco.

Out for dinner, we ate Italian, then stayed in an old restored hotel, the Lenna of Hobart. It was very cold there. An electric heater barely kept up, and the hallway was ice cold. Our beds had electric pads under the sheets!

July 2

We drove through hops country, where I took several pictures of the oast houses where the hops were processed. We took an hour's walk in Tall Tree National Park. It had several waterfalls and the climate was quite damp. We saw a tiny kangaroo-like animal in the forest. After a great lunch, I took some reflective pictures at an old farm where everyone saw a platypus and lots of geese—some black and some white. The man who started the hops farm was religious, so Bible quotes were visible on the outside of the building.

We got back to Hobart by mid-afternoon and went shopping—I bought a set of mugs along with creamer and sugar bowls, to be shipped—then had dinner at the home of Margaret and Wayne. He was a carpenter, and she had been a realtor for 25 years. He did the cooking, and she was glad! They invited the tour group in every week, which they had done for the last 3½ years. The meal Wayne cooked included chicken, fish, chips, coleslaw, carrots, corn, and two desserts. We took our own wine, and I brought a merlot that had a house with a scene on the label.

July 3

More shopping with a lunch at Merles Fish and Chips. We took a morning tour of the city, which I found very interesting. There were many beautiful old buildings in Hobart, but there were also new, very modern ones going up. The real estate here was skyrocketing. The island itself was very wet and humid.

Back at the Lenna, we got ready to catch our flight to Melbourne in the afternoon.

July 4

After stopping at the Box Hill Gardens, we went on to see Captain Cook's Cottage, then shopped one more time. Our last dinner was at an Italian place where we were offered two desserts, one made by Tess that was a meringue that had sparklers in it for the Fourth of July.

July 5

We flew home, which took all day.

Seventy-Five and Alive

In younger days I worried not
If I was 20, 30, 40, or plumb shot.

There always was another day,
No time to fall asleep in the hay.

I took each year as a chance to see
If I could earn a different degree.

The one I sought was World Traveler,
No time to be a youthful idler.

I took to Europe by foot and train,
Hiked the Milford Track in pouring rain.

There was Peru and Mount Chinchey,
Rappeling the Maiden on belay.

Exploring canyons and climbing cliffs,
Searching for Algerian glyphs.

Rafting rivers, diving for pearls,
Jumping rope with Indian girls.

Then on to Nepal and breathless heights,
Also Alaska and mosquito bites.

I saw Morocco, Turkey, and the Chinese,
India, Pakistan, Egypt, Taiwanese.

Now, one would figure time's running out,
Something would slow me, perhaps the gout.

I've been hit from behind while riding my skis,
And being knocked from my bike was not a breeze.

The horse that threw me, down in Peru,
And the donkey I fell from should have been a clue.

I'm losing my teeth, a toe bothers me,
But I can't stop yet, there's more to see.

—Julia Johnson

2003 Monument Valley
Plane Ride
with Gene Fouchet

A Wedding!

Would you believe that I had no travels to some far-off exotic country this year?! But what I can report was that there was a wedding at 2:00 p.m. on April 4, 2004. Yes, indeed!! Brad finally found that very special young lady he wanted to spend the rest of his life with.

I must say that I wasn't surprised, because my new daughter-in-law—Rosmery (correctly spelled)—was a dear, sweet person. Anyone who met her immediately fell in love with her. I felt so very fortunate. Brad had met Rosmery about six years ago in Peru while guiding one of his trekking groups. He took people to Machu Picchu with a couple nights spent in Cusco to get acclimated. Rosmery was from Cusco, and they met in the Hotel Monastario where she was delivering a flower arrangement made by her mother. Rosmery's cousin worked in the hotel and, through her, Brad kept track of Rosmery over the following years. He finally located her in Miami and convinced her to move to Boulder, go to the International English Institute to learn English, then come to Ridgway to try life together to see if a relationship would work.

Well, work it did! About a year later, they decided to tie the knot. It was almost springtime but in Ridgway, the weather was still "iffy." Sometimes it rained, sometimes it snowed, and it was still cold. It kind of surprised me that they were actually going to get married. I had just left there and been home in Boulder only a day or so when they announced that the following weekend, on Sunday, April 4, they would marry at a place called "Inspiration Point," about a thousand feet above the floor of Pleasant Valley.

Brad and Rosmery's neighbor, Bill Allred, escorts her down the aisle.

It had a spectacular view across the valley south to the east-west San Juan Mountain range with 14,000-foot Mount Sneffels right in the middle.

So I hurried back to Ridgway on Tuesday, a 360-mile drive, and proceeded to help Rosmery plan a small wedding. This was no easy feat in this town of 700 where the streets (there are no sidewalks) were rolled up at 5:30 every day. The 30-minute drive north brought us to the main shopping area at a Walmart or a Home Depot, but no wedding dress stores, and only a City Market florist and bakery. You get the picture.

Believe it or not, in 3½ days, Rosmery and I had ordered flowers (designed by Rosmery) and a cake from City Market; found a man (who turned out to be someone Brad knew and was a climber) to marry them (no minister in town was free); and made a

Brad and Rosmery exchanging vows with George Gardner officiating.

Everyone's happy the ceremony is over! From left: Scott Thorburn, Brad, George, Rosmery, and Rosmery's friend, Ursula Crystal.

long-distance call to Miami to their Ridgway neighbors, who lived there part-time and had just returned from several months in Roatan (building a house). Would Bill, the husband, drive Rosmery to the wedding site and usher her in to the overlook? He was delighted and honored to be asked, and they would arrive in Ridgway the night before the wedding. A restaurant for a wedding reception dinner was chosen after much discussion as to which one of the two to choose from had the better margaritas. But the neighbors who were not yet home from Roatan/Miami offered their home, rather than the restaurant, for the finale of cake and champagne.

Rosmery wore a size ZERO! Do I have all you ladies' attention? Yes, *zero*. So trying to purchase a wedding dress in "Podunk country" was out of the question. She and Brad decided on a sequin-covered, peach, off-the-shoulder dress that Brad liked her in. With everything pretty much taken care of, Rosmery and I actually had time to make little nettings tied with peach bows and filled with birdseed for everyone to throw after they said, "I do." We also bought 18 box cameras so everyone could take pictures.

The day of the wedding, I put up signs directing folks to Inspiration Point above the valley floor and discovered that the trail, about 50 yards up a slight hill, was nothing but muddy clay! Announcing this to Brad and that we had better have the wedding at the neighbors' home, he took a look. Someone he knew had recently cut down a tree and conveniently chipped the remains, so he and a friend, with wheelbarrow and shovels, distributed the chips along the trail, put a large 4X5 entrance

Peter Appenzeller, a friend of Brad's since childhood.

Left to right: Larry Lane, Blues Voisard, Rosmery, Brad, Carl Darnell, and Jaime.

Left to right: Dale Johnson and his wife, Frandee, Rosmery, Brad, me, and Carl Darnell.

floor mat from their garage where he wanted them to stand, and—voila! It was perfect!

They had written their own vows, pretty much identical. Brad's were in English, Rosmery's in Spanish. The day came, the guests came, the time came, and everyone found their way to the appointed spot. The sun, which we had not seen all week long, came out for one hour between 2:00 and 3:00 p.m. It was warm enough for Rosmery not to be cold in her off-the-shoulder dress. It couldn't have been better.

How many folks do you know who would go to an outdoor hot springs pool following a wedding? Well, everyone had brought their swimsuit, and they headed south to Ouray to the pool before having dinner back at the Adobe in Ridgway, followed by cake and champagne at the neighbors' home. What a lovely affair!

The happy bride and groom.

WHEELING AND DEALING IN REAL ESTATE

For me, 2005 was the year of real estate wheeling and dealing. I had purchased 35 acres several years ago about a 15-minute drive from where Brad lived, but now there were some very unfriendly neighbors who had bought land just to the east of mine. First, they put locks on two of my gates in my newly erected fence. Then they planted tall trees between me and where my house was going to be built, blocking my view of the Cimarron Range. They refused to let me or my neighbors to the west clean out irrigation ditches which brought water to our pastures. When they wrote me a letter just before Thanksgiving telling me to install a weir in the irrigation ditch and install a new fence with half on their side and half on my side, with locks on both sides—that was the straw that broke the camel's back!

I had heard through the grapevine that someone wanted my land bad enough to pay me twice what I had paid for it. My western neighbors had told me they would like first right of refusal if I ever decided to sell. Aha! So I went to them and said, "I'm going to sell! Do you want it?" They did, and in a matter of five months, I had located the owners of the land across the road from Brad. I agreed to the price they wanted, knowing what I would get for the 35 I was selling. In April, we closed on the 35 and I bought 44. No neighbors, just more than a 180-degree view of the entire valley and spectacular views of the entire San Juan range of mountains—much better than on the 35.

So then I could build my new home just a five-minute walk from Brad's front door. Everyone was happy, especially me, since I did two real estate deals without a realtor's commission, plus the townhouse I sold a year ago in Frisco without using a realtor. I was smelling like a rose! All the local realtors were mad at me. One even called and said, "I think you should go to work for us."

I'd been in Ridgway since late

Brad with a Peruvian friend, Jaime.

Several of Rosmery's family surprised us by showing up at the airport. Left: Brad, Rosmery, and Aunt Doris. Right: Rosmery with her mom, Ayda.

April when Brad left for Peru. Rosmery went with him this year, as she could now leave the U.S. and return without immigration problems. It was the first time in four years she had been back to see her family. They went a couple weeks prior to when Brad's treks started so they could attend a wedding and spend a week with her family. As it turned out, her mom was giving a family barbecue for them on May 4, my 77th birthday. When they realized that, they insisted I fly down also. It was the first time the two of them were there together, making the barbecue special for everyone to meet the newlyweds and the new mother-in-law.

It was a grand affair, high on a hillside overlooking

Above: The view of Cusco from Rosmery's uncle's house.
Below: The chefs keeping an eye on the barbecue.

Entrance gate and rope bridge at Rosmery's uncle's house where the barbecue was held.

Trying to maintain the birthday pisco sour custom! I just couldn't do it.

the sprawling city of Cusco. There were about 40 people there—aunts, uncles, cousins, cousins' children, etc. One uncle in the family owned this very large home overlooking the valley where they always held annual family gatherings. Everyone crowded around a huge barbecue pit with stone tabletops and seats surrounding the oversized grill, where chicken and pork sizzled. The scent of cooking meat wafted through the crowd. The national drink, pisco sours, was plentiful, along with beer and wine.

When it came time for dessert, a very large, gorgeously decorated cake with 77 candles flaming was brought out. The custom was for everyone to clap and sing happy birthday while the birthday person chugalugged a frigid pisco sour. The drink was so cold that it made my temples and forehead ache! I just couldn't do it. Rosmery's aunt had made the cake, and her mom presented me with a lovely bouquet of roses.

The following five days were a whirlwind of activities, trying to see and do everything. We rode 10 hours in a chauffeured van to another village where Rosmery's brother and sister-in-law ran the in-laws' hotel. We drove over a 12,000-foot pass on a very bumpy dirt road through farm country full of tiny villages and beautiful mountain terrain. Mother's Day was spent there with the family.

Finally, I returned home with fond memories of Rosmery's family and the adventures we had together. I was in Ridgway for only a few days when I flew to Wisconsin for my family reunion. I was there just four days when I started coughing. A quick trip to Urgent Care at the hospital resulted in a chest x-ray which said I didn't have pneumonia. So I was given the strongest antibiotic known to man, Z-Pak. I was to take two to start and one each day for four more days.

Top left: The hotel Rosmery's brother and sister-in-law managed.
Top right: Rosmery's brother, David's, sons on their way to school.
Bottom left: Rosmery with her dad and her brother, David.
Right: A lovely hibiscus bloom.

It didn't faze my cough. Back in Ridgway, I saw a second doctor who gave me Cipro, which was not the thing to take: It was for intestinal problems. So I coughed 24 hours a day from May 21 until July 29. I lost 12 pounds, and it about killed me. Finally, after I stopped coughing, I saw a pulmonologist in Montrose who said I'd had whooping cough! Then I discovered that Boulder had had the highest number of whooping cough patients anywhere in the U.S., and the area around Ridgway had had an epidemic the previous year. Now there was a national epidemic. If you had a vaccination as a kid but never had whooping cough, you needed to get a booster shot.

Finally well again and back in Ridgway, I eagerly awaited the day my foundation would be dug and the house would get started. It wasn't until fall that things began to take place. I had taken pictures of every step. Having waited 4½ years for this to happen, you'd think I would have chosen all the fixtures, tile, cupboards, etc., but that wasn't the case. I was soon on the hunt for all the things that go into a newly built

2000   2001   2002   2003   2004   **2005**   2006   2007   2008   2009

Ridgway house construction and finished interior/exterior views.

house, and to do that in Ridgway wasn't easy: I only had access to a Walmart and Home Depot in Montrose for such supplies.

On December 27 I was back in Boulder, shuttling back and forth to Denver to look for faucets, kitchen cabinets, etc. In early January, I drove back to Ridgway and started skiing at Telluride. Perhaps you'd heard about the record amounts of snow that had fallen at Vail, Copper Mountain, Breckenridge, and the other ski areas on the Front Range? Over a 100 inches! Unfortunately, Telluride hadn't received enough to make skiing enjoyable. Pleasant Valley, running east and west outside of Ridgway and surrounded by high peaks, had also somehow missed those storms. When it snowed, it had been just in the mountains, not in the valley. That was great for building a house, but not for skiing. The one big storm we had left 18 inches. They didn't have the roof on the house yet, so Brad and I shoveled 3,000 square feet of snow off the pre-floor of my house. It took us three hours! Later, I ran into a friend who was also building. She said they hired someone to shovel theirs to the tune of $900! We were glad that WE had done ours and saved that money.

May I come in, please?

New Home, Europe, Peru

I finally got settled here in Ridgway, Colorado. One room was still in somewhat of a mess and may end up staying that way. It was meant to be a projection room where I could show slides, but I have yet to do that. Also, I no longer take regular pictures with a camera that uses film; like most everyone else, I'd gone to digital.

Needless to say, I hadn't been doing much traveling, but since you last heard from me, I think I took my new daughter-in-law to Florence, Italy, and back. It was a University of Colorado alumni trip which I felt was too short and

Trevi Fountain, the Colosseum, and the Roman Forum were some of the sights I saw on the trip to Italy with Rosmery.

2000   2001   2002   2003   2004   2005   **2006**   2007   2008   2009

not very well organized, as far as getting people from Denver to Florence and back. The guides we had were excellent. Rosmery, my daughter-in-law, was an artist and, of course, was very interested in all the art, but we didn't have enough time to really digest it.

Then in June, I took my second grandniece, Ali Faris, to Peru. I started something four years ago when I offered to take her older sister anywhere in the world that she might want to go as a high-school graduation present. I should've known that she didn't really want to go when she couldn't come up with a destination. Therefore, when it got to be April and we needed to make reservations, I decided to make it easy on myself and have Brad organize a trip for us to Peru and Machu Picchu, one of the wonders of the world. I believe strongly that all kids need to visit a foreign country, preferably a Third World country, when they graduate from high school. It made them appreciate what they had and realize how lucky they were to be an American, living in a country that had running water, central heat, electricity, and enough money to buy food.

Unfortunately, this grandniece didn't seem interested in anything we were going to do. She didn't even apply for her passport until April 5, and we were leaving June 1. When May rolled around and she still didn't have a passport, I spent hours and hours on the phone trying to figure out how to get it in time for our departure. On Memorial

Day Weekend, I heard that President Bush was not at his ranch, so I called the White House and asked to speak to him. I didn't even get laughed at but was cordially told to call back on the Tuesday after Memorial Day. I did that and got the Comment Department and a very nice lady who patiently listened to my tale. She said she

Below: One of our accommodations in Peru.

would tell the President. I asked her, "When?" She said she would tell him that night. "Liar, liar!" I felt like saying.

My grandniece's father contacted their congressman who knew our family and who my brother had helped get elected. Even HE couldn't do anything and said we needed to go to Chicago to the Federal Building. Chicago was a three-hour drive from where my niece lived. By the time we realized we were stuck with having to make that trip, she was having finals, and then there was graduation. That left just one day, a Friday, before the Monday when we were leaving for Peru.

So after graduation, we left home at 11:30 and drove into the teeth of a tornado between Milwaukee and Chicago. The semis roared by, spraying the windshield with water so we couldn't see the road. It was a wonder we even got there at 3:30! We had reservations in a nearby hotel and had a 4:30 wake-up call. We had been told to be at the Federal Building early. We thought if we were there around four, we might be first in line, but we were

Hot springs pools.

On our trip we met up with Rosmery, who was visiting her mother, Ayda. Ayda lived in an area of Peru where there really wasn't anything—no stores or schools—so she started a small school near her home. When we were there, it just happened that they were having school that day, and Ayda had asked Rosmery to show the children some pictures on a calendar from Utah. That's when I snapped this picture.

The pictures on the next several pages are from the trip to Machu Picchu with my grandniece, Ali Faris.

about 250th! People were asleep in sleeping bags and lying on lawn chaises, had coolers and blankets, and it looked like they were waiting for some big concert. We took up ranks and waited and waited. I went around the building to the head of the line to see what time the person first in line had gotten there. He had driven from Cincinnati, Ohio, and arrived at 2:00 a.m. I had written on those tiny 1X2-inch Post-it notes the telephone numbers of the White House and the Comment Department. I must have had about 35 Post-its. When people were sufficiently awake, I stood in front of about 50 sleepy people and asked, "Are you as upset as I am about having to come here and sleep on the sidewalk in order to get a passport?" Heads nodded and someone said, "Yeah!" "Well," I told them, "I called the White House, and I think if we all called the White House and told the Comment Department what we've had to go through, it might make an impression on someone there. Do any of you want the phone number?" I handed out all 35 Post-its to people who said they would have their entire family call!

Then I returned to my place in line, which was now going around in back of the Federal Building, and I couldn't believe the scene to get a passport that had been applied for two months earlier! I called the *Chicago Tribune* and asked to speak to a reporter. I told them to get someone down to the Federal Building and see what was going on. They asked if I hadn't read the paper,

because they had had several articles about people trying to get their passports. I told them I was not from the area, hadn't read the paper, and doubted if any of the articles indicated how many hundreds of people were sleeping on the sidewalk with a line that would soon go entirely around the building. They needed to GET A REPORTER DOWN HERE! I hung up. About 30 minutes later, there was a reporter with a cameraman taking pictures, and I was told later that the report had hit national TV news that night.

About 10:00 a.m., we finally were allowed into the building. I asked one of the female gun-toting guards if there was a restroom we could use. I was loudly told, "Get over there in line; we are not here to answer questions. Do you have food there? Get rid of it! You can't have food in here! What is that? Coffee? Take it outside. Be quiet!" Everyone felt like we were in Germany and being talked to by the Gestapo. Some folks felt there was going to be a riot any minute.

At the security entrance, like what you go through at the airport, they announced that if anyone was leaving in MORE than two weeks, they should go home. They were only giving passports to people who were leaving in less than two weeks. I didn't say anything because I knew I'd be reprimanded, but I wondered why they hadn't sent someone outside and told the long lines of people who had been there since 2:00 a.m. that.

We were ushered into a large room with rows of chairs and given a number. Because we went in and then went out the same way we had come in, we lost our place by about 25 people, but we didn't dare complain. Then we went up to the eighth floor and lined up in a long unventilated hallway. We stood here for 30 to 40 minutes until

Opposite page: An example of the rugged, terraced landscape around Machu Picchu.

Two brightly dressed locals.

Left: Content child on mom's back.

Below left: Ali doing a little shopping.

there was space for a few at a time to go into another room, where there were 10 theater-type, inch-thick ticket windows where the applications were being taken. There were only seven people working, so there were three windows not even operating. Because my niece was having finals that last week, the only time she could get a passport picture taken was when she was wearing her strapless graduation dress. They wouldn't accept that, because she looked like she was naked. So she and her father had to go out onto the streets of Chicago and find a place where she could get another photo taken. After another hour, which now put it at about eleven in the morning (we had been there since four), she was finally given a piece of paper to get back into the building at three. She and everyone else had to come back at three, even the guy who got there at 2:00 a.m. They didn't have facilities for printing the passports and had to send them out across town to be printed. We had lunch, roamed around town, returned at two, and were told to come back at three. At three, only she and her father could go upstairs, where at four, they finally got her passport.

Now it was rush-hour traffic time, and we had to go out into it to head up north like everyone else in the summer did on a Friday afternoon. At least we had two days over the weekend to recover.

Finally, on Monday morning, we flew from Milwaukee to Lima, Peru. As I said before, my grandniece wasn't interested in anything. She was a very bad traveler who was only interested in getting back to the hotel and the computer so she could e-mail her boyfriend. I won't go into any details of the trip.

When we got back home on June 20, I stayed with her family through the weekend. On Sunday morning, my nephew hollered to me that the congressman who wouldn't help us was swimming the length of the lake. He lived on the lake and, usually on Sundays, he swam from his home to out in front of ours. I jumped into the canoe and paddled out to him. "Are you Congressman Petri?" I asked. He was. I told him who I was, for he would know my family. I said, "I've got you right where I want you." Then I proceeded to tell him about our experience in getting my niece's passport, and I wanted to know what they (back in Washington, D.C.) were going to do! He didn't have much to say except that it was a mess. By then, I had been circling him in the canoe while he dog-paddled. I decided to stick with him until he got to a shallow place. I didn't want him to drown. I wanted him to return to Washington the next day and let everyone know THERE WAS A PROBLEM!

My family couldn't believe what I'd done, but it just goes to show that it helped to blow off steam—call the White House, paddle a canoe around a drowning congressman, do whatever it took to make them hear us. Given the opportunity again, I would do it all over.

My grandniece started college the fall of 2006. We had returned late June, and it wasn't until January that I received a written "thank you" from her. I think when she got to college, her new friends asked her what she had done over the summer. When she told them her aunt had taken her to Peru, they were all astonished and probably said they wished *their* aunts had taken them on a trip to Peru. Little by little, I think she finally realized what a lucky young lady she was.

Now, I was getting ready to spend 10 days in San Juan, Puerto Rico. Her family, my daughter-in-law, and I were going there instead of spending Christmas together in cold Wisconsin. We were all excited and eager to get into some 80-degree temperatures.

Since living here in God's Country and the area called the "Switzerland of America," I played a lot of golf, hiked some, biked, and kept busy enjoying my new home. I have two guest rooms I hope will get a lot of use. You would have to give me a call and see when they would be available, because I want all of you to come visit.

Taos Pueblo with Marge, October

I had an interesting experience recently that I thought you would enjoy. Years ago, in fact, about 1982 or 1983, I happened to be in Taos. There on their central plaza sat an Indian who appeared to be in his mid-fifties. I observed that he was always there, every day. So before I left town, I asked if he would mind if I took his picture. I was doing black-and-white photography at the time. I developed it and came up with a very large print of him. A few years later, I happened to be back in Taos and looked for him on the plaza, but he wasn't there. A nearby department store owner had a picture of him hanging in their store, which I'd noticed when I was there before and had taken the photo. So I dropped in there and asked where he was. It turned out that two years after I had taken the photo, he'd had a hernia operation and died!

For years, that picture hung in my downstairs room where I had all the other black-and-white prints I'd taken and made over the years. Now, in moving, I no longer had a place for that photo, so I decided to search for his relatives.

A few weeks ago, I went to Santa Fe to visit Fred and Marge Quist. After we did all the other things I wanted to do while there, I asked Marge if she would go with me to Taos on Saturday. I was leaving the next day, on Sunday, to come back home. So we went in search of this unknown Indian's family.

First, we went to the store where I had seen the picture of him. There was a new owner and the woman suggested we go to the Taos Pueblo. As we strolled around the plaza, I carried the framed picture with me. When I noticed two Indians in one of the shops, I showed them the picture and asked if they knew him. Yes, they knew him and actually had a name—Frank! So on we went, ending up at the Taos Pueblo where we had to purchase tickets to enter (you didn't used to have to pay to enter). I showed the picture to the lady who sold us the tickets. She knew Frank and said his daughter and granddaughter owned a shop just around the corner, but she was sure they weren't there that day. So we looked and—sure enough—it was closed.

There was a lady in the plaza selling fry bread, and I suggested we buy some. Unfortunately for us, there was a lady ahead of us who was the guide for about 15 people from the Czech Republic, and she was buying fry bread for all of them. So we waited while the cook made 15 fry breads in her one pot. Her daughter was with her, and I showed her the picture to pass the time away. They both knew Frank and, in fact, the young girl had a phone number for the family. Hurray! After getting all stuck up with fry bread, we went back into town to make a phone call. Now we were armed with Frank's last name: Lujan. We stopped at the nearest hotel for a phone book. After calling three numbers, it was the last one that was successful. "Where are you?" the man asked. "Oh, you're very close. Just go toward the Pueblo, take the first right turn, and look for a white motor home and a horse trailer. That's where you'll find his daughter." He thought her name was Shirley.

Now headed back to the Pueblo, we were sure we would find the daughter. There were only three houses on that road, and none of them matched the white motor home and horse trailer description. What a disappointment. As we were about to depart that short road, a young boy on a bike rode toward us. I rolled down the window and asked if he knew anyone by the name of Lujan. He pointed to one of the houses, where we immediately drove.

The young boy followed us and went into the house. Soon he came back out and asked me to come in. Instead of being ushered into the living room, I was ushered into a hallway that led to the bedrooms. There, by the side of a well-slept-in bed, stood an elderly man in his BVDs. I told him what I wanted, and he said, "Oh, you want to go across the road!"

Back in the car, across the road we went. There were two pickup trucks parked there, so we were certain we would find someone home, at last! Well, no one responded to the knocking on the door or the window. Obviously, they weren't there. What a disappointment, after all that time and after showing the picture to so many people who knew Frank.

So Marge and I went back to Santa Fe. I decided that instead of going home through Española the next day, I would go to Taos to stop there one more time, then cut over on the highway to the north.

As I approached the house where the two pickups had been the day before, one of them wasn't there. I thought, "NO, someone *was* there the day before and didn't hear my knocking!" Drat! But just as my heart fell, the white pickup driving right in front of me turned in there! Oh, maybe all was not lost! I followed it in and stopped right behind it so they couldn't leave. I introduced myself and showed the man Frank's picture. Hallelujah! He was Shirley's husband, and Shirley was Frank's daughter! He invited me into the house where he showed me a portrait that someone had done before Frank died. I left the picture with him and said I was really sorry that I wasn't able to give it directly to Shirley.

Days passed and there was no word from Shirley, even though the husband and I had exchanged addresses, phone numbers, and e-mail addresses. Finally, I couldn't stand it any longer and called her. She was very apologetic but appreciated that I had left the picture. We talked for quite a while. She told me that the doctors who operated on Frank had cut something they weren't supposed to cut. He died because of it, and they sued the doctors. They had to go to another state to get a lawyer who would represent them, but they won. She didn't tell me how much, but they were satisfied. Shirley's husband told me about their daughter who had the shop at the Pueblo, and that she was soon going to play the violin in a symphony in Telluride.

Not long afterward, I got an e-mail from the daughter, granddaughter to Frank. She told me she would be in Telluride, so we made plans to meet, and I took her to lunch. We rode the gondola to Mountain Village, which she didn't know existed. She told me that Frank's name was really Romera. No wonder we had such a time finding him! I really enjoyed the concert, which was a lovely ending to quite an adventure.

A Year of Visits, My 80th Birthday, Riding in a Stemme Sailplane

January 2008 saw me in San Juan, Puerto Rico, with my niece, Anne Faris, her husband, Jeff, and their three lovely daughters, Liz, Ali, and Jenny. They had a friend who owned a two-bedroom condo which we stuffed ourselves into. Besides sunning on the

An inviting beach and a friendly iguana.

The Faris family in Puerto Rico.

Left: The Farises go for a horseback ride on the beach. Right: A local cemetery.

beach and the girls being eyed by some young boys, we had a great tour of the Bacardi Rum facility. We all got stoned!

February and March was filled with a lot of skiing with local friends. I managed not to fall!

April 4 was Brad and Rosmery's fourth anniversary, so I planned a hot air balloon ride for all of us. Toward the end of that month, they left for Peru and the beginning of Brad's summer guiding season.

80th Birthday and Finding Pepper

May 4 was the BIG EVENT of the year, MY 80th BIRTHDAY! I planned to put a swing together and asked a worker at the local hardware store what days of the week he had off. It turned out that he only had Sundays off, and my birthday was on a Sunday. Despite that, I asked him if he would help me put a swing together. Now, this is no ordinary swing that you envision from a large tree branch. It was a swing for three people with a cover and two little side glass tables to set a drink on. WELL, I was sure my muscular friend thought it would only take about an hour of his only day off, but let me tell you...it took us three hours! Poor guy!

But that wasn't really the big event of the year. Brad phoned from Peru and said he was calling to wish me a happy birthday. Immediately, I wondered where his group was and if Rosmery was OK. Yes, everyone was fine. They weren't far from a highway, and he thought it would be great to hike down and call me. *Well!* I knew he wasn't telling the truth, and a week later he called again from his mother-in-law's and told me that he'd been carrying a Peruvian mountain puppy six miles downhill so it wouldn't get killed on the Inca Trail.

At first I was speechless, but after I heard the full, TRUE story, I understood. Two dogs—a mother and her puppy—had followed his group over a 16,700-foot pass almost to where they would connect with the Inca Trail. The mother decided to go back to wherever she had come from but the pup, who became known as Pepper because of the color of her coat, had stayed with the group. Brad knew they couldn't let her continue on the Inca Trail, because eventually she would be killed. Dogs weren't allowed on the trail and, in fact, Brad found out later that her mother had been killed.

What to do, what to do... Brad, of course, had seen Machu Picchu many times, and therefore was elected to take the dog out. Out to where? He decided to adopt the dog and bring her back to the U.S. So he hadn't hiked out to call me on my 80th birthday after all: It just happened to be the day he was carrying the dog out.

Once Brad hiked out and got to the highway, he had to hitch a ride. In Peru, you get into what's called a "*colectivo,*" which is a half-size VW bus with crouching room only. Brad's 6'2" frame made it even worse. He had the dog, a duffel bag, and a backpack. There were no free seats, so he was crouched over with a quivering, frightened dog in his arms. He asked if any of them would please give up their seat to him, but no one offered. He finally said, probably in Spanish, "Awe, come on! Someone give me your seat. Can't you see I have a problem here?" Finally, the mother of a little girl told her to give him her seat. Whew!

The next hurdle was how to get himself, the dog, and his gear to his mother-in-law's. A young boy sitting near him was talked into helping when Brad said he'd pay him. It was probably some miniscule amount in U.S. dollars, but in soles, it was a day's worth of work.

Finally at his mother-in-law's home in the Sacred Valley, he put a collar on Pepper, which frightened the poor dog, and she ran off! But she came back. The next test was a leash, which sent her running off again,

Pepper when she was still a puppy.

because the leash made unfamiliar noises behind her. She came back a second time. Meanwhile, I looked up on the Internet to see what Brad would need to do to get Pepper into the States. Everyone thought there would be a quarantine period, but Brad found a vet who knew what to do, i.e., shots, delousing, a bath, etc. In just one day, it was all done! Then there was the purchase of a kennel for her on the plane. More money.

Then another call to Mom: What are you doing next week? As it turned out, I was going to Wisconsin. Oh, no! Now he would have to buy a $580 ticket for the dog to get from Cusco to Albuquerque, where a couple who was on his trip would pick her up. He also had to buy a round-trip ticket for himself from Cusco to Lima, because he had another trip to lead.

This all took place in mid- to late May when the Albuquerque couple drove not only Pepper to Ridgway, but their own cat and two dogs. Pepper stayed with her new parents until the first part of August when Brad finally returned. Needless to say, she was in seventh heaven with two dogs and a cat to play with on 70 acres of ranch land, no rocks or sticks being thrown at her, and people who loved her at every turn.

Initially, Pepper wouldn't eat, but when the vet told us that some dogs don't like to eat from a bowl, it only made sense. She had been killing her own food or eating lying down whatever was thrown out for her. Now she eats lying down and from a paper plate...ravenously!

2000   2001   2002   2003   2004   2005   2006   2007   **2008**   2009

Botswana: Kalahari, Delta, and Beyond

Dave Luck, our guide for this trip.

On March 4, Brad, Rosmery, and I went on our first trip to Botswana, organized and run by Natural Habitat Adventures. Brad's birthday was the very day of our departure. Our guide was Dave Luck. And were we lucky! He had grown up in Africa and knew the animals, their habits, and the noises they made. He knew where to look for them.

Our first stop was in Atlanta. We had a long layover—two hours—with not much to do. We found our gate and a very large flat baggage platform where we could lie down and take a nap. We thought our papers were in order and we had our boarding passes, or so we thought.

Finally, our flight was announced and since we had been there so long, we decided to be first to board. Brad took our passports and boarding passes and we all stood aside, waiting for permission to board. Much to our surprise and dismay, Brad was told that his passport didn't have enough pages in it, and he would not be able to join us until it had six more pages! Had we known this two hours earlier, Brad could've gotten those pages right there in the airport. Now it was late, and people had gone home for the day. He would have to stay overnight and get to the office in the morning. We hoped he could find a flight that would have room for him to meet us the next day. Horrors!

Rosmery and Brad had packed so that some of their things were in the other one's suitcase, so they had to unpack and repack again in the large luggage area where we had spent the last two hours. With the commotion that was going on, I'm sure everyone knew what was happening with us. Finally, Rosmery and I took our things and went over into the line to go through boarding a second time. By that time, the other passengers had lined up and many had already boarded.

As we walked down the ramp leading to the plane, and as I took the first corner leading us out of Brad's sight, it suddenly occurred to me that he had all our money for the trip! I dropped my luggage and ran back, darting the opposite way through the check-in area. This caused a buzzer to go off, alerting the check-in people that someone was going back into the boarding area. They stopped me from running after Brad. Knowing we needed the money, I hollered as loud as I could, "BRAAAAAAD! THE MONEY!!!" Everyone was shocked.

Fortunately, everyone figured out what was going on. Brad heard me and came back with the money. Would you believe that he gave it to someone near the end of the line and they passed it forward until I got it?

So we finally boarded the plane. When we got settled, the lady in front of us offered us her cell phone so we could call Brad. We got in touch with him before we took off. By then he had found where he had to go for more pages in his passport and said he'd go first thing in the morning. He'd see us the next day.

Rosmery and I managed to sleep a good bit on the long flight to Johannesburg. We spent that night there and got our flight to Maun, Botswana, the next morning. This was the part of the entire trip that Brad was really looking forward to, and he was missing it! There, we waited a short time for our four-hour flight to the Adventure Camp in Deception Valley.

Our private campsite was a 9X9-foot, well-ventilated dome tent with a mini veranda. Everything was provided—beds, crisp linen, duvets, pillows, towels, and amenities. There also was a shared bedside table with a lantern. The tents were large enough to stand up and move easily around in, even with mini-luggage benches. All tents had a private en-suite, open-air bathroom accessible through a zippered door at the rear. Yes, there was a short-drop toilet, an old style tin bucket shower (hot water on request), and a hand basin.

Adventure Camp in Deception Valley. Left: An example of their food presentation.

This park had a healthy population of cheetahs.

Hurricane lanterns and a good campfire lit up the camp in the evening. Delicious meals were prepared around our campfire by our safari staff, creating a great atmosphere. The dining area was under the stars, although if it rained, there was a bush dining tent where we could eat.

Within the remote environs of this little-visited national park, animal movements seemed to be dictated by nature and the rains. We tracked them on extended game drives, studying the desert ecology along the way. The famous black-maned Kalahari lion resided there, as well as a healthy population of cheetahs.

Rosmery holding up an elephant!

After two nights there, we were taken to the airstrip where we boarded a small plane to fly to the next camp, Little Vumbura in the Okavango Delta. There, we searched for elephant herds in the forests, buffalo in the wetlands, and a range of other plains game which attract a variety of predators.

At the end of our second day there, word came that

Brad's welcoming committee.

Brad was going to arrive that evening. The help knew before we did and were out by the parking area with pots and pans, large spoons, etc., to welcome him. When he drove up, they began to drum on the pans and sing a welcoming song as they performed a dance. Of course, Brad had a big smile and was relieved to catch up with us, appreciating the welcome.

We only had one more day there before moving on to the next camp, so Brad had missed the entire time we spent at Little Vumbura Camp on the Okavango Delta.

Again, we were taken to another light aircraft which flew us to the secluded

Pictures of our various accommodations.

The pictures on this page are from our tour of the Okavango River Delta.

Victoria Falls.

Savuti Camp, called "Linyanti Concession." It was one of Botswana's premier private reserves with fully equipped tents, a thatched dining area, pub, and plunge pool, all laid out on wooden decks. Again, we were there just two nights and days.

With just a week behind us, our next destination was in Chobe National Park, famous for its massive herds of elephants, of which we saw many. There our camp, called "Toka Leya," was on the Zambezi River. All of the camp was on wooden walkways snaking through the trees between spacious safari-type tents. Each tent had wood flooring with a tasteful décor in earthy hues, climate-controlled for a cool summer haven close to the river with many sights and sounds of birds, elephants, and hippos.

Besides daily safari animal drives, we were able to take numerous pictures of Victoria Falls which was on our last safari drive. And to top it all off, we had a heli-flight around the area. What a trip!

But we weren't going home yet. Our next destination again required flying from Livingstone to Windhoek, Namibia. The flight was so long that we had dinner on the plane before landing close to Windhoek. There, we were taken to our one-night stay in the Alice

Uh-oh, stuck in the mud!

2000   2001   2002   2003   2004   2005   2006   2007   2008   **2009**

331

Grove Guesthouse, which was close to the city center. It had all the conveniences we might need—even TV, which we hadn't had for the past weeks, and a computer. In the morning, we were driven back to Eros Airport where we met our pilot and were transferred by light aircraft to the Okonjima Luxury Bush Camp of eight thatched, African-style chalets.

   We were at this camp just two nights. During the day, we took excursions on foot to look for cheetah footprints. Our guide used telemetry to monitor the animals. The AfriCat Foundation was developed to house and feed injured and orphaned animals. One day, we were driven out to the area where the fenced-in animals were fed. A pickup truck drove up and the animals rushed to the fence, knowing they would get something to

The AfriCat Foundation facility we visited.

eat. A fellow in the back of the pickup grabbed large hunks of meat and threw them over the fence. The animals leaped to catch them then ran off into the woods to devour the pieces. If you didn't throw something over the fence, the animals would come up to the barbed wire and just peer at you. Sometimes they would growl. It was rather scary, and Rosmery was happier inside the vehicle we had come in.

After two days at Okonjima, hunting for the animals and watching them be fed, we were on our way back to Windhoek and the Olive Grove for a final night's rest before beginning six days in the dunes and desert of the Namib Desert. This

Left: A hissing lioness warning us away.
Below: One of the many incredible African sunsets I witnessed.

The Namib dunes.

time we were flown across the expanse of desert to Sossusvlei Wilderness Camp. We were told that the Namib was the world's oldest desert with the world's tallest sand dunes. The word *namib* in the Nama language meant "vast," and vast it was! On our drives, we saw lone oryx, ostrich, and other wildlife as they traversed the massive golden dunes.

Sossusvlei Wilderness Camp was 20 kilometers from the park's entrance to the dunes. The towering dunes rose more than 1,000 feet above the plains and were easily climbed by the tourists, such as us.

Besides climbing the dunes, we flew due west to Meob Bay on the Skeleton Coast. The scenery was spectacular where the dunes and the desert met at the Atlantic Ocean.

Flying up the coast, the pilot pointed out the shipwreck of the *Shawnee* while we were over Sandwich Harbour and its famous lagoon to finally land at Swakopmund Airport. Surprisingly, we were transferred to Walvis Bay Harbour and given a boat ride which allowed us to see seals and schools of dolphins swimming right alongside the boat. We also saw turtles, sunfish, and penguins, and one of the seals actually leaped up onto the boat where the boatman fed it while we took pictures and petted it. Rosmery actually fed it! At the end of the day, we flew up the Huab River Valley to our last camp, Damaraland. The next day, we were flown back to Windhoek where we caught our final flight back to the U.S.

An incredibly friendly seal.

Leopard, Botswana 2009.

2010-2017

ANTARCTICA WITH OLAF & PATSY, OCTOBER

I can't believe that everything went OK. I didn't goof, nor did I lose anything. In Denver, the time was short, but then I had five-plus hours in Dulles and the same in Buenos Aires. I took half an Ambien and slept eight hours. The flight into Ushuaia was incredibly beautiful. I didn't realize there were so many mountains all around. They had snow, or perhaps since it was spring here, the snow was melting off. At any rate, as we approached landing, we flew along a very long waterway, made a huge half-circle, and then—very low—came across the water until we finally landed right next to it, with the water on the left and the town on the hillsides to the right. I had a heart attack about half an hour out when I couldn't find a baggage claim ticket and thought I'd have to deal with it if the bag didn't arrive. But it was there, with all the orange tape tied everywhere so I couldn't miss it.

And what a surprise to have Olaf holding up one of the Quark signs to greet people! He had practically run from the hotel they were staying in to the airport, which was farther than he thought, but he got there just as I was coming out with my suitcase.

The Quark transportation bus took everyone to his hotel first, then to mine. We were to meet in the morning at 9:00 a.m. and decide what we were going to do. I hoped I could convince them to go to Tierra del Fuego where there was a lot of hiking. If they didn't want to go, I would do it by myself.

I had dinner with two very young people, married, who were working in Tanzania for Barrick Gold Mining Company. The fellow had the

Our base.

THE CURIOUS PENGUIN

This fellow was very interested in the tripod, but shortly after giving it the once over, he skedaddled back to the rookery.

same camera I had. We ate dinner together, but another passenger talked too much.

I'd been using the tape recorder I brought along to record what happened day-to-day. After getting settled in the Albatros Hotel and having dinner, I took a quarter of an Ambien and slept really good, so I was ready for whatever happened.

Olaf and Patsy arrived about 9:15 the next morning and we went to the local prison, which was really interesting. It was built by the prisoners themselves and was very large.

It was really windy and cold, so I actually wore my old large Frostline jacket. It was amazing how many sporting goods stores were there. I didn't count, but I'll bet there were at

Pictures from the emperor penguin rookery we visited.

least a dozen. Signs in the windows read Lowe, North Face, etc. I think North Face did a lot of advertising down there, as everyone wore a North Face jacket. There was a small ski area there which really was a surprise. If there wasn't enough snow, there were all kinds of hiking trails off the lift.

My hotel was right in the heart of town, which had one-way streets because it was so small and the streets were so narrow. The ships were right out in front of the hotel. I was surprised that there actually were flowers in bloom. Spring must've come before we got here.

The airport had only three commercial parking places, and when we arrived, we were the only other commercial plane there. I saw two small Cessna-like planes parked off to the side, and today one flew over. Boy, would it ever be something to get a ride in one!

In the morning, we put our tagged bags out in the lobby by 9:30 for pickup and had several hours for breakfast and exploring before we boarded our ship around 5:30. That would be interesting. My roommate, whose name was Ellen, would arrive that night. That was all I knew. I just hoped she didn't talk too much and wasn't way overweight. The ship's cabin we would be sharing was very small. We were also to have an orientation meeting later at 6:30.

The ship came in early, and the passengers onboard registered in our place and had their breakfast. I roamed around some then decided to just stay at the hotel until the afternoon, when it would be time to board.

Everyone, I mean *everyone*, who had been on the ship had their own computer. Now they were in the computer room, logged on and talking with their families.

I couldn't believe they could actually see each other, probably on Skype, and were telling their families what they'd seen. People were from all around the world—Asia, Scandinavia, South America, Europe—you name it, they were there. The world was no longer a big place.

As I wrote this, one fellow was seeing his children and his wife on the computer screen and they were talking to each other.

We didn't go aboard the ship until 5:00, so I tried to write again before then.

A Chinaman who was on the ship stopped by and said the ship didn't have stabilizers, so it was very "rolly." Also, they had only two good days and didn't see that many penguins. Oh, well. Maybe we'll be luckier.

We were about to go aboard when I noticed that there were more young people than people my age. Really interesting. Brad had mumbled something to me about not going along because the other passengers would all be in wheelchairs or on crutches. Not so! Too bad. One fellow who just got off of the last trip was going out again on ours because of a last-minute cancellation.

The food was great, and there were interesting programs in the auditorium. The first day out, we had incredible weather with a long march through melting ice, over one mile to a rookery. I took many pictures, but not enough. I was in the radio room on our second day out of three when we were planning to visit Snow Hill Island. We ended up with three days of sailing through very rough seas. We were breaking sea ice, with the winds so high that we couldn't fly, so we were going around in circles just taking pictures of immense icebergs. There was one night I couldn't sleep because of the rocking. We finally flew out on a helicopter.

We just arrived back in Ushuaia and put our feet on solid ground. It wasn't moving, but we still were!

WINTER TRAIN TRIP

The only train trip I had ever been on was during the Wetherill–Grand Gulch Research Project, when we took the train from Denver to Chicago to do research in the museum there. It was overnight, so we sure didn't see much.

When my neighbor, Olaf Rasmussen, a "train buff," asked if I would like to join him and his wife, Patsy, on a unique, one-time-only, steam-powered winter train excursion, I said "yes" and found it to be like no other train trip.

Olaf's love of old-time, steam-train railroads began as a kid in Remscheid, Germany, after the war. Despite his young age, he was allowed to ride many of the trains and got hooked.

After Olaf moved to the U.S., he became acquainted with how the U.S. trains operated and even spent time refurbishing old trains. The trip that he'd chosen to share with me started in Alamosa, Colorado, and headed for the La Veta Pass line of the San Luis and Rio Grande Railroad. There had been more than 50 years of freight-only operations on that scenic route, which went over the Sangre de Cristo Mountains. It could be traversed in the summer months, but it wasn't quite summer when our steam-powered train was going to take this route. There was still snow on the ground and the tracks! That didn't seem to bother the engineers, who were in control.

I know nothing about trains, whether they're powered by steam or travel narrow gauge or normal track. So I was about to learn a few things.

At this time, the trains taking this line were soon to be powered by diesel locomotives. For a few years, steam engines were used, and this trip was the last "mid-winter" excursion doing this. And WE WERE ON IT!

After spending the night in Alamosa, we boarded the train with Steam Engine 18, which included a club car, two dome cars (meaning seated up high where you could see out as the train chugged along), and a well-chilled, open

Patsy enjoying the train ride.

observation car (no windows, all open!). The route crested the Sangre de Cristo range at a siding called "Fir." After we passengers got off the train, the engine and cars backed up about a mile around the looping tracks on the west side of the pass. We passengers stood in the snow by the tracks and waited until the train started back so we could take pictures of it as it returned.

Back on board, we stopped in La Veta for a short lunch, then the train turned for the long, steep climb back over the snowy pass to Alamosa. Needless to say, it seemed everyone had enjoyed this once-ever winter adventure via Steam Engine 18. We felt special, as it sure *was* special.

ALAN MULALLY LETTER

After seeing an episode of *Charlie Rose* that aired July 27, 2011, I wrote the following letter to a man who was interviewed, Alan Mulally, CEO of Ford Motor Company at the time:

August 23, 2011

Dear Mr. Mulally,

I watch *Charlie Rose* and was delighted to be watching the night you were on his program. My enthusiasm comes from the fact that my father brought the first Ford car into the state of Wisconsin about 1911. The local farmers and lookers laughed and said, "That dad-burned machine can't even go up the courthouse steps." I have a picture of him driving up those steps, which went from ground level to the third floor where a policeman awaited him. He spent the night in the local jail.

His name was Thomas Wakefield Meiklejohn. After he got his business, called Service Motors, set up in Fond du Lac, Wisconsin, Henry Ford visited the new business and found my dad under a car. Henry gave a slight kick to Dad's leg and said, "Get out from under there and get a suit on. You're the boss here." Needless to say, the business thrived and grew to Illinois, Michigan, and all of Wisconsin.

I have pictures and stories of his adventures in one model or another of the Ford then. I even own a 1930 Model A five-window Ford Coupe with a rumble seat. Right now, our local fair and rodeo are coming up, and I plan to give $5 rides to anyone who wants one for a local fundraiser. I guess I should tell you that I am no longer a spring chicken but a little over 83, and I still get a kick out of driving the "A."

Listening to you and your excitement over what you have been able to do as President and CEO excited me. I felt I had to tell you how much I enjoyed the program and how much I am still enjoying the "A."

Let me know if you can use any of the Ford history I might have. If not, continued good luck to you and your endeavor with Ford.

Sincerely,

Julia M. Johnson

DALE JOHNSON'S MEMORIAL SERVICE

Brad and his wife, Rosmery, had been taking care of Dale, my husband of 30 years, for weeks when he finally passed. A memorial service was to be given in Chautauqua Park in Boulder, Colorado. As far as Brad and I were concerned, the room where it was to be held was way too small. However, we had no say. So I decided that Dale and his life were so important to friends and the people of Boulder that I would give a speech telling about his life, which few had known, including his second wife, Frandee.

Needless to say, my arrival that day was a shock to her, for who would have thought I would attend? At the top of the steps, she stood with her arms outstretched, waiting to greet me as if I was an old friend. Ha, ha! Little did she know what was to come. I had a conversation with the emcee, Peter Birkeland, asking him if he would call my name and get me up to the microphone very close to the beginning of the service.

I found myself a seat right in the front row so I wouldn't disturb anyone when I got up, and I would be right where I could walk up to the stand and the mic. I presented the following remembrances:

"Hello, everyone. Thank you for coming. I am Julia Johnson, but Dale called me 'Julie.' My life today is due to what Dale's life was. So I'd like to share with you my memories of Dale's life, beginning in 1954.

"Dale was many things, but when I first met him, he was a miner working nights at Climax Molybdenum Mine north of Leadville. Right out of college, he chose that job so he could work nights and hike in the mountains he so dearly loved during the day. He was one of those fellows who set the dynamite and called out 'FIRE IN THE HOLE!'

"His teen summers had been spent in the Teton Range where he lived with his Aunt Jo and Uncle Charles. There, he and a buddy dreamed of being married in the Church of the Transfiguration in Moose, Wyoming. Not a very romantic name, but standing at the altar, the Tetons rise up before you through the large picture window. We were married there.

"He never dreamed of being a telephone techie, but the Army taught him that right after we married.

"As a father, before our son, Brad, learned to walk, Dale introduced him to camping in our Ford station wagon in a Georgia dump while in the service. After we returned to Boulder, when Brad was still in diapers, Dale carried him in his backpack to the top of the

Third Flatiron. A bit later, we decided to camp on top of a peak west of Boulder. Carrying all our gear as well as Brad, what should greet us at the top but two parked cars! We could have driven up there! Much later, at Vail, it was in the back bowls in knee-deep powder where Brad called out: 'I CAN'T DO THIS!' But he did, and he does. Later in life, that lesson took us heli-skiing in Canada about five times.

"As a CMC climbing instructor, I was one of Dale's first students, and he taught me how to rappel, of all places, from the Maiden. I well remember seeing the void below me on the first lead. The belayer, Cary Houston, called out to Dale, 'She's crying! What should I do?' Dale called back, 'Let her cry!' I realized not too long after that experience that Dale was preparing me for a climb up Shiprock, hoping I would be the first female to do so. When we checked the CMC register, we were all disappointed, because I was second. Worst of all for me, though, there were nine rappels.

"I guess this is as good a place as any to say that right from the start of our marriage, Dale was a great lover…of pancakes! When we divorced, he asked me for my recipe.

"Most importantly, Dale was a designer, which started when I became a seamstress for Gerry Cunningham. Friday nights, Gerry came for dinner and brought several items for me to sew. I guess I did OK, because he had me sew 20 Gerry Himalayan tents to be used on Everest, K2, and Makalu. Somehow I managed to do that in our 9X12 bedroom, and sometimes we couldn't find the bed. But all those Friday-night dinners resulted in the opening of Boulder's first Gerry Store with Dale as manager and partner. Ten years later, Gerry asked Dale to open a store in California, but we wanted to stay in Boulder.

"That resulted in Dale's developing his own extremely successful business of Frostline Kits. While riding to and from his Denver job at U.S. National Bank as a teller, he put the bank's loans on their first computer which, in those days, was room-size. All of that while he was on the bus designing jackets, vests, packs, and sleeping bags. A lady on the bus asked him why he was the only one not sleeping. When he told her what he was doing, she became very excited. She was a Boulder schools home economics teacher and, not long after their meeting, Boulder's Home Ec classes offered Home Ec for boys using Frostline Kits.

"During the years with Gerry, and followed by many more with Frostline, our lives were filled with incredible experiences. As co-leaders with Harold and Sadie Walton, we led 40 CMCers on a climbing expedition to Peru; the following year, after feeling we had learned the ropes, Dale organized the first CMC European Outing with 48 CMCers. That wasn't enough punishment, so we took 30 CMCers to Africa and, finally, 28 to New Zealand where we mourned the loss of Dale's favorite pin-covered hat when it was blown off while on a boat.

"Dale was also a great friend, fishing with Ben Chidlaw in Wyoming, hiking Utah desert canyons, and biking across half of Canada. Having opened a store in Alaska—one of 18 wholly owned Frostline stores—Dale's Durango High School buddy, Frank Pinkerton, who lived in Anchorage, urged us to get our floatplane licenses. That took us on a northern Alaska float trip to help Frank get his bighorn sheep. They got it, but then the plane was heavy. We took turns piloting, and it was my turn. Frank questioned whether I thought I could get the plane off the tiny lake we had landed on, but I did it, and Dale patted me on the back.

"Little did Dale realize what a successful businessman he would become, going from the basement of our home to two places east off Valmont Road, followed by a big move to the first industrial park west of Broomfield, before the final move to an expansive building with 225 employees in Thornton. Never did he dream of a huge business like Johnson's Wax wanting to buy our 10-year-old business. He said he couldn't do it…it was like selling Brad. And it was even more surprising that a razor company, Gillette, would be the one to bring our business journey to an end after 14 years.

"Those 30 years were filled with a world of never-thought-of experiences, like being guests of the huge YKK Zipper Company in Japan and climbing Mt. Fuji, or reaching the top of 20,000-foot Tocllaraju in Peru or Kilimanjaro in Africa.

"A miner, a dreamer, a father, an instructor, a designer, a very successful businessman, a friend. Dale will be remembered by many.

"Before I close, I wish to thank, from the bottom of my heart, our son, Brad, and his lovely gem of a wife, Rosmery, for staying by Dale's side during his last 23 days."

Jasmine Reece and Fiji Biking through Ridgway

It was toward the end of the day when I stopped at Ridgway's Panny's Pizza for an ice cream cone, chocolate mint. Who should I meet there but a friend, Judy Darwick, and her friend, Jimmy. They, too, were having ice cream cones. I noticed a heavy-set young black gal and her dog at one of the tables. She had ridden her bike from somewhere, and I didn't know where until we struck up a conversation with her. I discovered that she had biked all the way from New York pulling a child's wagon that held her personal belongings, plus a bag of dog food with a violin on top. She was headed to the West Coast. She had an appointment to interview for a job—I've forgotten doing what. We couldn't believe that she had gotten directions as to the best way to get across Colorado from a bike touring outfit in New York. I told her they must have never been to Colorado, because the route took her right through the middle of Western Colorado and Utah's Indian Country, where there would be no people, no stores, absolutely nothing! She shouldn't go that way! The only other way would be to go north to Moab, but that would put her on I-70, where bikes are not allowed.

We asked her where she'd been staying. She said she'd had a tent, sleeping bag, etc., but it had all gotten lost. She lost them when a very nice person had picked her up when she had a flat tire. The tailgate didn't get closed all the way, and all her belongings fell out the back end. In Ridgway, she had

Jasmine and Don, unloading his truck at Lizard Head Pass.

Sign on Jasmine's bicycle.

booked a room in the one and only motel, but they'd given her room away so she wasn't sure where she was going to stay.

Judy, Jimmy, and I had a quiet conversation, and it was decided that she could stay with me, even though I never let dogs stay with any friends who came to visit. Jimmy was in a pickup, so he could take her, her belongings that were left, plus the dog up to my place, which was uphill from where we were. So off we went.

My home was on a hillside, but you can't see that unless you're standing on the deck and looking out over the valley. Once inside, I opened one of the doors, and out flew Fiji, the dog, leaping off the deck at a squirrel that was scurrying away. Because the land went downhill beyond the deck, Fiji didn't land right and hurt one leg. So I called our traveling veterinarian, Michelle Dally. She couldn't come until the next day, but that was OK. Fiji decided to just lie around after that.

My home overlooked the valley north of the San Juan Mountains, a view that captured you every time you looked out. Jasmine was taken with it, which was no surprise. Once settled, we just chatted, and I asked many questions in order to get to know her. She had been going to college in Missouri and had a job with an eye clinic there where people also tried to lose weight, and Jasmine needed to lose weight. That led her to think about riding her bike from the East Coast to the West Coast, and thereby lose some weight. She had lost 40 pounds so far.

She contacted a bike tour agency in New York for help in planning the route she should take to get from New York to San Diego, California. When she told me she was headed for Cortez and across the desert west of there, I was shocked! West of Cortez there was nothing—no stores, few settlements, not even any Indians! I had to convince her to go another way. But what way? She couldn't go through Telluride or Norwood. The long steep hill up to Norwood would take her west to where there was nothing! If she went to Telluride, it would be difficult first going over Dallas Divide and, later, over Lizard Head Pass.

About then, another friend of mine dropped by with some guests. It was Don and Terri Bell from South Carolina. They wanted their guests to meet me and see my home, as well as my 1930 Model A Ford my brother had given me years ago. They had two teenaged children with them.

That turned out not only to be entertaining, but laughable. When they saw the violin, they wanted her to play it. Then they kept eyeing my old car. I finally asked the young children if they wanted a ride. When I told them to get into the back end and showed them how to do it so as not to step on the shiny fender, they were very surprised. No one had ever put them in the "trunk of a car" and given them a ride. So off I went with them in the rumble seat, which they had never heard or dreamed of.

When Don and Terri got ready to leave with their guests and two children, Don took me aside and said he had a pickup and would be delighted to take Jasmine and all her stuff to Lizard Head Pass, because it seemed that would be the only way she could go.

The next day, Vet Dally couldn't believe Fiji. She said she had never worked with a dog as "tough and solid." In fact, before she could examine her, she had to give Fiji three shots so she would relax enough to be examined. It turned out that the leg wasn't broken, just injured. Jasmine would have to put Fiji in the wagon so she wouldn't have to walk on it for a few days.

Later that day, Don called. Jasmine and I told him we would sure appreciate him taking her and all her belongings to Lizard Head Pass. I had called a friend of mine who lived in Cortez, Fred Blackburn from the Wetherill Project. He said that, by all means, she was welcome to spend that night with them and decide what to do next.

I think it was late morning the next day that Don arrived with his pickup. We all drove over to Lizard Head Pass and helped Jasmine get her things off the pickup and back together on her trailer to start downhill to Cortez.

We called Fred to let him know that she'd started down to Cortez from Lizard Head. When Jasmine made it to Rico, a small town southwest of Lizard Head Pass, she called Fred to let him know where she was and that she had made it that far with no problems. About 30 minutes later, Jasmine had a flat tire. She had lost her equipment back in Iowa and never got any new to replace it, so she had no way to fix the tire. She hoped someone would stop and help her, but no one did. The only thing she could do was walk, pushing the bike with Fiji in the wagon along with all her belongings, a large bag of dog food, and—finally—her violin.

When the day started to get dark, Fred decided to drive up and see where she was. He finally found her at Stoner, a wide spot in the road southwest of Rico. Jasmine had walked about 22

miles after she had the flat. Needless to say, she was very grateful that Fred had decided to go look for her.

Surprisingly enough, after getting back to Fred's, a longtime female friend of his showed up at his home, stopping by just to say hello. She had a very large vehicle, so Jasmine asked where she was headed. Yup! She was headed for Moab, *the* place Jasmine couldn't go because the only route west of there was on I-70. But there was no stopping her: She was sure she could figure out something once she got there. And that she did.

Jasmine and Fiji loading everything up. Back on the road again!

How, I haven't heard, but I will tell you what I do know.

I had told her to go to the airport and see if she could get a flight west. She did that, and they told her she had to go to Grand Junction because flights out of Moab were way too expensive. Back in town, she decided to put ads on Craigslist and in the newspaper. I guess it must have been printed soon after, because she got a phone call from a lady in Grand Junction who saw it and—being a biker herself—decided to see what she wanted.

The Grand Junction lady said she realized Jasmine couldn't backtrack, but if she was ever in that area at a later time, she could stay with her and her husband anytime. No sooner had she finished that conversation when,

somehow, Jasmine met a young woman in Moab who was going to Grand Junction for a dental appointment, and her car was large enough for Jasmine, Fiji, her bike, and all. So off they went.

While all this was going on, Jasmine called the lady in G.J. and told her she had a ride, and would she help her rent a vehicle large enough for all her things. Jasmine let me know and gave me that lady's phone number, and I called her. I told her I was as honest as the day was long, and I would appreciate her helping Jasmine get a car and help her on her way west through Salt Lake. I would send her a check for whatever the car rental was. Turned out the car rental place wouldn't have a car until the next day, so Jasmine had to stay overnight—apparently OK with the G.J. folks.

The next day, the husband of the G.J. lady took Jasmine to the car rental place so they wouldn't decide they didn't want to rent to her, and that worked. They got the car, paid for it, were told if she didn't get to Sacramento, California, in 12 hours, it would cost another $100! Returning to the home of the G.J. folks, they helped her load everything into the rental, and Jasmine was off to the West.

Somehow, I will never know, she made it to Sacramento in less than 12 hours! How she stayed awake or if she stopped for a short nap, she never told me. From Sacramento, she biked the coastline highway to San Diego, where she had an interview scheduled for a job. What kind, again, I don't know. But when I finally got in touch with her, she was biking to L.A. From there, she hoped to find a ride back to Indianapolis, Indiana, where she had lived before starting this grand trip. Believe it or not, she found a young girl with a vehicle who would take her, the bike, Fiji, etc., right where she wanted to go. There, she played with the Indianapolis Symphony for a while.

It seemed like many months had passed when I heard that she got back on her bike and somehow made her way to the southeastern U.S., then biked diagonally northwest to Seattle. She was planning to bike across Canada and back to N.Y. Quite some young gal! She was even preparing to bike across Asia.

BRAD'S ACCOUNT OF HIS CLIMB OF MT. EVEREST

It had been almost two weeks since my last e-mail of May 4, 2013. A lot of things had happened since then.

Playing the waiting game in the days leading up to our planned departure date of May 18 for our summit push weighed heavily on all of us. For me, I found that I became more and more nervous. I also went through phases of doubt and fear—fear of the unknown terrain above Camp Three, worrying about high winds at the South Col, being cold and miserable. Also, there were times that I really worried about what would happen on summit day and if I would be able to keep my feet warm. Deep down I knew that I shouldn't let my mind get the best of me. Once I was out of the tent each day and climbing, everything would become automatic for me, and I would be able to take care of myself and make the right decisions. Still, I felt that somehow I wouldn't make the top, while other people who had little or

Mount Everest.

The photos in this story were taken by Brad Johnson.

no experience climbing would just do what they were told and follow the fixed line and their Sherpas to the summit. I'm sure each member of our team went through their own doubts and anxieties.

In the dining tent, conversation always seemed to center around people who were already making summit attempts—some successful, others having turned around due to high winds. Since we were camped next to the Everest base camp medical tent, we would hear that people were coming down off the mountain with frostbitten hands or feet. All this only kept us on edge, more nervous than necessary, and we would check the weather forecasts twice a day to see if the weather windows of the 22nd and 23rd were still looking like the best days to go for the summit.

Our plan was to depart base camp on May 18, which we did. We departed about 3:00 a.m. and climbed through the Khumbu Icefall. It had been two weeks since we had last been through the icefall, and it was easy to see how many areas of it had changed. There were areas of the glacier the size of football fields that had collapsed by as much as 100 feet. This was

Top: The team.
Right: Climbing through the Khumbu Icefall between base camp and Camp One.

2010   2011   2012   **2013**   2014   2015   2016   2017

Left: Eric Meyer crossing a crevasse between Camp One and Camp Two. Above: Eric Meyer and Brad Johnson.

rather shocking and very sobering. Our previous acclimatization trip on the mountain had helped, as we now were able to go faster and with fewer rest stops in the riskier areas. We climbed as fast as we could through the danger zones to limit our exposure of being in an area that might collapse.

The trip from base camp to Camp Two took us between six and nine hours, with most of us arriving at Camp Two around 9:00 a.m. I was a little worried about the slower members in our group, as their times would only get slower higher up on the mountain.

We planned to have a rest day at Camp Two on May 19. I wasn't too excited about spending basically two full days and two nights at Camp Two. I always felt that I wasn't eating well there, and that it was a sinkhole for me energy-wise. In the long run, it was good that we had that time there. It had been two weeks since I'd slept at the 21,000-foot camp, and I felt that I regained some acclimation again.

During our time hanging out at Camp Two, we heard of a Taiwanese climber—Mr. Lee—who had climbed Mt. Lhotse without bottled oxygen a few days earlier. On the descent from the summit to his high camp, Mr. Lee sat down in exhaustion and didn't get up again. He spent several nights out in the open at 26,000 feet before someone discovered that he was still alive and managed to get him down to a tent at high camp. In a coma, his only chance of survival was an organized rescue team that would put him in a sketch (a plastic sled) and lower him 3,000 feet down the Lhotse Face to Camp Three. There, a helicopter rescue might be possible. While a rescue team was getting organized, a B3 helicopter was sent up to try and pluck Mr. Lee off the Lhotse Face in what was called a "long-line" rescue. Three times, the helicopter tried to hover over the camp with the line dangling below, but the winds were too strong and this rescue failed.

Top: Looking up the Western Cwm on the way to Camp Two.
Below: Brad at Camp Two.

Mr. Lee's third night on the face passed with some climbers giving him oxygen and Dexamethasone to help keep him alive, but since he was not responsive and couldn't be given fluids, he died in the night before the rescuers could get there.

On May 20, we awoke at 3:00 a.m., had a light breakfast, and headed up the glacier to climb the Lhotse Face to Camp Three. We wanted to get there before the sun hit the face. Once in the sun the temperatures rose dramatically, and it felt like we were in an oven. Believe it or not, even at 23,000 feet, we were lying around in our tents in our long underwear, the sun beating down on us. We focused on eating and staying well hydrated as we watched over a hundred people descend from their summit climb of the South Col that day or the previous day. I say "previous day" because some people who summited Everest the previous day took too long and didn't have the time or the strength

2010   2011   2012   **2013**   2014   2015   2016   2017

to descend from the South Col on the same day that they summited, so they spent a second night at the South Col and then descended the next morning.

We watched the sun set over the many high peaks to the west and the afternoon winds blowing off the top of Everest. By 7:30 p.m., we were all in our sleeping bags and asleep. The plan was to wake up at 3:00 a.m. and depart by 4:00 a.m. to begin the 3,000-foot climb to Camp Four at the South Col, 26,000 feet.

Everyone on the team slept using bottled oxygen and began the climb to the South Col using bottled oxygen, as well. Both Eric (Meyer) and I decided to do the same. We decided that our best chance of climbing both Everest (29,035 feet) and Lhotse (28,000 feet) back to back would only happen if we used bottled oxygen. Rather than climb to the South Col without oxygen and use up a tremendous amount of energy,

Top: Starting up the Lhotse Face to Camp Three.

Above: Eric Meyer approaching Camp Three.

Right: High winds blowing off of Mt. Lhotse.

we chose to climb using oxygen. At first, I felt a little guilty doing so, as I had never used bottled oxygen before on all of my other 8,000-meter expeditions, including having climbed to 27,000 feet to the summit of Cho Oyu without bottled oxygen. Once I had the mask on my face and began climbing, I gave up my sense of "climbing by fair means," a phrase coined by Reinhold Messner during his quest to become the first person to climb all 14 8,000-meter peaks without bottled oxygen.

Leaving Camp Three first at 4:00 a.m. and using bottled oxygen, I arrived at the South Col at 9:00 a.m. with two of our climbing Sherpas. It was two hours later before the rest of the team finally arrived at our Camp Four.

I was amazed by the number of tents that were pitched at the South Col. It seemed like there were 50 yellow tents pitched on the flat, barren, windswept, rocky saddle between Mt. Everest and Mt. Lhotse. Teams that had summited Everest that morning were taking down most of the tents, and the Sherpas were in a hurry to descend down to Camp Two that same day. At the same time, people were putting up tents for their attempt at summiting that night.

I have to say, the volumes of garbage that had been left behind shocked me: It was truly the world's highest trash dump. Piles of broken tent poles, empty fuel canisters, uneaten food, plastic wrappers, skeletons of destroyed tents, thin sleeping mattresses, some empty oxygen bottles—

Top: Brad and Eric Meyer resting in Camp Three.

Above: Climbing from Camp Three to the South Col camp on the Lhotse Face.

2010   2011   2012   **2013**   2014   2015   2016   2017

those latter are very valuable, and the climbing Sherpas will take them down, as they are paid for every oxygen bottle they bring off the mountain.

It was obvious that Camp Four was only a place to spend as little time as possible and everyone was in a state of survival, especially those returning to the South Col from climbing Everest. In this situation, most "clients" were so exhausted from their climb that all they could do was sit or lie down and rest. Finding the energy to eat and rehydrate, let alone collect your garbage and pack your belongings, was too big a task. The result was that each team's climbing Sherpas were mostly interested in packing up tents and loading their packs with oxygen bottles, stoves, full gas canisters, mattresses, and clients' sleeping bags, then getting down off the mountain as quickly as possible. Trying to pick up trash and numerous small things that clients had brought up was just too time-consuming. It was quite sad to see what was left behind.

Tent city at the South Col (Camp Four) 26,000 feet.

Arriving at the South Col with our climbing Sherpas, I spent some time drinking and eating snacks and taking care of myself. I then began helping our Sherpas clear tent platforms on the rocky plateau and helped them pitch several tents. In order to do this, I took off my oxygen mask and found that I didn't have any problems performing work in the rarified air of 26,000 feet. By the time the entire team arrived, all of the tents were pitched. We were lucky to have perfectly calm winds in a place where they normally blow hard on a regular basis. As the day wore on, the winds slowly picked up until we were getting an almost-continuous 40 mph. Doubts of being able to go for the summit that night began creeping into our minds.

Chris Klinke, our expedition leader, was able to get new weather forecasts from base camp. These forecasts showed that the jet stream was now coming down over Everest and that by 3:00 a.m., the winds above 28,000 feet would be too strong to climb in. The forecast also showed that the following night, May 22-23, the winds would be much calmer. We decided not to depart that night, but to sleep and spend a second day at the South Col and depart the next night in hopes of reaching the summit on the morning of May 23. We had brought just enough oxygen that everyone could sleep on oxygen at .05 liters per minute and spend the next day on oxygen. When we departed on the night of May 22 for our summit climb, we could switch to fresh bottles, and each climber would then have three bottles of oxygen to climb to the summit and get back down to the South Col. If the regulator was set to 2.0 liters per minute, one bottle would last eight hours, meaning that three bottles would last 24 hours. This was by far more than enough bottled oxygen than anyone should need to get to the top and back down to the South Col.

Chris wanted everyone to climb on 2.0 liters a minute. I planned on using 4.0 liters a minute to help me stay warm and climb faster. My friend, Adrian Ballinger of Alpenglow Expeditions, who had summited Everest six times, had told me, "If you're going to use O's, then you might as well put it on 4.0 liters a minute, climb faster, and stay warmer." He went on to say, "It's not a game of who can climb on the lowest number of liters per minute. No one's up there checking your regulator to see how much oxygen you're using. It's all about staying warm, making the right decisions, and being safe, not about seeing if you can climb in a more rarefied oxygen state."

We spent a windy but comfortable night at the South Col with three people to a tent. The following day, May 22, was somewhat boring, as we spent most of the time in our tents out of the wind. Looking up at Everest and the huge plume of windblown snow coming off the peak, it was obvious that the weather forecast was accurate. Our climbing Sherpas worked tirelessly all day to melt snow and provide everyone with fluids to drink and soup and other things to eat. We couldn't climb Everest without all their hard work.

"It's not a game of who can climb on the lowest number of liters per minute. No one's up there checking your regulator to see how much oxygen you're using. It's all about staying warm, making the right decisions, and being safe, not about seeing if you can climb in a more rarefied oxygen state."

As the day wore on, the winds began to pick up until around 4:00 p.m., when we were getting hit with gusts of 50 to 60 mph. It was bad enough that we had to hang onto the poles while sitting in the tents to help keep them from getting flattened, but...would these winds die down??? We all wondered if we were going to get a chance at the summit or not. The weather forecast called for a calm night, but for three hours, we were being battered by these incredibly strong winds with no sign of it letting up.

At 7:00 p.m. on the evening of May 22, as if someone was in charge and had just flipped a switch, the winds suddenly ended and everything was dead calm outside. No more wind, only a night sky full of stars. We were all a little shocked at how suddenly the winds had quit. Excitement went through camp, as it appeared that we might actually get a chance at the summit.

The plan was for everyone to depart at 8:30 p.m. and begin their summit push. I had convinced Chris to let me depart at 10:30 p.m. because I had consistently been two hours faster in climbing than the rest of the team. I really didn't want to climb in the dark and cold any longer than I had to. I wanted to be able to climb at my own pace to keep my feet warm and, hopefully, be able to climb the last part of the peak in the sunshine to help stay warm. I hoped that I could reach the summit at 6:00 a.m.

Chris had told everyone to set their regulators to 2.0 liters per minute to make sure the slower climbers had plenty of oxygen for the climb. I decided I was going to take Adrian's advice and climb on 4.0 liters per minute of oxygen flow. I asked my climbing Sherpa to set my regulator to 4.0 liters, and he said OK. I could always turn it back down if I needed to, but I didn't think I'd be climbing that slowly.

Leaving at 10:30 p.m. and having a 6:00 a.m. summit goal meant that I had 7½ hours to climb the 3,000 feet to the summit. In reality, I wanted to leave at midnight, as I really thought that I could reach the summit in six hours. Chris and our head climbing Sherpa didn't want me to leave that late, thinking that I'd be too far behind the group. Part of my deal with Chris was that I agreed to carry two oxygen bottles so that my personal climbing Sherpa wouldn't have to carry his two bottles and two bottles of mine. That way, he could climb faster.

I departed at 10:30 with my climbing Sherpa, Dumai, and we set a steady pace. The first goal was to climb from the South Col (26,000 feet) to the Balcony (28,000 feet) on the southeast ridge. I calculated that I would have to reach the Balcony in five hours, which seemed like an awfully long time to climb 2,000 feet. Then I would have 2½ hours to climb the final 1,000 feet to the summit, equally a long time for such a short distance.

Departing the South Col, we walked across the flat, rocky expanse until we reached permanent snow and ice and could put our crampons on. From that point, we gained 300 feet up a blue ice hump to a small plateau and up a gradual snow slope to the base of what was called the "Triangular Face." The main difficulty was climbing 1,000 feet of bands of shale rock at about 50 to 60 degrees in steepness. Once past the rock bands, the route became snow again, climbing diagonally up and right for 800 feet to the ridge crest and a point known as the Balcony. Rope was fixed all the way, so we clipped our jumar to the rope and began carefully climbing up through the rock bands of loose shale. I could see a line of headlamps leading up the Triangular Face and then diagonally right to the Balcony. There were even headlamps above the Balcony on the ridge leading to the South Summit.

Although I had left camp completely warm, my pace actually made me feel a little sweaty, which worried me. As time went by, I began to feel cold creep into my toes and the bottoms of my heels, which worried me even more. Gradually, Dumai and I caught up with and passed climbers above us. There were about six climbers who passed us on their descent; they had apparently decided to turn around because they were too cold. My feet continued to get colder, making me want to climb faster to try and warm them, but I didn't want to climb so fast that I would be reaching the summit in the dark. Our steady pace brought us to the Balcony by 1:30 a.m., a full two hours ahead of my five-hour goal. *Shit!!* At this pace, I would be at the summit by 3:30 a.m., an hour and half before the sun came up! I wanted to be able to see the sights—the Hillary Step, the final summit ridge, and Makalu—at sunrise.

In 1970, a Japanese man by the name of Yuichiro Miura had become the first to try and ski down Mt. Everest. They made a movie about this venture called *The Man Who Skied Down Everest.* It really should have been titled *The Man Who Fell Down Everest and Survived.*

Five years ago Mr. Miura, at the age of 75, became the oldest person to summit Mt. Everest. This record didn't last, as someone older climbed Everest a few years later. This year, at the age of 80, Mr. Miura was attempting his third Everest summit climb with the intention of once again becoming the oldest person to climb Mt. Everest. Starting in base camp, Mr. Miura used bottled oxygen and, with the help of eight Japanese climbers and Sherpas, slowly worked his way up the mountain. Because of the long distance of climbing 3,000 feet from the South Col to the summit, Mr. Miura's team had a plan to make a Camp Five on the balcony at 28,000 feet. This was an incredibly cold and windy place to camp, but with oxygen, it was possible, and it would also shorten his summit day to only 1,000 feet.

When Dumai and I reached the Balcony, we found the two big tents of Miura's team. They were all just getting out of their tents, getting their crampons on, and getting Mr. Miura ready to depart for the summit. By now, my feet were really too cold, and so I asked Mr. Miura and his Sherpas if I could enter one of the tents to take my boots off and adjust my socks. Back at the South Col, I had inserted some temporary heated insoles (similar to the little chemical pads

The summit ridge looking from the South Summit toward the Hillary Step, 28,700 feet.

people put in their ski gloves to keep their fingers warm), which were supposed to heat for seven hours. It didn't feel like they were working, and I wanted get them out and make more room in my boots.

I crawled into one of the tents, took my boots off, removed the sticky insole from the bottom of my socks, and rubbed my feet. My socks were damp with sweat, and I was angry that I had forgotten to grab my extra pair of dry socks from the tent at the South Col. To be able to put fresh, dry socks on now would have solved my cold-feet problem. Instead, I put my boots back on and got out of the tent and back to my oxygen mask and pack.

It was customary to switch oxygen bottles when you reached the Balcony. This gave you a fresh bottle that should easily get you to the South Summit. The old, mostly empty bottle was stored at the Balcony to be picked up on descent. When I checked my oxygen regulator, I saw that it was set at 2.0 liters per minute, not 4.0 as I had asked Dumai to set it. He was following Chris's order of setting all regulators to 2.0 liters per minute. Even though I had asked him to set mine to 4.0, he didn't, but told me he had. I think this greatly contributed to my getting cold feet. Once I had switched bottles, I set my regulator to give me 4.0 liters of oxygen a minute. I figured this might be just what I needed to get my feet warm again.

Dumai and I departed the Balcony at 2:00 a.m. When we had first arrived there, I could see most of our team just beginning the steep snow ridge above the Balcony. Now they were 30 minutes ahead of me again, and just their headlamps were visible on the ridge above.

The South Summit was only 700 feet above me, with the main summit another 300 feet beyond that. With three hours before the sun was to rise, it seemed obvious to me that I would be getting to the top in the dark. I began to climb slowly to try and delay my arrival and time it with the sunrise.

Do you know how hard it is to make yourself climb extra slow? At least for me, it was hard to do that. I began a technique of climbing up about 10 feet then stopping and just stomping my feet in one place, until a 30-foot gap was created between myself and the climbers ahead of me. Then I would repeat the process. The combination of breathing 4.0 liters a minute of oxygen and stomping in one place slowly began to warm my feet. The rest of my body and hands were completely warm.

Dumai began to get angry with me, asking me why I was climbing so slowly. I told him I didn't want to arrive at the summit in the dark. He told me that I was going to run out of oxygen. I said no, I wasn't, because I had only been climbing one hour above the Balcony and I had at least three hours of oxygen left in my bottle, and the South Summit was not three hours away. I told Dumai that if he wanted to climb fast, he could go on ahead and I would see him at the top. In a fit of anger, he took off up the rope only to descend back to me about 30 minutes later to check on me and tell me I was climbing too slow. I again told him that I didn't want to reach the summit before the sun came up. I said that this was the only time I was going to climb Everest, and that I wanted to enjoy the views, see the ridge we were climbing in the daylight, and that I had spent a lot of money to come here and wanted to do it in daylight, not darkness. He had already climbed Everest nine times, and views to him weren't important—only getting up and down the mountain quickly.

About halfway up the ridge between the Balcony and the South Summit, in a steep part of the ridge, the shape of a man lying in the snow came into view of my headlamp. As I got closer, I could see that he was lying/hanging upside down off of one of the anchors of the fixed rope. When I arrived at this place, the man was dead and half buried by snow. People were calmly getting to this point and unclipping their jumar from the rope below the body and clipping it back into the rope above the body. I later learned that he was a Bangladeshi man who, only two days earlier, was descending from the summit alone and in very windy conditions. It appeared that he had tripped and fallen from a distance above the anchor and fell headfirst down the slope until his carabiner and slings stopped him at the next anchor. He had stopped abruptly and, with the weight of his pack and oxygen bottle, ended up upside down. He didn't have the strength to right himself and get untangled from the anchor, and he didn't have a personal climbing Sherpa to help him. He was stuck and exhausted, and just hung there hoping someone would come by to help him, which didn't happen. He stayed there in that position until he died. Now he was a permanent fixture on the mountain unless someone cut him free, but that didn't seem to be a priority now. Climber after climber walked past on his or her mission to get up or down the mountain. When I passed him, I thought about taking a photo to document the situation. Since it was dark out, I decided I'd do it on the way down from the summit, but that didn't happen. I felt a sense of indifference to the body, maybe because I didn't know the person, maybe because he was just a lifeless body and there was nothing I could do to reverse the situation, or maybe because I have witnessed so many deaths in the mountains before that I now felt detached from the reality of what had happened to him and accepted it as a mistake someone else had made. I thought that that wasn't a mistake that I would make...

Dumai came back down the rope looking for me and again was angry that I was climbing so slowly. I said, "OK, I'll climb fast," and got back into my normal climbing pace. I passed Dumai and shortly thereafter caught up with two climbing Sherpas who were assisting a woman. She seemed to be climbing quite slowly and was especially slow and clumsy with her jumar and safety carabiner. As I passed her on a steep rocky section, I showed her how she was using the jumar and safety carabiner incorrectly and how I was using mine, then I continued on up the ridge.

By now it was almost 4:00 a.m. and the eastern horizon was becoming a sliver of morning light. The curvature of the earth was apparent from 28,600 feet. I realized that it would be only another hour before the sun came up. Fifteen minutes later, I topped out on the South Summit at 28,700 feet. From here, I could see the final knife-edge ridge leading to the Hillary Step and, above that, the summit ridge. There were a handful of climbers moving across the ridge between the South Summit and the Hillary Step and a few above that. The combination of a ridge crest barely lit by the morning light, yet dotted with headlamps, was truly a perfect photo, but without a tripod, my attempted photos only came out blurred.

Up until now, everyone had been climbing in almost completely calm air. I thought this would last all the way to the summit, however once I turned the corner and went up over the South Summit, I was hit in the face with a stiff, 25 mph icy wind. It was a bit of a wake-up call and made me pull the hood of my down suit up.

From the top of the South Summit, it was a 30-foot drop down into a notch. It was here that people once again changed their oxygen bottles. Dumai and I stopped in a place out of the wind to do this. Here, I met the lead climbing Sherpa from the Russell Brice team. His name was Phurba Tashi and he was 300 feet from summiting Everest for his 21st time, tying the record that Apa Sherpa held. I was 300 feet away from my *first* Everest summit! I congratulated Phurba and told him I would see him on the summit.

After switching oxygen bottles, Dumai and I began the narrow traverse that led across to the Hillary Step. There were only a few people ahead of us, which was a good thing, as I had heard stories of people waiting 1½ hours for their turn at climbing the step and getting up on the final summit ridge. I wouldn't have had the patience to wait if we had been in that situation, and I'm sure that I would have figured out some way to pass people.

Climbers on the Hillary Step.

It was now beginning to get light enough to see the surrounding peaks and valleys below us. I looked down the southwest face of Everest, the route that Doug Scott and Dougal Haston and the British expedition had pioneered 30 years earlier. I was impressed by how steep the terrain was and remembered reading that Doug and Dougal had stood on the summit of Everest, watching the sun set, only to spend the night out under a rock overhang at the South Summit, hoping they would survive the night. They spent the night with their boots off, rubbing each other's feet to stay warm and awake.

The Hillary Step, which in all the photos I had seen of it was usually a steep snow step, was this year a steep rock step with several ropes hanging down over it. Climbing the step required a few steps of rock climbing and pulling hard on the ropes. Beyond that was another 30 feet of rock scrambling before the snowy summit ridge continued. I could see to the east and realized that any minute now, the sun was about to break the horizon. I wanted to hurry to reach the summit and witness sunrise from the highest point on earth, but we were blocked by a group of 12 people moving incredibly slow in this final stretch. Eventually we got to a place where I decided to unclip from the fixed line and just walk on the hard snow on the uphill side of the line of people. Dumai and I passed everyone and, around a corner, the summit of Everest came into view with all the prayer flags lying in the snow. There were about 30 people already gathered on the summit in a bit of disarray, congratulating each other and taking photos. Dumai and I arrived at the summit of Mt. Everest at 5:20 a.m. on May 23, 2013.

It was impossible to actually stand on the top because there were too many people already there. I tried to find a point on the Tibet side of the summit where I could get close to the top and asked someone to take my photo. It all seemed surrealistic to me. I wanted to just stand there and take

The final summit ridge with the summit in the distance.

Climbers on the summit of Everest.

in the views. I felt a need to somehow touch something that confirmed I was standing on top of Everest. The aluminum tripod that the Chinese had put on the summit so many years ago wasn't there to grasp. The fact that no other point was higher had to be proof. The wave of emotion that I expected to overcome me didn't occur. I almost felt an anti-climax.

2010   2011   2012   **2013**   2014   2015   2016   2017

There were specific summit photos that I wanted, and needed, to take and found a few people to take the photos with my camera. Finally, Dumai found me and said it was time to go down. I said, "No, not yet. There's something very important that I want to do." I walked down the slope 30 feet to a spot that I could have away from the large group of people celebrating on the summit. Dumai kept insisting that we go down, but I told him to just wait a minute, that I had something very important to do. I dug into the top pocket of my pack and brought

Left; View of Mt. Makalu and climbers from the summit of Mt. Everest, 29, 035 feet.

Below: Brad Johnson on the summit of Everest, May 23, 2013, 6:00 a.m.

2010   2011   2012   **2013**   2014   2015   2016   2017

out a plastic bag with six film canisters—three with my father's ashes and three with my best friend's...his name was Blues...ashes. I explained to Dumai what I intended to do. With ashes in hand, I tried to say something profound for both Dad and Blues but ended up only saying I love you and I miss you, then threw the ashes to the wind. Now I had tears in my eyes and Dumai, seeing this, wiped the tears from my cheeks and apologized for not understanding before. I then found Eric Meyer nearby and congratulated him on his second Everest summit. His first had been in 2004 when he climbed from the Chinese side up the northeast ridge. We hugged each other, then I turned to descend with Dumai.

We passed a few people on their way to the summit, but most people were now headed down. There were no traffic jams and, in no time, we were back at the South Summit. Small groups of people were stopped in various locations to put on their goggles or sunglasses. I quickly did the same at the South Summit, then continued up and over it and began the long descent down to the Balcony. Forty feet down from the South Summit, I came onto Mr. Miura leading his party of climbers and Sherpas, one step at a time, up the ropes. About two hours later he, too, summited Everest for his third time and became the oldest person to climb Mt. Everest at age 80. Now, that was impressive!

It was good to be climbing down in sunshine and have my feet and everything warm. In no time, I was back at the Balcony. Here, Dumai and I stopped to eat and drink and take a few photos, then we headed down to the South Col. I had left the summit at 6:00 a.m. and returned to the South Col camp at 8:00 a.m. Winds were calm and it was nice and sunny. Two of our team members were resting in their tent there. One guy, Bart, from Poland had turned around at the bottom of the Triangular Face at 10:30 p.m., saying that he was too tired and that his oxygen mask wasn't working. There was a whole other story about Bart that I could write, but really his mask worked fine, and he needed some excuse for not summiting. The second guy in camp was Thor from Sweden. He had left at 8:30 p.m. with everyone else and had climbed too fast, arriving at the summit at 3:10 a.m. in the dark, with no views of anything. Then he descended quickly back to the South Col.

After resting, rehydrating, and packing up all of my belongings, Thor and I departed the South Col at 10:30 a.m. just after the rest of the team had returned safely. We were ready to get down to Camp Two and its relative luxury. By 1:00 p.m., the rest of the team began their descent from the South Col to Camp Three, arriving either just before or just after dark. The descent from Camp Three in the heat of the afternoon sun became quite difficult. Many of the ice screw anchors were melting out, and I spent time replacing about seven different anchors to safeguard everyone descending behind us.

It was good that all the climbing members and the climbing Sherpas were able to make it from the summit to Camp Two the same day. Now we only had to worry about the final descent the next morning down to Camp One, and then down through the icefall to base camp.

We were all off the next morning by 7:30 a.m. and arrived an hour later in Camp One. Our packs were full of everything that we had brought up the mountain, including clothing, sleeping bags, mattresses, food, trash, and I even packed out my human waste in a special bag that we each had brought along for that use.

The icefall had changed again, and the anchors were also showing signs of melting out. We felt that we weren't getting off the mountain any too soon. Being near the end of May, the temperatures were getting too warm to safely travel through the icefall much longer. Later that night, Dumai fell into a crevasse while crossing a ladder bridge because the anchors on one side of the crevasse pulled out, sending him plunging into the gaping hole. Fortunately, he had clipped into both safety lines, and the only thing he lost was his pack with all his personal belongings and the dining tent from Camp Two. The Sherpas hoped to go back up through the icefall the next day and rappel into the crevasse to retrieve his pack.

All members were down in base camp by the afternoon of May 24. I was too tired to do more than eat and change my clothes. I figured I would take a shower the next day. May 25 was a rest day, and we packed all our duffel bags in anticipation of departing base camp the next day.

On May 26, everyone except Eric, Chris, and me began the three-day walk to Lukla. The three of us paid to have a helicopter pick us up at base camp and fly us to Lukla, then on to Kathmandu. This sounded simple, but it took all day with many shuttles of other groups before we were on the last helicopter to Kathmandu, arriving there at 6:00 p.m. that evening. When we landed in Kathmandu, the warm, moist air hit us in the face: The monsoon was approaching.

So I was in Kathmandu for two nights, going on two days. The rarified air and views from 29,035 feet seemed like a long time ago, but it had only been five days. How quickly we settled into the life of hotels, restaurants, an Internet connection, and cold beer...

I should arrive home June 2 for two days before heading to Peru on June 6 to guide a group of 10 people around the Cordillera Huayhuash for three weeks.

Thanks for all your support,
Brad Johnson

6/02/13—Brad's E-mail Update on the Everest Climb

This will be my final e-mail regarding Everest. It's not a short e-mail.

Keeping a written journal on a long trip like this is very time consuming, and my original intent was to just send a series of e-mails to keep everyone up to date on what was happening. Looking back on my e-mails, I see that I didn't talk about the other people who were on the expedition with me; I mostly talked about what was happening with me.

I went to Everest with a Nepal-based company called "Rolwaling Excursion." Three years ago, when I went to climb Makalu, the same company provided the logistics for the entire expedition. On that trip, I signed on with a group of six French and three Americans. I didn't know any of the people who were going, but I really wanted to go back to Makalu. It turned out the three Americans on that trip all lived in Colorado. Robbie Klimek was a flight paramedic living in Grand Junction; Eric Meyer was an anesthesiologist living in Steamboat; and Chris Klinke worked in upper management for a climbing equipment company in Boulder called "Trango." We all ended up having a great trip together.

This year's Everest trip included both Eric Meyer and Chris Klinke, and they invited me to join the expedition. Both Eric and Chris had climbed Everest before via the northeast ridge from the Chinese side. They had tried to climb K2 together in 2008 but turned around on summit day. This year's Everest trip, Chris Klinke was the expedition leader and Eric was team doctor. We also had a team of 11 climbing Sherpas and a kitchen staff of about five people.

Aside from Eric and Chris, there were also two young guys from Indonesia, Fadre and Martin. Fadre had tried to climb Everest last year but didn't get above the South Col camp due to poor weather and strong winds. This year, Martin was on Everest for the first time. Both of them were attempting to climb all of the "seven summits," the highest peak on each of the world's seven continents. They both had climbed six of the seven, with Everest being the last one to do. Martin didn't speak much English and was fairly quiet; Fadre spoke a lot more English. Both had numerous sponsors for their seven-summit quest and had been given over $1,000,000 USD in sponsorship money. They both said they were climbing for national pride, as only a couple of other people from Indonesia had climbed the seven summits, including Everest. When I first met Fadre and Martin in Kathmandu and heard that the only climbing experience they had was six out of the seven summits, I felt that they were a perfect example of the majority of people who come to climb Mt. Everest. They want to say that they climbed it but don't want to put in the many years of experience required to be qualified to climb Mt. Everest. I felt that they both didn't know what they were getting themselves into on Everest.

In addition to Fadre and Martin, there were also two climbers from Poland, Peter and Bartolomeu (or Bart). Peter told us at the beginning of the trip that he was a historian when it came to Mt. Everest, and that he had read almost every book dealing with the mountain. He also had been climbing in Poland for the past 10 years but really didn't consider himself an accomplished climber. Frequently, Peter would entertain us with some history regarding the first ascent of Mt. Everest. He would always start his speech by saying, "In 1953...." By the end of the trip, we started calling him "1953" instead of Peter.

Bart, who taught law at a university in Poland, said that he had been climbing for 25 years, although watching him climb through the icefall, it was hard to believe that he'd been climbing very long. He didn't have any natural skills or balance. Bart had tried to climb Mt. Everest last year from the Chinese side of the mountain via the northeast ridge. He managed to reach 8,300 meters (27,232 feet) but said that he had to turn around because his oxygen system didn't work. At the beginning of this year's trip, he talked a lot about the mistakes he'd made on last year's expedition, and he complained frequently about the services on this year's trip. He let everyone know that he had a contract with Rolwaling Excursion, which included a personal climbing Sherpa for the whole trip. When Chris told Bart that his personal climbing Sherpa wouldn't be available to him until the final summit push (because all Sherpas would be carrying loads up the mountain prior to that), Bart became very upset and threatened to sue Rolwaling Excursion. On the entire trip, Bart was a negative drain on the whole team and always complained about something. In the end, he didn't summit Everest again and blamed it on a faulty oxygen mask or regulator. Funny thing is that it was the same oxygen mask and regulator that he had no problem with while climbing from Camp Three to the South Col, then spent 36 hours breathing on while resting at the South Col. When he came off the mountain with the rest of us, he refused to tip any of the kitchen staff or his personal climbing Sherpa. In addition, once in Kathmandu, he filed a lawsuit against Rolwaling Excursion for twice the amount of money that he originally paid to go on the trip. Sounded like something a sleazy lawyer from Poland would do!

In addition to the above-mentioned climbers, we had a climber from Sweden by the name of Thor. Thor really had little-to-no climbing experience, but he was strong, was a fast learner, and had a great attitude. Thor was the crazy one on the trip who brought a lot of energy and humor to the team on a daily basis. On summit day, Thor left camp at 8:30 p.m. with the rest of the group but climbed too fast, reaching the top at 3:10 a.m. in the dark, and didn't get to see a thing. He was back in the South Col camp by the time the sun came up.

There was also a 27-year-old American climber by the name of Hari who had come to climb Mt. Lhotse without oxygen. Lhotse is the fourth-highest mountain in the world at just over 8,500 meters (28,000 feet). Hari used to be an elite college distance runner, competing in 5K and 10K runs and running some of the fastest times in world at those distances. Hari had only been climbing about five years but had already climbed some 7,000-meter peaks in Russia, solo and very quickly. He was hoping to use his speed to climb Lhotse quickly without oxygen on May 22, the same day we had planned to climb Everest. Unfortunately, the winds ruined his attempt, and he chose not to go on oxygen, rest another day, and try again the next day. Instead, he descended all the way to base camp on the 23rd.

The team as a whole seemed to look up to Eric, Chris, and me as the most experienced climbers in the group. We were frequently asked our opinions about climbing certain parts of Everest and our approach to climbing it. Except for Bart, the whole team became a very tight group of friends, and hopefully we'll all stay in touch now that the trip is over.

Everest is like no other mountain that I have been to. It attracts more people from around the world than any other of the 8,000-meter peaks. When I first arrived at Everest base camp, I couldn't believe how many expeditions were there to climb the mountain. I couldn't believe the sea of tents that spread over a mile and a half on the glacier at Everest base camp. It felt like a circus show, not a climbing trip. Each team expedition flew their national flags representing the country they were from. There were teams from most countries, including Spain, China, Russia, Taiwan, Bangladesh, Korea, Indonesia, Morocco, South Africa, England, and India.

India was well represented at base camp. It seemed that the economic growth India had gone through had created a new middle class that had money to burn. Now that they could afford to go to Everest, they were coming by the dozens. There were even two identical 21-year-old twin sisters from India who had come to climb Everest, and the only mountain they had climbed prior was Mt. Kilimanjaro. They wanted to be the "first" twin sisters to climb Mt. Everest. There was always a new "first" for Mt. Everest. There was even a group of about 15 high school kids from India between the ages of 15 and 18. They looked like a group of Boy and Girl Scouts on a weekend outing.

I met a 19-year-old girl from Pakistan, a princess from Saudi Arabia, and an actor and actress from Kathmandu. The Nepali Army and Pakistani Army each had a team

> *Everest is like no other mountain that I have been to. It attracts more people from around the world than any other of the 8,000-meter peaks. When I first arrived at Everest base camp, I couldn't believe how many expeditions were there to climb the mountain. I couldn't believe the sea of tents that spread over a mile and a half on the glacier at Everest base camp. It felt like a circus show, not a climbing trip.*

on the mountain. There were climbers from Colombia, Ecuador, Peru (I knew this guy from Huaraz), Brazil, Chile, Argentina, Mexico, and—of course—many climbers from the USA. There was even an armless man trying to climb Everest. How he got through the icefall, let alone up the thousands of feet of fixed rope on the Lhotse Face and above the South Col to the summit, is beyond me. I hear that he had Sherpas to push and pull him. I'm not sure if he made the summit or not, but I did hear that he needed a rescue high on summit day.

Base camp was a small city and, at night, it hummed with the sound of gas-powered generators creating electricity to light up all the kitchen and dining tents and provide electricity for the DVD players that projected the movies on the makeshift screens set up in dining tents. Everyone had solar panels set up to charge large batteries that, in turn, charged the thousands of cell phone batteries, camera batteries, iPods, iPads, laptops, movie cameras, GoPro movie cameras, headlamps, handheld radios to be used on the mountain, and any number of other battery-powered items. A view of base camp at night revealed hundreds of yellow, orange, red, and blue tents lit up from within by electric lights.

Cell phone reception was possible from most places around base camp. Someone discovered that if they walked out into the center of the glacier about a quarter mile, where they were within direct line of sight of Gorak Shep, the last village, you could get 3G internet reception. This spot became known as the "G" spot.

With around 400 paying climbers, there were at least one or more climbing Sherpas to help carry all the necessary food and supplies up through the Khumbu Icefall to Camps One, Two, Three, and Four. In addition, each expedition had a kitchen staff at base camp (cook, kitchen boys, and sirdar or base camp manager). Because Camp Two was the staging area for climbing the upper part of the mountain, it became a secondary base camp with kitchen tent, dining tent, and tents for all members to sleep in. This was our home away from base camp, and everyone's Camp Two had a second kitchen staff with at least one, if not two, cooks who lived at the camp for the entire expedition to cook meals for all the teams, climbers, and climbing Sherpas. At 21,000 feet, this was a hard place to live for the cooks, as they didn't get to come off the mountain to rest at base camp like everyone else did.

With the large number of paying climbers that came to climb Everest, it seemed inevitable that there were going to be accidents and deaths on the mountain. History has shown that the majority of deaths and accidents occurred on teams run by Nepali companies, not Western companies. By Western, I mean the big commercial teams owned and operated by American or English companies. These companies are very well organized, providing plenty of oxygen, and have a strong climbing Sherpa staff that pays close attention to the paying customer, especially on the summit push. In the past, most all of the deaths and accidents had occurred on understaffed Nepali-run companies, where the paying customer was either not looked after or abandoned on summit day, resulting in people running out of oxygen, getting exhausted and sitting down, and dying somewhere up high on the mountain. Last year, in 2012, there were 12 fatalities, all by Nepali-run companies. This year, because of all the good weather for summit attempts, the death toll was only six on the south side of the mountain. Three of these deaths were climbing Sherpas, the other three were Western clients who died because they were alone and not accompanied by a Western guide or a climbing Sherpa.

On the South Col, I met a young American from L.A. who chain-smoked. He had summited Everest using five bottles of oxygen on summit day and had taken 15 hours just to get to the summit. He said that Everest was the only mountain he had ever climbed in his life, and now that he had done it he could quit, sell all his gear, and do something else more fun.

There was a Nepali company called "Seven Summits Treks" who had 72 clients, each paying roughly $18,000 to $20,000 USD to climb Everest. Most of the clients were very inexperienced climbers, learning how to use their crampons and ice axes and how to jumar and rappel for the very first time at the beginning of the trip. The company had set up a ropes course with ladders in the lower part of the icefall just outside of base camp. It was here that all the inexperienced climbers practiced before heading up the mountain. It was this team in particular that all the Western companies were worried about causing lots of accidents and fatalities on the mountain. In the end, because of the week-long stretch of good weather for summit attempts, all of the Seven Summits clients succeeded in getting to the top and back down in one piece. If the weather window had only been a couple of days long at the end of the trip, and if the weather had been a lot worse, I think that there would have been a lot more fatalities. This only shows you that if all goes well with the weather and everyone has plenty of time to get up and down the mountain, even the most inexperienced of climbers can climb Everest and go home to boast about it. They don't realize how lucky they were to have summited.

Helicopter rescue on Everest became commonplace this year. From my understanding, in 2012, there were rescues done out of Everest base camp and possibly out of Camp One above the Khumbu Icefall. In 2012, there wasn't a permanent helicopter pad constructed and maintained at base camp. This year, there were three helicopter pads at Everest base camp. With the introduction of the new B-3 helicopter that is capable of flying to at least 28,000 feet, flights into base camp became an everyday occurrence. Not only did the helicopters come in to pick up injured or sick clients, but expeditions were paying to have fresh fruit, vegetables, meat, and other supplies flown directly into base camp.

The helicopter business is now booming in the Everest region, and many times helicopters flew to Camp Two at 21,000 feet to pick up someone with frostbitten hands or feet, or to pick up the bodies of the few people who had been killed on the upper part of the mountain. We even witnessed an attempted "long-line" rescue at the Lhotse high camp at 25,800 feet. If that had been successful, it would have been a world record for high-altitude rescues.

Helicopters are rapidly changing the nature of climbing Mt. Everest. I have to admit that Eric and I even took advantage of the system. After coming off the mountain from our first acclimatization rotation to 23,000 feet, Eric had a really bad chest cold, and I wasn't feeling much better. Oftentimes, respiratory infections spell the end to someone's chances at climbing Mt. Everest. It isn't possible to recover from an infection in base camp at 17,000 feet. The only way to get healthy is to go to a lower altitude, but that can be problematic, because it could take you two to three days just to walk down to 12,000 feet, and then you have to walk back up again once you're recovered. Now, with the use of helicopters, it's possible to pay a reasonable fee to get picked up at Everest base camp and flown down to Namche Bazaar at 11,000 feet in only 10 minutes. You can eat well, sleep well, and recover in no time, then pay for another flight back up to base camp. You haven't lost any acclimatization and haven't used up valuable time and energy walking in either direction. Your chances of success have been greatly increased.

Crowding on Everest for me is almost a bigger concern affecting my safety than anything else on the mountain, especially going through the icefall and also on summit day. It isn't uncommon to have more than 100 people trying to climb to the summit, especially if there are only a few summit days available at the end of the season. In 2012, the weather provided only two or three opportunities to summit, and 150 people were trying for the summit on each of these days.

Crowding on Everest for me is almost a bigger concern affecting my safety than anything else on the mountain, especially going through the icefall and also on summit day.

This year, there were a total of eight days that were good enough to summit, allowing more people to try for the summit on different days. Still, there were a few days around May 19, 20, and 21 where there were more than 100 people going for the summit, causing long lines and waits of 1½ hours just to climb the Hillary Step to gain the summit. If the weather had closed in and the winds come up on any of those days, it would have been a nightmare followed by catastrophe. Instead, everyone got lucky and survived their 12- to 18-hour summit days, way too many hours in my mind to be climbing 3,000 feet to the summit of Mt. Everest. I would say that the majority of those who summited on those days were inexperienced climbers who didn't have a clue as to how lucky they were to have reached the summit and returned safely to high camp. They just followed the fixed rope and did what their climbing Sherpas told them to do.

It seems that society has become one of instant gratification. Nobody wants to put in the years of work and training to gain the necessary experience to be "qualified" to climb Mt. Everest. Instead, if they have enough money, they think all they have to do is sign up and go climb it. Some people are a little more responsible and climb a few 14,000-foot peaks in the U.S. or take a course on Mt. Rainier, then climb maybe Denali or Aconcagua, and they think they're ready for Everest. Others, like the twin sisters from India, thought that hiking up Mt. Kilimanjaro was a good way to see how they do at altitude, then go to Everest. A few people decide that they will try to climb an "easy" 8000-meter peak like Cho Oyu, and then they're ready for Everest. This final option is a good choice: at least you're climbing to 27,000 feet and have the chance to try using oxygen.

2010   2011   2012   **2013**   2014   2015   2016   2017

Not all guide companies, just a few of the big Western guide companies, have minimum climbing requirements before you can sign on to a trip. Most companies, especially the Nepali-based companies, just take your money and sign you up. The only way to limit the masses going to Everest, and limit the possible fatalities and the crowding, is for all companies to follow a standardized set of rules, requiring all clients to have at least some minimum number of years of climbing experience and have previously climbed other mountains, such as Denali, Aconcagua, Cho Oyu, etc., prior to being accepted on any Mt. Everest permit. This has and is continuing to be discussed, but money speaks louder than words or requirements.

The question to ask the masses that want to come to climb Mt. Everest is this: When the shit hits the fan on summit day and the weather turns for the worst, do you have enough climbing experience to climb instinctively and get yourself down, or do you have to rely on someone else to tell you what to do? In my mind, if your movements and actions are not instinctive, then you don't belong there in the first place.

I was impressed by how big Everest is. Using oxygen definitely made climbing it easier. With all of the media attention that Everest gets, it's no longer a mountain for the "elite." It's become a money-making machine, another check mark on people's "bucket lists," and an endless reason for another "first something" on Everest. Although 99% of climbers couldn't climb Everest without the enormous help of the Sherpas, as they do all the work, it's also turned into a playground for the Sherpas who try to outdo each other by racking up more summits than their neighbor. The current record for the most summits climbed on Mt. Everest is 21, held by Apa Sherpa and Phurba Tashi Sherpa. I'm sure next year that record will be broken again.

I came back from Everest happy that I was able to get to the top and see all the iconic landmarks that I had read about and seen photos of for the past 45 years of my climbing career. It was amazing to think that I was standing at 29,035 feet with the world spread out below me. You really feel high when you're on the summit, everything else is so far below you. I wish that I had been able to spend more time on the top and take it all in. There didn't seem to be enough time to take the photos I wanted and look at the scenery, too. I feel like I need to go back for another look.

Everest for me may not feel like my most significant climb, but it *is* my highest. I think that maybe the fact that so many people have climbed Mt. Everest (it's in the thousands now), and so many of those ascents were done by people who didn't know what they were doing, that somehow the significance of it for me was diminished.

How can a sacred mountain like Mt. Everest be torn down to insignificance? Maybe I need to climb the north side, the way Mallory and Irvin were trying to do back in 1924.

Thanks for all your love and support,
Brad Johnson

Sent from my iPad

2010   2011   2012   **2013**   2014   2015   2016   2017

Hawaii with Rosmery and Brad

In early January of 2014, Rosmery, Brad, and I took off for a week in Hawaii. We were in the Kihei area for about a week. The only thing I remember about it was that if we wanted to go somewhere in our rented car, we spent more time in the car than we did anywhere else. Hawaii needed to limit the number of cars they allowed on the islands. Their roads were so narrow and so close to the buildings on either side that it was impossible to pass anyone. So the only thing you could do was bring along a book to read while you waited in line for the traffic to move.

The first thing we did was drive to a natural area reserve called "Ahihi Kinau" where we tried to snorkel. Brad and Rosmery didn't have any trouble but, for some reason, I couldn't do it without being afraid of drowning. Years ago I'd been to the islands southeast of Florida where I had snorkeled with no problem.

Paia, on the north side of the island, was where we went to see the sea turtles, which are REALLY big. Good night! They were at least three feet across! While there, we watched some young and inexperienced surfers try their luck at surfing. We also found a nice local coffee place called "Island Fresh Coffee."

Brad wanted to bike up Haleakala Volcano, which involved getting up early and getting into and out of the traffic I mentioned earlier. It really

bugged me, but I got him out to the starting point and told him I would return to pick him up if I could get there in the traffic. He did this twice.

We were in an area where if you went out in a larger boat, you might see the humpback whales. We decided to sign up for a tour, because they knew just where to go. We sat on the side of the boat so if there was anything close by, we would have a good place from which to see it. Well, we were almost ready to return to shore when the captain of the boat said to look directly over the side, because there was a whale there! Wow! That was scary but incredible, because it just slowly

swam under the boat, one side to the other. If it had decided to switch its tail, we would have been food.

One evening, we went to the Grand Wailea Luau where we watched the different South Pacific dances, drank mai tais, and had dinner. It was a beautiful evening with gorgeous ocean views and the setting sun. Later, we made our way back through traffic to our rooms.

The rest of the time we spent hanging out on the beach, eating fresh fish, plus trying a plate called "poke," which was made with raw fish. Of course, we spent time in the sun getting tan. Brad rode his bike almost every day, and Rosmery found a place to do CrossFit training every morning.

A great time was had by all of us and I hope Hawaii does away with some of their cars.

2010   2011   2012   2013   **2014**   2015   2016   2017

2014 Birthday Poem

Julie Johnson, it's your Day!
'Bout time we shared a meal,
When you don't have to cook,
When you don't have to pay!

Alex & I miss you,
We don't see you much.
You could come over anytime
Please stay in touch.

We wanted to give you a dog
For your Birthday.
We could babysit,
And Pepper wants to play!

But thought we'd better ask,
And see what you think.
'Cause if we'd just done it,
You might raise a stink.

We should go flying,
We should do something fun,
Just hangin' out's enough,
'Cause we love you a ton!

Happy, Happy!
Xxxooxooxoooxxxxxx—John & Alex

John and Alex Tucker with me.

Mother's Day Poem

OK, Julie,
Here we go:
You think Brad's your only kid?
Well, that's not so.

You know about Rosmery,
And Pepper, too,
The Tuckers are putting in a claim,
And the Thorburn/Nelsons, too!

There's probably twenty or thirty others
In this line
To claim you as family
(But I'm doing it in rhyme!)

So have a Happy Mother's Day,
And when you're through,
Think of us a little,
'Cause we're thinking of you!

—John Tucker

Fireside Remembrances

Day 5 by the light of a brilliant moon
Round a circle we gathered for a tale by June.

She read us letters from '83
Of a cowboy life unlike thee or me.

Of ruins and glyphs seen high on the walls
And roping in horses after their falls.

Then stars appeared in the darkened sky
No satellite was spotted tumbling by.

As each found a spot to lay down for the night
The moon in the water reflected its light.

Soon the voices did fade 'mid the song of a frog
One might think they were weary from too much grog.

But it was eating too much and rowing the raft,
It was loading and unloading the laden craft.

Up go the tents then down they must come,
And each night's dinner is so yum-yum!

Kayaks, dip sticks, poop box, and flags,
Hikes up the canyons and over the crags.

Citronella and tiki stakes
And watching the Dutch oven bake a cake.

—Julia Johnson

Second Trip to Botswana, November

I had already been to Botswana in 2009 with Brad and Rosmery. It was such a great trip and our guide, Dave Luck, was so incredible that we wanted to go again. We used Natural Habitat again for organizing everything.

Our first flight was from Montrose to Denver. Of course, United flights out of Montrose were almost always early morning if you planned to connect in Denver with another flight. So after the usual three-hour-and-14-minute wait in Denver, we finally headed for Washington, D.C., at 3:16.

Would you believe we were to be in business class?

After another long wait, this time only two hours and 24 minutes, we boarded a South Africa Airways flight at 5:40 a.m. headed for Johannesburg. We were seated in business class again, thank goodness! After the usual dinner, and having plenty of room in business class, we all slept. Our arrival in Johannesburg was 12 hours later at 5:50 p.m.

We stayed in a hotel very close to the airport because, after a couple of days, we would be leaving again on another South African Airways flight to Maun, Botswana, where our tour would start.

Sure enough, Dave Luck, our expedition leader on our trip in 2009, was going to be our guide. We were taken by light aircraft to our first camp, called "Kalahari Plains," which was in a remote area of the Central Kalahari Game Reserve. This time of the year, we were told we would see Africa's best wildlife. The reserve was the largest conservation area in Botswana and one of the largest protected wildlife areas in the entire world, meaning NO HUNTING!

The camp had about 10 Meru-style canvas tents, each with every facility one would

Our fearless expedition leader, Dave Luck.

This page and the next nine show pictures of our accommodations and the variety of wildlife we saw.

need plus a rooftop sleeping area to enjoy the amazing night sky. Like all other camps, there was a lounge, dining area, and bar. Everything was raised off the ground on wooden platforms to catch the breeze and take in the sweeping, spacious view across the Kalahari. We were told to watch for the black-maned lion, the Kalahari's most famous wild animal, along with the brown hyena, cheetah, giraffe, warthog, wild dog, leopard, and herds of wildebeest, eland, gemsbok, kudu, and red hartebeest that converged in the grassy riverbeds to feed.

Soon we were headed for the Okavango Delta and Xigera (Kee-jera) Camp. We were in a deluxe tented camp in the heart of the delta within the famed area called "Moremi Game Reserve."

We could see from the plane that we were in an area of complete isolation. No other camps were around, and there was unparalleled wilderness. We were on an island in the heart of the delta. In a dugout canoe piloted by a local Okavango-born guide, we glided through purple and white water lilies and wind-rustling reeds with African fish

2010   2011   2012   2013   **2014**   2015   2016   2017

This fellow, a Kalahari tribesman, showed us how to start a fire using two sticks and dry grass, then demonstrated how they catch scorpions, which they then cook and eat. The people of the Kalahari are a hunter-gatherer society and must forage for their food.

eagles flying above. After the canoe ride, we started out into the wilderness in hopes of seeing the wildlife the area was full of.

Our most exciting time was when we spotted a leopard crouched in the high grass and creeping in the direction of several impala. It went along the side of our vehicle then along the edge of the road ahead of us where some bushes kept the impala from seeing it or us. Suddenly, it leaped in the direction of the impala, which we couldn't see because

of some bushes. We could hear a lot of thrashing in the underbrush and, finally, silence. Our guide moved us ahead of the bushes so we could see what was happening. The leopard had the impala in its mouth and started dragging it across an expanse of open grass. It appeared that the impala was pregnant, which made dragging it difficult. Periodically, the leopard would stop for a few minutes to take a breath, then bite the body in another place and continue on to the other side. It stopped many times for a breath.

Once at the edge of the wooded area, the

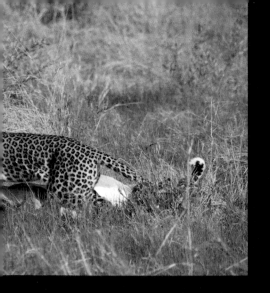

Leopard vs.
Impala vs.
Hyena

Photos by Brad and Julia Johnson.

leopard put the body down, but suddenly there was a commotion. A hyena had been watching what was going on and waited for the leopard to get to the other side of the expanse, then it frightened the leopard off and started eating the catch. We couldn't believe the scene! Not many tourists got to see something like that.

After two nights at the delta, we again flew in light aircraft to Chitabe Main Camp. We were told that the Chitabe Concession had the widest range of habitats in the Okavango Delta, from savannah to tree-filled islands and flooded plains. The housing was in spacious Meru-style tents on elevated

wooden decks beneath a canopy of indigenous trees. Again, each suite had all the modern facilities, even an outdoor shower for those who preferred to shower under the stars. Most evenings, we gathered around a flickering campfire and relaxed as we listened to the sounds of the African bush.

Our last stay was nearby at Lediba Camp. Besides all the usual facilities, the dining area and lounge had a shading thatched roof where, in the evening, we could sit and watch for the enormous elephants known to be in the area. A nearby waterhole attracted a multitude of wildlife.

Our last day involved flying from Chitabe Camp back to Maun for our connecting flight home.

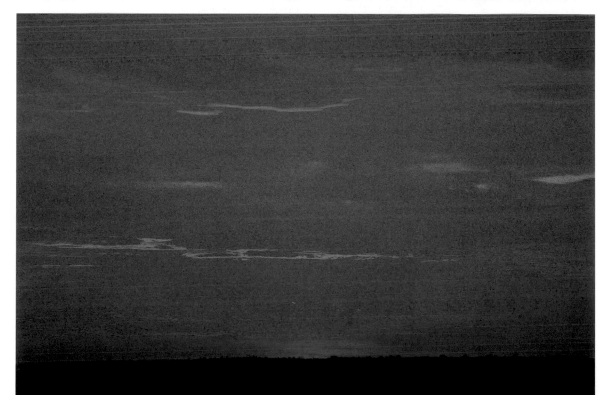

87th Birthday Poem

Well, Julie Johnson,
You're standing tall!
Even though your son
Is stuck in Nepal!

Africa, Peru?
I can't keep track—
You Johnsons travel
The world and back.

Where do you think
That next you will go?
How 'bout a vacation in Delta?
(It's out of the snow!)

I hope you'll consider
Staying close to home,
Though truthfully I've heard
The food's good in Rome.

Stop! Look around you.
It don't get no "bettah."
Your friends here are true—
Not just in fair weather.

Every one of us
Is happy to be with you
For this, your birthday
(Is it Number 72?)

Maybe you have
been up to some tricks—
Was last year really
Number 86?

Well, be it 86
Or 104,
You're honored and well-loved
And that is for shore!

xxxxooxxoooooxxx—John Tucker

LIZ AND STEVE'S WEDDING

Liz, my grandniece, and Steve's wedding was on September 5, 2015, at the American Club in Kohler, Wisconsin. For their rehearsal dinner, we went to the Blind Horse Winery in Sheboygan on September 4, 2015.

The wedding took place on a Saturday and was in the courtyard/garden of the American Club. Guests sat on the left and right sides with an aisle of gorgeous plants and flowers in the middle. Steve was Jewish, so they incorporated Jewish tradition by standing underneath a chuppah (canopy) that was covered in flowers as a judge married them (I cannot remember her name). During the ceremony, the two lit individual candles, then used each to light a larger candle bearing their names that sat in the middle of the two individual ones. At the conclusion of the ceremony, once the judge pronounced them man and wife, Steve incorporated another Jewish tradition of breaking the glass by stepping on it. The many pieces of broken glass symbolize the many years they will happily live together.

Following the ceremony, guests migrated to the other side of the garden/courtyard for a cocktail hour. Liz and Steve chose the old fashioned as their "signature cocktail" during this time, but guests were able to order other beverages as well.

After the cocktail hour, guests were asked to make their way down to one of the ballrooms inside for the reception. Before sitting down to eat we had the grand

The courtyard of the American Club, where the ceremony took place.

Liz and Steve, the bride and groom.

Liz's parents, Jeff and Anne Faris.

march, where the band Liz and Steve hired—Big Sam's Funky Nation from New Orleans (one of Steve's favorites that he saw often when he went to school at Tulane)—announced the wedding party. Following the grand march, the band played a couple of songs while guests danced, then everyone was seated for the first course. Each course was broken up with either a speech or a song/dance, so it kind of forced everyone to stay awake and moving rather than getting sleepy from sitting for so long during the meal. Jeff, Alison, Megan Svoboda, and Carmine DiCosmo were among those who spoke during the reception.

Julia Johnson: "Quite a Woman"

I first met Julia a decade or so ago and have really gotten to know and appreciate her for who she is. I'm not sure if it's her entrepreneurial spirit, her ability to speak her mind, or the fact that she's from the Midwest that have rendered a close working relationship over the years. She's been a good landscaping client who appreciates what I have to offer and isn't afraid to call me up for the strangest of tasks.

You see, I first met Julia when she called upon my professional services to fix a leaking water feature. This isn't one of my favorite types of jobs, as it usually involves adopting or inheriting a project that wasn't installed correctly in the first place. She has a way about her that left me unable to tell her no (and they say a good businessman knows when to say no). I found out later that a large buck deer (or was it an elk?) that was caught cooling off in the small watering hole had led to the need of having to repair some holes in the bottom of the rubber liner. We were able to revamp the entire feature and rebuilt the waterfalls and rocks surrounding the pond to make it a "natural piece of art" that enhances her backyard landscaping. It was all worthwhile when she exclaimed, "Where have you been all my life? I've needed someone like you for years to help me with my projects, and here you are!"

Well, that was that, and I've enjoyed many years since then of assisting in all sorts of outdoor (and indoor, replumbing a leaky water tank) projects, from cleaning gutters to pressure washing decks to planting high-dollar chipmunk and squirrel food in the form of wildflower sod in her large rock walls. She has a method to clear the varmints out that she's perfected by using live-trap wire cages and spray painting their butts bright orange to let them know they're not wanted, then haul them off to Timbuktu with the hope of them never returning. We have had fun clearing and pruning trees to enhance the view while offering some privacy from wind and attracting the variations of wildlife for viewing from in the house and around the patio. It's really refreshing as a contractor to have a client who is as savvy as she is, knows what she wants, and has the good old-fashioned determination to have it done her way. (It's a good thing we think alike!) We have also done fire mitigation work, hauling brush for burn piles down below for marshmallow and "wienie bakes."

Julia is a very colorful gal with an even more colorful past, and I really enjoy our time together. She treats us with consideration and pleasantries whenever we connect. She will always be a dear friend, and I look forward to being there for whatever needs she may have in the future. I also made a connection to her from the past, in that we had numerous Frostline Kits from their factory that we sewed and customized when I lived in Rockford, Illinois. This is real close to Wisconsin where she was born and raised and where I spent many years while growing up. Then we also realized that she lived in Boulder, where I would spend my weekends off from working in Winter Park, skiing. She's a great friend and we'll be there till the end (and beyond). We look forward to many more years to come!

Love you,

Dan and Sabine Zaugg, Ben, Nicole, Josh, and Jonny

89th Birthday Poem

Julie Johnson, You're 89!
Gawd Ah' Mighty, Girl!
You're lookin' fine!

You got some friends here
Who all love you dear.
They show up for your birthday
(Especially, if Brad has beer.)

Everyone we know
We know through you,
'Cause those friends you got
They all love you true.

So tell me, Julie,
What would be fun?
Messican food?
A trip to the sun?

We don't need to travel,
Just come by for eggs
And some good conversation,
Don't make us beg!

A starstruck life
You've had in spades.
Can't wait for the book
To see what you've made.

Though experience and travel
Are both very good,
It's the light in your eyes—
That's the stuff that's so good.

So happy birthday, Julie,
You're getting up there.
Thank you for everything,
For the life that you share!

—John Tucker

SURPRISE BIRTHDAY BREAKFAST FOR ROSMERY

Several weeks prior to June 19, Rosmery's 48th birthday, Brad made flight plans for her mom, Ayda, to come for a visit. She would come the day before, June 18, and stay with me so Rosmery would have no clue. Now that all seems pretty easy, but let me tell you, I was exhausted after it all happened.

First, I don't speak Spanish anymore—used to years ago. My hair stylist said if I had a smartphone, there was a Spanish-to-English app that worked pretty well. All I had to do was trade in my flip phone for a smartphone. I told Brad about this, and he thought it was a good idea. We just had to go to Verizon and trade in my flip phone.

As usual, Brad didn't take the time to go to Montrose until the week prior to when Ayda would arrive. It was Wednesday, and it took five days to do a transfer of information from the flip phone to the smartphone. I didn't want to be without my phone that long, so we didn't do any more than buy a new phone for Brad, and he gave me his old phone. I had to learn how to use it before we could do the transfer, which now would have to wait until after the surprise birthday party.

The more I thought about it, the more I realized I was going to need someone who spoke Spanish. I had a Mexican hot tub serviceman, so I called him to see if one of his children might be just the ticket. And sure enough! He had an 18-year-old daughter who liked to help people. He volunteered to meet me with her at our local downtown Montrose City Market, which was on my way to the airport to pick up Ayda on Sunday.

I had traveled many times to the Montrose airport from where I live and knew when I would need to leave in

order to make that stop and still get to the airport at 1:00 p.m. When, after 10 minutes from home, I arrived at the main highway to Montrose and rounded the first corner, I couldn't believe my eyes: Traffic was at a dead standstill, backed up for what appeared to be about four miles ahead of where I needed to go.

After thinking for just a couple of minutes, I decided to turn around and go the only other way there was to get from Ridgway to Montrose: County Road 1. Surprisingly, there were five others who had decided to turn around, and now I was faced with none of them going over the speed limit of 25 and, later, 35 miles an hour. Even going this way, I was going to be late. Much to my relief, when we finally got up County Road 1 and away from town, those ahead of me were going at least 60, which really made me feel OK. On we went on a paved road until, finally, it turned to gravel.

What none of us realized, because I'm sure those ahead of me rarely traveled County Road 1, was that the road was being re-graveled. Once off the pavement, the dust was such that you couldn't see the car ahead of you, nor could we see ahead to know if there was traffic coming from the other direction. I had to stay behind these five cars until we hit pavement on the other end of the road where it connected at Colona with Highway 550 on into Montrose.

I knew I was going to be late, but not as late as if I had stayed at the end of the backup. Fifteen

Surprise!

2010   2011   2012   2013   2014   2015   2016   **2017**

minutes late, I arrived at the market and my friend introduced me to his daughter. She was a delight! I said a million thanks, and off we took for the airport.

Another flight had just arrived from Denver while we waited for Ayda's flight from Houston. I finally had to sit down. We weren't paying much attention when suddenly I heard "Jew Lee"! It was Ayda, waving from the luggage ramp. It was so great to see her. She right away introduced me to a young lady who had sat next to her on the airplane who also spoke Spanish! Incredible! I couldn't believe it. However, she had to leave as soon as her bag came, for she was going to Norwood, a town west of us.

Jeff Wheeler, left, was visiting Rosmery and Brad.

My Spanish-speaking 18-year-old, Alejandra, did quite well, and before we knew

it, we had the luggage and were on our way. Ayda had boarded the flight at midnight so she certainly was tired, but we all needed lunch. We stopped at Applebee's, ate, then went back home.

It wasn't long after getting home that Ayda indicated she wanted to go to bed. I understood. Alejandra and I just sat around for a few hours, waiting for her father to show up to service my hot tub. His wife and their other children were with him. I hadn't known the family except for his son, who always came with him to learn how to service hot tubs.

They all chattered amongst themselves as their dad worked. After they left, I checked on Ayda, who was still sleeping, so I took the time to get my large table set for breakfast the next morning. Brad had two friends staying with them and they had met Ayda years ago when she visited here. To surprise

2010   2011   2012   2013   2014   2015   2016   **2017**

Rosmery, I set the table for five, not six. There were Brad and Rosmery, Jeff and Signe, and me. I got my best dinnerware out along with wine glasses for orange juice. I put out, in a very obvious place, only five white coffee cups.

Next morning, Ayda was up before I was, having caught up on her sleep. We were anxious for Brad, Rosmery, and their friends to arrive. Brad called to say they were on their way, which was only across the road about five minutes. When I saw them turn into my driveway, I motioned to Ayda to go into the nearest bedroom and stay in the bathroom until I knocked on the door, telling her to come out. There were many windows where one could see into that bedroom as you approached the front door, and

we didn't want Rosmery to see Ayda in there.

They greeted me and I greeted them, and wished Rosmery a happy birthday. I could see her look at the table and the cups and see there were only five. They stood at the far end of the living room out of sight of the bedroom, laughing, talking, and taking pictures. Finally, I got Ayda out of the bathroom and quietly ushered her into the living room, where she stood next to Rosmery who was looking the other way, posing for a picture. So she never saw that her mom was in the picture until it was taken, and she turned to see who was standing next to her.

Her eyes were the widest I had ever seen them, and her mouth was open as wide as it would open! Then the tears came, and she hugged her mom over and over and cried and was unable to say much, she was so surprised. WE DID IT! WE SURPRISED HER FOR HER 48TH BIRTHDAY! Everyone was in tears and more pictures were being taken. It couldn't have been any better. A great breakfast was had by all on that amazing day.

Trip to Wilson, Wyoming, to see the Eclipse

Thursday, August 19, 2017, I picked Brad up at the Montrose airport. He had helped Rosmery's mom, Ayda, get back home in Peru after she had come to surprise Rosmery for her 48th birthday. Then he'd planned to take two couples on a short trek that started out of Huaraz, Peru. His plan was to stay on for a month or more when the trek was over. However, when he heard about the upcoming eclipse and Wilson, Wyoming, being one of the best places to see it, he changed his reservation and came back earlier. I wish it had been even a couple days earlier than it was, but it wasn't.

We were to quickly pack the van after his return with what we would need to camp out for two nights at his friend, Jeff Foott's, six acres near Wilson.

Almost immediately, Brad began to set up tents on the grassy lawn to see which would work the best. I can't tell you when I had last slept on the ground in a tent. I wasn't looking forward to it, and I'd asked friends if they had a collapsible cot for camping. It looked like I was in for it until I had Leif Juell of Alternative Power come to see why my monthly solar production report via my solar panels was at zero. Just making conversation, I mentioned that I was looking for a foldable cot for camping, and he had one! Hooray! So I went over to his home and picked it up. It was perfect, because it folded in half, making it small enough to go in Brad's van. It would stand in the rear on one side, held in place with shock cords. Even more importantly, it fit into my tent.

I had given up trying to find a collapsible table about the size of two card tables together to use for our camp kitchen. In my back room where I've kept all my photography, I discovered that one of those tables actually folded in half, just like the cot did. But once everything was removed so I could see the underside of the table, there was a very large label saying not to put anything hot on the top, because it would melt the plastic. Well, we planned to use a two-burner Coleman stove, so I had to find something! After searching for and failing to find a couple of 4X4 fence posts, friends suggested I use one of my travertine floor tiles left from tiling my expansive floor. It was just the right size for the Coleman stove. Perfect! So we were set.

Jeff and Judith's home in Wilson, Wyoming.

Rosmery and I organized all the food we would need for the trip. We would put everything in the van the night before and just have our personal things to gather in the morning.

Well, Brad forgot to change his watch from Peruvian time to Colorado time (a one-hour difference), and when I arrived at their home the next morning at 6:45, they weren't up yet. Oh, well...we left at 8:00 a.m. instead.

We had 510+/- miles to drive to reach Wilson, Wyoming. We had expected a lot of traffic, as everyone who knew what we were going to do cautioned us about the thousands of people and cars that were headed to Jackson. As it turned

Viewing the eclipse.

2010   2011   2012   2013   2014   2015   2016   **2017**

Above and below: The total eclipse.

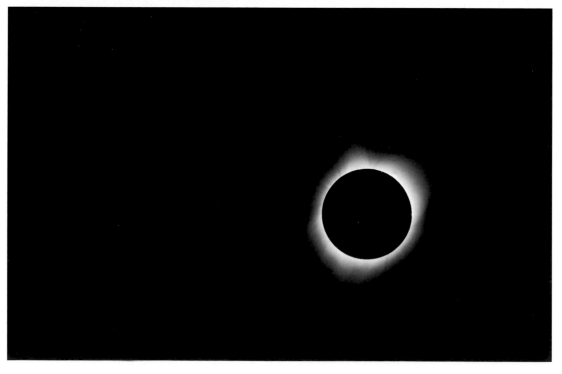

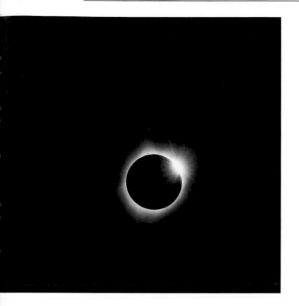

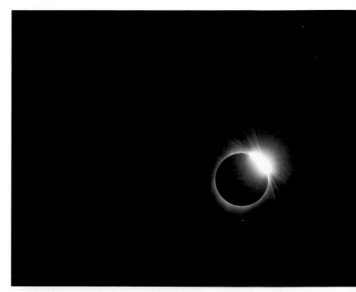

Sun emerging at the edge of the moon after totality.

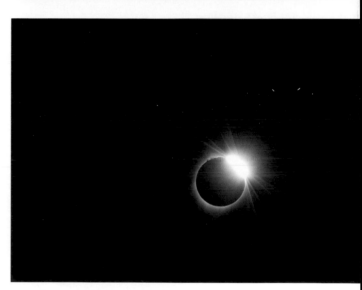

out, there was no traffic on the route that we had chosen, and we only ran into traffic when we arrived in the outskirts of Jackson. Brad and Rosmery had been there before and knew where to turn onto a road into a tree-covered valley. The road went gently uphill to finally arrive at what appeared to be an old red barn with a garage door on the right and a walk-in door on the left. We parked off the side of the graveled road near an

Eclipse photos by Brad Johnson.

area that looked like we might be able to pitch our tents in the meadow.

Jeff and Judith came out to greet us and showed us into the building, taking us through what might have been a tool shop, up a couple steps onto a landing, where there were more steps that led up to their second-floor apartment. Out back of the barn was a lovely deck next to a small stream. There was a round metal table with chairs, and a smaller table used to set food off from the larger one. What had once been a covered woodshed on one corner of the building now held a queen-sized mattress, which was sleeping quarters for Judith's daughter, Allison, and her boyfriend, Luke. They both

Jeff Foott, our host.

were lying in a hammock which hung close to the stream.

I had taken my beef stew dinner up the steps to their kitchen to heat it up, which then was added to what Judith had for dinner. When everything was ready we ate out on the deck, which was lovely. I had wrapped the first copy of my book for Brad because I had told him he would get the first copy. So after dinner he opened it, and pictures were taken with me standing beside him, smiling away.

Not long afterward, everyone helped clear the dishes, and we headed to our tents for the night, eager for morning to come when it would be time to watch the eclipse.

I had bought a large bucket and put a trash bag in it for me to use as a toilet, because I certainly didn't want to go across the driveway into the garage and up the stairs to use their facilities. I was sure I would have no trouble using the bucket in the night. It was colder than I thought it would be, so I was a bit cold. The second night, I used my larger down sleeping bag and, with my flannel jammies plus booties, I was toasty.

Rosmery viewing the eclipse.

2010   2011   2012   2013   2014   2015   2016   **2017**

After breakfast on the 21st, everyone gathered their camera, eclipse-watching glasses that Jeff provided, regular sunglasses, and chair to sit out in a large field east of where their home was and our tents were. Time ticked on when, finally, we could see the moon begin to cross over the sun. It was a slow process but interesting to watch. The surroundings began to get dark but it was still light enough to see. Once the moon covered the sun completely, the air temperature was cold enough for light down jackets, and we didn't need to use the special glasses again. The sky was a dark blue, around the edge of the moon were red solar flares, and we began to see some stars. One was Venus. The corona of light around the moon was diamond shaped and quite spectacular. Both Jeff and Brad frantically took photos of the event, hoping something would turn out. During the total eclipse, the horizon had a sunset while the sky was a dark blue.

The corona of light around the moon was diamond shaped and quite spectacular.

Totality only lasted a quick two minutes and, suddenly, the sun broke the edge of the moon and began to bring back daylight. In no time at all it began to get warm, and life around us started acting normal again, with birds chirping and insects flying around. Another hour went by and the moon had passed completely from the sun. We all wished that the totality had lasted longer, as everything we witnessed seemed to happen too fast with too many things to take in all at once.

We sat in the sun eating cheeses and crackers, drinking beer and wine, and talking about this incredible experience that was rarely seen unless you were a total-eclipse chaser going to far-off countries each year to see the event.

Another night was spent camping out. We departed early the next morning and headed for home, arriving after a long 10-hour drive.

Polar bear, Churchill, Canada, 1994.

Rwanda, 1990.

Grizzly bear, Alaska, 1988.

A Last Word

Whew! I can't believe that the end has finally arrived, but I'm at last finished with Volume 2.

As I'm sure you know, it's taken months and many beloved folks to get through these two volumes, and there were many who helped along the way. I couldn't have done this without the computer help of my dear friend, Fred Quist. He has more patience than I have! Friends like Fred Blackburn, Ann Phillips, and many others who were part of the Wetherill–Grand Gulch Research Project were able to remember what I couldn't and answer my many questions. My son, Brad, who has also written a book, was able to answer many questions about our trips of long ago to help fill in the gaps. And I had no idea the book would be *soooo* long! But the book's designer knew and advised that we go to two volumes because, otherwise, the spine would break under the weight of more than 500 pages. The first volume weighed close to four pounds and cost $4.10 book rate to ship to friends in the U.S. And for those who have been asking, the designer, Laurie Casselberry of Durango, did an excellent job of working the years these volumes cover into a very attractive and comprehensive chronology, and I agree that the book is gorgeous! Thank you, everyone. Without your help, this would not be, and I'm grateful to one and all. I hope you've read both volumes and traveled parts of the world with me through my stories. I'd really like to know if you enjoyed it, so send me an email: juliamj28@gmail.com

—Julia M. Johnson

Clouds over the San Juans.

Mountains I Have Climbed

Year	Area	Mountain Climbed/Route	Leader/Companions
1954	Colo. Rockies	Longs Peak (14,259') Alexander's Chimney	D. Johnson, Cary Houston, Bob & Ginny Sutton
1956	Colo. Rockies	James Peak	Dale Johnson, Dave, Jan, Phil Robertson, Maggie Powers
1957	Front Range, Colo. Rockies	Third Flatiron	Dale Johnson, Brad Johnson
		Maiden North Face	Dale Johnson, Cary Houston
	New Mexico	Shiprock, Normal Route	Dale Johnson, Wes Nelson, Cary Houston, Dick Bird, Dal Jackson
	Montana Glacier Pk.	Mt. Reynolds South Face	Dale Johnson
1958	Front Range	Dome Rock	Dale Johnson
1959	Front Range Colo. Rockies	N. & S. Arapahoe Peaks South Maroon Peak Ascent: South snow and ice couloir. Descent: Eastern Dividing Couloir	Dale Johnson Leader: Dale Johnson Others: Ken Wright, Karl Pfiffner
1960	Colo. Rockies	Crestone Needle, Ellingwood Arete	Leader: Dale Johnson Others: Ken and Ruth Wright
		Capitol Peak	Dale and Brad Johnson, Howard Snyder, Ben Chidlaw
		Navajo	Ken & Ruth Wright, Dale Johnson
		Kiowa & Arikaree	Ken & Ruth Wright, Dale Johnson
		Devils Thumb	Ken & Ruth Wright, Dale Johnson
1961	Europe, Bernese Alps	Jungfrau South Ridge Route	Dale Johnson Incomplete, dangerous conditions
1962	Colorado	The Matron	Ken & Ruth Wright, Dale Johnson
		Wetterhorn (14,021')	Mike O'Brien, Bob Baumgartner, Dale & Brad Johnson
		Little Matterhorn	Brad Johnson
		Lady Washington	Solo
1963	Peru	Co-Leader with Dale Johnson on Colo. Mtn. Club Expedition led by Dr. Harold and Sadie Walton	
	Cordillera Blanca	Nevado Chinchey (20,300')	Unsuccessful, stopped at 18,500' high camp.
		Tocllaraju (19,800') 3 day ascent	Leader: Dale Johnson. Others: Joe Fullop, Sue O'Brien, Dick Lamm, Roger Neave, Francis Chamberlain Carter

Shiprock, New Mexico.